# Learning Design Pattern Unity

CW00919660

Craft reusable code with popular software design patterns and best practices in Unity and C#

**Harrison Ferrone**

# Learning Design Patterns with Unity

Copyright © 2024 Packt Publishing

*All rights reserved.* No part of this book may be reproduced, stored in a retrieval system, or transmitted in any form or by any means, without the prior written permission of the publisher, except in the case of brief quotations embedded in critical articles or reviews.

Every effort has been made in the preparation of this book to ensure the accuracy of the information presented. However, the information contained in this book is sold without warranty, either express or implied. Neither the author, nor Packt Publishing or its dealers and distributors, will be held liable for any damages caused or alleged to have been caused directly or indirectly by this book.

Packt Publishing has endeavored to provide trademark information about all of the companies and products mentioned in this book by the appropriate use of capitals. However, Packt Publishing cannot guarantee the accuracy of this information.

**Senior Publishing Product Manager:** Larissa Pinto
**Acquisition Editor – Peer Reviews:** Gaurav Gavas
**Project Editor:** Meenakshi Vijay
**Content Development Editor:** Tanya D'cruz
**Copy Editor:** Safis Editing
**Technical Editor:** Tejas Mhasvekar
**Proofreader:** Safis Editing
**Indexer:** Pratik Shirodkar
**Presentation Designer:** Rajesh Shirsath
**Developer Relations Marketing Executive:** Sohini Ghosh

First published: May 2024

Production reference: 1270524

Published by Packt Publishing Ltd.
Grosvenor House
11 St Paul's Square
Birmingham
B3 1RB, UK.

ISBN 978-1-80512-028-5

www.packt.com

# Contributors

## About the author

**Harrison Ferrone** was born in Chicago, Illinois, and was raised all over the U.S. He's worked at Microsoft, PricewaterhouseCoopers, and a handful of small start-ups, but most days you can find him creating instructional content for LinkedIn Learning or working on new projects. He holds various fancy-looking pieces of paper from the University of Colorado Boulder and Columbia College Chicago. Despite being a proud alumnus, these are stored in a basement somewhere. After a few years as a full-time iOS and Unity developer, he fell into a teaching career and never looked back. Throughout all this, he's bought many books, been owned by several cats, worked abroad, and continually wondered why Neuromancer isn't on more course syllabi.

*Completing this book wouldn't have been possible without the loving support of Kelsey, my wife and partner in crime on this journey.*

# About the reviewers

**Charles Haché**, also known as Oz, is a seasoned game development teacher with extensive experience at both the high school and university levels. As a technical mentor for graduates and individuals seeking to upskill, he specializes in Unity, C# OOP, architecture, design patterns, VR, AR, instructional design, and leadership. In addition to his teaching roles, Oz has contributed to various game development projects and has been instrumental in shaping curricula that bridge the gap between academic theory and practical application. He has worked with several esteemed organizations, including the University of Victoria as a Unity Certified Instructor, Mastered Studios Inc. as a technical mentor, and Pearson as a subject mattter expert in Unity. His expertise has been sought after for technical reviews and consultations on several notable publications within the game development community.

*In working on this book, I would like to extend my heartfelt gratitude to my wife, Kari, for all the support she has given me over the past 12 years. I look forward to sitting on a porch with her, holding hands, now that this book is finished.*

**Luiz Henrique Bueno**, also known as Rick Good, began his career in Brazil, focusing on smart home and IoT projects. This laid the groundwork for his expertise in software architecture and design patterns, leading to proficiency across iOS, macOS, Windows, and XR platforms. By 2016, he had become one of Brazil's first Unity Certified Developers, showcasing his depth in game development. After moving to the USA in 2017, he founded Toodoo Studio, where he successfully launched several game titles, including *Global Destruction VR*, *Blondie on the Road*, *Thomas' Tales*, and *Food Chase*, using Unity and Unreal Engine. His contributions extend to authoring and technically reviewing Unity books and creating educational content on Unity and Unreal development. His technical skills span from C++ and C# to Swift, React, and Node.js. He has ventured into XR applications for Apple Vision Pro and Meta Oculus devices, continuing to push the boundaries of interactive technology. For a closer look at his projects and achievements, visit his portfolio at https://rickgood.me.

# Join our community on Discord

Join our community's Discord space for discussions with the author and other readers:

https://packt.link/gamedevelopment_packt

# Table of Contents

## Chapter 17: Simplifying Subsystems with the Façade Pattern 541

## Chapter 18: Generating Terrains with the Flyweight Pattern 557

# Preface

Design patterns have been around for a very, very long time (decades in fact), lighting the way through dark and troubled waters where scale, flexibility, access, communication, and optimization try to capsize your best coding efforts at every turn. You'll see these concepts taught and embedded in most, if not all, Computer Science curriculums around the world, but they're conspicuously missing from many a young game programmers toolkit (mine included when I first started out).

Maybe these skills are traditionally taught by more experienced developers and mentors over the course of a programmer's career. Maybe games are supposed to be fun to make, leaving the more *serious* work to the engineers who specialize in creating large accounting systems, traffic monitoring algorithms, or global trading platforms. Maybe this skill gap has simply been overlooked in favor of game mechanics and amazing animations (not that those aren't important bits – we'd be nowhere without them).

Whatever the reason, we need to break the current pattern of sending young developers off into the wilds with swords but no potions and start training for reality – a reality where games are still only *play*, but the underlying game systems need to be just as complex, flexible, and well architected as the software products we use in our daily lives!

## Who this book is for

I'm going to daringly assume that you're a programmer, hobbyist, software engineer, game designer, or unicorn hybrid of all the above. You might be looking to advance your C# and/or game programming knowledge, getting ready for a promotion, or just trying to make your code more reusable, flexible, and professional.

The goal of this book isn't to specifically teach you how to build applications, games, the ins-and-outs of the Unity engine, or even C# for that matter; it's to teach you how to think, problem-solve, and implement systems in your code. C# is a great Object-Oriented language,

Unity is an engaging visual environment, and games are a fun way to learn, but these are all tools for us to learn and design better systems (with the help of design patterns).

Even though design patterns aren't for complete programming beginners, once you have a basic competency in C# and Unity, it's never too early to start thinking and learning about good software architecture. Chances are that the way you're writing code right now could use a boost of optimization, flexibility, and efficiency. And that's why you're here, right?

# What this book covers

*Chapter 1, Priming the System*, starts off with a brief trip into software architecture, software design, and design pattern categories, all while getting comfortable with the why and when of implementing these solutions. We'll also go over the common pitfalls of using design patterns for the first time and the example projects used throughout the book.

*Chapter 2, Managing Access with the Singleton Pattern*, begins by laying the groundwork for uses-cases where globally accessible classes are needed (like persistent game managers) and moves on to generic singleton classes, thread-safety, and converting singletons into ScriptableObjects.

*Chapter 3, Spawning Enemies with the Prototype Pattern*, takes a deep dive into efficiently creating objects without the memory overhead by copying instead of instantiating new instances. We'll also cover the differences between shallow and deep object copying in C#, clone prefab objects, and build a generic cloning script component.

*Chapter 4, Creating Items with the Factory Method Pattern*, introduces the concept of object factories that can produce a variety of products, different factory variations we can use to make our code more efficient and flexible, and scale factory production with Reflection and LINQ.

*Chapter 5, Building a Crafting System with the Abstract Factory Pattern*, details the process for creating factories of factories, working with families of related and independent (or dependent) products, and finally exploring Abstract Factory variations for niche scenarios.

*Chapter 6, Assembling Support Characters with the Builder Pattern*, delves into an assembly line approach to creating complex objects using the same construction processes to pump out different products. We'll also add GameObjects to the mix and use the fluent Builder pattern variation for cleaner code.

*Chapter 7, Managing Performance and Memory with Object Pooling*, introduces the concept of recycling batches of objects for reuse instead of creating new instances from scratch while incorporating thread-safety and Unity's own generic ObjectPool class.

*Chapter 8, Binding Actions with the Command Pattern*, starts with an overview of actionable requests and pre-packaging everything a command may need to be executed. We'll also dive into the differences between coupled and uncoupled commands, their respective use cases, and how to build a complete undo/redo system from scratch.

*Chapter 9, Decoupling Systems with the Observer Pattern*, takes a more in-depth look at communication strategies between objects, how to effectively separate message senders from receivers, and the performance pros and cons of using native C# events versus Unity events.

*Chapter 10, Controlling Behavior with the State Pattern*, dives into the concept of managing an objects' state, transitioning between states, and the basic theory behind state machines. We'll also explore different configurations of state machines, including Finite state machines, Hierarchical state machines, and Concurrent state machines, as well as how to track and store state history.

*Chapter 11, Adding Features with the Visitor Pattern*, gets you ready to add new behaviors to existing objects without changing the underlying object in any way by creating a simple saving system. We'll also learn how to deal with composite elements (objects with children) and how to convert our save system to use ScriptableObjects.

*Chapter 12, Swapping Algorithms with the Strategy Pattern*, explores how to configure classes and objects with interchangeable behaviors (or algorithms) at runtime by building a simple turn-based battle team example. We'll also learn how to optimize these strategies for efficiency and update them to use ScriptableObjects.

*Chapter 13, Making Monsters with the Type Object Pattern*, takes a deep dive into separating common data that a group of related objects share and then creating different configurations of those objects with the least amount of classes using a flat hierarchy. We'll also look at memory allocation and inheritance optimizations and learn how to incorporate ScriptableObjects as configurable data containers.

*Chapter 14, Taking Data Snapshots with the Memento Pattern*, introduces a system for storing, managing, and restoring an object's internal state at any point in time using data snapshots without breaking the object's encapsulation by building a character builder UI example.

*Chapter 15, Dynamic Upgrades with the Decorator Pattern*, offers solutions for dynamically adding behaviors to existing objects without subclassing, making a completely optional opt-in system for new upgrades and features.

*Chapter 16, Converting Incompatible Classes with the Adapter Pattern*, dives into creating shared interfaces for two or more classes that aren't part of any shared hierarchies to work together. We'll also touch on two variations (class and object adapters) and how to map properties in mismatched hierarchies.

*Chapter 17, Simplifying Subsystems with the Façade Pattern*, details a common solution for creating a wall between client code and complex (and often interdependent) subsystems by creating a simple auto-save feature. We'll also get hands-on experience with adding multiplefaçade methods for clients to access and talk about creating abstract façade classes for certain scenarios.

*Chapter 18, Generating Terrains with the Flyweight Pattern*, introduces the concept of shareable state, which makes object creation (especially in large quantities) more computationally efficient if objects don't have to store duplicate data. We'll also discuss adding factories to this design pattern and how to correctly chose between the Flyweight and Type Object patterns.

*Chapter 19, Global Access with the Service Locator Pattern*, details a centralized solution for storing and locating systems in your projects that need to be globally accessible. Like singletons, these services may need to be persistent and accessible from anywhere, which means putting them into a single registry not only makes initialization easier, but it also makes them less prone to abuse.

*Chapter 20, The Road Ahead,* finishes with a look at the SOLID design principles, the design patterns we didn't cover, and resources to take your programming skills to the next level.

# To get the most out of this book

My north star is always making my content accessible to as many people as possible, which means I naturally try and keep prerequisites and barriers to entry fairly low or non-existent. However, design patterns are an intermediate programming topic, which means you need some foundational competencies to get going and feel confident with the material being presented.

Whatever brought you here, we need to lay out some basic requirements for getting the best possible experience from reading this book, so we're all on the same page. Here's what you'll need before getting started:

- Know how to write C# and its basic language components like variables, types, access modifiers, and control flow.
- Understand and use Object-Oriented Programming concepts like classes, objects, interfaces, generics, events, delegates, inheritance, and encapsulation.

- Be comfortable with Unity and the Unity editor, including navigation, creating scripts, and adding objects to the scene. You should also be comfortable with coroutines and basic Unity events like Awake, Start, and Update.

I don't want all of this to sound discouraging, so just know that if you've been playing around with Unity and C# for a few months, maybe watched some tutorials, or even made a simple playable prototype or two - you can absolutely continue reading. This book is a reference, which means you'll likely need to revisit chapters more than once to get things cemented in your mind. Don't feel obligated to read the book in sequence either – the right tool for the job is the mainstay of everything you'll learn here.

You'll also need the current version of Unity installed on your computer—2023 or later is recommended. All code examples have been tested with Unity 2023.1 and should work with future versions without issues.

| Requirements for the chapter exercises | Version |
| --- | --- |
| Unity | 2023.1 or later |
| Visual Studio | 2019 or later |

Before starting, check that your computer setup meets the Unity system requirements at `https://docs.unity3d.com/2023.1/Documentation/Manual/system-requirements.html`.

# Download the example code files

The code bundle for the book is hosted on GitHub at `https://github.com/PacktPublishing/C-Design-Patterns-with-Unity-First-Edition`. We also have other code bundles from our rich catalog of books and videos available at `https://github.com/PacktPublishing/`. Check them out!

# Download the color images

We also provide a PDF file that has color images of the screenshots/diagrams used in this book. You can download it here: `https://packt.link/gbp/9781805120285`.

# Conventions used

There are a number of text conventions used throughout this book.

`Code In Text`: Indicates code words in text, database table names, folder names, filenames, file extensions, pathnames, dummy URLs, user input, and Twitter handles. For example: "`Manager.cs` stores our score and loads the next scene."

A block of code is set as follows:

```
using System.Collections;
using System.Collections.Generic;
using UnityEngine;

public class Item: MonoBehaviour
{
    void OnCollisionEnter(Collision collision)
    {
        if (collision.gameObject.tag == "Player"){

            // 1
            Manager.Instance.score++;

            Destroy(this.gameObject);
            Debug.Log("Item collected!");
        }
    }
}
```

When we wish to draw your attention to a particular part of a code block, the relevant lines or items are set in bold:

```
public class Item: MonoBehaviour
{
    void OnCollisionEnter(Collision collision)
    {
        if (collision.gameObject.tag == "Player")
        {
            // 1
            GenericManager.Instance.score++;

            Destroy(this.gameObject);
            Debug.Log("Item collected!");
        }
    }
}
```

**Bold**: Indicates a new term, an important word, or words that you see on the screen. For instance, words in menus or dialog boxes appear in the text like this. For example: "Navigate to **Assets | Scenes**, and double-click on **SplashScreen**."

Warnings or important notes appear like this.

Tips and tricks appear like this.

# Get in touch

Feedback from our readers is always welcome.

**General feedback**: Email feedback@packtpub.com and mention the book's title in the subject of your message. If you have questions about any aspect of this book, please email us at questions@packtpub.com.

**Errata**: Although we have taken every care to ensure the accuracy of our content, mistakes do happen. If you have found a mistake in this book, we would be grateful if you reported this to us. Please visit http://www.packtpub.com/submit-errata, click **Submit Errata**, and fill in the form.

**Piracy**: If you come across any illegal copies of our works in any form on the internet, we would be grateful if you would provide us with the location address or website name. Please contact us at copyright@packtpub.com with a link to the material.

**If you are interested in becoming an author**: If there is a topic that you have expertise in and you are interested in either writing or contributing to a book, please visit http://authors.packtpub.com.

# Share your thoughts

Once you've read *Learning Design Patterns with Unity*, we'd love to hear your thoughts! Scan the QR code below to go straight to the Amazon review page for this book and share your feedback.

https://packt.link/r/180512028X

Your review is important to us and the tech community and will help us make sure we're delivering excellent quality content.

# Download a free PDF copy of this book

Thanks for purchasing this book!

Do you like to read on the go but are unable to carry your print books everywhere?

Is your eBook purchase not compatible with the device of your choice?

Don't worry, now with every Packt book you get a DRM-free PDF version of that book at no cost.

Read anywhere, any place, on any device. Search, copy, and paste code from your favorite technical books directly into your application.

The perks don't stop there, you can get exclusive access to discounts, newsletters, and great free content in your inbox daily.

Follow these simple steps to get the benefits:

1.  Scan the QR code or visit the link below:

https://packt.link/free-ebook/9781805120285

2.  Submit your proof of purchase.
3.  That's it! We'll send your free PDF and other benefits to your email directly.

# 1

# Priming the System

As programmers, our job is to design, build, and integrate software features into cohesive products that are useful and hopefully bring joy to our users. And somewhere in all of that, the software has to work. Our job can be anything from building a login feature or networking layer to a subscription and payment portal. In games, we're thinking of moving a playable character, building an adaptive AI enemy, or adding a random level generator. The big idea that should pop out at you is that these elements don't exist in a vacuum. In fact, they tend to wither and die of boredom if they're not connected to each other.

When you think of the code powering your applications and games, you're thinking about a collection of systems built around specific features or mechanics, but more importantly, around specific problems that come with making those features work as expected. If I could manage it, I'd have the word *systems* jump off the page and do a little dance to get your attention, because that's what this entire book is about: *games (and applications) are made up of systems – the more these systems grow and interact with each other, the more complicated things get.*

Systems may not be anything new to you, and they're certainly not new to the programming industry, but there are problems that you'll repeatedly run into that are directly related to systems running and interacting. And that's really what I want to drive home before we get started: design patterns provide *reusable* solutions to problems we face in our everyday software lives and offer a common vocabulary for understanding and talking about best practices.

Now the real work starts – how do we identify the parts of our code that could benefit from a design pattern? How does all this relate to software architecture? How can I adapt these patterns for game development in Unity?

These are big questions, which is why we're spending this first chapter getting a holistic feel for the following topics:

- Software architecture vs software design
- Design patterns and the categories they belong to (creational, structural, and behavioral)
- Why use design patterns at all?
- When to use design patterns
- Common pitfalls
- Starter projects for this book

By the end of the chapter, you'll have the necessary foundation to dive into design pattern implementations and a big-picture view of the flexibility, reusability, and structure they can add to your projects. But first, let's make sure you know what to expect from this book and that you're coming to the table with the prerequisites for getting the most out of the experience.

 At the time of writing, all chapter examples and project files were built using Unity 2023.1.5f1. Unity is the visual tool we're using to make the learning process more inviting, but the bones of the design pattern content are still 100% applicable to C# projects. The main differences that come into play between Unity, C#, and design patterns are how objects are created (new classes vs **MonoBehaviours**) and assembled (inheritance vs **GameObjects** and **Components**). Don't worry, we'll cover these variations in each pattern. Learning how each design pattern works as a system doesn't depend on a specific platform or language – it's all problem-solving skills!

## A word about software architecture

Software architecture is a big topic and shouldn't be confused with software design even though they both deal with "patterns." When we talk about architectural patterns, we're talking about big-picture solutions to problems that are typically focused on how multiple components work together at the application level, as well as conventions, best practices, and principles that guide the overall development process. When we talk about software design patterns, we're talking about problems that crop up when you're building those internal components. *Figure 1.1* provides a simplified example of the key difference we're talking about: *Process A* is made up of multiple internal components (the software design portion) while managing and organizing how these internal components fit together (the architectural portion).

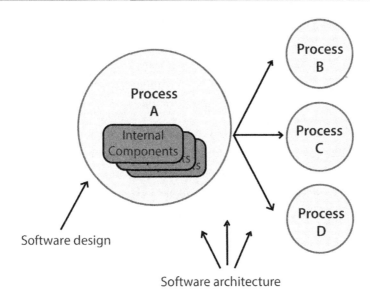

*Figure 1.1: Example diagram of software architecture vs design*

Clear as mud? OK, let's take a more relatable example: if we think about building a house, the architectural patterns are focused on how the *entire* house fits together and how the component parts (electrical, plumbing, insulation, etc.) come together into a functioning structure you can live in. Think LEGO (because that always helps me): architectural patterns deal with problems affecting the overall structure you're building, while design patterns focus on the individual LEGO blocks that make up the final structure. You ideally need both types of solutions in a great application or game, but they solve fundamentally different problems, which is why I bring this distinction up so early in our journey. We'll be focused on the software design aspect of things, but you can (and should) continue your journey into architectural waters after or in conjunction with this book.

In your everyday life, when you open Twitter (or whatever app you go to first thing in the morning), you're involved in what's called the **Client-Server** architectural pattern – the client (the app on your phone) consumes information from a server somewhere in a basement and displays it to you in a way you can understand. But it's not concerned with how the app remembers your login credentials or uses face recognition to log you in. Those are software design problems because they focus on the internal features of the application.

Before we get to the why, when, and how of design patterns, we need to agree on a basic understanding of what *good* software design is to see the benefits of design patterns. Books on software design are everywhere. Amazon thinks you want them, and your co-workers probably have a few gathering dust on their desks right now. Hell, your computer monitor might be sitting on a few of them at this very moment. This isn't one of those books.

I like to think of software design as a tool that might make things harder in the moment but easier in the long run, like going to the gym. It's a pain to use the Stairmaster every day, but being healthy has far-reaching benefits throughout a lifetime. The same is true of approaching a project with an eye to software design. With that in mind, let's set up a simple definition for ourselves as a kind of guiding light for what *we* mean by good software design:

*A codebase that is flexible, maintainable, and reusable is the product of good software design.*

This is easier said than done no matter how well-intentioned you or your team start off developing your game. Decoupling your code can speed up your development process, but it adds overhead and maintenance time. On the other hand, interdependent code can be costly when you want to make changes, big or small. It's all about balance, even if you can't have everything you want all the time. Fast, good, or cheap – you can only ever have two.

With a working definition of *good* software design, we can move on to talking about what design patterns are, how they're categorized, and how they fit into Unity projects.

# What are design patterns?

If I haven't harped on this point enough, I want you to keep thinking to yourself "Design Patterns are systems" over and over. Let's say that again, design patterns are systems, and systems are designed to solve specific problems. It doesn't matter if it's the brake system in your car, the biological systems that run our bodies, or the banking system in *Figure 1.2*. They're all systems and they're all trying to solve a problem or keep their respective system organized and balanced (and sometimes both).

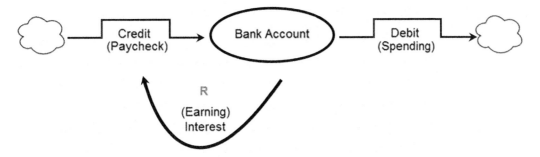

*Figure 1.2: Diagram of how bank accounts work using credit and debit*

More than anything, design patterns focus on making code more flexible and reusable, two tenets we'll hammer away at throughout this book. Just keep repeating our mantra every time we dive into a new pattern: design patterns are systems!

## The Gang of Four

Back in 1994, a group of four daring engineers banded together to better tackle OOP practices and recurring problems that kept popping up in their programs; *Design Patterns: Elements of Reusable Object-Oriented Software* written by Erich Gamma, Richard Helm, Ralph Johnson, and John Vlissides is the product of that team-up. The book covers 23 design patterns split into three categories according to their core functions, with examples written in C++ and Smalltalk. While the book was and continues to be an important resource, these patterns have been adapted and expanded since 1994, leaving some more (and some less) relevant depending on your chosen programming language and environment.

There are also those who have pointed out that a fair few of the patterns are replacements for perceived missing features in the C++ language. However, this argument has never resonated with me when I look at my code in other languages (whether it's C# or something like Swift) because wearing my systems-thinking glasses has always made me think more critically and write code more intentionally.

You've likely heard the phrase "Gang of Four" whispered with quiet reverence (or loud and angry fist-shaking, depending on who you're talking to), but with topics like this, I've found it's best to learn design patterns as a skill before making judgments. There are impassioned programmers on both sides of the aisle, which means getting your hands dirty is the best thing you can do for yourself. A lot of the debate gets lost in theoretical or pedagogical minutiae (and personalities) but the core skillset behind design patterns has always been a useful tool for programming.

## Pattern categories

There are three categories that all original design patterns fall into – **Creational**, **Behavioral**, and **Structural**. As with all things, additional patterns have evolved since 1994, resulting in useful patterns that were not included in the original Gang of Four book that we'll cover on our journey and a few honorable mentions (because we can't cover every design pattern in a single book).

Before we get into the category details, I feel it's important to address a problem that crops up at the beginning of most journeys into design patterns – how do I find the right pattern for the problem I'm facing? Do I need to read and memorize every pattern, or is there a better way to navigate this topic?

The answer might surprise you, but no, this isn't a memorization game and you don't get extra points for knowing everything about every design pattern – systems thinking is a learned skill, not a closed-book test. It's almost a detective game: first, knowing what problems each pattern category addresses is *super* important because it narrows the field you have to search. Second, reading the first few pages of each chapter in the applicable category will show you pretty quickly if you're in the right place. From there, the more you use design patterns, the more you'll get a feel for the problems and effective solutions out in the wild. As you'll see, design patterns offer solutions to well-documented problems, but they're not set in stone; it's up to you to adapt them to your project.

Now that we know the basics, let's dive into the nitty-gritty of each design pattern category and what specific problems they aim to solve.

# Creational patterns

**Creational patterns** deal with creating objects that are uniquely suited to a given situation or use case. More specifically, these patterns deal with how to hide object and class creation logic, so the calling instance doesn't get bogged down with the details. As your object and class creation needs become more complex, these patterns will help move you away from hardcoding fixed behaviors toward writing smaller behavior sets that you can use to build up more complex features (think LEGO). A good creational pattern black-boxes the creation logic and simply hands back a utility tool to control what, who, how, and when an object or class is created.

The creational patterns we'll cover are listed in the following table:

| Pattern | Description |
| --- | --- |
| Singleton | Ensure a class has only one instance and provide a global point of access to it – commonly used for features like logging or database connections that need to be coordinated and shared through the entire application. |
| Prototype | Specify the kinds of objects to create using a prototypical instance and create new objects from the "skeleton" of an existing object. |
| Factory Method | Define an interface for creating a single object, but delegate the instantiation logic to subclasses that decide which class to instantiate. |
| Abstract Factory | Define an interface for creating families of related or dependent objects, but let subclasses decide which class to instantiate. |
| Builder | Allows complex objects to be built step by step, separating an object's construction from its representation – commonly used when creating different versions of an object. |
| Object Pool | Avoid expensive acquisition and release of resources by recycling objects that are no longer in use – commonly used when resources are expensive, plentiful, or both. |

*Table 1.1: List of creational design patterns with descriptions*

## Behavioral patterns

**Behavioral patterns** are concerned with how classes and objects communicate with each other. More specifically, these patterns concentrate on the different responsibilities and connections objects have with each other when they're working together. Like structural patterns, behavioral patterns use inheritance to divvy up behaviors between classes, which gives you the freedom to let go of any white-knuckled control flow responsibilities and focus on how objects can work together.

The behavioral patterns we'll cover are listed in the following table:

| Pattern | Description |
|---------|-------------|
| **Command** | Encapsulate a request as an object, thereby allowing for the parameterization of clients with different requests and the queuing or logging of requests. |
| **Observer** | Define a one-to-many dependency between objects where a state change in one object results in all its dependents being notified and updated automatically. |
| **State** | Allow an object to alter its behavior when its internal state changes. The object will appear to change its class – commonly used when object behavior drastically changes depending on its internal state. |
| **Visitor** | Define a new class operation without changing the underlying object. |
| **Strategy** | Define a family of interchangeable behaviors and defer setting the behavior until runtime. |
| **Type Object** | Allow the flexible creation of new "classes" from a single class, each instance of which will represent a different type of object. |
| **Memento** | Capture and externalize the internal state of an object so it can be restored or reverted to this state later – without breaking encapsulation. |

*Table 1.2: List of behavioral design patterns with descriptions*

## Structural patterns

**Structural patterns** focus on composition, or how classes and objects are composed into larger, more complex structures. Structural patterns are heavy on abstraction, which makes object relationships easier to manage and customize. Patterns in this category will use inheritance to let you mix and match your class structures as well as create objects with new functionality at runtime.

The structural patterns we'll cover are listed in the following table:

| Pattern | Description |
| --- | --- |
| **Decorator** | Attach additional responsibilities to an object dynamically keeping the same interface. |
| **Adapter** | Convert the interface of a class into another interface clients expect. An adapter lets classes work together that could not otherwise because of incompatible interfaces. |
| **Façade** | Provide a unified interface to a set of interfaces in a subsystem. Facade defines a high-level interface that makes the subsystem easier to use. |
| **Flyweight** | Shares common data between similar objects to limit memory usage and increase performance. |
| **Service Locator** | Provide a global access point for services without coupling client code to the concrete service classes. |

*Table 1.3: List of structural design patterns with descriptions*

The goal with each of these problems is to use a solution that is coherent, reusable, and above all, designed for efficient change.

# Why use design patterns?

In four words – reusability, flexibility, and maintainability. You'll see these concepts pop up around software architecture and code complexity topics, but they are the central beneficial tenets of design patterns. For example, if you need to create variations of the same object in your game, it makes more sense to create a build system instead of individual hard-coded objects. *Figure 1.3* illustrates an assembly line that turns out little robots, with each step fulfilling a specific function in the object creation process.

This is a simplified but effective mental model for the Builder pattern:

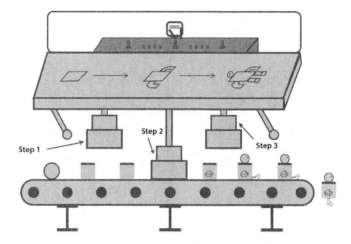

*Figure 1.3: Reusable Builder pattern creating objects*

Let's start with reusability, which OOP principles like encapsulation, abstraction, and inheritance already address and are the cornerstones of many design patterns in this book. There's no better feeling than sitting down with a new feature task to implement and realizing you already have the building blocks you need to get it done. Your only real task is to stack them together into a form that makes the feature work and test it out. With design patterns, you have the option of using class inheritance, delegation, and object composition to create reusable components for your game code. Each has its pros and cons, which we'll get into later, but they can also give you an efficiency bump when you're writing new code.

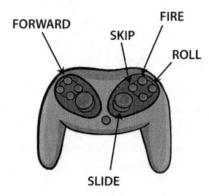

*Figure 1.4: Flexible control scheme diagram using the Command pattern*

In terms of flexibility, design patterns can help you structure your code for the future, and by the future, I mean change. When we talk about change and reusability, we're talking about code that can handle changing requirements *and* changing scales. No program you will ever write is going to be static, because no code is perfectly balanced on the first try. If you don't build in flexibility, the first strong wind is going to snap your project in two, and that means redesigns, feature implementations, and new rounds of testing.

The beauty of correctly using design patterns is that you don't just have to choose one – you can mix and match to get the desired result. For example, your game will always need player controls like in *Figure 1.4*, but what if you want to switch out individual commands or button assignments? Your code would be more flexible if you could separate the control input from the implementation, which is something the Command pattern is great at.

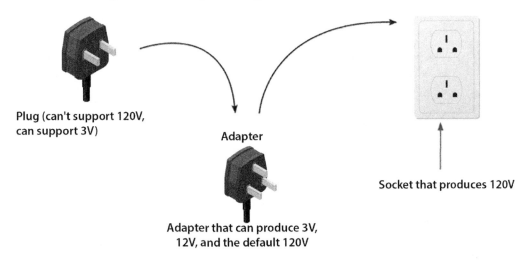

Plug (can't support 120V, can support 3V)

Adapter

Adapter that can produce 3V, 12V, and the default 120V

Socket that produces 120V

*Figure 1.5: Adapter pattern as an example of designing for change and easy maintenance*

Finally, we come to maintainability. The ideal is to have working code that has the *right* level of architecture and complexity; not only does this make our code readable, it's easier to debug if each component or class has a defined role we can isolate. I italicized "right" because it's a tricky task. On the one hand, you want enough structure in your project to make updating the code as easy and efficient as possible. On the other hand, too much complexity can needlessly clog up a project, having the exact opposite effect. Correctly identifying design patterns that'll help you achieve the former instead of the latter is the balancing act of code maintenance.

# When to use design patterns

You know you're doing something interesting when the answer to the question of why or when is both maddeningly simple and complex. The answer you'll hear the most about design patterns is that you should only use them when they're needed. Helpful, right?

The easiest way to know if you should use a design pattern is if you identify a concrete problem area in your code. Symptoms of a problem include code smells like tightly coupled classes, monolithic subclass hierarchies, and dependencies on specific operations, object representations, and hardware. Hardware and software dependencies are particularly acute in game development when you need to port your code to different devices or systems.

**NOTE**

If *code smells* are a new concept, don't worry, they're just a fancy industry term for characteristics of your code that might point to a deeper problem. Code smells can include huge, bloated classes, misuse of Object-Oriented principles, changes in one place necessitating changes in other places in your application, and excessively coupled objects.

All those symptoms are related to the idea of designing for change, and how easy or hard it is to make changes to your code. This is a topic we'll explore with each pattern individually, but here are a few high-level red flags to look out for:

- Is a class hard to add to or maintain?
- How much knowledge does the programmer making a change need to have of the entire system they are working on?
- Is it difficult to create slightly different objects from existing classes?
- Does a change in one area crash a secondary or even unrelated part of the codebase?
- Can your code satisfy an operational request in only one way?
- If you're working with algorithms, does changing the implementation break the object using the algorithm?

If any of these questions ring a bell, then your code could use some design pattern love. But design patterns aren't all fun and games (pun intended); there are pitfalls with any tool – software or physical – that we have to address before diving in.

# Common pitfalls

We can get to a well-architected state with less stress if we keep an eye on some common pitfalls. You'll notice as you read this book that it's not so much a step-by-step tutorial as it is a reference for when you need to implement a design pattern. Half the skill is learning if, and when, to use one at all.

Let's summarize:

- *Don't use a design pattern just for the sake of using it.* Impressing a review team or someone on GitHub isn't worth it. If a part of your game needs some abstraction and decoupling, absolutely do it.
- *Only add complexity where it's needed.* If you find that your project is overly architected, ask yourself if your codebase wouldn't be cleaner and easier to read without it.
- *Good software architecture is never free.* Abstracting code takes time to learn, write, and maintain, and you may take runtime hits to performance and speed.

So why do any of this design pattern nonsense in the first place? Because complexity isn't a bad word, performance can be improved later on, and the efficiency bump in your development process is well worth the up-front investment. You won't get it right the first time, so enjoy the iteration. It's all part of the process. And if you're like me, using design patterns is like a puzzle, and when that code runs, it's like finding that last pesky piece your cat hid under the couch – it's magic.

# About the example projects

When I first started learning about design patterns, I found the wealth of resources, tutorials, and applicable scenarios overwhelming (if this has happened to you too, I hope finding this book will make your journey much, much easier). The problem wasn't the technical information that I was finding, but the way it was presented. More often than not, the design pattern content seemed to be shrouded in dry, overbearing technical language, complicated examples, or just plain old incorrect solutions.

One of my main goals in writing this book was to present the foundation of these wonderful tools with as little fluff as possible. However, this turns problematic when trying to find a balance between teaching the design pattern itself and getting it to run in a meaningful way – because just like design patterns, new skills wither and die in a vacuum. This is all to say that I've created the starter projects for each chapter as simply and meaningfully as I possibly can. The balance is delicate, and you might find the examples weighted to one side or the other, but it's always been with the intention of making the design pattern the star.

## Client code

Some of the ways I've implemented UI code, client scripts, or any of the simple systems around *using* each design pattern are not production-ready or best practices – they are the simplest way of using the pattern with context. On the flip side, I've given as much thought and page count as possible to pattern variations, extensions, and best practices so you have concrete tools to bring to your own projects.

Again, this book isn't about Unity (although it's a delightfully fun learning environment), but rather how we can learn problem solving skills and apply them to software.

## Old vs new input system

As you'll see in the next chapter and onwards, I'm using Unity's old Input System rather than the new Input System. Why? Because it's the simplest way to get the client code running with a minimum amount of setup and screenshots for you to follow. I love the new input system (I feel I need to put this on the record or risk banishment), but it does require a little specialized knowledge and experience that doesn't contribute to design patterns. As always, I encourage you to experiment with implementing the design pattern solutions in whatever context works best for your project. For learning, I've found the old Input System works best.

## Art assets

I love beautiful Unity projects that are full of life, sound, ambiance, and thematic feeling, but these things don't help us learn new skills – in fact, they tend to distract at best and hinder at worst. All example projects use the most basic primitive objects and materials possible (essentially white boxing everything), not only to keep things consistent but to keep you focused on the design patterns. And who knows, the lack of excitement in our projects might just inspire you to deploy your new skills in ways you hadn't thought of before.

I hope the simplicity of the examples I've prepared doesn't make you nervous, because it should really make you hopeful. The fact that we can use these patterns as systems to be plugged in and interchanged with the UI, clients, or any other aspect of application development only strengthens the very first point of this chapter – design patterns are systems!

# Summary

I know this was a lot of logistics and theory to get through – congratulations on sticking with it even if you were itching to start coding. This chapter has a lot of useful resources and content that you can (and should) refer to as you continue your design pattern adventure. Remember, we defined good software as flexible, reusable, and maintainable, so keep that at the forefront of your mind when reading each chapter.

Design patterns are internal systems that solve specific problems, and half the battle is matching the problem you have to the pattern that solves it best. There's a time and place to use design patterns, but overusing (or misusing) them can lead to complexity you don't need and time costs you don't have to spend. Your ultimate job (which is down to me) is to come out of the other end of this book literate in the language of design patterns.

In the next chapter, we'll dive into our first official design pattern – the Singleton pattern – and get a taste of thinking in systems!

# Further reading

If any of these topics sounds foreign, you can take a step back and check out the resource list I've put together below or push through and learn as you go along.

- For C#, I'd recommend starting with my beginner-level book *Learning C# by Developing Games with Unity (7th Edition)*. I wrote it specifically to get new programmers up to speed with core programming skills from the ground up using C# and Unity, and you can find it at `https://www.amazon.com/Learning-Developing-Games-Unity-coding/dp/1837636877`.

- For a deeper dive into the C# language, Mark Price's book *C# 11 and .NET: Modern Cross-Platform Development Fundamental* is fantastic, which you can find at `https://www.amazon.com/11-NET-Cross-Platform-Development-Fundamentals/dp/1803237805`.

- For Unity content, I'd recommend *Hands-On Unity 2022 Game Development* by Nicolas Alejandro Borromeo (`https://www.amazon.com/Hands-Unity-2022-Game-Development/dp/1803236914`) and *Unity 3D Game Development* by Anthony Davis, Travis Baptiste, Russell Craig, and Ryan Stunkel (`https://www.amazon.com/Unity-Game-Development-design-beautiful/dp/1801076146`).

# Leave a review!

Enjoying this book? Help readers like you by leaving an Amazon review. Scan the QR code below to get a free eBook of your choice.

# 2

# Managing Access with the Singleton Pattern

In the last chapter, we went over the core of what design patterns are, the common problems they solve, and how we'll go about learning and implementing each of them throughout our adventure. In this chapter, we'll start our practical journey by exploring the Singleton pattern, which helps when you want a single instance of a class to be globally accessible. For applications and games, you'll commonly see this type of functionality with manager or service classes that keep track of global state or provide access to system-wide utilities. However, we need to be aware of potential risks with global state (and how to protect our newly accessible data), which we'll discuss later in the chapter.

Anytime you bring up the Singleton pattern in programming circles, you're likely to hear an audible sigh, some hushed booing, and maybe even an angry shout or two. And that's precisely why I like to teach this pattern first! It's one of the easiest design patterns to understand and implement (and, thus, abuse) but the hardest to use *correctly* (because, as we all know, there's only one way to do things *correctly* in programming, right?). I might even go so far as to say the Singleton pattern is more useful with Unity-specific features like ScriptableObjects than the original implementation could have anticipated (more on that later).

Like all design patterns, the Singleton pattern has its specific uses, pitfalls, and practical implementation, which we'll explore in the following topics:

- Defining, diagraming, and analyzing the pros and cons of the Singleton pattern
- Updating a MonoBehaviour script into a persistent singleton class

- Creating a flexible generic singleton class using lazy instantiation
- Making the generic singleton class thread-safe
- Creating singleton instances as `ScriptableObject` assets

Throughout this chapter, we're going to actively avoid typecasting the Singleton pattern as the big, bad boogeyman of design patterns. Instead, we'll focus on identifying areas where the pattern can help make your code more flexible, reusable, and maintainable while maintaining safety and encapsulation.

# Technical requirements

To get started:

1. Download or clone the GitHub repository at `https://github.com/PacktPublishing/C-Design-Patterns-with-Unity-First-Edition`.

2. Open the `Ch_02_Starter` project folder in Unity Hub.

3. Navigate to **Assets | Scenes**, and double-click on **SplashScreen**.

The starter project for this chapter has two scenes – a splash screen with the title of our little game and a button to start the adventure. When you click **Start,** the game transitions to a new scene, where you can move a capsule around a small arena and collect spheres.

As for the scripts:

- `Item.cs` is attached to each `Item` prefab that is responsible for destroying itself when there's a collision.
- `Manager.cs` stores our score and loads the next scene.
- `Player.cs` is responsible for moving our character around the scene using the *WASD* or arrow keys.
- `ScoreUI.cs` stores a Text object so that we can set an initial score value on our scene canvas.

We'll also be using some Unity and C# language features to take our code the extra mile. Don't worry if you're not familiar with these, as I've included links for the basics, and I'll explain how they apply to our use cases as we go along:

- Generics (`https://learn.microsoft.com/en-us/dotnet/csharp/fundamentals/types/generics`)

- ScriptableObjects (`https://docs.unity3d.com/Manual/class-ScriptableObject.html`)

- Multithreading (`https://learn.microsoft.com/en-us/dotnet/standard/threading/using-threads-and-threading`)

Our job in this chapter is to transform `Manager.cs` into a singleton class that can be referenced from `ScoreUI.cs` and `Item.cs`, which will keep the score value in sync with the UI. Don't worry about `Player.cs`, as you won't have to update any code there. Once you're done testing the starter project, we can move on to the pattern theory and then get into some code of our own!

# Breaking down the pattern

First, it's important to recognize scenarios where the Singleton pattern is useful and doesn't just add unnecessary complexity to your code. The original Gang of Four text says you should consider using the Singleton pattern when:

*You need to limit a class to a single instance and have that unique instance be accessible to clients through a global access point.*

For example, your computer should only have one filesystem, in the same way that your body should only have one heart (for best performance). A global variable can take care of the accessibility, and in the case of C#, a static variable fits the bill nicely. When you put it all together, a singleton class is responsible for initializing, storing, and returning its own unique instance, as well as protecting against duplicate instance requests.

*Figure 2.1* describes a game scenario where a manager script stores game state data and maybe some shared functionality.

In this case, implementing the manager as a singleton provides a global point of access to the manager so that other components like the UI, player controls, and event system can easily access it.

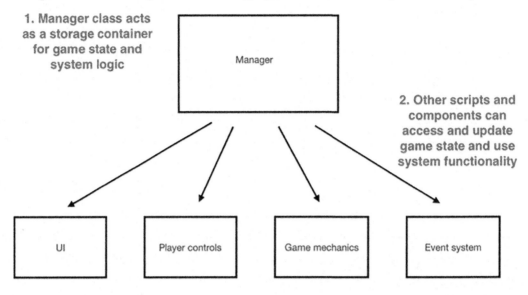

*Figure 2.1: Example scenario of multiple scripts accessing a single manager class instance*

The Singleton pattern also ensures that there's only one instance of the class at any given time. Without a singleton, you might end up with multiple manager instances running around in your application, making it difficult for other scripts to know where the single source of truth is. This can lead to mismatched information and unexpected states down the line, which are notoriously hard to debug. *Figure 2.2* shows a possible scenario where the UI, player controls, and game mechanics access Manager 1, while the event system pulls from Manager 2. This setup leads to data synchronization errors, mismatched class data, and unintentioned functionality.

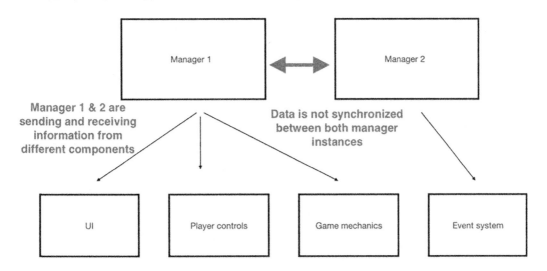

*Figure 2.2: Example of two manager instances being active at the same time*

In Unity, there are two additional features to a singleton class. First, the singleton is responsible for destroying any GameObject with a duplicate singleton class script component. Again, we don't want multiple instances of the same singleton in our applications, so if someone on your team mistakenly creates one, the existing singleton will destroy the duplicate. Second, the singleton is responsible for keeping itself active through the full application lifecycle, as shown in *Figure 2.3*. When the game starts, the manager instance is created and persists as different scenes are loaded. The manager is only destroyed when the application quits. If the manager were reinitialized in each scene, it wouldn't be updated with the data from the previous scenes (which would defeat the whole reason we started down this path in the first place).

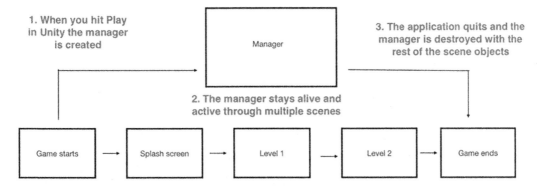

*Figure 2.3: Ideal lifecycle of a singleton class that persists from the start of a game session*

We'll discuss the finer pros and cons of the Singleton pattern later in this section. For now, we have enough to dive into a more technical definition of the pattern and start mapping out visual diagrams of how it works in code.

## Diagramming the pattern

*Figure 2.4* lays out the Unified Modeling Language (UML) diagram for the Singleton design pattern. The client asks for the instance from the singleton object, which checks if one already exists. If there's an active instance, the singleton object returns it; if there's no active instance, a new one is created and returned.

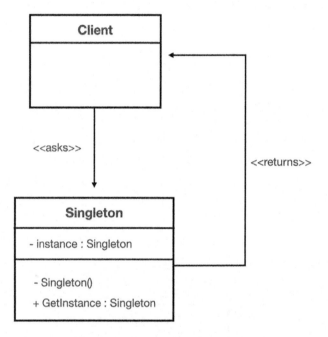

*Figure 2.4: UML diagram of the Singleton design pattern*

As I mentioned at the beginning of the chapter, there are not many moving parts to this design pattern, but it's still extremely useful if you're aware of the potential costs and benefits, which we'll get into in the next section.

## Pros and cons

Any information you'll find in the wild about the Singleton pattern usually comes with a warning label: *use with great care and moderation*. The fear is that a Singleton lets us black-box any manager class into a globally accessible instance, which then snowballs into a codebase full of singleton manager classes with the following consequences:

- **Increased coupling between classes is generally not a good outcome in programming.** This is especially true in an environment like Unity where everything is based on components and entities. Globally accessible singletons compromise decoupled code by offering up an easily accessible global state for any client class to couple with. However, if you look closely, you'll notice this isn't enough to nullify the potential benefits of the pattern. If the concept of coupling is new to you, think of it as connections between classes or objects, which can come in various degrees of strength or interdependence.

- **Unit testing can become very difficult when dependencies are everywhere.** For instance, if we have singleton classes for several managers in a game with dependencies on each other, it's hard to separate them out to individually test them. This problem is doubly dangerous because it won't crop up when you're initializing the dependent singletons, as that works just fine. The problem only arises when you've built out your interconnected systems. Dependency injection of mock testing can be a useful solution to this problem, and we'll discuss how to make singletons into ScriptableObjects later in the chapter, which can make testing more accessible.

While keeping the potential consequences in mind, the pattern offers the concrete benefits listed below:

- **It saves resources** by only initializing itself when first asked, which means we won't have an unused singleton taking up our valuable memory.

- **It is initialized at runtime** and has access to information only available after the game is running.

Finally, there are two outcomes of the Singleton pattern that we could put into either the pro or con column, depending on your scenario:

- **Global access is a double-edged sword.** It sounds efficient when you look at it from the client's perspective – you always know how and where to access it. But from a data perspective, global access can make it extremely hard to debug global state. If it's easily accessible to any client class, then global singleton data can also be modified from anywhere. It's hard to find the modifying culprit when everyone has a key.

- **Global state doesn't play well with concurrency.** A singleton's global point of access is stored in memory, which can be accessed and used by any thread. This can lead to aggravating threading bugs like synchronization errors, deadlocks, and race conditions. However, you can also see the singleton's innate ability to limit concurrency as a silver lining when you need to protect shared resources.

Now that we've covered the Singleton pattern theory, it's time to implement a singleton class into our starter project, which we'll do in the next section.

## Updating a MonoBehavior into a persistent singleton

Imagine you are building a platforming game where the player collects items through multiple levels. Your team lead asks you to create a manager script to track the player's score, handle scene transitions, and ensure there's always one unique instance in a scene. Our first task is to ensure that the game manager class in the starter project only ever has one active instance.

Open `Manager.cs` and update the code to match the following code, which sets the singleton instance or destroys the `GameObject` that the script is attached to if an instance already exists:

```
using System.Collections;
using System.Collections.Generic;
using UnityEngine;
using UnityEngine.UI;
using UnityEngine.SceneManagement;

public class Manager : MonoBehaviour
{
    // 1
    public static Manager Instance;

    public int score = 0;
    public int startingLevel = 1;

    // 2
    void Awake()
    {
        // 3
        if(Instance == null){
            Instance = this;
            Debug.Log("New instance initialized...");
        }
        // 4
        else if(Instance != this)
        {
            Destroy(this.gameObject);
```

```
                Debug.Log("Existing instance found, deleting self...");
        }
    }


    public void StartGame()
    {
        // ... No changes needed ...
    }
}
```

Let's break down the code:

1. First, we declare a public static variable to hold the only Instance of the Manager class. Creating a static variable means it can be accessed without creating an instance of the class, which is perfect for a singleton.

2. Then, we use the Awake method to set the instance when the script instance is being loaded.

3. Inside the Awake method, we check if the Instance is null – if it is, we set Instance to this instance of the class and print a debug log.

4. Finally, if Instance is not equal to this instance of the class (that is, if there's a duplicate), we destroy the GameObject and print a different debug log.

To start testing the singleton, update ScoreUI.cs to match the following code, which will reference the game manager's static instance and pull the real-time score data when you run the game:

```
using System.Collections;
using System.Collections.Generic;
using UnityEngine;
using UnityEngine.UI;

public class ScoreUI : MonoBehaviour
{
    public Text score;

    void Start()
    {
        // 1
        score.text += Manager.Instance.score;
    }
```

```
    void Update()
    {
        // 2
        score.text = "Score: " + Manager.Instance.score;
    }
}
```

This new code replaces the hardcoded values that came with the starter project, which means once we update the item collection logic, our score value will always be in sync with the UI display.

 For simplicity, we're checking for score updates in the Update method in the code above. However, in production code, a better solution is to add events for these kinds of updates and register listeners for scripts that want updated data. We'll discuss events and listeners in *Chapter 9, Decoupling Systems with the Observer Pattern,* subscribing and publishing events with the Observer pattern.

Now, update Item.cs to match the following code, which increases the score when an item is collected using the Manager singleton:

```
using System.Collections;
using System.Collections.Generic;
using UnityEngine;

public class Item: MonoBehaviour
{
    void OnCollisionEnter(Collision collision)
    {
        if (collision.gameObject.tag == "Player"){

            // 1
            Manager.Instance.score++;

            Destroy(this.gameObject);
            Debug.Log("Item collected!");
        }
    }
}
```

Run the **SplashScreen** scene in the starter project, and you'll see a console log shown below:

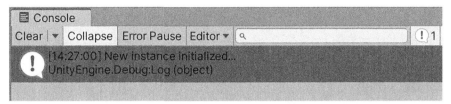

*Figure 2.5: A new instance of the Manager class is instantiated, and the confirmation log is printed out*

However, if you press the **Start** button in the scene and transition to the Level_01 scene, the Game Manager with the Manager script component attached won't persist in the **Hierarchy** when the new scene is loaded, as shown here:

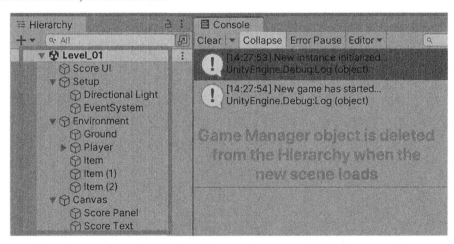

*Figure 2.6: The Game Manager object does not persist in the Hierarchy when the new scene loads*

Next, we'll add code to make sure the singleton isn't destroyed when new scenes load and finish off the section by testing the duplicate deletion logic.

## Persisting the singleton between scenes

For the next part of our example scenario, imagine your team lead specifies that the game manager instance needs to persist through the entire game session, even when new scenes are loaded. Since the Manager script is attached to a GameObject, we can mark that object to not be destroyed when a new scene is loaded. However, the object will still be destroyed when the game session ends, which fits into our ideal singleton lifecycle from *Figure 2.3*.

Go back to Manager.cs and update Awake() to match the following code, which persists whatever GameObject our Manager script is attached to:

```
void Awake()
{
    if(Instance == null)
    {
        Instance = this;
        Debug.Log("New instance initialized...");

        // 1
        DontDestroyOnLoad(this.gameObject);
    } else if(Instance != this)
    {
        Destroy(this.gameObject);
        Debug.Log("Duplicate instance found and deleted...");
    }
}
```

When Unity loads a new scene, all objects from the previous scene are destroyed, so what we've done here with DontDestroyOnLoad is mark the GameObject as being safe from those deletions. This allows the GameObject to pass through to the new scene and work normally in that environment.

> Unity loads all GameObjects present in a scene into memory when the scene is loaded. When the scene is unloaded or when a new scene is loaded, all GameObjects associated with the old scene are destroyed and removed from memory unless marked with DontDestroyOnLoad. This method is Unity's way of making sure that GameObjects are persistent, allowing them to survive scene transitions and continue existing in the new scene.

Run the **SplashScreen** scene again, and you'll see the Game Manager has been moved to the DontDestroyOnLoad section of the **Hierarchy**, as shown here:

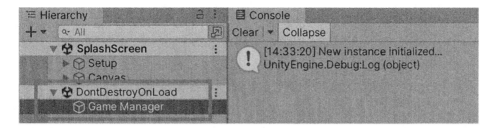

*Figure 2.7: Game Manager moved to the persistent DontDestroyOnLoad section of the project Hierarchy*

If you press the **Start** button, the scene will switch to Level_01, but the Game Manager will stay active in the DontDestroyOnLoad section of the new scene **Hierarchy**, as shown next:

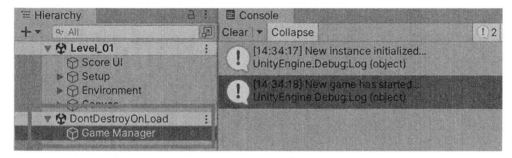

*Figure 2.8: Game Manager persists in the DontDestroyOnLoad section of the Hierarchy when a new scene is loaded*

Now, we have the bones of our singleton working, but we still need to test if checking and deleting duplicate instances works, which we'll do next.

## Testing for duplicate managers

Now that the Manager script is persisting on the Game Manager object between scenes, we can test how well our duplicate checking logic works in two different scenarios: how the singleton reacts when it detects a duplicate **in another scene** versus when it detects a duplicate **in the same scene at runtime**.

For the first scenario:

1. Open the **Level_01** scene, create an empty GameObject in the **Hierarchy**, and name it Duplicate Manager.

2.  Attach the Manager script as a component.

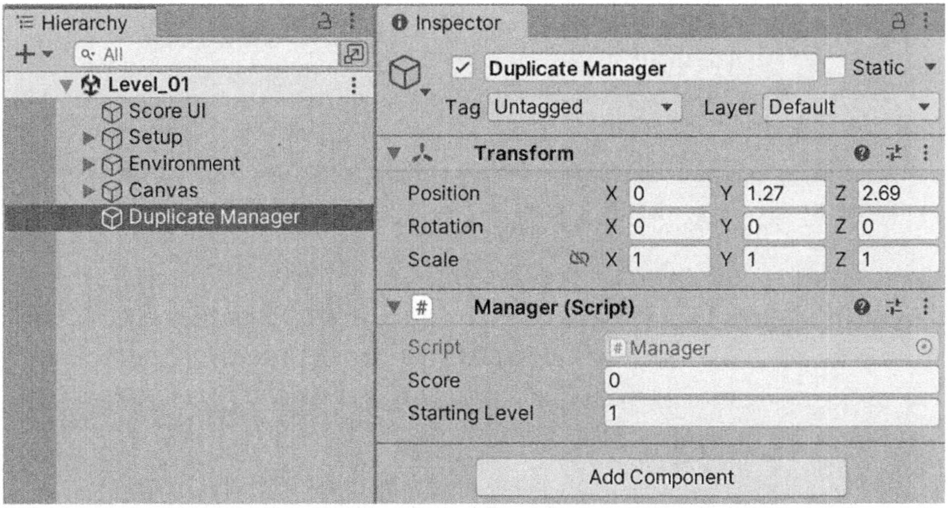

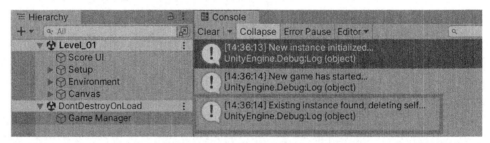

*Figure 2.9: Adding another manager object to the Level_01 Hierarchy to test duplicate deletions*

3.  Go back and run the **SplashScreen** scene and press **Start**. You'll see an additional console log that says a duplicate was found and deleted itself, which preserves the existing instance as the only active singleton, as you can see here:

*Figure 2.10: Example output of a duplicate manager class being found and deleted from the Hierarchy*

We can see from the console logs that our duplicate deletion logic is working as expected, which is great! However, as we'll see with our second test scenario, hardcoding a singleton in a MonoBehaviour class isn't going to give us the best results.

For the second scenario:

1.  Open the **SplashScreen** scene, create an empty GameObject in the **Hierarchy**, name it Duplicate Manager, and attach the Manager script as a component.

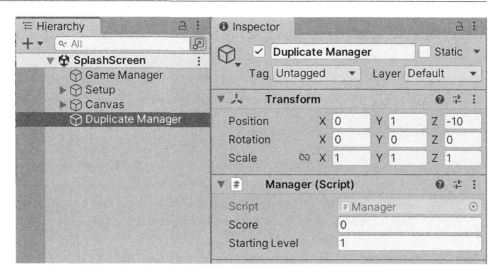

*Figure 2.11: Adding another manager to the SplashScreen Hierarchy to test duplicate deletions*

2.  When you run the scene this time around, you'll see that the original Game Manager was deleted and the Duplicate Manager was persisted, as shown here:

*Figure 2.12: Example output of a runtime race condition between duplicate managers*

Not being able to easily control the order in which the **Hierarchy** objects are created at runtime can have undesirable effects. In the starter project, the StartGame method in Manager.cs is connected to the **Start** button's OnClick method in the **Inspector**. If the wrong duplicate singleton is deleted, it breaks our scene.

The game manager class is now working as a singleton, but it lacks reusability and flexibility. If your singleton has to be hardcoded into the implementing class, it's not much use past the prototyping stage. In our second solution, we'll pass all our singleton logic to a generic class for any MonoBehaviour to inherit and use lazy instantiation to head off any race conditions, ensuring that the wrong duplicate is never deleted.

# Creating a generic singleton

Imagine you want to make the singleton more flexible, reusable, and maintainable. The previous implementation works, but it's hardcoded into Manager.cs, which won't help us if we want different classes to act like singletons. A better solution is to write a generic singleton that other classes can easily subclass.

 We're using a generic approach instead of subclassing the singleton class because we want the same design pattern implementations applied to different types. If we wanted the same functionality implemented in different ways across different singletons, subclass and traditional Object-oriented inheritance would be the way to go.

*Figure 2.13* describes a generic singleton script that other manager classes can inherit from. Each subclassed manager has the same underlying Singleton structure, but each one can also add its own unique functionality and variables.

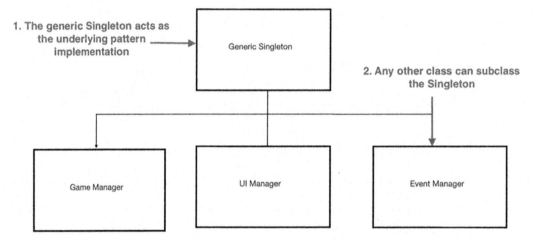

*Figure 2.13: Multiple manager classes inheriting from the same generic singleton class*

In the **Scripts** folder, create a new C# script named Singleton and update the code to match the following code, which will create a generic singleton class for any MonoBehaviour to subclass:

```
using System.Collections;
using System.Collections.Generic;
using UnityEngine;

// 1
```

```
public class Singleton<T> : MonoBehaviour where T: MonoBehaviour
{
    // 2
    private static T _instance;
    public static T Instance
    {
        get
        {
            // 3
            if (_instance == null)
            {
                _instance = FindAnyObjectByType<T>();

                // 4
                if(_instance == null)
                {
                    var singletonGO = new GameObject();
                    singletonGO.name = typeof(T).Name + " (Persists)";
                    _instance = singletonGO.AddComponent<T>();

                    DontDestroyOnLoad(singletonGO);
                    Debug.Log("New instance created!");
                }
            }

            // 6
            return _instance;
        }
    }
}
```

Let's break down this chunk of code:

1.  First, we declare a generic singleton class of type T where "T" is a MonoBehaviour, which makes sure that we never create a singleton class that can't be attached to a GameObject.

2.  Then, we add a private and public instance variable of type T with a get property, which are great places to put construction or initialization logic, especially when you have criteria that need to be checked when the variable is referenced from another script. Having a public variable with a private backing variable also gives you more control and safety when deciding what other scripts (if any) can make changes.

3.  We check if the private instance is null and return any active objects of type T.

4.  If the private instance is still null, we create a new singleton GameObject, attach a component of type T (our singleton type), and assign this new instance to our private instance. We also persist the new singleton object using DontDestroyOnLoad.

5.  Finally, we return the private instance to whatever script is asking for it.

We're using MonoBehaviour as the generic type in the code above, but you can specify the Component class as T, since the script will be attached to a GameObject. You can also use any custom subclass you might have if it inherits from either MonoBehaviour or Component.

 **Lazy instantiation** defers object creation until its first use, which improves performance and limits unnecessary computations. We've written our own lazy instantiation logic in our generic singleton code above, but C# also has a Lazy<T> wrapper, which you can find at https://docs.microsoft.com/en-us/dotnet/api/system.lazy-1?view=net-5.0. However, lazy instantiation creates objects when they're needed, and we lose the ability to control the specific time and place those objects are created. This is a potential red flag for singletons when you need fine-grained control over memory management.

Create another new C# script in the **Scripts** folder, name it GenericManager, and update its code to match the following code, which will provide all the singleton logic we've just written but with a much cleaner class implementation:

```
using System.Collections;
using System.Collections.Generic;
using UnityEngine;

// 1
using UnityEngine.SceneManagement;

// 2
public class GenericManager : Singleton<GenericManager>
```

```
    {

        public int score = 0;
        public int startingLevel = 1;

        public void StartGame()
        {
            Debug.Log("New game has started with generic manager...");
            SceneManager.LoadScene(startingLevel);
        }
    }
}
```

Here, we've created a manager script that's almost identical to Manager.cs with one major addition – we've declared GenericManager as a generic singleton. We could have easily updated the existing Manager.cs class to be generic, but I find it's easier to learn design patterns if implementations or variations are kept separate. This way, you'll have concrete examples to look back at any time you need.

We won't need any of the existing manager objects now that we can create them programmatically, so before moving forward:

1. In the **SplashScreen** scene, delete Game Manager and Duplicate Manager (or mark them inactive).

2. In the **SplashScreen** scene, select **Canvas > Button** and delete the OnClick event.

3. In the **Level_01** scene, delete Duplicate Manager (or mark it inactive by deselecting the checkbox next to its name in the **Inspector**).

Now, since generic singletons are only instantiated when they're first referenced, we can't drag and drop the StartGame function onto the **Start** button's OnClick event because there's no GameObject to drag and drop. You can solve this problem several ways, but for simplicity and easy testing:

1. Go back to the **SplashScreen** scene.

2. Create a new empty GameObject in the **Hierarchy** and name it Scene Control.

3. Create a new empty object in the **Hierarchy** named Scene Control.

4. Create a new C# script, name it SceneController, and attach it to the Scene Control object in the **Hierarchy**.

5.  Update the SceneController script to match the following code, which binds our **Start** button action with the StartGame method in GenericManager.cs:

```
using System.Collections;
using System.Collections.Generic;
using UnityEngine;

// 1
using UnityEngine.UI;

public class SceneController : MonoBehaviour
{
    // 2
    public Button start;

    void Start()
    {
        // 3
        start.onClick.AddListener(GenericManager.Instance.
StartGame);
    }
}
```

Let's break down our code:

1.  First, we add the UnityEngine.UI using a directive to access the Button class.

2.  Next, we declare a Button variable to connect to our **Canvas** button in the **Inspector**.

3.  Finally, we assign the GenericManager's StartGame method to the **Start** button's OnClick event, which will instantiate the generic singleton when it's referenced in the Awake method.

Make sure to drag and drop the **Start** button from the **Canvas** onto the SceneController script in the **Inspector** as seen here; otherwise, we won't have a reference to bind our singleton methods:

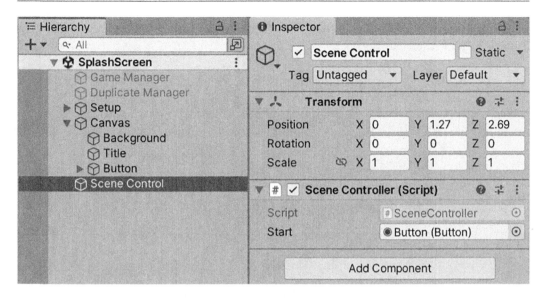

*Figure 2.14: The Scene Control object with the SceneController script and Start button configured*

Update the ScoreUI script to use a GenericManager instance according to the following code, which will pull the starting score and any score updates directly from the generic manager and display them in the scene's UI:

```
public class ScoreUI : MonoBehaviour
{
    public Text score;

    void Start()
    {
        // 1
        score.text += GenericManager.Instance.score;
    }

    void Update()
    {
        // 2
        score.text = "Score: " + GenericManager.Instance.score;
    }
}
```

Finally, update Item.cs to increment the score using the GenericManager instead of the hardcoded game manager in the following code:

```
public class Item: MonoBehaviour
{
    void OnCollisionEnter(Collision collision)
    {
        if (collision.gameObject.tag == "Player")
        {
            // 1
            GenericManager.Instance.score++;

            Destroy(this.gameObject);
            Debug.Log("Item collected!");
        }
    }
}
```

Now that the generic manager implementation is complete, we can test how the game program-matically creates a singleton class using lazy instantiation. Run the **SplashScreen** scene and press **Start** to see our generic singleton in action.

When you press **Start**, the singleton is created and added to the **Hierarchy**, as shown here:

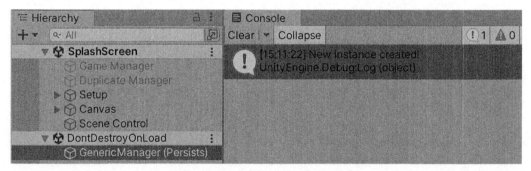

*Figure 2.15: The singleton object is created and added to the Hierarchy*

The singleton then persists into the **Level_01** scene, as shown next:

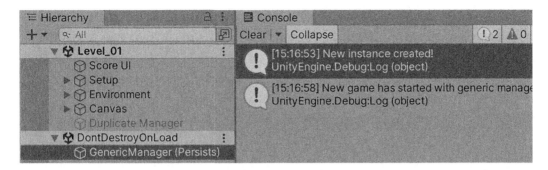

*Figure 2.16: The singleton object persists between scenes*

There's no need to check for duplicate objects because lazy instantiation ensures that we only ever allow one instance to be programmatically created. This is an efficient solution if you and your team agree that singletons are only instantiated in code, and never manually created and added to the scene **Hierarchy**.

However, there is still the matter of making sure there's no unusual or unintended activity in the event of multiple threads trying to create a singleton at the same time, which we'll talk about in the next section.

# Adding thread safety to the generic singleton

In this section, we're going to focus on making our generic singleton thread-safe by guarding against different threads potentially creating more than one instance of the singleton. For example, imagine you need to process an algorithm that finds all enemies within a set distance, as well as their positions and orientations. Doing this on the main thread might decrease your frame rate and slow down other processes in your game. However, if you separate the algorithm into a separate thread, Unity's main thread is free to keep running the essential parts of the game while the sub-thread does its work.

 Thread safety in multithreaded environments is a huge topic and has additional implications when using Unity APIs. For a deeper dive, check out *.NET Multithreading* by Alan Dennis at https://www.manning.com/books/net-multithreading.

If you're new to the concept of threading, it helps to think of your game as a river. Streams and tributaries can branch off and fold back in, but the water all started from the same place. In a multithreaded application, there can be several streams, or threads, running at the same time but doing different tasks.

This means there are situations where multiple threads access the same class or script component. Normally, the application environment handles these kinds of situations under the hood, but if you're actively taking control of multiple threads, you can end up competing for computational resources, global state updates, and class access. In our example, if multiple threads try and access a singleton for the first time, there could be more than one created.

I should point out that Unity's main engine runs in the main thread and most Unity API functions are not thread-safe – meaning they should only be called from the main thread. I'm adding a thread-safety solution to our example in case you find yourself in a multithreaded C# application, or in an advanced scenario where you use multithreading in Unity.

## Thread locking during lazy instantiation

Our next goal is to implement a locking mechanism in our singleton to limit access to one thread at a time.. As a secondary goal, we want to avoid slowing down our code by unnecessarily locking out our singleton if there's an active instance we can return. The lock keyword grabs a lock on an object, executes whatever code block we want to be locked, and then releases the locked object. While the object is locked, no other thread can access or execute logic on the object.

You can find more information about locking threads in the C# documentation at https://docs.microsoft.com/dotnet/csharp/language-reference/keywords/lock-statement.

Update Singleton.cs to match the following code, which locks the singleton instance to a single thread during lazy instantiation. This technique is called **double-checked locking**, meaning that we don't lock down a thread until we know there's no active singleton instance. Double-checked locking saves on computation time and overhead by only locking a thread when necessary:

```csharp
public class Singleton<T> : MonoBehaviour where T: MonoBehaviour
{
    // 1
    private static readonly object _threadLock = new object();

    // 2
    private static bool _isQuitting = false;
```

```
    private static T _instance;
    public static T Instance
    {
        get
        {
            // 3
            if (_isQuitting)
            {
                return null;
            }

            if (_instance == null)
            {
                _instance = FindAnyObjectByType<T>();

                // 4
                lock (_threadLock)
                {
                    if(_instance == null)
                    {

                        var singletonGO = new GameObject();
                        singletonGO.name = typeof(T).Name + " (Persists)";
                        _instance = singletonGO.AddComponent<T>();

                        DontDestroyOnLoad(singletonGO);
                        Debug.Log("New instance created!");
                    }
                }
            }

            return _instance;
        }
    }

    // 5
    public void OnDestroy()
```

```
    {
        _isQuitting = true;
    }
}
```

Let's break down the previous code:

1.  First, we add a `private readonly` variable to lock thread access.
2.  Next, we add a `boolean` to track if the application is in the process of quitting.
3.  Inside the get property, we check if the application is quitting and return `null` if it is.
4.  After checking for existing generic objects, we lock the thread when creating a new singleton instance.
5.  Finally, we set `_isQuitting` to true when the `MonoBehaviour` calls `OnDestroy`.

 When a Unity application quits, objects are destroyed in a random order. This should work for our Singleton as well, but there's always a chance that the instance gets called by a client after it's been destroyed. This will create a ghost object in the Editor after the game quits, which is why we use the `OnDestroy` method to set a `boolean` flag.

Running the game after these updates doesn't change anything because we don't have any testable conditions, where there might be multiple threads trying to create a Singleton at the same time. However, if a little defensive programming only costs a few lines of code in our generic singleton, I say, go for it!

In our final solution, we'll go in the opposite direction and exclusively create our singleton objects as `ScriptableObject` assets.

## Creating singletons as ScriptableObjects

Imagine you and your design team need to create, configure, and test singleton classes in the Unity Editor. Using `ScriptableObjects` as data containers not only frees you from attaching your scripts to `GameObjects` but also gives you the freedom to create singleton assets from the **Asset** menu. Both added features make scriptable objects a good fit to address testing concerns with the Singleton pattern, and it is much easier for non-programming members of your team to work with them.

Your last task in this chapter is to create a generic singleton as a `ScriptableObject` asset in the project. In the **Scripts** folder, create a new C# script, name it `ScriptableSingleton`, and update its code to match the following code. This script creates a generic `ScriptableObject` class that we can use to fetch a unique instance from the project resources when queried:

```csharp
using System.Collections;
using System.Collections.Generic;
using UnityEngine;

// 1
public class ScriptableSingleton<T> : ScriptableObject where T :
ScriptableObject
{
    // 2
    private static T _instance;
    public static T Instance
    {
        get
        {
            // 3
            if (_instance == null)
            {
                T[] singletons = Resources.LoadAll<T>("");

                // 4
                if(singletons == null || singletons.Length < 1)
                {
                    throw new System.Exception("No " + typeof(T).Name + "
singleton objects found...");
                }
                // 5
                else if(singletons.Length > 1)
                {
                    Debug.LogWarning("More than one " + typeof(T).Name + "
singleton object found...");
                }
```

```
                    // 6
                    _instance = singletons[0];
                    Debug.Log(typeof(T).Name + " singleton instance
fetched!");
                }

            return _instance;
        }
    }
}
```

Let's break down the code:

1.  First, we declare a singleton class of type T, where T is a ScriptableObject.

2.  Next, we add a private and public instance variable of type T with a get property.

3.  Now, we can check if the instance is null and load any objects of type T from the project resources.

4.  If the instance is still null or no ScriptableObjects were found, throw a system exception.

5.  If more than one asset of type T is found, print out a debug warning.

6.  Finally, we set the private instance to the first object in the resources array, print out a console log, and return the private instance to the get property.

If you're not used to throwing exceptions when managing unexpected behavior, check out the documentation at https://learn.microsoft.com/en-us/dotnet/ csharp/fundamentals/exceptions. Throwing exceptions can be computationally expensive if you're using them in your game's update loop, but in the preceding case, it's not going to have a noticeable impact. However, feel free to address the problem in another way if you'd rather stay away from exceptions – they aren't part of the actual design pattern.

Let's test our new singleton by creating one last script in the **Scripts** folder, naming it SOManager, and updating its code to match the following code so that we can create ScriptableObjects from the **Assets** menu and add them to a folder in our project:

```
using System.Collections;
using System.Collections.Generic;
```

```
using UnityEngine;

// 1
using UnityEngine.SceneManagement;

// 2
[CreateAssetMenu(fileName = "Game Manager", menuName = "ScriptableObjects/
Game Manager")]

// 3
public class SOManager : ScriptableSingleton<SOManager>
{
    // 4
    public int score = 0;
    public int startingLevel = 1;

    public void StartGame()
    {
        Debug.Log("New game has started with SO manager...");
        SceneManager.LoadScene(startingLevel);
    }
}
```

Let's break down our code:

1.  First, we add the SceneManagement namespace so that we can switch scenes.

2.  Next, we add a CreateAssetMenu attribute and specify the filename and menu name to be listed in the **Assets/Create** submenu.

3.  Then, we declare SOManager as a subclass of ScriptableSingleton, of type SOManager.

4.  Finally, we add variables for the score and starting level index and a method to load a new scene.

 Adding scriptable objects to the **Assets** menu is a great way to streamline your object management, especially when you want to abstract functionality away from your code.

Since our `ScriptableSingleton` is looking for scriptable objects in the project resources, we need to:

1.  Create an empty folder in our **Assets** and name it `Resources`.
2.  Select the **Resources** folder and select **Assets | Create | Scriptable Objects | Game Manager**.

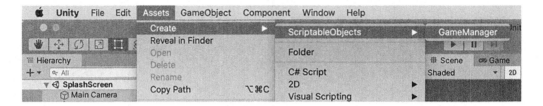

*Figure 2.17: The Assets menu with a new custom item to create ScriptableObject singletons*

You'll see a new asset in the **Resources** folder named Game Manager, as shown in the following screenshot:

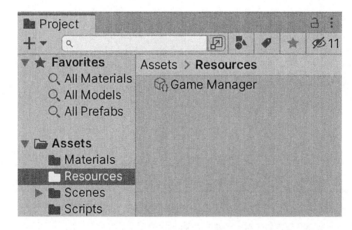

*Figure 2.18: The Game Manager ScriptableObject created and added to the Resources folder*

For testing, we need to change the `SceneController` script to reference the `SOManager` in the following code, which will load the Game Manager ScriptableObject from our project at runtime:

```
public class SceneController : MonoBehaviour
{
    public Button start;

    void Start()
    {
```

```
        // 1
        start.onClick.AddListener(SOManager.Instance.StartGame);
    }
}
```

Now, update ScoreUI.cs one last time according to the following code, which will use the new ScriptableObject asset as the singleton instance:

```
public class ScoreUI : MonoBehaviour
{
    public Text score;

    void Start()
    {
        // 1
        score.text += SOManager.Instance.score;
    }

    void Update()
    {
        // 2
        score.text = "Score: " + SOManager.Instance.score;
    }
}
```

Now that the score text is initializing and updating from the SOManager, we also need to update the Item class to increment the score using the unique SOManager instance, as shown here:

```
public class Item: MonoBehaviour
{
    void OnCollisionEnter(Collision collision)
    {
        if (collision.gameObject.tag == "Player"){

            // 1
            SOManager.Instance.score++;

            Destroy(this.gameObject);
            Debug.Log("Item collected!");
```

```
            }
        }
    }
```

Everything works the same as the generic singleton but with the added advantage of a configurable singleton asset in the editor. When you play the game, you'll see a debug log showing the SOManager instance running, as you can see in the following screenshot:

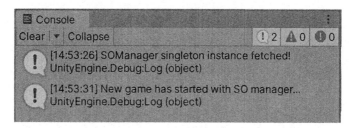

*Figure 2.19: The ScriptableObject singleton created with lazy instantiation and added to the scene Hierarchy*

We can also test our item collection to make sure everything still works as expected, as shown in the following screenshot:

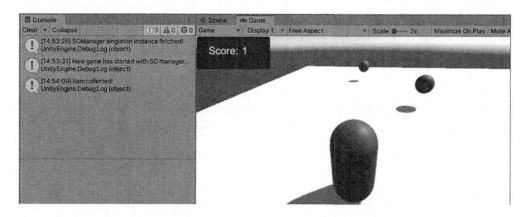

*Figure 2.20: Item collection and score updates referencing the ScriptableObject singleton instance*

If you're creating your own editor tools, you know how important scriptable objects are. Unity has added a generic scriptable object subclass called `ScriptableSingleton` that does everything we covered in the *Creating Singletons as ScriptableObjects* section but can also persist data between game sessions. Unfortunately, this subclass is only available in the Unity Editor. However, if you're building your own editor tools, be sure to check out the documentation at `https://docs.unity3d.com/2023.2/Documentation/ScriptReference/ScriptableSingleton_1.html`.

And that's our first design pattern completed – make sure to fully digest all the pros, cons, pitfalls, alternative options, and practical implementations of this pattern. As with any design pattern, half the battle is figuring out if the added complexity will pay efficiency dividends in the future or needlessly bog down your code.

## Summary

If this was your first foray into design patterns, congrats and welcome to the club! We've covered quite a bit in this chapter, from a super-vanilla singleton hardcoded into a single class all the way to lazy instantiation, generics, and thread safety – not to mention using `ScriptableObject` assets as containers for design pattern code.

Keep in mind that your singleton classes are most useful when you only want a single class instance, a global point of access, and persistence throughout the Unity game lifecycle. You have the choice of lazily instantiating your singleton objects, which helps with accessing information your project may only have after compiling (not to mention the singleton itself won't be created until it's needed). You can also go for a generic solution, which can be a subclass or even a `ScriptableObject`!

However, it's important to remember that any globally accessible objects can have adverse effects if you're not careful. They can lead to increased coupling between classes, difficulty tracking down global state bugs, and inefficient unit testing. Globally accessible state is also not thread-safe, but we've covered how to add thread-locking code to your singleton to address threading issues.

In the next chapter, we'll work on creating (or cloning) objects with the Prototype pattern, using traditional C# implementations, Unity prefabs, and even a generic `GameObject` component script. Let's keep it going!

# Further reading

- Generics open up a whole new world of programming possibilities (which is why I included a generic solution in this chapter), but I'd recommend reading up on the topic at `https://learn.microsoft.com/en-us/dotnet/csharp/fundamentals/types/generics`.

- `ScriptableObjects` are the perfect way to create data containers in your Unity projects (and we'll use them in almost every chapter going forward), but I'd also recommend checking out the documentation at `https://docs.unity3d.com/Manual/class-ScriptableObject.html`.

- Multithreading is a bit of an advanced topic outside the scope of this book, but being able to perform multiple operations at the same time is a useful tool in your toolbox. If you want to know more about this topic, head over to the documentation at `https://learn`.

# Leave a review!

Enjoying this book? Help readers like you by leaving an Amazon review. Scan the QR code below to get a free eBook of your choice.

# 3

# Spawning Enemies with the Prototype Pattern

In the last chapter, we dove head-first into our first design pattern – the Singleton. We talked about its strengths, weaknesses, and practical implementations with C# and Unity-specific APIs (while simultaneously trying not to vilify the poor thing). In this chapter, we'll learn how the Prototype pattern can help you define and manage objects you want to copy while avoiding the computational overhead that comes with creating new objects (because we should all aim to be frugal programmers when it comes to memory).

The idea is to take the original object (called a – you guessed it – Prototype or prototypical instance) and return copies of it whenever needed. Think of games where procedural enemies are spawned with a base state and modified later during gameplay; it would be great if we didn't have to create a new enemy from scratch every time they popped up to harass our character.

One important concept to keep in mind with this pattern is how objects are copied in C#, specifically the differences between a shallow and deep object copy. A shallow copy will clone every object field except reference types, while a deep copy will include the object's reference type properties. When we copy Unity objects, everything is duplicated.

For this chapter, we're going to start with a C# implementation, then move on to cloning Unity prefabs to add a visual component, and end our discussion with a generic cloning script that can be attached to any GameObject in our scene. To that end, we'll be focusing on the following topics:

- Defining, diagramming, and analyzing the pros and cons of the Prototype pattern
- Implementing shallow and deep object copying

- Programmatically cloning Unity prefab objects at runtime
- Creating a generic cloning script component

By the end of the chapter, you'll have a range of Prototype solutions to fit different scenarios. More importantly, you'll be comfortable with how object copying works in C# and Unity and be able to adapt the pattern to your own projects.

# Technical requirements

Before you dive in:

1.  Download or clone the GitHub repository at `https://github.com/PacktPublishing/C-Design-Patterns-with-Unity-First-Edition`

2.  Open the **Ch_03_Starter** project folder in Unity Hub.

3.  In **Assets | Scenes**, double-click on **SampleScene**.

Now that you're ready to go let's look at the starter project, which is a single scene with an empty ground plane ready for enemies to be spawned and a set of pre-made scripts to make life easier.

As for the scripts:

- `DataSpawner.cs` is attached to an empty `GameObject` in the scene called `Enemy Spawner` and right now there's only one `Ogre` created with its stats printed out.
- `Enemy.cs` is the base class for our future C# objects.
- `BaseEnemy.cs` is the base class for when we clone prefabs.
- `AshKnight.cs` and `Ogre.cs` are two concrete enemy types that inherit from `BaseEnemy`.

 We'll be creating different spawning scripts for prefabs and generic components later in the chapter, but I'll explain that in detail when we get to each one.

We'll also be using some Unity and C# language features to take our code the extra mile. Don't worry if you're not familiar with these, I've included links about the basics, and I'll explain how they apply to our use-cases as we go:

- Generics: `https://learn.microsoft.com/en-us/dotnet/csharp/fundamentals/types/generics`
- Interfaces: `https://learn.microsoft.com/en-us/dotnet/csharp/fundamentals/types/interfaces`

- Reflection: `https://docs.microsoft.com/dotnet/framework/reflection-and-codedom/reflection`

Our job is to start implementing a system for shallow and deep object copying with the `Enemy` and `BaseEnemy` subclasses that are ready to go!

# Breaking down the Prototype pattern

As part of the creational family of design patterns, the Prototype pattern gives us control over how we make copies of common base objects, making it effective when:

- A system needs to be independent of how its objects are created, composed, and represented.
- The objects you're creating need to be specified at runtime.
- You want to avoid parallel class hierarchies of factories and objects.
- You want to specify the kind of objects you're creating by defining a prototypical instance and copying it.

A useful mental model for this scenario is a photocopier (remember those?), shown in *Figure 3.1*. If we had a memo to pass around the office, it wouldn't be efficient to create a new memo for each employee; instead, we'd simply duplicate the original memo and hand out copies (or use email, whichever ends up being faster).

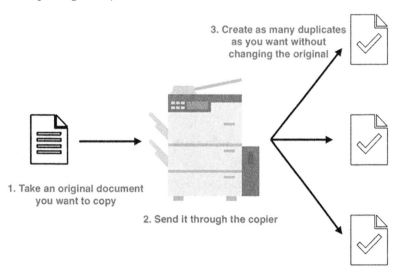

3. Create as many duplicates as you want without changing the original

1. Take an original document you want to copy

2. Send it through the copier

*Figure 3.1: Photocopy machine example*

Rather than spending valuable memory resources, the Prototype pattern lets us specify an original object (called a prototypical instance) and create a copier of our own that can spit out duplicate C# objects or Unity prefabs as many times as needed without changing the original instance.

*Figure 3.2* illustrates the different efficiency levels for creating objects with and without the Prototype pattern. The example on the left shows a client that creates a brand-new object in memory each time it needs a new instance, while the example on the right shows a client requesting a copy from a prototypical object and getting a duplicate in return. From an optimization standpoint, the workflow on the left is much more expensive because it creates 3 objects from scratch, unlike the workflow on the right, which only creates one object in memory and reuses it whenever new copies are needed.

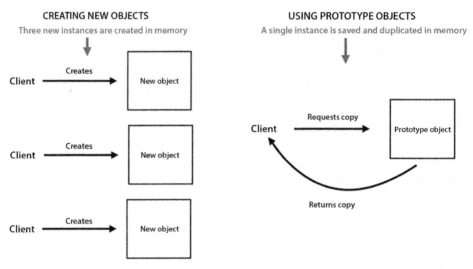

Figure 3.2: Comparison scenarios for creating new objects vs copying a prototypical instance

The same goes for C# data structures, Unity prefabs, and components. In a game where waves of enemies are continuously generated, creating new objects for each enemy could significantly drop the framerate of the game at a crucial time for your players. Using prototype enemy objects in this scenario reduces our computational load and keeps game memory free. And yes, I know computers are *very* powerful nowadays so you may not think this is necessary, but you'll thank me when you're trying to spawn a thousand little pixel fruits for people to slash on their cellphones without crashing the app (or your users rage, quitting in frustration)!

We'll discuss the finer pros and cons of the Prototype pattern later in this section. For now, we have enough to dive into a more technical definition of the pattern and start mapping out visual diagrams of how the pattern works in code.

## Diagraming the pattern

*Figure 3.3* shows the structure of the Prototype pattern, which has three main components:

- The **Prototype** interface, enabling objects to copy themselves
- The **Concrete Prototypes** that implement the self-cloning logic
- The **Client**, which creates new objects by asking prototypes for clones of themselves

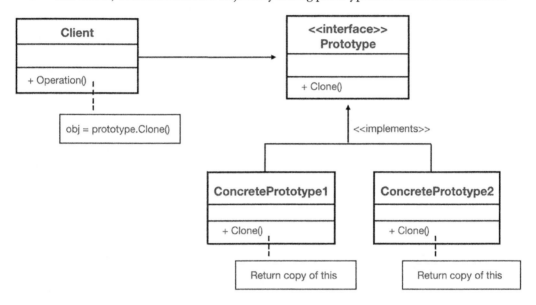

*Figure 3.3: Diagram of the Prototype design pattern*

We'll also be using an optional variation called a **Prototype Factory** class, which stores a single instance of each prototypical object we want to clone as shown in *Figure 3.4*:

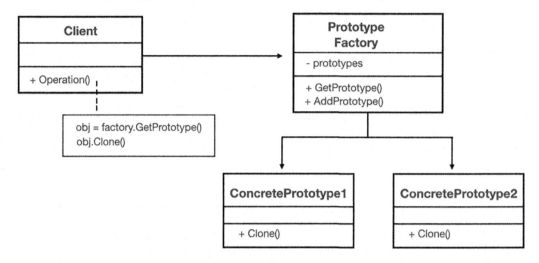

Figure 3.4: Diagram of a Prototype factory being used to store objects in memory for cloning.

The addition of a `factory` class can help scale a growing array of prototypical objects in your game and makes your pattern implementation more intentional. Now that we've covered a bit of the theory behind this pattern, let's go over some of the pros and cons and then get into the code!

## Pros and cons

Both implementations come with their own set of pros and cons, as does the pattern itself. Let's start with the potential benefits of the Prototype pattern:

- **Bulit-in initialization overhead and memory management**: Clones of prototypical instances don't need to be instantiated over and over, and reusing the prototypes already in memory to create new copies is a big optimization boost.

- **Easy adding and removing of new prototypical objects at runtime**: Any new prototype object only needs to implement the cloning interface and instantiate a single instance of itself in the Prototype factory or with the client directly.

- **Ability to create new objects with different values and structures from the same prototypical objects:** A prototype with the right variables can be used as a base for creating a wide array of different objects without the need to extensively subclass. Likewise, objects built out of parts and subparts can be prototypes if they implement the Prototype interface and cloning method. These composite objects can even have prototype subparts.

- **Safer self-duplication**: Prototype objects are responsible for copying themselves, which makes the duplication process safer and standardized.

However, here are two pitfalls you should be aware of if you're going to put the pattern into production code:

- Be mindful of the internal structures of your prototypical objects. When your C# objects are complex, their internal structures may not support cloning without custom implementations.

 Check out the native C# `ICloneable` interface (`https://docs.microsoft.com/en-us/dotnet/api/system.icloneable`) and object serialization (`https://docs.microsoft.com/en-us/dotnet/csharp/programming-guide/concepts/serialization`) for more information.

- Destroying the prototypical object instance before making a copy will not increase your memory efficiency. This type of workflow is common when using the Prototype pattern with Object Pooling and can lead to unwanted race conditions.

Now that we've covered the Prototype pattern in theory, it's time to implement a prototype enemy spawning system, which we'll do in the next section.

# Implementing shallow and deep object copying

Imagine you're building **role-playing game (RPG)** where a truly ungodly variety of monsters can pop up in your path and wreak havoc. Your project already uses a base enemy class with properties for the enemy's name, damage, and battle cry, you've already created several enemy subclasses, and there can be multiple instances of each enemy. Your goal is to build a system where new enemies are created without having to initialize new objects, but where you can still configure their properties at runtime. You also need to future-proof your solution by handling any reference properties your enemy classes need later on, which means deep and shallow copying.

## Adding a prototype interface

Our first task is creating an interface with cloning methods that all cloneable data structures will eventually implement. The official pattern only has one cloning method, but since we can either shallow or deep clone C# objects, let's be thorough and add two methods.

Open the `Enemy.cs` script and update the code to match the following code, which adds a proto-type interface with method definitions for shallow and deep cloning:

```
using System.Collections;
using System.Collections.Generic;
using UnityEngine;

// 1
using System;

// 2
public interface IPrototype
{
    // 3
    IPrototype ShallowClone();
    IPrototype DeepClone();
}
```

 Best practice dictates we always put new interfaces or classes in their own files (which you should absolutely do), but I'm including the `IPrototype` interface inside `Enemy.cs` to make things easier to understand while we're learning.

Let's break down the code:

1.  First, we include the `System` namespace so we have access to exceptions for debugging purposes.
2.  Next, we declare a `public interface` to store all prototype methods for cloning objects.
3.  Finally, we add two methods for returning shallow or deep copies of `IPrototype` objects.

Update `Enemy.cs` to match the following code, which allows `Enemy` to inherit from `IPrototype`, adds the required `DeepClone` and `ShallowClone` interface methods, and returns the current instance as a placeholder:

```
// 1
public class Enemy : IPrototype
{
    public int Damage;
    public string Message;
```

```csharp
    public string Name;

    public Enemy(int dmg, string msg, string name)
    {
        this.Damage = dmg;
        this.Message = msg;
        this.Name = name;
    }

    public void Print()
    {
        Debug.LogFormat($"{Message}! {Name} can hit for {Damage} HP.");
    }

    // 2
    public IPrototype DeepClone()
    {
        return this;
    }

    // 3
    public IPrototype ShallowClone()
    {
        return this;
    }
}
```

Let's break down the code:

1.  We add the IPrototype interface to the Enemy class declaration.
2.  We then implement the DeepClone interface method and return a placeholder value.
3.  Next, we implement the ShallowClone interface method and return a placeholder value.

For the moment, we'll have both our IPrototype methods return the current Enemy instance using the this keyword, but we'll learn how to clone objects and the difference between shallow and deep copies in the next section.

# Making shallow object copies

When we say shallow copies, we're talking about making new copies of objects that don't have any reference properties. In our Enemy class, we only use int and string properties to store data. A shallow copy of an Enemy instance will be totally separate from the original instance and keep any changes to the original instance from trickling down into cloned objects. You don't want a damaged enemy affecting *all* enemies in your game (or maybe you do – who knows – it could be a cool status buff).

Update the ShallowClone method in the Enemy.cs script to match the following code, which uses a try-catch statement to return a shallow copy of the object with the MemberwiseClone method. MemberwiseClone copies all nonstatic and value type fields to a new object and returns it:

```csharp
public IPrototype ShallowClone()
{
    // 1
    IPrototype newPrototype = null;

    // 2
    try
    {
        // 3
        newPrototype = (IPrototype)this.MemberwiseClone();
    }
    // 4
    catch (Exception e)
    {
        Debug.LogError("Error cloning: " + e);
    }

    // 5
    return newPrototype;
}
```

Let's break down the code:

1. It creates a temporary IPrototype variable to hold the shallow copied object.
2. It then declares a try statement to hold the shallow copy logic.

3.  Then calls `MemberwiseClone` on the base object and explicitly casts it to the `Iprototype` type.

4.  Goes on to declares a `catch` statement to log any errors thrown from the cloning process.

5.  Finally it returns the shallow object copy.

 I err on the side of caution when programmatically creating objects, so we're using a `try-catch` statement to catch any thrown exceptions from the cloning process. However, we could have simply returned the cloned object if you're not concerned with edge-case errors.

Now that the Enemy class can copy and return a shallow copy of itself any time we want, we can update `DataSpawner.cs` to clone a new ogre enemy instead of instantiating a new one, as shown in the following code. When you run the game, you'll see two debug logs in the console with the same properties, but only one new object is taking up memory:

```
using System.Collections;
using System.Collections.Generic;
using UnityEngine;

public class DataSpawner : MonoBehaviour
{
    void Start()
    {
        Enemy ogre = new Enemy(10, "RAWR", "Ogre");
        ogre.Print();

        // 1
        IPrototype clonedPrototype = ogre.ShallowClone();

        // 2
        if (clonedPrototype is Enemy clonedEnemy)
        {
            clonedEnemy.Print();
        }
```

```
// 3
else
{
    Debug.Log("Failed to clone ogre. Cloned object is not an
Enemy...");
}
}
}
```

Let's break down the code:

1.  Assigns the result of ShallowClone to a new IPrototype variable
2.  Tries to cast the cloned object from IPrototype to Enemy and calls Print
3.  If the cast fails, prints out an error message to the console

While we could assume ShallowClone will always return an IPrototype object, this might not always be the case. It's better to safely guard against runtime exceptions and fail or succeed gracefully when casting is involved.

Run the game and watch our code create and assign a new enemy variable with a shallow copy of the original ogre instance while debugging both enemy properties as shown in the following figure:

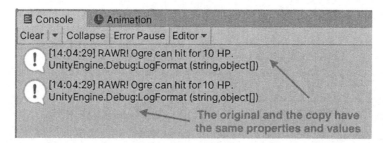

*Figure 3.5: Console output with an original and cloned enemy object*

Since our Enemy class doesn't contain any reference properties, our second ogre in the preceding figure is a separate copy and won't have any trickle-down effects from updates to the original instance. To test this out, update the original enemy's name and damage values in DataSpawner.cs to match the following code and notice that the cloned properties don't reflect the change:

```
void Start()
{
    Enemy ogre = new Enemy(10, "RAWR", "Ogre");
    ogre.Print();
```

```
IPrototype clonedPrototype = ogre.ShallowClone();

if (clonedPrototype is Enemy clonedEnemy)
{
    clonedEnemy.Print();

    // 1
    ogre.Name = "Monstrous Ogre";
    ogre.Damage = 30;

    // 2
    ogre.Print();
    clonedEnemy.Print();
}
else
{
    Debug.Log("Failed to clone ogre. Cloned object is not an
Enemy...");
}
    }
}
```

All we've done here is manually update the Name and Damage properties of the original ogre instance and debug both ogres to see the differences, as shown in the following figure:

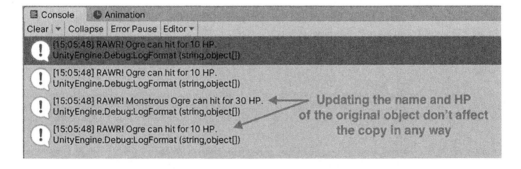

*Figure 3.6: Console output showing the original object properties doesn't affect the clone*

As can be seen, the original ogre's properties are updated, but the cloned enemy retains its original values. However, if our prototype classes have their own reference properties, a shallow copy will keep the reference from the original object (creating a data connection between cloned objects and their originator). In the next section, we'll learn how to copy reference properties when we clone prototype objects through deep copying.

## Making deep object copies

Now imagine all our enemies are also carrying an item that can damage the player (on brand for monstrous enemies trying to take you down). If we continue to use shallow copying, all our enemies will retain the same item reference as the original, which wouldn't allow each enemy to have its own unique item. Instead, we want each cloned enemy to start with a copy of the original enemy's item but not its reference, which will allow each enemy to hit us in annoyingly creative ways.

In the **Scripts** folder, create a new C# script named Item and update its code to match the following snippet, which adds a new Item class with a Name property:

```
public class Item
{
    public string Name;
    public Item(string name)
    {
        this.Name = name;
    }
}
```

Update Enemy.cs to match the following code, which adds an Item property and updates the Print method with our new information:

```
public class Enemy : IPrototype
{
    public int Damage;
    public string Message;
    public string Name;

    // 1
    public Item Item;

    // 2
```

```
public Enemy(int dmg, string msg, string name, Item item)
{
    this.Damage = dmg;
    this.Message = msg;
    this.Name = name;

    // 2
    this.Item = item;
}

public void Print()
{
    // 3
    Debug.LogFormat($"{Message}! {Name} has a {Item.Name} and can hit
for {Damage}  HP.");
}

// … No other script changes needed …
}
```

Let's break down the code:

1.  Adds an Item field to the Enemy class
2.  Updates the constructor arguments and sets the Item value
3.  Updates the Print method to reference the Item name

With this new field, shallow copies will hold the same reference to the Item. This behavior is okay in some cases, but we want the option to decouple reference fields when cloning our enemy objects.

Update DataSpawner.cs to match the following code, which adds an Item parameter to the ogre enemy constructor and changes the Name after the enemy is cloned. Our base item is going to be a Poison dart, but we'll see how we can set this for other cloned enemies in just a minute:

```
public void Start()
{
    // 1
    Enemy ogre = new Enemy(10, "RAWR", "Ogre", new Item("Poison dart"));
    ogre.Print();
```

```
      IPrototype clonedPrototype = ogre.ShallowClone();
         if (clonedPrototype is Enemy clonedEnemy)
         {
             clonedEnemy.Print();
             ogre.Name = "Monstrous Ogre";
             ogre.Damage = 30;


             // 2
             ogre.Item.Name = "Potion";


             ogre.Print();
             clonedEnemy.Print();
         }
         else
         {
             Debug.Log("Failed to clone ogre. Cloned object is not an
Enemy...");
         }
}
```

Our prototypical enemy now has an Item reference that we've set to Poison dart, which means our clone will also have the same reference. However, when we change the original objects' Item.Name value the Item for both objects is now a potion instead of one potion and one poison dart.

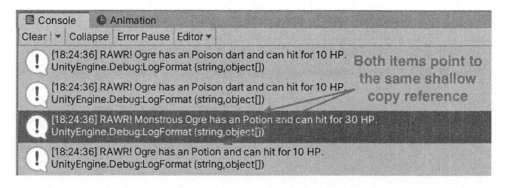

*Figure 3.7: Console output showing the reference property in the clone is not a deep copy*

This coupling isn't ideal for changing the reference properties in our prototypical enemy, so let's decouple that properly and copy the reference Item by initializing a new one after the original object is copied.

Update the DeepClone method in Enemy.cs to match the following code, which will create a shallow copy of the object and then add a new Item reference property using the base object's item name:

```
public IPrototype DeepClone()
{
    // 1
    Enemy newPrototype = (Enemy)ShallowClone();

    // 2
    newPrototype.Item = new Item(this.Item.Name);

    // 3
    return newPrototype;
}
```

Let's break down the code:

1.  It creates a temporary enemy and assigns it a shallow clone of the base object.
2.  It assigns the temporary enemy's Item property to a new Item instance using the shallow clone's Name in the class constructor.
3.  It returns the temporary enemy.

Update DataSpawner.cs to match the following code, which uses the DeepClone method instead of ShallowClone to copy our prototypical enemy instance. When you run the game, you'll see all properties are disconnected from the original base object enemy, including the Item field!

```
public void Start()
{
    Enemy ogre = new Enemy(10, "RAWR", "Ogre", new Item("Poision dart"));
    ogre.Print();

    // 1
    IPrototype clonedPrototype = ogre.DeepClone();

    if (clonedPrototype is Enemy clonedEnemy)
    {
        clonedEnemy.Print();
```

```
            ogre.Name = "Monstrous Ogre";
            ogre.Damage = 30;
            ogre.Item.Name = "Potion";
            ogre.Print();
            clonedEnemy.Print();
        }
        else
        {
            Debug.Log("Failed to clone ogre. Cloned object is not an
Enemy...");
        }}
```

Even though each enemy has a reference Item property, deep cloning produces a duplicate that includes a new item created with the same base values but no longer holding the original enemy's item reference. In the following figure, you can see that all updated values in the original enemy are no longer trickling down into the copy:

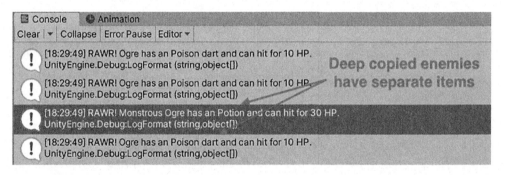

*Figure 3.8: Console output showing the deep object copy and its unchanged properties*

Now, before we move on to working with prefabs and script components, there's a final piece of the Prototype pattern to add to our code – the prototype factory!

## Adding a prototype factory

A prototype factory class is exactly what it sounds like – an access point for storing and retrieving our raw prototype materials, or in our case an instance of each cloneable object. This part of the Prototype pattern is completely optional and not always recommended unless you're dealing with enough base objects to make the added abstraction worthwhile.

In the **Scripts** folder, create a new C# script, name it Factory, and update its code to match the following snippet. This will create a generic factory class with a dictionary of objects stored by key, which can be stored or retrieved by using an indexer (which lets you access classes, structs, and even interfaces like they're arrays). For a prototype factory, this cuts down on the boilerplate code we'd have to write to get and set our dictionary of base objects:

```
using System.Collections;
using System.Collections.Generic;
using UnityEngine;

// 1
public class Factory<T>
{
    // 2
    private Dictionary<string, T> objects = new Dictionary<string, T>();

    // 3
    public T this[string key]
    {
        // 4
        get
        {
            if (objects.ContainsKey(key))
            {
                return objects[key];
            }
            else
            {
                throw new KeyNotFoundException("Key not found: " + key);
            }
        }

        // 5
        set
```

```
        {
            if (objects.ContainsKey(key))
            {
                objects[key] = value;
            }
            else
            {
                objects.Add(key, value);
            }
        }
    }
}
```

Let's break down the code:

1.  Creates a `Factory` class that accepts a generic type `T` when initialized
2.  Adds and initializes a `dictionary` of `string` and type `T` objects
3.  Adds an indexer for type `T` values that takes in a `string` key parameter
4.  Uses a get property to return an object if it's present or throw an exception if it's missing
5.  Uses a set property to set a value if the key exists or add a new key-value pair

 We're using a generic type for the factory to make testing easier, as we'll cover multiple examples with different implementations in the rest of the chapter. If you only have one type of prototype object in your project, a generic solution might be an unnecessary level of abstraction.

Now that we can add and retrieve instances of our base prototype objects, we can test this new feature by commenting or deleting all the code in the `Start` function of `DataSpawner.cs` and replacing it with the following code. This creates a new `factory` instance that stores `IPrototype` objects, adds two enemies, and clones them by requesting the base objects from the factory:

```
void Start()
{
    // 1
    Factory<IPrototype> factory = new Factory<IPrototype>();

    // 2
    factory["Ogre"] = new Enemy(10, "RAWR", "Ogre", new Item("Poison
dart"));
```

```
        factory["Knight"] = new Enemy(15, "To Arms!", "Ash Knight", new
    Item("Shuriken"));

        // 3
        IPrototype ogrePrototype = (Enemy)factory["Ogre"].DeepClone();
        IPrototype knightPrototye = (Enemy)factory["Knight"].DeepClone();

        // 4
        if(ogrePrototype is Enemy ogreEnemy)
        {
            ogreEnemy.Print();
        }

        if(knightPrototye is Enemy knightEnemy)
        {
            knightEnemy.Print();
        }
    }
```

Let's break this down step by step:

1.  Creates a new factory instance that stores IPrototype values
2.  Initializes and adds two enemy instances to the factory using string keys
3.  Requests an instance of both base enemies from the factory and deep clones them
4.  Prints out the properties of both cloned enemies in the console

You can see each enemy has been deep cloned in *Figure 3.9*, by making a request from the prototype factory. This is an added level of complexity, but when you're dealing with a system that is bound to scale up during development, it's worth the extra code.

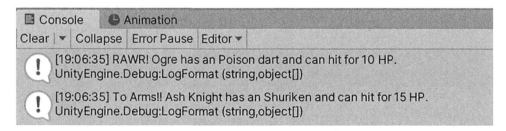

*Figure 3.9: Console output showing enemy clones managed by the prototype factory*

With C# data object cloning under our belts, it's time we moved on to some Unity-specific fun with prefabs, which we'll dive into in the next section.

# Cloning prefabs

Now that we've tackled a game with regular C# enemies, let's imagine we want to upgrade our game to an open world where enemies are procedurally generated at random positions on a map. You've already created an abstract enemy class to store basic enemy data, which you've subclassed as MonoBehaviours for each enemy type and attached to their respective prefabs. Your job is to create an enemy spawning system that can take in multiple prefabs, assign them to a prototype factory, and clone them whenever necessary.

Our first task in our new scenario is to declare a public interface in the BaseEnemy.cs file with a method for copying prefabs, as shown in the following code. We'll also have the abstract BaseEnemy class implement the new interface and add custom cloning logic, with each enemy Prefab randomly placed in the scene and parented to the Enemy Spawner object that already exists in the **Hierarchy**:

```
using System.Collections;
using System.Collections.Generic;
using UnityEngine;


// 1
public interface ICopy
{
    public ICopy Copy(Transform parent);
}


// 2
public abstract class BaseEnemy : MonoBehaviour, ICopy
{
    [SerializeField] protected int Damage;
    [SerializeField] protected string Message;
    [SerializeField] protected string Name;

    public void OnEnable()
    {
        Debug.LogFormat($"{Message} - an {Name} entered the arena.");
```

```
    }

    public virtual void Attack()
    {
        Debug.LogFormat($"{Name} attacks for {Damage} HP!");
    }

    // 3
    public ICopy Copy(Transform parent)
    {
        // 4
        BaseEnemy clone = Instantiate(this);

        // 5
        var clonePosition = new Vector3(Random.Range(-7, 7), 0, Random.
Range(-7, 7));

        // 6
        clone.transform.SetParent(parent);
        clone.transform.localPosition = clonePosition;

        // 7
        return clone;
    }
}
```

Let's break down the code:

1.  Adds a public `interface` to copy and returns a base object with a `Transform` parameter
2.  Updates the `BaseEnemy` class to inherit from `ICopy`
3.  Declares the `Copy` interface method that returns an `ICopy` type object
4.  Creates a `clone` object variable and uses the `Instantiate` method to copy and return a base copy
5.  Creates a variable to hold a random enemy range using a `Vector3` variable
6.  Sets the clone's parent and the clone's local position to the random enemy range vector
7.  Returns the configured `clone` object

We're packaging the procedural positioning and parenting code straight into the copy method for simplicity, but in cases where you want to decouple the cloning logic from your other requirements, you can absolutely do that from the calling client.

To test out the Prefab generation, create a new script in the **Scripts** folder named PrefabSpawner and update its code to match the following code. Unfortunately, Unity doesn't allow interface types to be set in the **Inspector**, so we'll have to declare our base prefabs as BaseEnemy type variables instead of ICopy types:

```
using System.Collections;
using System.Collections.Generic;
using UnityEngine;

public class PrefabSpawner : MonoBehaviour
{
    // 1
    public BaseEnemy OgrePrefab;
    public BaseEnemy AshKnightPrefab;
    private Factory<ICopy> factory = new Factory<ICopy>();

    // 2
    void Awake()
    {
        factory["Ogre"] = OgrePrefab;
        factory["Knight"] = AshKnightPrefab;
    }

    void Start()
    {
        // 3
        for (int i = 0; i < 10; i++)
        {
            // 4
            BaseEnemy clone = null;
            var random = Random.Range(1, 3);

            // 5
            switch (random)
```

```
        {
            case 1:
                clone = (BaseEnemy)factory["Ogre"].Copy();
                break;
            case 2:
                clone = (BaseEnemy)factory["Knight"].Copy();
                break;
        }

        // 6
        if(clone)
        {
            clone.Attack();
        }
    }
  }
}
```

I'm not a huge fan of using switch statements in these cases where you might be adding a large variety of enemies to your project. I've used a switch statement to keep our focus on the learning objectives, but you can (and should) absolutely use Reflection, the number of keys in the Factory dictionary, or some other scalable solution.

Let's break down the code:

1.  Adds two variables to hold the enemy prefabs and a prototype factory to index them
2.  Uses the Awake method to set the enemy prefabs in the list of prototype factory objects
3.  Uses a for loop to generate ten random enemy prefab types
4.  Creates a local clone variable set to null and a random number range for choosing enemy prefabs
5.  Uses a switch statement to return either an ogre or knight prefab based on a random range
6.  Checks that clone is not null and calls Attack on every randomly generated clone from the BaseEnemy script

To test this out, use the following steps and make sure they match *Figure 3.10*:

1.  Deactivate the **Data Spawner (Script)** component on the Enemy Spawner in the **Hierarchy**.

2.  Attach the PrefabSpawner script.

3.  From the **Prefabs** folder, drag the Ogre and Ash Knight prefabs into the script variables in the **Inspector**.

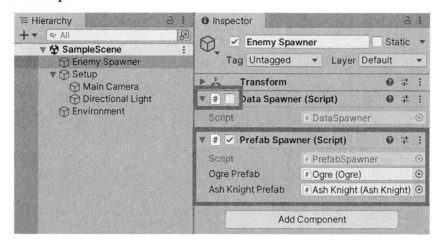

*Figure 3.10: Attach the Prefab Spawner script and assign the enemy prefab objects in the Inspector*

When you play the game now, your project will look something like *Figure 3.11* (although since we're doing everything randomly, the enemy positions will be different every time you run the game). Either way, you'll see a randomly generated group of enemies split between Ogre and Ash Knight Prefabs at random positions within the range we specified!

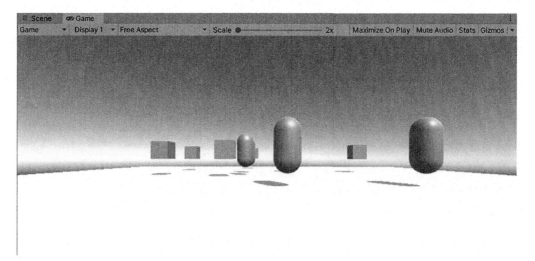

*Figure 3.11: Randomly generated enemies in the Unity scene*

You'll also see that each enemy is neatly parented to the Enemy  Spawner in the **Hierarchy**, as shown in the following figure:

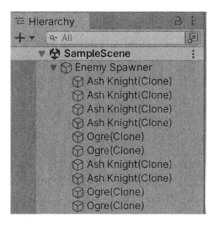

*Figure 3.12: Enemy prefabs are automatically parented to the Enemy Spawner when cloned*

While this solution is a complete implementation of the Prototype pattern in our Unity project, we're going to talk about a more generic, component-based solution before closing out the chapter. I've included this last scenario/solution combo to take advantage of Unity's inherently decoupled component architecture when constructing game objects.

## Creating a generic prototype component

Imagine that your game has more than a few enemy types, all of which need to be cloneable. If you were going to try and use the previous solution, you would quickly be underwater with the amount of BaseEnemy subclasses you'd be creating every time the game needed a new enemy type. Further, imagine that your team lead asks you to make any GameObject in the project cloneable with a single script component.

Our first and only task to satisfy the scenario requirements is to create a new MonoBehaviour with a single cloning method. In the **Scripts** folder, create a new C# script, name it Clone, and update its code to match the following code. This code will reuse the same random generation and parenting logic from the previous solution, but we'll also fetch and return the specified script component if it's attached to the base clone:

```
using System.Collections;
using System.Collections.Generic;
using UnityEngine;
```

```
// 1
public class Clone : MonoBehaviour
{
    // 2
    public T Copy<T>() where T : Component
    {
        // 3
        Clone instance = Instantiate(this);

        // 4
        GameObject spawner = GameObject.Find("Enemy Spawner");
        var enemyRange = new Vector3(Random.Range(-7, 7), 0, Random.
Range(-7, 7));

        // 5
        instance.transform.SetParent(spawner.transform);
        instance.transform.localPosition = enemyRange;

        // 6
        return instance.GetComponent<T>();
    }
}
```

If you've noticed that finding the Enemy  Spawner object in the **Hierarchy** could fail for a number of reasons (it doesn't exist, its name is misspelled, etc.), you'd be right! Like other optional parts of the examples throughout the book, this solution is meant to give you a jumping-off point for your own customizations, not necessarily a one-size-fits-all solution.

Let's break down our code:

1.  Declares a new MonoBehaviour class
2.  Adds a generic method to copy and return a cloned object of type T where T is a Component
3.  Creates a clone object variable and uses the Instantiate method to copy and return a base copy
4.  Creates a spawner variable and uses GameObject.Find to assign the Enemy  Spawner object by name

5. Creates a variable to hold a random enemy range using a Vector3 variable

6. Sets the clone's parent and the clone's local position to the random enemy range vector

7. Returns the component of type T from the cloned instance

Open the **Prefabs** folder and add **Clone (Script)** to both the Ash Knight and Ogre prefabs, as shown in the following figure:

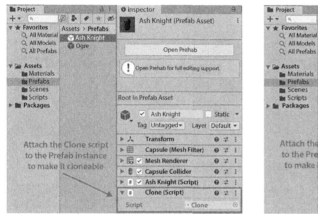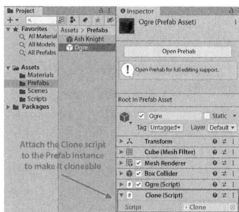

*Figure 3.13: Generic clone script added to both prefabs*

Since our client code is almost exactly the same as the PrefabSpawner, you can either update it or create a new script in the **Scripts** folder. I've created a new script called ComponentSpawner to keep things clearly differentiated, but whichever method you choose, you need to update the code to match the following snippet:

```
using System.Collections;
using System.Collections.Generic;
using UnityEngine;

public class ComponentSpawner : MonoBehaviour
{
    // 1
    public Clone OgrePrefab;
    public Clone AshKnightPrefab;
    private Factory<Clone> factory = new Factory<Clone>();

    // 2
    void Awake()
```

```
    {
        factory["Ogre"] = OgrePrefab;
        factory["Knight"] = AshKnightPrefab;
    }

    void Start()
    {
        // 3
        for (int i = 0; i < 10; i++)
        {
            // 4
            BaseEnemy clonedEnemy = null;
            var random = Random.Range(1, 3);

            // 5
            switch (random)
            {
                case 1:
                    clonedEnemy = factory["Ogre"].Copy<Ogre>();
                    break;
                case 2:
                    clonedEnemy = factory["Knight"].Copy<AshKnight>();
                    break;
            }

            // 6
            if(clonedEnemy)
            {
                clonedEnemy.Attack();
            }
        }
    }
}
```

Let's break down our new spawning code:

1.  Adds two variables for objects with the Clone script attached and a prototype factory to index them

2.  Uses the Awake method to set the enemy prefabs in the list of prototype factory objects

3.  Uses a for loop to generate ten random enemy prefab types

4.  Creates a local clone variable set to null and a random number range for choosing enemy prefabs

5.  Uses a switch statement to return either an Ogre or AshKnight component based on the random range

6.  Checks if clonedEnemy is not null and calls the attack method on every randomly generated clone from the BaseEnemy script

 Using a switch statement to choose which enemy gets spawned isn't the most scalable, but for our example, it's a workable solution. However, if you want to make this more flexible in your own code, Reflection is going to be your best friend, as well as basing the random number generator on the number of keys in the factory. You can find concrete examples of this solution in *Chapter 4, Creating Items with the Factory Method Pattern*.

Before you test this out, use the following steps and make sure they match *Figure 3.14*:

1.  Deactivate the **Data Spawner** and **Prefab Spawner** components on the Enemy Spawner object (we don't need that many enemies rushing at us all at once).

2.  Attach the ComponentSpawner script.

3.  Drag the Ogre and Ash Knight prefabs into the script variables in the **Inspector**.

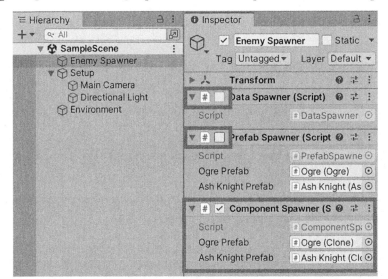

*Figure 3.14: Component test spawner script added to the Enemy Spawner object in the Hierarchy*

When you run the game for the last time, you'll see the same randomly generated and positioned enemy clones in the scene and each enemy parented to the Enemy  Spawner in the **Hierarchy**, as shown in the following figure:

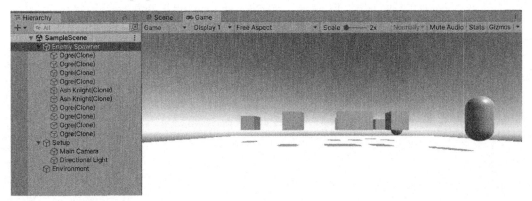

*Figure 3.15: Randomly generated prototype enemies using the generic cloning script*

While the result is the same using the PrefabSpawner and ComponentSpawner solutions, the Clone script will let you clone ANY GameObject without having to adopt any interfaces or create extensive class hierarchies.

# Summary

That wraps up our journey into the Prototype pattern! As always, it's important to decide if adding a prototype layer of complexity to your game is worth the overhead, rather than simply using the Instantiate method. In my experience, if your game is dealing with a vast array of cloneable objects, and if the optimization you gain by cloning rather than creating new objects from scratch outweighs the added Prototype pattern abstraction code, it's worth the effort.

Remember, the Prototype pattern is going to give you the most bang for your buck when you want to specify the kind of objects you're creating by defining a prototypical instance and copying it. C# data structures can either be shallow or deep copied – a shallow copy includes references to reference fields, while deep copies create new reference variables (and Unity prefabs can be made into prototype objects and cloned just like C# data structures)!

In the next chapter, we'll create an assembly line with the Factory Method pattern that can dish out different types of objects without the client being aware of what the actual objects are. This approach shifts the burden of creating objects from the object itself (like in the Prototype pattern) to a fully functioning factory. Let's keep it rolling!

# Further reading

- Generics open up a whole new world of programming possibilities (which is why I included a generic solution in this chapter), but I'd recommend reading up on the topic at `https://learn.microsoft.com/en-us/dotnet/csharp/fundamentals/types/generics`.

- Interfaces are a great way to create groups of related functionality (with or without default implementations) that can be adopted by any class or struct. These are especially handy when you want to have a class inherit from multiple groups of functionality, which is called object composition. For more, check out the documentation at `https://learn.microsoft.com/en-us/dotnet/csharp/fundamentals/types/interfaces`

- Reflection lets you get an inside glimpse at the classes, structs, and other types that are present in your project's assembly and can be used to create instances of any of those types at runtime. Like multithreading, going too deep into this topic is a little outside the scope of this book, but if you'd like to learn more, head over to `https://docs.microsoft.com/dotnet/framework/reflection-and-codedom/reflection`.

# Join our community on Discord

Join our community's Discord space for discussions with the author and other readers:

https://packt.link/gamedevelopment_packt

# 4

# Creating Items with the Factory Method Pattern

In the last chapter, we built an enemy-spawning system using the Prototype pattern, Unity prefabs, and C# generics. In this chapter, we'll learn how the Factory Method pattern not only lets you specify a common interface for any objects you're creating but also lets the subclass decide the actual class being instantiated. Think of games you've played or built that used NPCs – wouldn't it be nice if there was a mechanism that could create NPCs using a single underlying class but that could also defer the concrete type (a quest giver or random village person) that rolls off the assembly line? Well, that's exactly what the Factory Method pattern does!

Before we dive in any further, we should talk about two design patterns related to factories: the Factory Method and Abstract Factory patterns. The Factory Method pattern allows you to make objects without specifying the exact class being instantiated, while the Abstract Factory pattern combines groups of related factories without specifying the concrete factory classes that are rolling out the items.

How to choose between these two patterns is a question of categories and scale (and you should absolutely ask yourself these questions). How many kinds of items do you need? Can they be grouped into families of related products? Will composition work better than inheritance for your scenario, or vice versa? Don't worry, we'll address these questions in this and the following chapter, as the Abstract Factory pattern deserves its own focused coverage.

In this chapter, we'll focus on using a factory with a small variety of items to:

- Create a product interface and concrete products

- Build different creator class and factory method variations
- Scale factories with reflection and LINQ
- Integrate Unity prefabs in to product and creator classes

If you looked at the page count for this chapter and thought "nope, nope, nope," that's totally normal. We're covering a ton of different pattern variations; don't feel like you need to implement all of them in your project at once. I'm showing complete examples of each one to give you the best tools for common scenarios you may run into. Let's dive in!

 The example code in this chapter is also focused on programmatically implementing the Factory Method pattern using Unity components and APIs. This isn't the only way to do things, but I've found that client code is much cleaner this way and GameObject management in the project **Hierarchy** is minimized.

# Technical requirements

Before you start:

1. Download or clone the GitHub repository at https://github.com/PacktPublishing/C-Design-Patterns-with-Unity-First-Edition.

2. Open the **Ch_04_Starter** project folder in Unity Hub.

3. In **Assets | Scenes**, double-click on **SampleScene**.

The project for this chapter has a character standing at attention right in front of the camera, ready to be modified based on items we'll create and use, and a simple UI display with a **Stats** panel for the character's health and boost multiplier, as well as an **Inventory** panel for showing our future items!

As for the scripts:

- Client.cs just holds a reference to an **ItemButton** prefab we'll be using to programmatically fill out the UI panel:

    - The **Inventory** panel has the Client.cs script attached to it, which has a connection to the ItemButton.cs script we've attached to the **Button** prefab (in the **Prefabs** folder).

- ItemButton.cs configures each factory item by assigning the GameObject name, OnClick event, and button Text.

- `Manager.cs` has get and set properties for updating the **Stats** panel values and is attached to the `Manager` GameObject in the **Hierarchy**.

- `Player.cs` has a method to change the GameObject's material color when called and is attached to the `Player` GameObject in the **Hierarchy**.

We'll also be using some Unity and C# language features to take our code the extra mile. Don't worry if you're not familiar with these; I've included links for the basics and I'll explain how they apply to our use cases as we go:

- Interfaces (`https://learn.microsoft.com/en-us/dotnet/csharp/fundamentals/types/interfaces`)

- ScriptableObjects (`https://docs.unity3d.com/Manual/class-ScriptableObject.html`)

- LINQ (`https://docs.microsoft.com/dotnet/csharp/programming-guide/concepts/linq`)

- Assembly (`https://docs.microsoft.com/dotnet/standard/assembly`)

- Reflection (`https://docs.microsoft.com/dotnet/framework/reflection-and-codedom/reflection`)

Now it's your (our) job to implement a basic factory that can churn out items for us to use on our character!

# Breaking down the Factory Method pattern

As part of the creational family of design patterns, the Factory Method pattern gives us the power to create objects through an interface without having to specify the exact class that's getting instantiated. The Factory Method pattern is useful when:

- Your class can't specify the class objects it's required to create.

- Your class needs its subclasses to determine the objects it's required to create.

- You need a common method or operation among all objects for instantiation.

Consider a real-world company that manufactures a variety of products as shown in *Figure 4.1*. A customer orders a product or products, the factory manufactures the order, and then the factory ships it back to the customer. The company's management system doesn't necessarily need to know the details of how each and every product is made (it doesn't care how fidget spinners or computers are put together). In fact, that would create a lot of unnecessary overhead, which could potentially slow down production and incur additional costs.

Instead, the company only needs factories that know that each product plays by the same basic rules when being created but takes care of its own details (gadget factories know how to make gadgets, and technology factories know how to make different devices).

*Figure 4.1: Simplified example of a real-world customer/factory interaction*

The same is true in the gaming example we'll build out in this chapter. Games almost always have in-game items, and there's usually a lot to choose from, as shown in *Figure 4.2*. It's going to be a headache if you have to worry about how each different item is created every time you want to put one onscreen, especially if you're constantly adding items to your game. Instead, every item decides how it's instantiated, and we simply request a new instance when we need one. We can even add GameObjects to further customize each item, which we'll see later in the *Adding GameObjects to the mix* section.

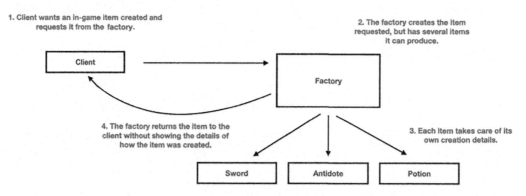

*Figure 4.2: Example scenario with a client asking a factory to create in-game items*

The main takeaway for this pattern is deferment – we can have as many different objects as we want, but if they all implement the common interface, we can treat them the same in our client code. This is extremely useful when you're creating more complex objects, especially in games, where you want the actual instantiation logic hidden in a black box with only the common methods exposed (those common methods are called the factory methods, which is where the pattern gets its name from).

Now that we have enough theory to get started, let's get some visuals to put the pattern into perspective.

## Diagramming the pattern

*Figure 4.3* shows the structure of the Factory Method pattern, which has four components:

- The Product interface for all objects our factory method can create.
- Concrete Products that implement the Product interface.
- A Creator class, which declares the factory method and returns a Product object. This class can also provide default factory method logic that returns a default Product object.
- A Concrete Creator class that subclasses the Creator and overrides the factory method to return specific Concrete Product instances.

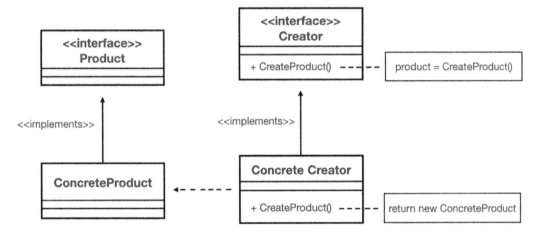

*Figure 4.3: Diagram of the Factory Method pattern components*

You can see in the preceding diagram that this pattern depends heavily on interfaces and abstract classes. We have a Product interface that all Concrete Products implement and an abstract Creator class that all Concrete Creator classes inherit from.

Once the structure is set up, our client code becomes streamlined by working with the Product interface and abstract Creator classes no matter what concrete objects we want to use!

Notice the Creator depends on its concrete subclasses to specify the exact Product object to create and return, which results in a parallel class hierarchy between concrete products and concrete creators. In cases where a parallel class hierarchy would create too much overhead every time a new product is added to the game, it's useful to understand the different variations of the Factory Method pattern:

- A Concrete Creator class can be declared without a parent class and simply have default factory methods for each of its products. This is only scalable and flexible if there is a set number of products or product tiers.

- A Concrete Creator class can be declared with a factory method that takes in an argument specifying the product you want to be returned. This is the most common variation, but it can quickly get out of hand when scaling products. We'll talk more about maximizing scalability and efficient maintenance with reflection in the *Scaling factories with reflection and LINQ* section.

## Pros and cons

Like all design patterns, there are pros and cons. Let's start with the benefits of the Factory Method pattern:

- **No more binding** specific classes in your client code; everything goes through the Product interface. Adding new products is as easy as implementing the Product interface.

- **Black-boxing object creation** into product subclasses keeps everything together but hidden. This is especially flexible and scalable when you're creating complex objects and need to expand a factory's duties.

However, be careful of the following pitfalls when using the pattern in your projects:

- **Extra code means extra time** spent handling your product and factory relationships, which is why we'll spend considerable time in this chapter talking about the three variations this pattern offers to remove some of that extra abstraction overhead. For example, a project with products being added all the time isn't going to be scalable with the original pattern implantation; instead, the concrete or parameterized variations would be a more maintainable choice. Choosing the right type of product-to-factory relationship is essential to making this pattern work for you.

- **The Factory Method isn't the Abstract Factory** – these are different patterns, and they have different implementations, pros, and pitfalls. The Factory Method lets you make objects without specifying the class being instantiated, while the Abstract Factory pattern combines groups of related factories without specifying concrete factory classes. Ask yourself what the end goal is and then choose between the two patterns rather than trying to create a Frankenstein's monster of both.

Now that we've covered the structure, benefits, and limitations of the Factory Method pattern, we can dive into building an inventory system in the next section.

# Declaring our inventory products

Imagine you are building an open-world RPG with a long list of in-game items, like health items, weapons, and armor. You and your team need a system for creating items from a central access point but don't want the actual instantiation logic in the client code. You also need to be able to change what types of items are created using subclassing. As you go, you'll want to display all available items in a UI list of buttons and execute actions when each button is pressed.

## Adding a product interface

The first component of the Factory Method pattern is a product interface, which in our scenario needs to be implemented by all in-game items. This is going to let us create any number of concrete products, or items, as we go along.

Open the **Scripts** folder and create a new C# script named Item, then update the code to match the following code. The IItem interface is pretty sparse since we only need an Equip method for every item to override and implement its own unique logic when selected from the UI list in the starter project:

```csharp
using System.Collections;
using System.Collections.Generic;
using UnityEngine;

// 1
public interface IItem
{
    // 2
    void Equip();
}
```

Let's break down our code:

1. Declares a new public abstract class named Item
2. Defines a public method called Equip for each item to implement

Your next task is to create three concrete products, so we have different items to play with in our example game.

## Creating concrete products

Update the Item.cs script to match the following code, which adds Pebble, CursedKnife, and Potion concrete item classes. Pay attention to how the code is implementing each item's Equip method differently:

- For the Pebble, it's a simple console message.
- The CursedKnife changes the player's capsule color.
- The Potion changes the player's color and updates its HP and Boost values in the UI.

```
...

// 1
public class Pebble : IItem
{
    // 2
    public void Equip()
    {
        Debug.Log($"You skipped your pebble at a nearby lake.");
    }
}


// 3
public class CursedKnife : IItem
{
    // 4
    public void Equip()
    {
        var player = GameObject.FindAnyObjectByType<Player>();
        player.SetColor(Color.magenta);
```

```
            Debug.Log($"Woops, you're cursed...");
        }
    }


    // 5
    public class Potion : IItem
    {
        // 6
        public void Equip()
        {
            var player = GameObject.FindAnyObjectByType<Player>();
            player.SetColor(Color.green);

            var manager = GameObject.FindAnyObjectByType<Manager>();
            manager.HP += 5;
            manager.Boost++;

            Debug.Log($"Potion healed you for 5 HP!");
        }
    }
```

Let's break down our item code:

1. Declares a concrete `Pebble` item class

2. Implements the pebble's `Equip` method and prints out a console message

3. Declares a concrete `CursedKnife` item class

4. Implements the cursed knife's `Equip` method to change the player object color

5. Declares a concrete `Potion` item class

6. Implements the potion's `Equip` method to change the player object color and stats

Now that each item oversees its own unique `Equip` logic, we can start setting up the factory class structure to defer instantiation to each `IItem`'s interface implementation in the next section.

# Working with different factory class variations

There are three variations of factory classes in the Factory pattern:

- The common *Abstract/Concrete* parallel factory structure

- The *Concrete-only* factory structure
- The *Parameterized* factory

We'll cover each one in the following subsections, but we're going to start with the classic implementation, which declares a factory for each product (or item). We've already noted that a parallel class hierarchy between products and factories doesn't necessarily scale well, but it's effective when you have a preset number of products in your game that aren't likely to change.

## Adding an abstract factory class

Open the **Scripts** folder, create a new C# script named AbstractCreator, and update its code to match the following code. The abstract creator is only responsible for declaring a factory method that all factory subclasses will implement on their own, in this case, the Create method, which returns an IItem object (which is why we declare it as an abstract class). As we've discussed, this defers item creation to concrete subclasses at runtime:

```
using System.Collections;
using System.Collections.Generic;
using UnityEngine;

// 1
public abstract class AbstractCreator
{
    // 2
    public abstract IItem Create();
}
```

**Optional default implementations and calling your own factory method**

You can add a default implementation for your factory method as shown in the following code if you want the option of returning a default product without overriding the factory method:

```
public abstract class AbstractCreator
{
    public virtual IItem Create()
    {
        return new Pebble();
    }
}
```

You can also add another layer of abstraction by calling the factory method from the abstract creator itself. This can also add another level of protection so the client script doesn't need to know about the factory method, but you lose the ability to create default factory methods:

```
public abstract class AbstractCreator
{
    protected abstract IItem Create();
    public IItem GetInstance()
    {
        return this.Create();
    }
}
```

Just like with our concrete items, we need to add a concrete creator class for each type of item. In our example, a pebble factory creates `Pebble` objects, cursed knife factories create `CursedKnife` objects, and so on.

Now we need to write concrete creator classes for each item product, which lays out the parallel class hierarchy we've been talking about so much. Open `AbstractCreator.cs` and update the code to match the following code, which adds new `AbstractCreator` subclass factories for creating pebbles, cursed knives, and potions:

```
...

// 1
public class PebbleFactory : AbstractCreator
{
    // 2
    public override IItem Create()
    {
        return new Pebble();
    }
}

// 3
public class CursedKnifeFactory : AbstractCreator
{
```

```
    // 4
    public override IItem Create()
    {
        return new CursedKnife();
    }
}


// 5
public class PotionFactory : AbstractCreator
{
    // 6
    public override IItem Create()
    {
        return new Potion();
    }
}
```

Let's break down our factory code:

1.  Declares a pebble factory that subclasses AbstractCreator
2.  Overrides the Create method and returns a new Pebble object
3.  Declares a cursed knife factory that subclasses AbstractCreator
4.  Overrides the Create method and returns a new CursedKnife object
5.  Declares a potion factory that subclasses AbstractCreator
6.  Overrides the Create method and returns a new Potion object

Notice that our inventory system now lets Item subclasses decide what to do when they're equipped, and creator subclasses decide what item is created. The important part is that we're not binding any of the creation logic to any concrete implementations, so customizing, subclassing, and building complex objects is possible without any hardcoding!

As mentioned earlier, this variation doesn't scale well for scenarios where you're adding product classes on a regular basis because you would need to add a sibling factory class for each new item. However, it would be perfect for locked-in products like level difficulty or item ranks.

Before testing:

•   Go to the **Scripts** folder, open ItemButton.cs, and uncomment the Configure method.

- Select **Canvas | Inventory** in the **Hierarchy** and make sure the **Button** prefab is assigned to the **Client (Script)** component, as seen in the following screenshot:

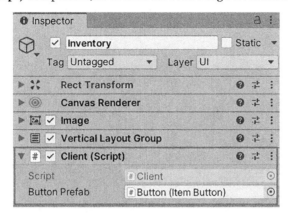

*Figure 4.4: Client script in the Inspector with Button Prefab assigned*

While still in the **Scripts** folder, open the `Client.cs` script and update the code to match the following snippet. This creates a list of factories, adds a new instance of each concrete factory we created in the code, and populates the UI list in the game scene by creating a new `ButtonPrefab` with each item's information:

```
using System.Collections;
using System.Collections.Generic;
using UnityEngine;

public class Client : MonoBehaviour
{
    public ItemButton ButtonPrefab;

    void Start()
    {
        // 1
        List< AbstractCreator> factories = new List< AbstractCreator>()
        {
            new PebbleFactory(),
            new CursedKnifeFactory(),
            new PotionFactory()
        };
```

```
// 2
foreach (AbstractCreator factory in factories)
{
    // 3
    var button = Instantiate(ButtonPrefab);

    // 4
    IItem item = factory.Create();

    // 5
    button.Configure(item);
    button.transform.SetParent(this.transform);
}
}
}
```

Let's break down the code:

1.  Instantiates a list of factories with an instance of each concrete factory class

2.  Loops through each factory in the factories list

3.  Instantiates a new button using the ButtonPrefab

4.  Creates an item using the Create method on each concrete factory

5.  Passes the new item to the button's Configure method and sets the item's parent

 We're segmenting each factory variation in the Client script to make building and testing easier, but this approach isn't linked to the Factory Method pattern itself.

Press **Play** and you'll see a list of items in the **Hierarchy** under an empty parent object named **Inventory**, along with a list of items in the **Game** view, as seen in *Figure 4.5*. Each factory class can be treated the same in this example since each one is responsible for creating a certain type of item. While the factories all share the same Create method, each specific Item takes care of its own internal construction.

Each item in the UI has an object in the Hierarchy

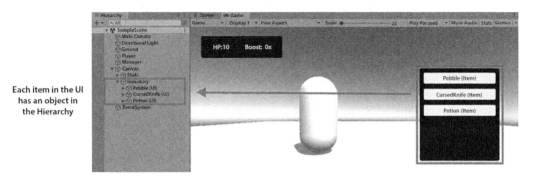

*Figure 4.5: UI list populated with items in the game view and Hierarchy from the Abstract-Factory class*

When you select each item from the UI list, you'll see their respective Equip method execute. When you click on the **Pebble (Item)** in the UI list, a console message prints out saying you've skipped it at a nearby lake, as shown in the following screenshot:

Selecting the Pebble executes it's Equip function

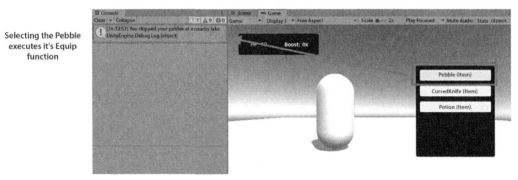

*Figure 4.6: Console output from selecting a Pebble from the UI list*

When you select the **CursedKnife (Item)** from the UI list, the player turns magenta and another console message prints out saying you're cursed, as shown in the following screenshot:

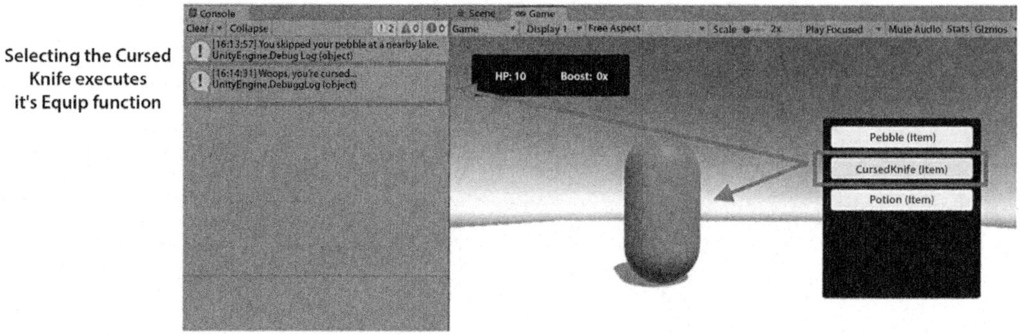

Selecting the Cursed
Knife executes
it's Equip function

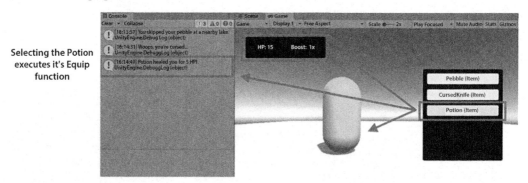

*Figure 4.7: Console output and Player capsule modifications from selecting a CursedKnife from the UI list*

Selecting the **Potion (Item)** turns the player green, adds 5 to the **HP** and 1 to the **Boost** values in the stats bar to the upper left of the player, and prints out another console message, as shown in the following figure:

Selecting the Potion
executes it's Equip
function

*Figure 4.8: Console output and Player capsule modifications from selecting a Potion from the UI list*

That completes our basic factory implementation, with each item deferring its Equip functionality to its subclasses while the factory class creates and returns a single type of item. This separation of concerns allows all our items to share the same interface and specify custom functionality while the factory classes simply instantiate their items.

Your next task is to implement the same functionality using a concrete parent factory class, which has several advantages in flexibility and scalability over the current solution that we'll tackle in the next section.

# Building a concrete factory

The abstract factory implementation we have right now is one of parallel hierarchies, in our example, between concrete item classes (pebbles, cursed knives, and potions) and their creator classes (pebble, cursed knife, and potion factories). However, each new item class we add to our game comes with a new factory class, which isn't ideal for scaling systems.

The concrete factory class variation lets you declare factory methods with default implementations, while still being able to override them in subclasses if necessary. The concrete parent factory is also a good choice when you have a set way of creating products. A classic example is programmatically creating a maze with set products like walls, rooms, and doors in a static configuration but with interchangeable products. In our example, we'll adapt the concrete factory class to populate an inventory list with one of each of our item types.

## Creating a concrete factory class

In the **Scripts** folder, create a new C# script named `ConcreteCreator` and update its code to match the following snippet. This code adds three factory methods for returning normal, rare, and healing items with default implementations and a `CreateInventory` method to set the inventory list. Notice that each factory method for returning an item is marked `virtual` so we can override any, all, or none of them in a subclass:

```
using System.Collections;
using System.Collections.Generic;
using UnityEngine;

// 1
public class ConcreteCreator
{
    // 2
    public virtual IItem NormalItem()
    {
        return new Pebble();
    }

    // 3
    public virtual IItem RareItem()
    {
        return new CursedKnife();
```

```
    }

    // 4
    public virtual IItem HealingItem()
    {
        return new Potion();
    }


    // 5
    public List<IItem> CreateInventory()
    {
        return new List<IItem>()
        {
            NormalItem(),
            RareItem(),
            HealingItem(),
        };
    }
}
```

Let's break down our code:

1. Creates a public class called ConcreteCreator

2. Adds a virtual method designed to return normal level items with the default return item set as a Pebble

3. Adds a virtual method to return rare level items and sets the default return item to a CursedKnife

4. Adds a virtual method to return healing items and sets the default return item to a Potion

5. Adds a public method to return a pre-configured list of inventory items and returns one of each item

 You could also add a constructor to the concrete creator class and make it call CreateInventory when it's instantiated, or even store a list of items in the ConcreteCreator itself to further abstract and black box the creation process.

Now that a single concrete factory can produce several different items and an inventory list, update the Client script to match the following code. Instead of populating the list of factories, we can simply call CreateInventory and programmatically create our UI buttons and set each item's Equip method to the button's OnClick event. This keeps the amount of information the client code needs to a minimum and simplifies the factory process:

```
using System.Collections;
using System.Collections.Generic;
using UnityEngine;

public class Client : MonoBehaviour
{
    public ItemButton ButtonPrefab;

    void Start()
    {
        // 1
        var creator = new ConcreteCreator();
        var items = creator.CreateInventory();

        // 2
        foreach (IItem item in items)
        {
            var button = Instantiate(ButtonPrefab);

            // 3
            button.Configure(item);
            button.transform.SetParent(this.transform);
        }
    }
}
```

Let's break down our new client code:

1.  Creates a new instance of the ConcreteCreator class and uses CreateInventory to return a list of items

2.  Loops through the items list and create a new button prefab for each

3.  Passes the new item to the button's Configure method and sets the item's parent

When you press **Play**, everything will still look and function the same as the classic abstract factory variation, as you can see here:

UI and Canvas
Buttons are the same
as the Abstract class

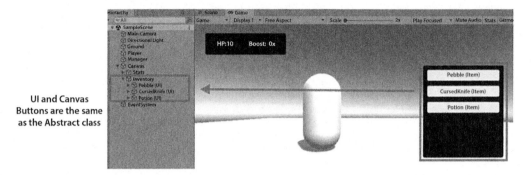

*Figure 4.9: UI list populated with items in the game view and Hierarchy from the Concrete-Factory class*

The console output from each button will print out as shown in the following screenshot. The bonus from this approach is we don't need to keep making concrete factory classes for each item type we may want to add (parallel hierarchies would be a headache with DLC).

**Button output is the same as the
Abstract class implementation**

```
Console
Clear | ▼ | Collapse | Error Pause | Editor ▼        Q

    [16:02:28] You skipped your pebble at a nearby lake.
    UnityEngine.Debug:Log (object)

    [16:02:29] Woops, you're cursed...
    UnityEngine.Debug:Log (object)

    [16:02:30] Potion healed you for 5 HP!
    UnityEngine.Debug:Log (object)
```

*Figure 4.10: Console output from selecting each item in the UI list*

Let's see this added bump in efficiency in action – let's say we wanted to create a factory that only produced healing items (i.e., just potions). Add the code in the following snippet to the bottom of ConcreteCreator.cs as a separate class, which overrides the NormalItem and RareItem methods to both return Potion objects while leaving the default HealingItem code alone:

```
...

// 1
public class HealingFactory : ConcreteCreator
```

```
{
    // 2
    public override IItem NormalItem()
    {
        return new Potion();
    }

    // 3
    public override IItem RareItem()
    {
        return new Potion();
    }
}
```

Let's break the code down:

1.  Declares a new subclass of ConcreteCreator called HealingFactory
2.  Overrides the default NormalItem method and returns a Potion instead of a Pebble
3.  Overrides the default RareItem method and returns a Potion instead of a CursedKnife

Update Client.cs to match the following code, which substitutes the new HealingFactory for our old ConcreteCreator and uses the parent class methods to populate and return a list of items. Notice that nothing else needs to change; we simply swapped out one creator for another, which is a great sign that our code won't fall to pieces when we need to make a change (brittle code is the worst):

```
using System.Collections;
using System.Collections.Generic;
using UnityEngine;

public class Client : MonoBehaviour
{
    public ItemButton ButtonPrefab;

    void Start()
    {
        // 1
        var creator = new HealingFactory();
        var items = creator.CreateInventory();
```

```
        foreach (IItem item in items)
        {
            var button = Instantiate(ButtonPrefab);

            button.Configure(item);
            button.transform.SetParent(this.transform);
        }
    }
}
```

When you press **Play**, all the items in our UI are potions as shown in the following screenshot (which won't help us beat the game, but we'll be super well cared for):

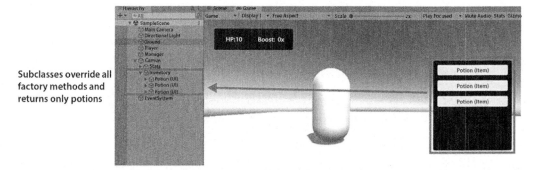

*Figure 4.11: UI list populated with items from the HealingFactory subclass*

When you look at the console output you'll see the output from each item being selected, as shown in the following screenshot:

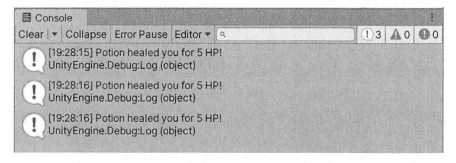

*Figure 4.12: Console output from selecting each item from the UI list*

Notice that throughout this entire section, we haven't touched our IItem interface or implementing classes, which is one of the main strengths of the Factory Method pattern. Decoupling the type of created item from how it's created is fundamental in a flexible, scalable, and maintainable factory system.

Now, the abstract and concrete factory class variations can be a great tool when applied to the scenarios that best fit them. But what if we want to create a factory class that can create any kind of item we have in our game? For that case, a parameterized factory variation is the best fit, which we'll build in the next section.

## Building a parameterized factory

Both the abstract and concrete factory variations we've built are good for specific, static products and factory hierarchies. But what if our game needs factories that can build a growing set of products? Luckily, there's a variation of the factory pattern called a parameterized factory, where we store products by key and simply request the item we want. While this might sound like the work we did in the last chapter on the Prototype pattern, adding argument parameters to a factory still uses the underlying separation of concerns between product and creator classes.

### Creating a parameterized factory class

In the **Scripts** folder, create a new C# script named ParameterizedCreator and update its code to match the following snippet. Continuing with our item scenario, our parameterized factory will have a single Create method that takes in a string parameter for the name of the item we want. Based on the item name we pass in, a new IItem instance will be created and returned. I've also marked the Create method as virtual so we can easily customize a factory by subclassing:

```
using System.Collections;
using System.Collections.Generic;
using UnityEngine;

// 1
public class ParameterizedCreator
{
    // 2
    public virtual IItem Create(string itemName)
    {
        // 3
        switch (itemName)
```

```
    {
        case "Normal":
            return new Pebble();
        case "Rare":
            return new CursedKnife();
        default:
            return null;
    }
  }
}
```

Let's break down the code:

1.   Declares a new public class named ParameterizedCreator

2.   Creates a public method that takes an item name parameter and returns an IItem

3.   Uses a switch statement on the item name parameter and returns a matching IItem instance

To use our new factory variation, update Client.cs to match the following code, which adds a ParameterizedCreator instance, a list of items using the Create method and the item names, and loops through all the items to populate the UI list in the game scene:

```
using System.Collections;
using System.Collections.Generic;
using UnityEngine;

public class Client : MonoBehaviour
{
    public ItemButton ButtonPrefab;

    void Start()
    {
        // 1
```

```
        var itemFactory = new ParameterizedCreator();

        // 2
        List<IItem> items = new List<IItem>()
        {
            itemFactory.Create("Normal"),
            itemFactory.Create("Rare"),
            itemFactory.Create("Rare")
        };

        // 3
        foreach(IItem item in items)
        {
            var button = Instantiate(ButtonPrefab);

            // 4
            button.Configure(item);
            button.transform.SetParent(this.transform);
        }
    }
}
```

Let's break down the code:

1. Creates a new instance of the `ParameterizedCreator` class

2. Adds a list of items and populates it using the `Create` method and the item's type

3. Loops through the list of items and creates a new button prefab with each item's information

4. Passes the new item to the button's `Configure` method and sets the item's parent

Since we're no longer limited to items of a certain type of factory or to default methods in a concrete factory class, we can pass a `string` item name, or even an enum or `class`, into the parameterized factory's `Create` method and get the item we need, as shown in the following screenshot:

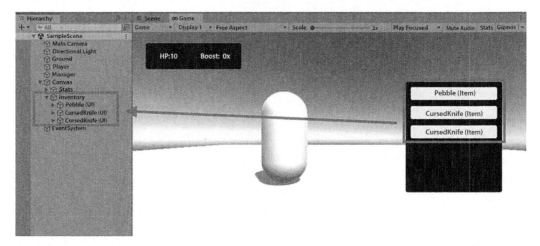

*Figure 4.13: UI list with items in the game view and Hierarchy using the ParameterizedFactory class*

For added flexibility, add the code in the following snippet to the end of the `ParameterizedCreator.cs` script to create a parameterized factory subclass that extends and modifies our creatable items. This is a great way to specify different factories without adding a huge amount of new code:

```
...

// 1
public class NoobFactory : ParameterizedCreator
{
    // 2
    public override IItem Create(string itemName)
    {
        // 3
        switch(itemName)
        {
            case "Rare":
                return new Pebble();

            // 4
```

```
                case "Healing":
                    return new Pebble();
        }


        // 5
        return base.Create(itemName);
    }
}
```

Let's break down the code:

1.  Declares a new `NoobFactory` class as a subclass of `ParameterizedCreator`
2.  Adds a `Create` method with a string parameter and uses a `switch` statement based on `itemName`
3.  Changes the `Rare` item case to return a `Pebble` instead of a `CursedKnife`
4.  Adds a new case for `Healing` items that return a `Pebble`
5.  Calls the base classes `Create` method to handle any other switch cases

We're using inheritance to our advantage here by calling the base `Create` method to handle any additional item cases we don't need to update or add. This gives us the ability to only handle new item cases by delegating items we've already handled to the base class.

To test out the new subclass, update the `Start` method in `Client.cs` to match the following code to use the `NoobFactory` and add a healing item to the inventory list in our game UI:

```
Void Start()
{
    // 1
    var itemFactory = new NoobFactory();

    List<Iitem> items = new List<Iitem>()
    {
        itemFactory.Create("Normal"),
        itemFactory.Create("Rare"),
        // 2
        itemFactory.Create("Healing")
    };

    foreach (Iitem item in items)
```

```
    {
        var button = Instantiate(ButtonPrefab);

        button.Configure(item);
        button.transform.SetParent(this.transform);
    }
}
```

Notice how easy it is to not only change an existing item case to return a different item in the case of the Rare items, but to extend a factory with new items as in the Healing item case, as shown in the following screenshot:

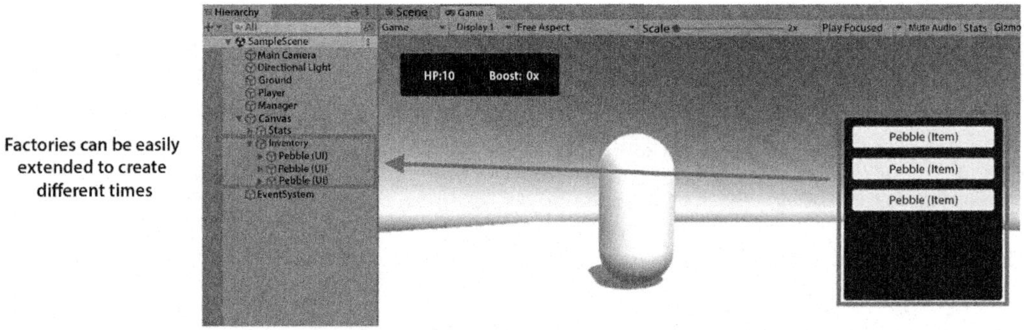

**Factories can be easily extended to create different times**

*Figure 4.14: UI list populated with items in the game view and Hierarchy from the NoobFactory subclass*

Not only is the parameterized factory a nice mix of functionality and flexibility we saw in the abstract and concrete factory variations, but it can also be efficiently scaled with judicious use of reflection and the LINQ API, which we'll build out in the next section.

## Scaling factories with reflection and LINQ

Using a parameterized factory class can quickly become a spaghetti nightmare of monstrous switch statements and unmanageable code if items are being added or updated at a fast pace. Luckily, C# has a System.Reflection namespace that can tell you about all the classes, interfaces, and value types your project has by looking through the project's assembly.

In addition to reflection, we'll be using the LINQ API, which stands for Language Integrated Query. Don't worry if you've never used LINQ before – think of it as a way to filter, sort, or otherwise manipulate a set of data. For example, if we had a list of player names but only wanted to see players with a specific first initial, LINQ would get us there fast!

You can check out more on the LINQ API at `https://docs.microsoft.com/dotnet/csharp/programming-guide/concepts/linq`.

Reflection lets you create type instances at runtime, just like we instantiate `GameObjects` in Unity. The great part about the `Reflection` namespace is that it has everything you need to programmatically find, filter, and populate a dictionary of objects at runtime that your factories can create. Any new products are automatically added to the list of creatable objects with no extra code, making the system much more scalable and maintainable in real-world projects.

Now before you run off and use reflection in every future line of code, it's important to know that it's not always the most performant option (it can actually be extremely slow, especially in Unity). This isn't to say that you mustn't use it but be aware that it's a specific tool for a specific job (you can read all about this aspect of the Reflection API with a quick Google search as it's outside the scope of this chapter).

**Resources on assemblies and reflection in C#**

Assemblies are the literal building blocks of any C# application, and this holds true for Unity projects as well. By default, new Unity projects only have one assembly, which you can access using the `Assembly` class.

 Reflection and assemblies are advanced topics in C#, so if you haven't heard of them that's no problem. We'll go through the basics in the code examples, but if you're interested in diving deeper check out the following resources:

- `https://docs.microsoft.com/dotnet/standard/assembly`
- `https://docs.microsoft.com/dotnet/framework/reflection-and-codedom/reflection`

We're going to create a new factory class for this example, so create a new C# script in the **Scripts** folder, name it `ReflectionFactory`, and update its code to match the following snippet. The idea for this factory class is to programmatically fill a dictionary with all item names and their class types using `Reflection`. We'll do this by declaring a dictionary of items, using the `Assembly` class to filter out all types that implement our `IItem` interface, and storing the type name and type as the dictionary key-value pairs:

```
using System.Collections;
using System.Collections.Generic;
```

```
using UnityEngine;

// 1
using System;
using System.Reflection;
using System.Linq;

public class ReflectionFactory
{
    // 2
    Dictionary<string, Type> _items = new Dictionary<string, Type>();
    public Dictionary<string, Type> Items
    {
        get { return _items; }
    }

    // 3
    public ReflectionFactory()
    {
        var itemTypes = Assembly.GetAssembly(typeof(IItem)).GetTypes();

        // 4
        var filteredItems = itemTypes.Where(item => !item.IsInterface &&
typeof(IItem).IsAssignableFrom(item));

        // 5
        foreach (var type in filteredItems)
        {
            _items.Add(type.Name, type);
        }
    }
}
```

Let's break down the code:

1.  Adds namespaces for System, Reflection, and Linq

2.  Creates a private and public Dictionary of strings and types

3. Adds a class constructor and uses the `Assembly` class to get all `IItem` class types in the project

4. Filters all types to discard interfaces and returns objects that have implemented the `IItem` interface

5. Loops through the list of filtered items and adds the temporary item's type name and type to the dictionary of items

> In a scenario where you might have multiple subcategories of items or products in your game, you could add a generic type for the entire `ReflectionFactory` class and use it in the constructor and `Create` method to only return that specific type of object instead of hardcoding our `Item` class as the default type in the preceding and following code blocks.

To complete our new factory, add a factory method to the `ReflectionFactory` class shown in the following code. This method takes in an item name and returns an instance of the item we're looking for if it exists in our dictionary of items that we filled in the previous code block. Since we only know the type of the object we want, we can use the `Activator` class to dynamically create and return an instance of the type we want at runtime, for example, a `Potion`, without having to know what specific item we're dealing with. This crucial method now replaces a huge `switch` statement you'd be forced to work with every time you added a new item:

```
...

// 1
public IItem Create(string itemName)
{
    // 2
    if (_items.ContainsKey(itemName))
    {
        // 3
        Type type = _items[itemName];

        // 4
        var item = Activator.CreateInstance(type) as IItem;

        // 5
        return item;
```

```
    }

    // 6
    return null;
}
```

Let's break down the code:

1. Adds a `public` method called `Create` that takes a string parameter and returns an `IItem`.

2. Checks if the item's name is in the `_items` dictionary.

3. If the item exists, we cast it as a new `Type` variable.

4. Uses the `Activator` class to create a new instance of the given type and cast it as an `IItem`.

5. Returns the cast item.

6. If the item doesn't exist, we return `null`.

To test, update the `Client.cs` script to match the following code, which creates a `ReflectionFactory` instance, fills a list of items using the factory's `Create` method and item name, and finally instantiates our UI list:

```
using System.Collections;
using System.Collections.Generic;
using UnityEngine;

public class Client : MonoBehaviour
{
    public ItemButton ButtonPrefab;

    void Start()
    {
        // 1
        var itemFactory = new ReflectionFactory();

        // 2
        List<IItem> items = new List<IItem>()
        {
            itemFactory.Create("Pebble"),
            itemFactory.Create("CursedKnife"),
            itemFactory.Create("Potion")
```

```
        };

        // 3
        foreach(IItem item in items)
        {
            var button = Instantiate(ButtonPrefab);

            // 4
            button.Configure(item);
            button.transform.SetParent(this.transform);
        }
    }
}
```

Let's break down the code:

1. Creates a new instance of the `ReflectionFactory` class
2. Adds a list of items and populates it using the `Create` method and the item's class name
3. Loops through the list of items and creates a new button prefab with each item's information
4. Passes the new item to the button's `Configure` method and sets the item's parent

Everything works exactly the same in the game scene, but the real magic happens when you create a new concrete item. Go ahead and try it out – create a new item class, implement the `IItem` interface and the `Equip` method, and then add a new item to the items list in the `Client.cs` script. Watch it appear in the UI list without you having to manually register it with the `ReflectionFactory`!

Now that our C# implementation for the Factory Method pattern is complete, it's time to incorporate some Unity-specific features into the mix with GameObjects.

## Adding GameObjects to the mix

`GameObjects` are a fundamental part of any Unity game, which makes them an essential addition to our Factory pattern implementation. For our example, we're going to add `GameObjects` to each `Creator` class variation we've already built so the items not only have a code component but also appear in the game scene.

Because the main building block of our item classes is the IItem interface, we're going to make each of our concrete items a MonoBehaviour so Unity treats them as components. We'll use the factories to instantiate new GameObjects based on the pre-made models in the starter project and show you how to build up complex objects from scratch. In an ideal world, we would have the item classes own their own GameObjects, but C# doesn't allow interfaces to have instance fields.

 If you're asking yourself why I don't just add an instance field to each item class and assign it a GameObject in its constructor, the answer is that it's a lot of overhead for every new item. In the next chapter, we'll see how an abstract item class can be used as an alternative solution.

Your next task is to upgrade each item to a MonoBehaviour and the Abstract Creator classes to deal with their own GameObjects for each item.

## Updating the Item class

For our example, each item is going to be its own component, which can be mixed and matched with whatever model GameObject we want in the game scene. This might seem like overkill for our simple example but consider if your product was made up of several Prefabs, components, or GameObjects. You'd want a factory to be able to put all that together into a complex object and return it to your client code.

Open the Item.cs script and update each concrete item to inherit from MonoBehaviour *before* implementing the IItem interface shown in the following code. This is very important, as Unity requires composed objects to be MonoBehaviors before anything else:

```
public class Pebble : MonoBehaviour, IItem
{
    //… No other changes needed …
}


public class CursedKnife : MonoBehaviour, IItem
{
    //… No other changes needed …
}


public class Potion : MonoBehaviour, IItem
```

```
{
    //... No other changes needed ...
}
```

Now each item can be treated as a component, we can start building our items in the concrete factories we've already created, which we'll cover in the next section.

## Updating the Abstract Creator class

Update the base `AbstractCreator` class with instance fields for spawner and model `GameObjects`, then assign their values in the class constructor as shown in the following code. The spawner object serves as the empty parent `GameObject` in the **Hierarchy**, which lets us have several different kinds of creators in the scene (and even multiple instances with the same model for better optimization):

```
using System.Collections;
using System.Collections.Generic;
using UnityEngine;

public abstract class AbstractCreator
{
    // 1
    public GameObject Spawner { get; protected set; }
    public GameObject Model { get; protected set; }

    // 2
    public AbstractCreator(GameObject model)
    {
        // 3
        Spawner = new GameObject();
        Model = model;
    }

    public abstract IItem Create();
}
```

Let's break down the code:

1.  Adds instance fields for `Spawner` and `Model` `GameObjects` with public get and protected set properties

2.  Declares a class constructor with a single argument taking in a GameObject

3.  Sets the Spawner to a new empty GameObject and the Model to the constructor parameter

Alternatively, you could pass in a GameObject to the create method instead of the class constructor, but I prefer to have a reference to the prefab so creating multiple items is more efficient after the factory instance is initialized.

Before we test out this new code, we need to update each of our concrete factory classes, as shown in the following code. This new code passes the constructor's GameObject argument in each concrete creator subclass up to the base AbstractFactory class, and then sets the spawner object's name. The important part is how the Create method is updated in each factory to instantiate and configure an item:

```
public class PebbleFactory : AbstractCreator
{
    // 1
    public PebbleFactory(GameObject prefab) : base(prefab)
    {
        Spawner.name = "Pebble Factory";
    }

    public override IItem Create()
    {
        // 2
        var pebble = GameObject.Instantiate(Model);
        pebble.AddComponent<Pebble>();
        pebble.transform.position = new Vector3(-2.2f, 0.3f, -7f);
        pebble.transform.SetParent(Spawner.transform);

        return pebble.GetComponent<Pebble>();
    }
}

public class CursedKnifeFactory : AbstractCreator
{
    // 3
```

```csharp
    public CursedKnifeFactory(GameObject prefab) : base(prefab)
    {
        Spawner.name = "Cursed Knife Factory";
    }


    public override IItem Create()
    {
        // 4
        var knife = GameObject.Instantiate(Model);
        knife.AddComponent<CursedKnife>();
        knife.transform.position = new Vector3(-0.6f, 0.3f, -7.6f);
        knife.transform.SetParent(Spawner.transform);

        return knife.GetComponent<CursedKnife>();
    }
}

public class PotionFactory : AbstractCreator
{
    // 5
    public PotionFactory(GameObject prefab) : base(prefab)
    {
        Spawner.name = "Potion Factory";
    }

    // 6
    public override IItem Create()
    {
        var potion = GameObject.Instantiate(Model);
        potion.AddComponent<Potion>();
        potion.transform.position = new Vector3(0.6f, 0.3f, -7f);
        potion.transform.SetParent(Spawner.transform);

        return potion.GetComponent<Potion>();
    }
}
```

I've hardcoded the individual positions of each GameObject so they are all laid out in front of the scene's camera, but these values aren't part of the pattern itself. If you wanted to have a more flexible system, you could pass in position coordinates into the Create method and set the item positions that way too!

Let's break down our new code:

1.  Declares a PebbleFactory constructor with the base class constructor and sets the object's name

2.  Creates and configures a Pebble object using the Model and returns the Pebble component

3.  Declares a CursedKnifeFactory constructor with the base class constructor and sets the object's name

4.  Creates and configures a CursedKnife object using the Model and returns the CursedKnife component

5.  Declares a PotionFactory constructor using the base class constructor and sets the object's name

6.  Creates and configures a Potion object using the Model and returns the Potion component

There's a lot of repeated code here since we're trying to keep things relatively straightforward but notice how easy it would be to construct each item in a different way. Further, if you wanted to keep the same creation logic as we have in the preceding code snippet, you could optimize the AbstractFactory with default or generic methods to streamline the process even more. Again, these implementations are templates rather than hard and fast rules (get creative and adapt them to your needs).

Now we can update Client.cs to hold variables for each type of model and pass them into their respective factories during instantiation, as shown in the following code:

```
using System.Collections;
using System.Collections.Generic;
using UnityEngine;
```

```
public class Client : MonoBehaviour
{
    public ItemButton ButtonPrefab;

    // 1
    public GameObject PebbleModel;
    public GameObject KnifeModel;
    public GameObject PotionModel;

    void Start()
    {
        List<AbstractCreator> factories = new List<AbstractCreator>()
        {
            // 2
            new PebbleFactory(PebbleModel),
            new CursedKnifeFactory(KnifeModel),
            new PotionFactory(PotionModel)
        };

        foreach (AbstractCreator factory in factories)
        {
            var button = Instantiate(ButtonPrefab);
            IItem item = factory.Create();
            button.Configure(item);
            button.transform.SetParent(this.transform);
        }
    }
}
```

To test the new GameObject implementation:

1.  From the **Hierarchy**, select **Canvas | Inventory**.

2.  Drag each model from the **Resources** folder into their respective variables on the **Client (Script)** component as shown in the following screenshot:

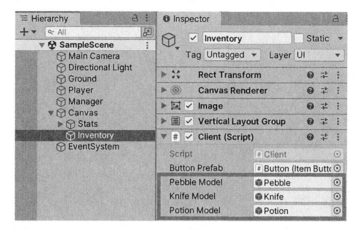

*Figure 4.15: Client script in the Inspector with each item model assigned to their respective variables*

Run the game and you'll see a different button for each item in the UI list and GameObjects on-screen at the foot of the player capsule, as shown in the following screenshot:

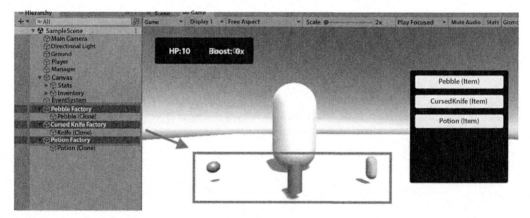

**Each factory creates a single type of item**

*Figure 4.16: Game view with multiple factories and items in the Hierarchy and scene*

Notice we only had to make minor changes to the Client.cs script to implement GameObjects, as all the work is done behind the scenes in our creator classes. In the next subsections, we'll update the other factory variations to use GameObjects and finish off the chapter with a quick word on ScriptableObjects.

# Updating the concrete factory

Each of the factory variations follows the same structure we set up in the previous subsection: we need a spawner object to act as the factory parent, models for each item, and a set of instructions on how to put the items together when they're created.

Open ConcreteCreator.cs and update the code to match the following snippet, which sets up instance fields for a spawner, models, and a list of protected items we can access from our client script. The main difference in this variation is loading the models directly from the **Resources** folder in the project instead of dragging and dropping them in the client script. I'm structuring this example for simplicity, but I'll leave further optimizations for you to implement in your projects:

```
public class ConcretCreator
{
    // 1
    public GameObject Spawner { get; protected set; }

    // 2
    public GameObject PebbleModel { get; protected set; }
    public GameObject KnifeModel { get; protected set; }
    public GameObject PotionModel { get; protected set; }

    // 3
    protected List<IItem> _items = new List<IItem>();
    public List<IItem> Items
    {
        get { return _items; }
    }

    // 4
    public ConcreteCreator)
    {
        Spawner = new GameObject();
        Spawner.name = "Concrete Factory";

        // 5
        PebbleModel = Resources.Load("Pebble") as GameObject;
        KnifeModel = Resources.Load("Knife") as GameObject;
```

```
        PotionModel = Resources.Load("Potion") as GameObject;


        // 6
        CreateInventory();
    }
}
```

Let's break down the code:

1.  Declares a new instance field for a spawner GameObject
2.  Adds three new instance fields for each item model GameObject
3.  Adds a protected list of items, initializes it to an empty list, and adds a public access variable
4.  Declares a class constructor, instantiates the spawner object, and changes its name
5.  Uses the **Resources** class to load each item model by name and cast each as a GameObject
6.  Calls CreateInventory to initialize default items

Once we have our models and spawner configured, all that's left is to update the default factory methods to match the following code. The object creation code is almost exactly the same as the previous example; we just add each item to the _items list before returning the IItem component to the client script, which lets us work with the running list of items outside the concrete factory:

```
public virtual IItem NormalItem()
{
    // 1

    var pebble = GameObject.Instantiate(PebbleModel);
    var item = pebble.AddComponent<Pebble>();

    pebble.transform.position = new Vector3(-2.2f, 0.3f, -7f);
    pebble.transform.SetParent(Spawner.transform);
    _items.Add(item);

    return pebble.GetComponent<Pebble>();
}


public virtual IItem RareItem()
{
    // 2
```

```
        var knife = GameObject.Instantiate(KnifeModel);
        var item = knife.AddComponent<CursedKnife>();

        knife.transform.position = new Vector3(-0.6f, 0.3f, -7.6f);
        knife.transform.SetParent(Spawner.transform);
        _items.Add(item);

        return knife.GetComponent<CursedKnife>();
    }

public virtual IItem HealingItem()
{
    // 3
    var potion = GameObject.Instantiate(PotionModel);
    var item = potion.AddComponent<Potion>();

    potion.transform.position = new Vector3(0.6f, 0.3f, -7f);
    potion.transform.SetParent(Spawner.transform);
    _items.Add(item);

    return potion.GetComponent<Potion>();
}
    public List<IItem> CreateInventory()
    {
        // ... No changes needed ...
    }
}
```

Let's break down the new code:

1.  Creates and configures a Pebble object using the Model and returns the Pebble component
2.  Creates and configures a CursedKnife object using the Model and returns the CursedKnife component
3.  Creates and configures a Potion object using the Model and returns the Potion component

 Any subclasses you create that inherit from ConcreteFactory will need updated instructions in the Create method if you want to include GameObjects.

Update Client.cs to match the following code, which instantiates a new ConcreteFactory instance and uses the IItems list to populate the UI list in the game scene. Notice that all the item creation work is hidden away in the class constructor, so our client code is especially clean and readable:

```
using System.Collections;
using System.Collections.Generic;
using UnityEngine;

public class Client : MonoBehaviour
{
    public ItemButton ButtonPrefab;

    void Start()
    {
        // 1
        var creator = new ConcreteCreator();

        // 2
        foreach(IItem item in creator.Items)
        {
            // 3
            var button = Instantiate(ButtonPrefab);

            button.Configure(item);
            button.transform.SetParent(this.transform);
        }
    }
}
```

Let's break down the code:

1.  Declares a new instance of the ConcreteCreator class

2.  Loops through the IItems list that's populated in the constructor and create a button for each

3.  Creates, configures, and parents a new button prefab with each item's information

Run the game and you'll see the items show up in the game view at the foot of the player capsule as shown in *Figure 4.17*. You'll also see a single factory parent object in the **Hierarchy** with each item as a child object, which decreases the clutter of our previous example that had a factory object for each item type.

The Concrete Factory can create multiple types of items

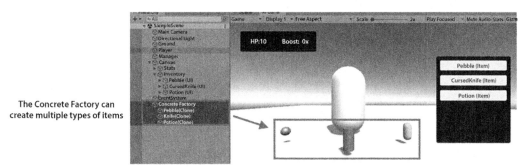

*Figure 4.17: Game view with a single factory and multiple items in the Hierarchy and scene*

The last updates we'll make are to the reflection variation, which will combine the tools we've already learned into a sleek, efficient, and scalable factory.

## Updating the reflection factory

Because we've already deferred so much work in the ReflectionFactory class to reflection techniques, our updates are more surgical. Open ReflectionFactory.cs and update the code to match the following snippet, which adds a spawner, configures it in the class constructor, and modifies the Create function with GameObject instantiation logic:

```
using System.Collections;
using System.Collections.Generic;
using UnityEngine;
using System;
using System.Reflection;
using System.Linq;

public class ReflectionFactory
{
    // 1
    public GameObject Spawner { get; protected set; }

    Dictionary<string, Type> items = new Dictionary<string, Type>();
    public Dictionary<string, Type> Items
```

```
    {
        get { return items; }
    }

    public ReflectionFactory()
    {
        // 2
        Spawner = new GameObject();
        Spawner.name = "Reflection Factory";

        // … No other changes needed …
    }

    // 3
    public IItem Create(string itemName, GameObject model, Vector3
position)
    {
        if (_items.ContainsKey(itemName))
        {
            Type type = _items[itemName];

            // 4
            var obj = GameObject.Instantiate(model);
            var item = obj.AddComponent(type) as IItem;

            // 5
            obj.transform.position = position;
            obj.transform.SetParent(Spawner.transform);

            return obj.GetComponent(type) as IItem;
        }

        return null;
    }
}
```

Let's break down the code:

1. Declares a spawner GameObject with public get and protected set properties
2. Initializes the spawner with a new GameObject and updates the name property
3. Updates the Create method to take in additional arguments for item model and position
4. Instantiates an item GameObject using the model parameter and adds the appropriate item script as a component
5. Sets the item object's position and parent, and then returns the item component script

The dictionary of item names and types pre-populated in the class constructor makes our programmatic code much more streamlined in the Create method, making this implementation the most scalable and maintainable in most cases.

To test, update Client.cs to match the following code, which adds a list of starting positions and passes each model and position to the item factory's Create method:

```
Using System.Collections;
using System.Collections.Generic;
using UnityEngine;

public class Client : MonoBehaviour
{
    public ItemButton ButtonPrefab;

    // 1
    public GameObject PebbleModel;
    public GameObject KnifeModel;
    public GameObject PotionModel;

    public void Start()
    {
        // 2
        List<Vector3> pos = new List<Vector3>()
        {
            new Vector3(-2.2f, 0.3f, -7f),
            new Vector3(-0.6f, 0.3f, -7.6f),
            new Vector3(0.6f, 0.3f, -7f)
        };
```

```
    var itemFactory = new ReflectionFactory();

    List<Iitem> items = new List<Iitem>()
    {
        // 3
        itemFactory.Create("Pebble", PebbleModel, pos[0]),
        itemFactory.Create("CursedKnife", KnifeModel, pos[1]),
        itemFactory.Create("Potion", PotionModel, pos[2])
    };

    foreach (Iitem item in items)
    {
        var button = Instantiate(ButtonPrefab);

        button.Configure(item);
        button.transform.SetParent(this.transform);
    }
}
}
```

Don't forget to drag each model from the **Resources** folder back onto the **Client (Script)** component, as shown in the following screenshot:

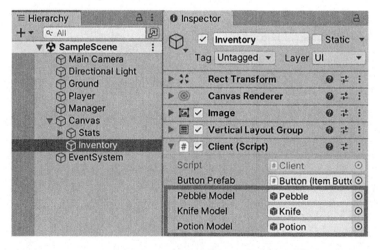

*Figure 4.18: Client script in the Inspector with each item model assigned to their respective variables*

Play the game for the last time and see everything looking and working the same, but now with the added benefit of reflection. Any new item you add to the project that implements the IItem interface can be created from the ReflectionFactory with no extra code in the underlying pattern implementation. Everything is done programmatically, and all information the items need to create themselves is being injected into the Create method.

## Extending products and factories with Scriptable Objects

As your factory classes start needing more and more information to create their objects, it's a good idea to incorporate ScriptableObjects into the landscape. For example, you could create a ScriptableObject class with fields for an item's name, model, and starting position, then pass them into the Create method. This would reduce the amount of information the client code needs to know, make it easier to script, and bring designers and other non-programmers on your team into the process. We've used ScriptableObjects in the previous two chapters, which you can use for reference.

# Summary

Phew, that was a monster chapter, folks! Congratulations on making your way through the ins and outs of the Factory Method pattern, complete with Unity implementations and a little reflection and LINQ syntactic sugar. The Factory Method pattern is one of those patterns that's sometimes overlooked in favor of just using Prefabs and doing everything in the Editor (that's one of Unity's best qualities), but when you want to automate or programmatically control your assembly lines, this pattern is a must.

Remember, the Factory Method pattern is most useful when you want to defer class instantiation to subclasses. There are several Creator class variations in the Factory Method pattern, including an abstract creator, concrete creator, and parameterized creator. Consider which option is best for your project – abstract factory method implementations lead to parallel hierarchies between concrete items and their creator classes, concrete factory classes let you declare factory methods with default implementations that can still be overridden, and parameterized factories can help scale your product inventory (and you can always use reflection and LINQ to make your job easier).

In the next chapter, we'll dive into the Abstract Factory pattern by building an upgraded spawning system where NPCs are paired with items when instantiated, which provides much-needed companion content to this chapter to form the whole factory picture!

# Further reading

- Interfaces are a great way to create groups of related functionality (with or without default implementations) that can be adopted by any class or struct. These are especially handy when you want to have a class inherit from multiple groups, which is called object composition. For more, check out the documentation at `https://learn.microsoft.com/en-us/dotnet/csharp/fundamentals/types/interfaces`.

- `ScriptableObjects` are the perfect way to create data containers in your Unity projects (and we'll use them in almost every chapter going forward), but I'd also recommend checking out the documentation at `https://docs.unity3d.com/Manual/class-ScriptableObject.html`.

- Reflection lets you get an inside glimpse at the classes, structs, and other types that are present in your project's assembly and can be used to create instances of any of those types at runtime. Like multithreading, going too deep into this topic is a little outside the scope of this book, but if you'd like to learn more head over to `https://docs.microsoft.com/dotnet/framework/reflection-and-codedom/reflection`.

- LINQ provides a set of features you can use for querying, sorting, and filtering your data however you want with minimal code. As you start to deal with more complex data requirements, you'll definitely want to check out the documentation at `https://docs.microsoft.com/dotnet/csharp/programming-guide/concepts/linq`.

- Assemblies are collections of types and resources built to work together and form a logical unit of functionality (the literal building blocks of C# applications). These can be executable (`.exe`) or dynamic link library (`.dll`) files, and they provide the common language runtime with the information it needs to be aware of type implementations. Since assemblies are an advanced topic, I'd encourage you to check out the documentation at `https://docs.microsoft.com/dotnet/standard/assembly`.

# Join our community on Discord

Join our community's Discord space for discussions with the author and other readers:

`https://packt.link/gamedevelopment_packt`

# 5

# Building a Crafting System with the Abstract Factory Pattern

In the last chapter, we built an item production system using the Factory Method pattern, Unity GameObjects, and reflection. In this chapter, we'll add some related content focusing on the Abstract Factory pattern for creating factories *of* factories. While the Factory Method pattern helped us hide the creation process of a single product (or type of product), the Abstract Factory pattern lets us black box the creation process behind families or related groups of products. As we noted in the last chapter, choosing between these two patterns largely depends on the scale and depth of your product hierarchies, but also their relationships to one another.

There are a few varieties the Abstract Factory pattern can take depending on the kind of product families you're creating and what (if any) relationships those product families need. Like the Factory Method pattern, the interfaces or abstract classes give our client code the flexibility to leave out the specifics of each concrete product class being created. This added level of abstraction lets the client treat every object factory the same way, regardless of what factory is being used or what family of objects it's popping out on request.

The examples we'll work with in this chapter follow a similar theme to what we built in the previous chapter (assembling items makes for great factory work after all), which will put the following topics in the same mental-model wheelhouse:

- Pros and cons of the Abstract Factory pattern
- Working with families of related but independent products
- Working with families of related and dependent products
- Exploring different Abstract Factory variations

Again, the design pattern variations we'll talk about don't need to be implemented together – you can pick and choose which one fits best. I'm showing the complete code in separate examples on the following pages to make sure you have the best options when you're choosing a direction for your projects.

## Technical requirements

Before you start:

1. Download or clone the GitHub repository at `https://github.com/PacktPublishing/C-Design-Patterns-with-Unity-First-Edition`.

2. Open the **Ch_05_Starter** project folder in Unity Hub.

3. In **Assets | Scenes**, double-click on **SampleScene**.

The starter project for this chapter is brutally sparse (we did a ton of work with visual components and Unity-specific features in the last chapter, so we're not going to recreate all that work). I've only created a ground plane and a `Crafting System` GameObject in the **Hierarchy** with an accompanying empty `CraftingSystem.cs` script attached.

We'll also be using some Unity and C# language features to take our code the extra mile. Don't worry if you're not familiar with these; I've included links for the basics, and I'll explain how they apply to our use cases as we go:

- Interfaces (`https://learn.microsoft.com/en-us/dotnet/csharp/fundamentals/types/interfaces`)

- Abstract classes (`https://learn.microsoft.com/en-us/dotnet/csharp/language-reference/keywords/abstract`)

So, why have I left you with such a bleak arena? Well, all the concepts we used in the last chapter are applicable to this chapter's content – I'll be guiding you through implementing the code for the Abstract Factory pattern, but it's your stretch goal to make it look interactive (think of this chapter as a sibling of the previous more than a completely new design pattern).

## Breaking down the Abstract Factory pattern

As part of the creational family of design patterns, the Abstract Factory pattern is all about using a common interface to create families of related or dependent products without knowing the concrete classes of the products being created. You'll find this pattern is most useful in scenarios where:

- You need a product creation system that's decoupled from how the products are created or assembled.

- Your creation system can be configured with a variety of product families.

- You need to explicitly constrain a family of related products designed to work together.

- You need a collection of products but only want the system to know about their interfaces instead of detailed implementation.

A common use case for the Abstract Factory pattern would be a look-and-feel scenario or anything to do with multiple configurations that need to be managed. For example, if you were developing a game or application for mobile and PC, iOS, and Android (or whatever combination you have), the Abstract Factory pattern would let you pre-configure a common system of interfaces for each platform or device. This could be a different GUI look and feel for each platform or a specific set of capabilities – either way, the Abstract Factory pattern would be a great fit. The following figure shows an example where a game can be played on mobile, desktop, or VR platforms, each with its own set of player input controls:

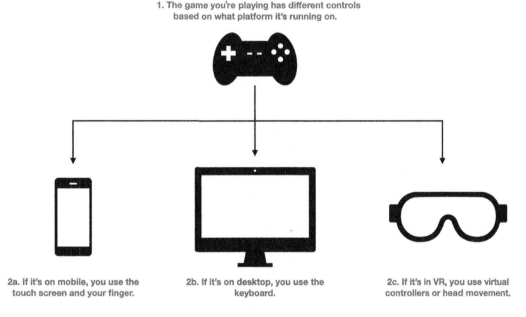

*Figure 5.1: Example of an application used on different platforms with unique control schemes*

Trying to build a central input system to account for all platforms would be hectic and complex, but more importantly, it would be tightly coupled and fragile.

With an Abstract Factory pattern, the main client code could detect which platform the game is running on and simply return the correct player input configuration *without* changing the actual underlying game mechanic code in any way. For example, a jump command on mobile might be a double-tap, while on desktop it's pressing the spacebar, and so on. The key is creating a set of interactions that work across all platforms but are implemented differently. To illustrate this visually, the following image shows a factory that produces different platform configurations for input controls and saving/loading data.

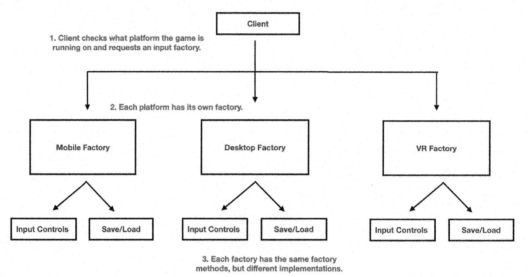

*Figure 5.2: Example scenario of a client creating a factory instance based on the deployed platform*

Like the Factory Method pattern, each product in this example implements a common interface (i.e., **Input Controls** and **Save/Load**, as you can see in the preceding figure), while each factory also implements a set of common interfaces for creating and interacting with those products. The main difference is that the Abstract Factory pattern handles families of related or dependent products with an added layer of abstraction.

There are also several variations to the Abstract Factory pattern that we'll dive into later in the chapter, but we have enough theory to move on to the pattern components in the following section.

## Diagramming the pattern

*Figure 5.3* shows the UML structure for the Abstract Factory pattern and the interactions of its five component parts:

- The **Abstract Product** defines the interface for each type of product, related or dependent.
- Each **Concrete Product** implements the Abstract Product interface and defines a type of product that can be created by its corresponding Concrete Factory.
- The **Abstract Factory** defines an interface for creating abstract products.
- Each **Concrete Factory** implements the Abstract Factory interface and creates a designated family of products.
- The **Client** only works with the **Abstract Factory** and **Abstract Product** interfaces, hiding all implementation logic.

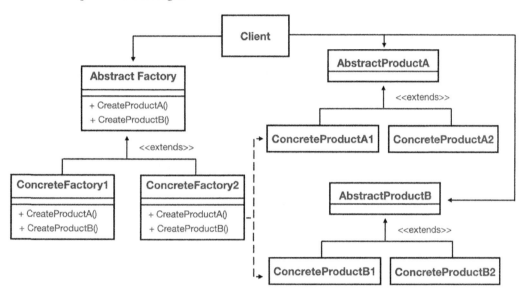

*Figure 5.3: UML diagram of the Abstract Factory components*

Notice that the client is only ever concerned with the Abstract Factory or product interfaces, never the concrete implementations. This decoupling makes factories and products interchangeable if they inherit or implement the required abstract classes or interfaces, making your client code significantly less fragile than a tightly coupled class hierarchy. While it's more work up-front, once the infrastructure is implemented, you'll be able to swap out item factories, character factories, or factories *of* factories whenever you want with very minimal code updates.

When you're trying to choose which pattern fits your problem best (between the Factory Method and Abstract Factory choices), it's important to remember the following:

- The **Factory Method** pattern encapsulates, or hides, the construction code for specific objects.

- The **Abstract Factory** pattern encapsulates the construction of groups of objects, usually referred to as object families. These objects are always related, but they can also be dependent on, and interact with, each other.

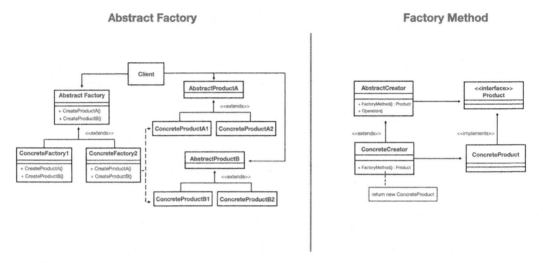

*Figure 5.4: Abstract Factory and Factory Method UML diagram comparison*

With the pattern logistics under our belts, let's move on to fleshing out the crafting system in the starter project.

## Pros and cons

Like all our design patterns, there are pros and cons to the Abstract Factory. Let's start with the benefits and go from there:

- Concrete **class creation is kept separate** from your implementation code, meaning you can control the kinds of objects that are being instantiated in your project. This separation also means client code is never aware of the concrete product classes, only their exposed interfaces. In our example, we'll create classes of blacksmiths and merchants, but the concrete types won't matter to the client because each blacksmith and merchant class shares an interface.

- **Switching entire product families is easy** – simply changing the Concrete Factory being used gives you an entirely new set of products to configure and spit out. You don't want to use the magical blacksmith anymore? No problem, switch it out for the elemental blacksmith instead (half a line of code).

- Enforcing **consistency between products** in the same family is built-in – they can work together efficiently, and you can keep track of which products aren't meant to be interacting by keeping them in separate product families.

However, be careful of the following pitfalls:

- **Adding new products can be time consuming** because Abstract Factory patterns usually have a fixed list of products they can create. Any new products would need code updates in the Abstract Factory classes and their subclasses. Never fear – we can plan for this type of situation by creating a parameterized Abstract Factory (which we'll build at the end of the chapter).

- **The Abstract Factory isn't the Factory Method** – these are different patterns, and have different implementations, pros, and pitfalls. Remember to ask yourself what the end goal is and choose between the two patterns rather than trying to create a Frankenstein of both.

Now that we've covered the structure, benefits, and limitations of the Abstract Factory pattern, we can get to building a system for buying and fusing (or upgrading) items in our inventory!

# Creating related but independent products

Imagine you're building an action platformer with two main crafting systems, one for regular items, armor, and weapons, and another for special fusion products. Each crafting system needs to have the same basic capabilities for buying, selling, crafting, and disassembling items. On top of that, your team needs to be able to interact with each crafting system through a common set of interfaces but be able to switch them out at any time without breaking existing code (whenever new DLC comes out, I'm guessing).

## Scripting product interfaces

The first component of the Abstract Factory pattern is the abstract product interfaces. In our example, we not only have two different sets of capabilities – buying/selling and crafting/disassembling, which leads to a nice (and sensible) separation of interfaces for our factories – we'll let the merchant products handle buying and selling, and the blacksmith products can take care of the crafting and disassembling.

In the **Scripts** folder, create a new C# script named RelatedFactory and update its code to match the following code block, which declares the two abstract products that our factory can produce for each crafting system configuration.

It'll be up to our concrete product classes to specify how each of these interfaces is implemented in the next subsection:

```
void Craft();
    void Disassemble();
}


// 3
public interface IMerchant
{
    // 4
    void Buy();
    void Sell();
}
```

Let's break down the code:

1. It declares a public interface for all forge products to implement.
2. It adds two interface methods for crafting and disassembling items.
3. It declares a public interface for all merchant products to implement.
4. It adds two interface methods for buying and selling items.

With the abstract products defined, we can go ahead and create concrete products for each crafting configuration we want.

## Adding concrete products

Update RelatedFactory.cs to match the following code, which declares a concrete blacksmith forge and a concrete fusion forge with different implementations of the abstract product interfaces. Notice that each concrete IForge class handles its own Craft and Disassemble logic, while the factory down the line will only care about the IForge interface:

We'll stick to just one of each in this chapter, but there's nothing to stop you from creating multiple concrete products (as a matter of fact, this is where the pattern really shines).

```
...

// 1
```

```
public class BlacksmithForge : IForge
{
    // 2
    public void Craft()
    {
        Debug.Log("Your item was created from raw materials!");
    }

    public void Disassemble()
    {
        Debug.Log("Item was broken down to its raw materials.");
    }
}

// 3
public class FusionForge : IForge
{
    // 4
    public void Craft()
    {
        Debug.Log("Your items were fused together!");
    }

    public void Disassemble()
    {
        Debug.Log("Fused item was returned to rare materials.");
    }
}
```

Let's break down the code:

1.  It declares a new concrete class for a blacksmith forge and implements the IForge interface.
2.  It defines the IForge interface methods for crafting and disassembling regular items with logs.
3.  It declares a new concrete class for a fusion forge and implements the IForge interface.
4.  It defines the IForge interface methods for crafting and disassembling fusion items with logs.

Before we can work with the abstract and concrete factories, we need concrete merchant classes for each crafting system. Update `RelatedFactory.cs` with the following code, which adds concrete classes for blacksmith and fusion merchants with their respective implementations of the buying and selling interface methods:

```
...

// 1
public class BlacksmithMerchant : IMerchant
{
    // 2
    public void Buy()
    {
        Debug.Log("Thanks for paying in gold!");
    }

    public void Sell()
    {
        Debug.Log("Would you accept gold for that item?");
    }
}

// 3
public class FusionMerchant : IMerchant
{
    public void Buy()
    {
        Debug.Log("We only accept soul chips for fusions.");
    }

    public void Sell()
    {
        Debug.Log("We can only pay you in soul chips.");
    }
}
```

Let's break down the code:

1.  It declares a new concrete class for a blacksmith merchant using the IMerchant interface.
2.  It defines the IMerchant interface methods for buying and selling regular items with custom logs.
3.  It declares a new concrete class for a fusion merchant using the IMerchant interface.
4.  It defines the IMerchant interface methods for buying and selling fusion items with custom logs.

Now that we have the products laid out, let's move on to creating the abstract and Concrete Factory classes for crafting system configurations.

## Creating abstract and Concrete Factory classes

Each crafting system needs a forge and merchant product class, but it doesn't need to know which specific concrete product to instantiate. By adding an Abstract Factory interface, our client code can communicate with any factory and any products in that factory using only interfaces (which is the main goal here, let's be honest). This black boxing coupled with concrete class deferment is the critical benefit of the Abstract Factory pattern.

Update RelatedFactory.cs with the following new code snippet, which declares the underlying factory blueprint containing two methods: one for returning a forge configuration and one for returning a merchant configuration:

```
...

// 1
public interface IAbstractFactory
{
    // 2
    IForge CreateForgeSystem();
    IMerchant CreateMerchantSystem();
}
```

Let's break down the code:

1.  It declares a new public interface for all concrete factories to implement.
2.  It adds interface methods for returning an instance of each abstract product.

Now, any Concrete Factory classes we create that implement the IAbstractFactory interface have a common set of underlying methods that can have different implementations, making them fully configurable within the boundaries we've set up. All we need to do now is create a Concrete Factory for each kind of crafting system!

Update RelatedAbstract.cs to match the following code, which declares a Concrete Factory for the blacksmith and fusion crafting systems, and then returns the concrete products for each configuration:

```csharp
...

// 1
public class BlacksmithFactory : IAbstractFactory
{
    // 2
    public IForge CreateForgeSystem()
    {
        return new BlacksmithForge();
    }

    // 3
    public IMerchant CreateMerchantSystem()
    {
        return new BlacksmithMerchant();
    }
}

// 4
public class FusionFactory : IAbstractFactory
{
    // 5
    public IForge CreateForgeSystem()
    {
        return new FusionForge();
    }

    // 6
    public IMerchant CreateMerchantSystem()
```

```
    {
        return new FusionMerchant();
    }
}
```

Let's break down the code:

1. It declares a new Concrete Factory for crafting regular items named `BlacksmithFactory`.
2. It implements the `CreateForgeSystem` Factory Method and returns a new `BlacksmithForge` instance.
3. It implements the `CreateMerchantSystem` Factory Method and returns a `BlacksmithMerchant` instance.
4. It declares a new Concrete Factory for the fusion crafting system named `FusionFactory`.
5. It implements the `CreateForgeSystem` Factory Method and returns a new `FusionForge` instance.
6. It implements the `CreateMerchantSystem` Factory Method and returns a `FusionMerchant` instance.

With two concrete crafting systems implementing the same Abstract Factory interface, we can write a client class to perform the same actions no matter which system we're using. A common scenario to visualize is a menu where the player can select between blacksmithing and fusion in a crafting menu but can still buy, sell, craft, and disassemble items in either system.

## Writing a client class using only interfaces

In the **Scripts** folder, create a new C# script named `Client` and update its code to match the following code. The client's only job is to interact with the abstract product and factory interfaces, so we'll inject a factory into the class constructor and do all our work from there. In this example, we'll simply create a forge and merchant from whatever factory is passed in and buy and craft an item, but this is a great place to tie everything into the UI of your project:

```
using System.Collections;
using System.Collections.Generic;
using UnityEngine;

public class Client
{
    // 1
    private IAbstractFactory factory;
```

```
// 2
public Client(IAbstractFactory factory)
{
    this.factory = factory;
}


// 3
public void ExecuteFactoryProcesses()
{
    // 4
    var forge = factory.CreateForgeSystem();
    var merchant = factory.CreateMerchantSystem();


    // 5
    forge.Craft();
    merchant.Buy();

}

}
```

Let's break down the code:

1. It declares a private variable to store the factory instance being passed into the constructor.

2. It adds a class constructor with a factory parameter and sets the instance field.

3. It creates a method to use the factory and product interfaces.

4. It requests a new instance of the factory's forge and merchant classes.

5. It calls the Craft and Buy methods on the forge and merchant products.

 Depending on your needs, you could also instantiate and store the individual factory products or a list of factory products in the client class constructor instead of the factory instance – totally up to you!

To test, let's update CraftingSystem.cs to match the following code, which creates a new factory instance, passes the factory instance into the client, and calls ExecuteFactoryProcesses on the client to simulate crafting and buying items:

```
using System.Collections;
using System.Collections.Generic;
```

```
using UnityEngine;

public class CraftingSystem : MonoBehaviour
{
    void Start()
    {
        // 1
        var factory = new BlacksmithFactory();

        // 2
        var client = new Client(factory);

        // 3
        client.ExecuteFactoryProcesses();
    }
}
```

Let's break down the new system code:

1.  It declares a new instance of the BlacksmithFactory concrete class.

2.  It creates a new client instance and passes the factory into the constructor.

3.  It calls the client method to execute the factory processes.

Play the scene in the Unity Editor and you'll see the crafting and buying logs printed out for the blacksmith factory, as shown in the following screenshot:

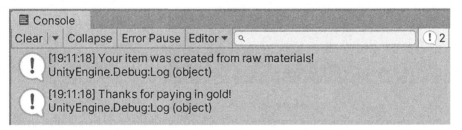

*Figure 5.5: Console output from the concrete blacksmith factory instance*

Notice that the client doesn't specify which factory we're using to create and manipulate our objects, only that it implements the IAbstractFactory interface. In a larger system, this additional flexibility means we can switch out factories anytime we want without breaking the factory system.

For example, we can update CraftingSystem.cs to match the following code by changing the factory to a FusionFactory instance. The client works exactly the same, but the factory products are different:

```
using System.Collections;
using System.Collections.Generic;
using UnityEngine;

public class CraftingSystem : MonoBehaviour
{
    void Start()
    {
        // 1
        var factory = new FusionFactory();
         var client = new Client(factory);

        client.ExecuteFactoryProcesses();
    }
}
```

Run the scene again and you'll see that the client code executes the same processes, but this time we'll get the logs from the fusion factory, as shown in the following figure:

*Figure 5.6: Console output from the concrete fusion factory instance*

That wraps up the traditional implementation of the Abstract Factory pattern, but there's another variation that's extremely important – creating families of related *and* dependent products. We'll spend the next section building out a different crafting scenario using this variation, one where we can check for material and item combinations to see whether they can be upgraded!

# Creating related and dependent products

Imagine your action platformer needs an upgrade system, one where your players can use raw materials to upgrade existing items according to preset recipes. To create, manage, and expand this system, your team needs a way to create different crafting configurations of products while hiding their implementation. Further, you need to be able to interact with each product and factory using the same interfaces, so the client code doesn't break when factories or items are switched out or updated.

## Writing dependent product abstract classes

In the **Scripts** folder, create a new C# script named DependentFactory and update its code to match the following code, which declares our two abstract products, one for raw materials and one for upgradeable items. Since we need dependent products for this example, each concrete UpgradeMaterial will be used to upgrade items, and each Item will accept an UpgradeMaterial to see whether it's a viable choice for the upgrade. This way, you can set rules for upgrades based on which materials you want to pair with which items without having to manage that dependency in the client code. The UpgradeMaterial abstract class doesn't need any methods because we're using a simplified example, but you could absolutely have a fully formed class here:

 We're using abstract classes here instead of interfaces to a different OOP approach to the pattern. You can see a full Unity implementation example using interfaces in the previous chapter on the Factory Method pattern. The choice between interfaces and abstract classes comes down to object composition versus inheritance. Use whichever option fits your project structure or personal style best.

```
using System.Collections;
using System.Collections.Generic;
using UnityEngine;

// 1
public abstract class UpgradeMaterial { }

// 2
public abstract class Item
{
    public abstract void Upgrade(UpgradeMaterial material);
}
```

Let's break down the code:

1.  It declares a public abstract class named `UpgradeMaterial` with no methods.

2.  It declares a public abstract class named `Item` and adds an `Upgrade` method with an `UpgradeMaterial` parameter.

Defining rules for your dependent products at the abstract or interface level is a great way to safeguard against unwanted interactions (especially in scenarios where one product's instantiation or capabilities need to execute before another, hint hint).

## Creating concrete products

Now that we have new abstract products, we need to define the different concrete product classes we want our factories to work with. Update `DependentFactory.cs` to match the following code, which declares the `Iron` and `Dragonscale` concrete classes, which both inherit the `UpgradeMaterial` abstract class:

```
using System.Collections;
using System.Collections.Generic;
using UnityEngine;

...


// 1
public class Iron : Material { }
public class Dragonscale : Material { }
```

For our concrete items, we're going to create a `Sword` and `Lance` that both inherit the `Item` abstract class and implement their own upgrade logic. Update `DependentFactory.cs` to match the following code, which declares our two new concrete items and overrides the `Upgrade` method. Each product is responsible for determining which materials it can use to upgrade itself:

```
...


// 1
public class Sword : Item
{
    public override void Upgrade(UpgradeMaterial material)
    {
        // 2
```

```
            if (material.GetType().Name == "Iron")
            {
                Debug.Log("Sword upgraded => Iron Sword!");
            }
            else
            {
                Debug.Log("You don't have the right upgrade materials.");
            }
        }
    }


// 3
public class Lance : Item
{
    public override void Upgrade(UpgradeMaterial material)
    {
        // 4
        if (material.GetType().Name == "Dragonscale")
        {
            Debug.Log("Lance upgraded => Dragonite Lance!");
        }
        else
        {
            Debug.Log("You don't have the right upgrade materials.");
        }
    }
}
```

Let's break down the code:

1.  It declares a new concrete Item class named Sword and implements the Upgrade method.
2.  It performs a check to see whether the correct UpgradeMaterial is available for the sword's upgrade.
3.  It declares a new concrete item class named Lance and implements the Upgrade method.
4.  It performs a check to see whether the correct UpgradeMaterial is available for the lance's upgrade.

Now that we have concrete items to work with, we can start working with abstract and concrete factories.

## Adding abstract and Concrete Factory classes

In our example, the upgrade functions only need to return a material and an item. Update DependentFactory.cs to match the following code, which adds a Factory Method for creating an UpgradeMaterial object and an Item object:

```
...


// 1
public abstract class AbstractRecipeFactory
{
    // 2
    public abstract Item GetItem();
    public abstract UpgradeMaterial GetMaterial();
}
```

Let's break down the code:

1.  It declares a new abstract class for all concrete factories to inherit.

2.  It adds Abstract Factory methods for returning an instance of each product type.

For simplicity, we're only going to add two concrete upgrade factories by updating DependentFactory.cs to match the following code. This isn't the most scalable or maintainable framework, but it's a good in-between solution when you don't need to constantly add concrete factories to your project (we'll talk about efficient scaling techniques in the *Parameterized factories* section, hold tight):

```
...


// 1
public class IronSwordUpgrade : AbstractRecipeFactory
{
    // 2
    public override UpgradeMaterial GetMaterial()
    {
        return new Iron();
    }
```

```
    public override Item GetItem()
    {
        return new Sword();
    }
}


// 3
public class DragoniteLanceUpgrade : AbstractRecipeFactory
{
    // 4
    public override UpgradeMaterial GetMaterial()
    {
        return new Dragonscale();
    }

    public override Item GetItem()
    {
        return new Lance();
    }
}
```

Let's break down the new code:

1.  It declares a new concrete sword recipe factory that inherits AbstractRecipeFactory.
2.  It implements the base class methods and returns a material and item accordingly.
3.  It declares a new concrete lance recipe factory that inherits AbstractRecipeFactory.
4.  It implements the base class methods and returns a material and item accordingly.

Now that we have different concrete factories to work with, we can update the client to use the new factory and product interfaces in the next section.

## Updating the client

Update the Client.cs script to match the following code, which changes the type of factory we store and initialize in the class constructor.

The new code also changes the factory methods being used, so we can create as many materials and items from a given factory as we need and then call the Upgrade method:

```
using System.Collections;
using System.Collections.Generic;
using UnityEngine;

public class Client
{
    // 1
    private AbstractRecipeFactory factory;

    public Client(AbstractRecipeFactory factory)
    {
        this.factory = factory;
    }

    public void ExecuteFactoryProcesses()
    {
        // 2
        var item = factory.GetItem();
        var material = factory.GetMaterial();

        // 3
        item.Upgrade(material);
    }
}
```

Let's break down the new client code:

1.  It changes the variable and constructor parameter factory type to AbstractRecipeFactory.

2.  It uses the factory method to create and store an item and material.

3.  It calls the Upgrade method on the item and passes in the material.

To test, let's update CraftingSystem.cs to match the following code, which changes the Concrete Factory instance passed to the client:

```
using System.Collections;
using System.Collections.Generic;
```

```
using UnityEngine;

public class CraftingSystem : MonoBehaviour
{
    void Start()
    {
        // 1
        var factory = new IronSwordUpgrade();
        var client = new Client(factory);

        client.ExecuteFactoryProcesses();
    }
}
```

Hit **Play** in the Unity Editor once again and you'll see the Sword get upgraded to an Iron Sword, as shown in the following screenshot:

*Figure 5.7: Console output from dependent sword recipe products interacting with each other*

Like the previous example, you can change the upgrade factory the client is using by updating CraftingSystem.cs to match the following code:

```
using System.Collections;
using System.Collections.Generic;
using UnityEngine;

public class CraftingSystem : MonoBehaviour
{
    void Start()
    {
        // 1
        var factory = new DragoniteLanceUpgrade();
        var client = new Client(factory);
```

```
            client.ExecuteFactoryProcesses();
    }
}
```

When you hit **Play** again, you'll see that the item gets upgraded successfully, as shown here:

*Figure 5.8: Console output from dependent lance recipe products interacting with each other*

Now, the fun really starts when you play around with the products the factories are creating. For instance, try and mix and match the materials and items so that they don't have the right combinations for an upgrade. You'll quickly find out that configuring your dependent factory products with predetermined limitations is a great way to enforce how interactions take place. This is also a great place to add your own safety checks for different combinations and dependencies!

Before we end the chapter, we still need to touch on two important variations to the Abstract Factory pattern – parameterized factories and factories that produce other factories!

# Optional factory variations

Like the Factory Method pattern, abstract factories have useful variations that you'll see pop up in the programming wilds. The two we'll talk about in the following subsections are the parameterized abstract and Concrete Factory, and the factory of factories (so meta).

## Parameterized factories

Firstly, the parameterized Abstract Factory is almost identical to the parameterized Factory Method variation we built in the last chapter. The idea is to have the methods in any Abstract Factory class take a parameter value specifying which object to create and return. For example, we could update the recipe factory to take a string name and use a switch statement inside each method to return the correct object, as shown in the following code:

 This isn't the most scalable approach but adding reflection or generics can greatly increase how flexible the parameterized factory can be. Again, we covered this extensively in *Chapter 4, Creating Items with the Factory Method Pattern*, so head back there for a refresher.

```
public abstract class AbstractRecipeFactory
{
    public abstract Item GetItem(string name);
    public abstract Material GetMaterial(string name);
}

public class WeaponUpgradeFactory : AbstractRecipeFactory
{
    public override Item GetItem(string name)
    {
        switch(name)
        {
            case "Sword":
                return new Sword();
            case "Lance":
                return new Lance();
            default:
                return new Sword();
        }
    }

    public override UpgradeMaterial GetMaterial(string name)
    {
        switch (name)
        {
            case "Iron":
                return new Iron();
            case "Dragonscale":
                return new Dragonscale();
            default:
                return new Iron();
        }
    }
}
```

## Creating a factory of factories

Secondly, you might run into a use case where you're managing a not-so-small list of factories and need a centralized point of access. In that scenario, a factory of factories comes in handy, especially as a static class method. For example, we could update our original blacksmith and fusion crafting system with an added abstraction layer like the following code. The MetaFactory would be the new access point when creating factory instances in a client or Unity editor script, and we'd simply pass in the string or enum value of the factory we wanted. This way, there's no need for your client code to know what kind of concrete products they are pumping out *or* the concrete factories that are doing the construction:

```
public class MetaFactory
{
    public static IAbstractFactory GetFactory(string name)
    {
        switch(name)
        {
            case "Blacksmith":
                return new BlacksmithFactory();
            case "Fusion":
                return new FusionFactory();
            default:
                return new BlacksmithFactory();
        }
    }
}
```

**Using Prototypes and Singletons in your factories**

If you've been thinking that the factory would be much easier if we used the Prototype pattern, you'd be right! The idea is to initialize a Concrete Factory instance with prototypical objects for each product the factory can produce and create them from there. We implemented something similar in *Chapter 3* with the Prototype Factory class.

Another pattern that plays well with abstract factories is the Singleton. Since a family of products typically only needs one instance of its Concrete Factory, a Singleton might make sense – especially in the case of a factory of factories.

**A word on reflection, generics, and Unity APIs**

Everything we've coded in the last two chapters can be expanded and layered into deeply complex abstracted systems using reflection and generics. The examples in this chapter can also be adapted to use Unity `GameObjects`, prefabs, components, `ScriptableObjects`, and `MonoBehaviours`. We've implemented each of these adaptions in previous chapters and I encourage you to reference them when creating your own custom implementations.

Again, the same advice and warnings go for this switch statement, which can quickly become unmaintainable – default objects and reflection are your best friends here yet again!

Like all pattern variations we discuss in this chapter (and other chapters), these are just options and aren't always necessary. Don't add them just to add them (unnecessary complexity is the ultimate bane of design pattern implementations), but keep them in mind for more niche scenarios you may run into.

# Summary

That wraps up our twin chapters on the Factory Method and Abstract Factory patterns! These two patterns, although related, are not the same and shouldn't be used interchangeably or smooshed together into a Frankenstein factory. Always pick the right tool for the job!

Remember, the Abstract Factory pattern lets us abstract the creation process of families of related products. These object families should always be related, but they can be dependent on or interact with each other, and we can always extend our factories with parameters and factories of factories if necessary. Picking which solution to use depends on scale, product hierarchies, and the relationships you may or may not need between your objects and object families.

In the next chapter, we'll explore how the Builder pattern helps separate the creation of complex objects from their representations and gives us the power of customized assembly lines!

# Further reading

- Interfaces are a great way to create groups of related functionalities (with or without default implementations) that can be adopted by any class or struct. These are especially handy when you want to have a class inherit from multiple feature groups, which is called object composition. For more information, check out the documentation at `https:// learn.microsoft.com/en-us/dotnet/csharp/fundamentals/types/interfaces`.

- Abstract classes can't be created on their own, but they are excellent solutions when you want a consistent base class blueprint that other classes can inherit from. Many of our solutions in this book rely heavily on abstract classes to provide an abstraction layer between class blueprints and their concrete implementations. You can find more information at `https://learn.microsoft.com/en-us/dotnet/csharp/language-reference/ keywords/abstract`.

- LINQ provides a set of features you can use for querying, sorting, and filtering your data however you want with minimal code. As you start to deal with more complex data requirements, you'll definitely want to check out the documentation at `https://docs.microsoft. com/dotnet/csharp/programming-guide/concepts/linq`.

- Assemblies are collections of types and resources built to work together and form a logical unit of functionality (the literal building blocks of C# applications). These can be executable (`.exe`) or dynamic link library (`.dll`) files, and provide the common language runtime with the information it needs to be aware of type implementations. Since assemblies are an advanced topic, I'd encourage you to check out the documentation at `https://docs. microsoft.com/dotnet/standard/assembly`.

- Reflection lets you get an inside glimpse at the classes, structs, and other types that are present in your project's assembly and can be used to create instances of any of those types at runtime. Like multithreading, going too deep into this topic is a little outside the scope of this book, but if you'd like to learn more, head over to https://docs.microsoft.com/dotnet/framework/reflection-and-codedom/reflection.

## Join our community on Discord

Join our community's Discord space for discussions with the author and other readers:

https://packt.link/gamedevelopment_packt

# 6

# Assembling Support Characters with the Builder Pattern

In the last chapter, we finished talking about encapsulating object creation logic with the Abstract Factory pattern. In this chapter, we'll work on assembling complex objects while separating the actual construction process from its representation. Not only is this a fun way to programmatically build, well, anything, but it also gives you the freedom to build different objects using the same construction process, plus finer control over how each component of the larger object is put together.

Like the other Creational patterns we've covered, the Builder pattern is sometimes overlooked in Unity in favor of more editor-focused processes to create complex objects. While Prefabs are great for static objects, the Builder pattern really shines when you need an encapsulated construction process AND abstractions to handle individual objects and their component pieces (the best of both worlds).

Think LEGO – you could have several different kinds of base blocks, but the color, position, and size might all need to be interchangeable. Likewise, you may want to assemble LEGO buildings using the same process (i.e., make a floor, build all the walls, and then add a roof), but each building needs to follow a different blueprint. The Builder pattern lets you direct the house-building procedure regardless of the blueprint you're using.

To those ends, we'll use this chapter to focus on the following topics and see if we can't get the Builder pattern and Unity to play nicely together in the same sandbox (who knows?

They might even complement each other):

- The pros and cons of the Builder design pattern
- Creating a base product and the builder interface
- Adding concrete builder classes
- Using a director class
- Integrating Unity `GameObjects`
- Exploring the fluent Builder pattern variation

By the end of the chapter, you'll have a strong foundation to construct complex objects and customize them all in the same workflow, and we'll even throw in some pattern variations for those niche scenarios we all run into from time to time.

# Technical requirements

Before you start:

1. Download or clone the GitHub repository at `https://github.com/PacktPublishing/C-Design-Patterns-with-Unity-First-Edition`.
2. Open the **Ch_06_Starter** project folder in Unity Hub.
3. In **Assets | Scenes**, double-click on **SampleScene**.

The project for this chapter mimics a generic assembly system – in this case, for support characters that can be deployed with you on playable missions. The main scene has a ground platform (ambiance is important) and a UI panel on the right-hand side where you can click **Create** to build whatever support character you want. When a support character is built, each of its component parts will be printed out in the UI panel as a blueprint.

As for the scripts:

- `Client.cs` has a `Text` field to print out the blueprint components.
- `ModelData.cs` is a utility script for creating `ScriptableObject` components for our support allies.
- The **Resources** folder has six pre-made `ScriptableObject` components (three for each ally type) for you to mix and match.

We'll also be using some Unity and C# language features to take our code the extra mile. Don't worry if you're not familiar with them; I've included links for the basics, and I'll explain how they apply to our use cases as we go along:

- Interfaces (`https://learn.microsoft.com/en-us/dotnet/csharp/fundamentals/types/interfaces`)

- ScriptableObjects (`https://docs.unity3d.com/Manual/class-ScriptableObject.html`)

- Resources (`https://docs.unity3d.com/ScriptReference/Resources.html`)

Our job is to use the Builder pattern to assemble these components into support allies in our scene, complete with their individual blueprints, shown in the UI for easy reference!

# Breaking down the Builder pattern

As part of the Creational family of design patterns, the Builder pattern focuses on creating different representations of a complex object while delegating the customized building instructions to concrete builder classes. You'll find this pattern is most useful in scenarios where:

- You need to separate the construction of complex objects from their representations.

- You want to build different objects using the same construction process.

- Finer control of each step of the construction process is necessary.

- You want to delegate creating the object to an encapsulated builder instead of directly creating them in the client.

The Builder pattern example that's familiar to most people is the assembly line – in this case, a car factory. When your favorite (or rival) car manufacturer sets up a factory, they can specify common production steps that all their different makes and models have to go through. This could include building the car frame, adding wheels (if you want to go anywhere), adding doors (if you want to stay inside), and installing an engine, as shown in the following figure:

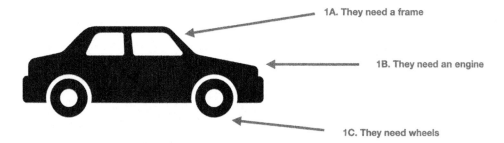

**1. All cars have a common assembly process**

**1A. They need a frame**

**1B. They need an engine**

**1C. They need wheels**

*Figure 6.1: Simplified example of the component parts in every car*

However, each of these production steps installs different parts depending on the model of the car, so a truck would have a large frame and truck bed, two doors, bigger wheels, and a higher output engine, while a sports car would have a lighter or smaller frame, four doors instead of two, and a higher performance engine. At a high level, your car manufacturer doesn't really need to know what component parts get installed in which car model, just the overall construction process. The important part is that a fully assembled car comes off the line at the end of all that work that can drive someone safely from point A to point B (and, maybe, have a nice red paint job), as shown in the following figure:

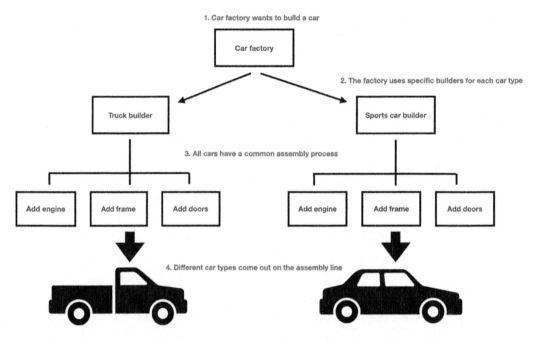

*Figure 6.2: Example of the car manufacturing process to create different car types*

In a gaming scenario, your character might have a customizable character system where they can specify the hair, eyes, facial hair, and body type of their playable avatar, and the game saves them each time as a complex object. It doesn't matter what character class, species, or type your player is building, only the way the character is put together. Orcs, humans, wizards, and elves all presumably need a head, eyes, and a body, all with optional facial hair on request.

Writing an ad hoc process to assemble and customize characters would be chaotic at best, but it can be solved by defining a common assembly process that all characters adhere to. Really, any situation where a larger complex object is composed of smaller component parts is a good candidate for the Builder pattern.

# Diagramming the pattern

*Figure 6.3* shows the UML structure of the basic Builder design pattern and the interaction of its four components:

- The **Director** initiates and manages all object creation using the builder interface methods, which removes any construction logic from the client.
- The Builder interface defines the common methods for building each part of the product.
- **Concrete Builders** (or Builders) are the corresponding builder classes for each different product representation.
- The Product is the base object created, which has a reference to all its component parts and can add new components.

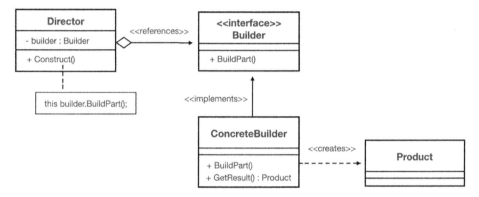

*Figure 6.3: UML diagram of the Builder pattern components*

All the client needs to do is ask the director to build the object or objects without any knowledge of how the tasks are executed. Like the factory patterns, the client is only concerned with the builder interface that each of the concrete builders implements. We'll talk about pattern variations, customization, and object optimization at the end of the chapter, but for now, we've got enough theory to lay out the basic Builder structure.

# Pros and cons

Like all design patterns, there are pros and cons, but let's start off with the positives of the Builder pattern:

- **Construction is hidden from the client**. The internal build process for each object, and the type of object being built, are both separated from the client code. This not only lets you vary how each object is assembled but also lets you swap out the object being put together without any client-side changes.

- **A step-by-step construction process**, which allows fine-grain control over how each part or component is built and added to the completed object. This can be exceptionally helpful when you need an object to be built in a specific sequence with individual components that may have custom or unique dependencies.

However, be careful of the following pitfalls

- **New objects increase code complexity**. Anytime you want to add a new object to the pattern, you'll need to manually program how that object is put together. This isn't a huge drawback, but it's definitely something to consider. If your objects aren't massively configurable, the Builder pattern might be more work than it's worth. On the other hand, if you're building a modifiable object system (like a character design system), the Builder pattern is definitely worth the extra code.

Now that we've covered the structure, benefits, and limitations of the Builder pattern, we can dive into the starter project and start building our support character assembly line!

# Creating a base ally and builder interface

Imagine you're making a tactical RPG where you can create a team from a variety of support vehicles and allies. You and your team need a system to create each different party member using the same base construction process. Further, you need to be able to build these objects from a central access point. As you go, you'll want to display each support member's blueprint and stats in the console, so your players know what components they have to work with! Before we can do any of that work, we'll need a product class and some kind of common interface that builds our allies in a specified order, which we'll do next.

## Scripting the product class

The first component of the Builder pattern is the product, which in our example is a base support ally. Since each support ally needs to have the same properties and methods, we can create a single class to handle all its functionality. The nice thing here is that the product class is just a container for the few processes that all support allies share. The concrete builders will take care of the custom construction logic.

In the **Scripts** folder, create a new C# script named SupportAlly and update its code to match the following code, which lays out the base structure for all allies, mostly concerned with what type of ally is being constructed and adding parts to a stored components list. We'll leave the actual component creation to our concrete builder classes:

```csharp
using System.Collections;
using System.Collections.Generic;
using UnityEngine;

public class SupportAlly
{
    // 1
    public string allyType;

    // 2
    public List<string> components = new List<string>();

    // 3
    public SupportAlly(string newAlly)
    {
        allyType = newAlly;
    }

    // 4
    public void AddComponent(string name)
    {
        components.Add(name);
        Debug.Log($"{name} component added!");
    }
}
```

Let's break down the code:

1.  Declares a `string` variable to hold the support `ally` type.
2.  Declares a list to store all component parts of the object during the construction process.
3.  Adds a class constructor that takes in and sets the `ally` type variable.
4.  Creates a method to add parts to the component list and prints the component name.

With the `ally` class keeping track of its component parts as they're added to the build, we need a way to print out a decent-looking log to display in our scene UI. Add the following code to the end of the `SupportAlly` class, which declares a method to create and return a list of all parts in the current blueprint:

```csharp
// This code goes below the AddComponent method from above
```

```
...

// 1
public string GetBlueprint()
{
    // 2
    if(components.Count == 0)
    {
        return "No components listed, use the Director class!";
    }

    // 3
    string blueprintLog = $"  Support type: {allyType}\n\n";

    // 4
    foreach(string component in components)
    {
        blueprintLog += $"     - {component} --- installed\n";
    }

    // 5
    return blueprintLog;
}

// Remainder of the SupportAlly class
```

Let's break down the code:

1. Declares a method to return a log of all components in the object.

2. Checks if the components list is empty, and if it is, we return with a warning message.

3. Adds a string to store the first line of the blueprint log with the object's type printed out.

4. Loops through each component in the components list and appends a string to the log.

5. Returns the completed blueprint log as a string.

Now that our ally class is ready to go, we can write an interface with build instructions for all concrete builders to implement, which we'll do in the next section.

# Declaring a common builder interface

Each support ally will need a few common building blocks, regardless of what actual ally we're building. In our example, all ally types are going to be a variation of a vehicle or machine type, like a tank or drone. While each of these objects is different, they all need a frame, motor, and, presumably, a weapon system of some kind. This kind of scenario should automatically signal a good use case for the Builder pattern – a common construction with different representations!

In the **Scripts** folder, create a new C# script named `Builder` and update its code to match the following snippet, where we declare the method for the three construction steps and a convenience method to return a fully assembled support ally:

```
using System.Collections;
using System.Collections.Generic;
using UnityEngine;

// 1
public interface IBuilder
{
    // 2
    void BuildFrame();
    void BuildMotor();
    void BuildWeapon();

    // 3
    SupportAlly GetAlly();
}
```

Let's break down the builder interface:

1.  Declares a new `public interface` named IBuilder.
2.  Adds methods for each construction step that concrete builder classes need to implement.
3.  Adds a method to return a product at any time in the construction process.

Any concrete builder classes need to implement the IBuilder interface to give our construction process some common processes. Again, the parts and assembly of the frame, motor, and weapon system of each ally are up to the concrete classes, not the base product. This frees up our code from keeping track of each specific ally type being created, instead focusing on the base construction process outlined in the IBuilder interface.

In the next section, we'll put together two concrete builder classes to assemble tanks and drones, each with its own separate component parts.

## Adding concrete builders

Our next task is to create the concrete assembly instructions for each of the support ally objects we'll be building (again, tanks and drones are presumably going to be doing all the real work in this game). Both objects have the same component categories, such as a frame, a motor, and a weapon system, but each individual component is different. We don't want heavy tank treads on a fiberglass drone hull, right?

Add the following code to the bottom of the Builder.cs script but outside the IBuilder interface declaration. Here, we specify the component parts we want to be assembled into a tank and return the SupportAlly object whenever GetAlly() is queried:

 You can create separate scripts for the concrete classes and the IBuilder interface if you like; I'm including them together for easier reference.

```
...

// 1
public class TankBuilder : IBuilder
{
    private SupportAlly _ally;

    // 2
    public TankBuilder()
    {
        _ally = new SupportAlly("Tank");
    }

    // 3
    public void BuildFrame()
    {
        _ally.AddComponent("Steel Frame");
    }
```

```
    // 4
    public void BuildMotor()
    {
        _ally.AddComponent("Heavy Treads");
    }


    // 5
    public void BuildWeapon()
    {
        _ally.AddComponent("Mortar");
    }


    // 6
    public SupportAlly GetAlly()
    {
        return _ally;
    }
}
```

Let's break down the code:

1.  Declares a new TankBuilder class that implements IBuilder and stores a private SupportAlly field.
2.  Adds a class constructor and instantiates a new SupportAlly with a "Tank" ally type.
3.  Declares the BuildFrame interface method and adds a "Steel Frame" component to the ally.
4.  Declares the BuildMotor interface method and adds a "Heavy Treads" component to the ally.
5.  Declares the BuildWeapon interface method and adds a "Mortar" component to the ally.
6.  Declares the GetAlly interface method and returns the _ally object.

Our new concrete builder now has fine-grain control over how every tank component is composed and configured without having to know much about the base SupportAlly class. This might strike you as an incredible amount of infrastructure and hardcoding, especially if it's all upfront. Don't worry – separating object construction from representation pays maintenance dividends down the road when you need to update or modify object components. It can even help you build customization functionality, as we'll see in the *Integrating GameObjects* section.

While each method or assembly step is required by the interface, each concrete builder isn't required to return or do anything in those methods. For example, if we wanted to build an attack bicycle (I know, why?), there wouldn't be a motor, but there would definitely need to be a frame and weapon system.

To illustrate how easy it is to switch the assembled object, let's script a concrete builder to put together drones before we test. Add the following code to the end of the Builder.cs script as a new class outside the interface and TankBuilder implementations. This class has the same structure as TankBuilder but with different components added at each construction step, dictated by the IBuilder interface:

```
...

// 1
public class DroneBuilder : IBuilder
{
    private SupportAlly _ally;

    // 2
    public DroneBuilder()
    {
        _ally = new SupportAlly("Drone");
    }

    // 3
    public void BuildFrame()
    {
        _ally.AddComponent("Titanium Hull");
    }

    // 4
    public void BuildMotor()
    {
        _ally.AddComponent("Fiberglass Wings");
    }

    // 5
```

```
    public void BuildWeapon()
    {
        _ally.AddComponent("Missiles");
    }

    // 6
    public SupportAlly GetAlly()
    {
        return _ally;
    }
}
```

Let's break down the code:

1.  Declares a new `DroneBuilder` class that implements `IBuilder` and stores a private `SupportAlly` field.

2.  Adds a class constructor and instantiates a new `SupportAlly` with a "Drone" ally type.

3.  Declares the `BuildFrame` interface method and adds a "`Titanium Hull`" component to the ally.

4.  Declares the `BuildMotor` interface method and adds a "`Fiberglass Wings`" component to the ally.

5.  Declares the `BuildWeapon` interface method and adds a "`Missiles`" component to the ally.

6.  Declares the `GetAlly` interface method and returns the `_ally` object.

Now that we have our two concrete builders, we can write a small director class to supervise all object construction using the `IBuilder` interface methods, which we'll do in the next section.

## Using a director class

The director class in the Builder pattern has one job and one job only – to use the builder interface methods to assemble a complex product object. The director class shouldn't know about anything other than the builder interface – not the product, not the concrete builders, not the client, nothing. This way, our director never needs to know what concrete builders it's using to construct which objects, making the client code less prone to breaking when you swap concrete builders.

In the **Scripts** folder, create a new C# script named `Director` and update its code to match the following snippet.

Here, we're adding a method that takes in any class that implements the IBuilder interface, so in this example our concrete builders, and executes the interface methods in a preset sequence. The methods can be called in any order you want, which is especially useful if some components need to be built before others to support dependencies:

```csharp
using System.Collections;
using System.Collections.Generic;
using UnityEngine;

// 1
public class Director
{
    // 2
    public void ConstructWith(IBuilder builder)
    {
        // 3
        builder.BuildFrame();
        builder.BuildMotor();
        builder.BuildWeapon();
    }
}
```

Let's break down the directory code:

1. Declares a new public Director class.

2. Adds a construction method that accepts an IBuilder parameter.

3. Uses the IBuilder argument to sequentially call each interface method.

**Storing concrete builders in a director class**

The director class we've written is lean and mean, but you might come across a director variation in the wild that stores a concrete builder instance on initialization. This is fine if you need to use the same concrete builder in more than one construction method, but it's over-optimization if you don't. Take a look at the following code to get an idea of when this might be useful:

```
public class Director
{
    private IBuilder _builder;

    public Director(IBuilder newBuilder)
    {
        _builder = newBuilder;
    }

    public void LoadoutA()
    {
        _builder.BuildFrame();
        _builder.BuildMotor();
        _builder.BuildWeapon();
    }

    public void LoadoutB()
    {
        _builder.BuildFrame();
        _builder.BuildMotor();
    }
}
```

If you have multiple construction methods, you'll need to implement your own defensive logic to ensure parts don't get overridden. You'll also need a way to reset the concrete builder class after each construction process if you're going to be interchanging concrete builders.

We now have all the pieces in place to build an actual support ally object, so let's test out the code by updating the Client script to match the following code. The starter project already has the Build() method hooked up to the UI button in the scene; our job is to create a director, pass it a concrete builder, and request the finished ally object. The director uses whichever concrete builder we pass in to assemble the object, which means we can get a list of its component parts directly from the concrete builder:

```
using System.Collections;
using System.Collections.Generic;
using UnityEngine;
using UnityEngine.UI;
public class Client : MonoBehaviour
{
    public Text BlueprintLog;

    public void Build()
    {
        // 1
        IBuilder builder = new TankBuilder();

        // 2
        Director director = new Director();

        // 3
        director.ConstructWith(builder);

        // 4
```

```
        var ally = builder.GetAlly();

        // 5
        BlueprintLog.text = ally.GetBlueprint();
    }
}
```

Let's break down the code:

1.  Declares a new concrete builder instance of the TankBuilder class.

2.  Declares a new Director instance.

3.  Passes in the concrete builder instance to the ConstructWith method to assemble the ally.

4.  Requests the finished ally product from the concrete builder instance and stores it locally.

5.  Sets the UI Text field in the scene to the string result from the ally's GetBlueprint method.

Like switching out concrete factory classes in the previous chapter, we can use any concrete builder class we want, and the director will have no problem building a different object. Run the scene and click **Build**, which prints out a message when a new component is added by the concrete builder. The following screenshot shows the order in which the components are added, which is dictated by the order we laid out in the director class:

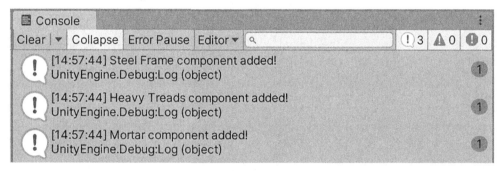

*Figure 6.4: Console output with each tank component name displayed when it's added*

The ally's blueprint log in the text UI also updates with the formatted string from the GetBlueprint method. The component order in the blueprints UI in *Figure 6.5* is the same as the console messages in *Figure 6.4*, showcasing the role of the director class as the architect of the complex objects we're building.

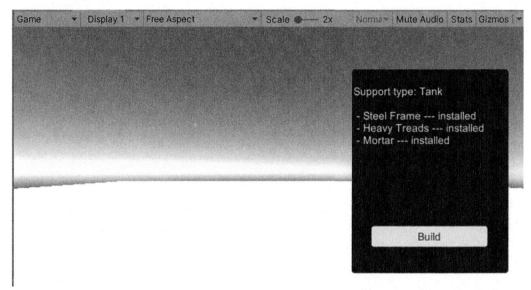

*Figure 6.5: Game view showing UI Text updated with the tank's component information*

Update the Client.cs script to match the following snippet, which uses a DroneBuilder instance instead of a TankBuilder instance:

```
public class Client : MonoBehaviour
{

    public Text BlueprintLog;
    public void Build()
    {
        // 1
        IBuilder builder = new DroneBuilder();
        Director director = new Director();

        _director.ConstructWith(_builder);
        var ally = _builder.GetAlly();

        BlueprintLog.text = ally.GetBlueprint();
```

```
    }
}
```

Run the scene again; when you press the **Build** button, the internal construction processes remain the same, but a drone ally is assembled. The following screenshot shows debug logs for each new component added:

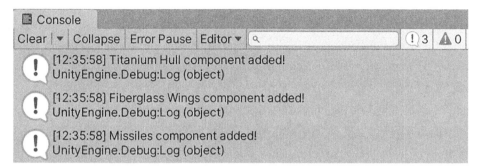

*Figure 6.6: Console output with each drone component name displayed when it's added*

Again, the ally's blueprint log in the text UI will update with the formatted string from the `GetBlueprint()` method, as shown here:

*Figure 6.7: Game view showing UI Text updated with the drone's component information*

With that, we have a totally different ally with the same assembly process – the construction separated from the representation! In the next section, we'll add Unity primitives for each component part and put the ally objects together piece by 3D piece.

# Integrating GameObjects

Suppose your tactical RPG needs to show a complex model for each support member, made up of primitive or **Prefab** GameObjects. Further, each ally's base class needs to keep track of its own component list and make each component part a child of a common parent when instantiated. Well, let's not just suppose; let's build that in!

Update the SupportAlly script to match the following code, which will now store a list of GameObjects, instantiate an empty parent object for each ally, and set new components as children of the parent whenever they're added by our concrete builders:

```
using System.Collections;
using System.Collections.Generic;
using UnityEngine;

public class SupportAlly
{
    public string allyType;
    // 1
    public List<GameObject> components = new List<GameObject>();


    // 2
    public GameObject parent;

    public SupportAlly(string newAlly)
    {
        allyType = newAlly;

        parent = new GameObject(newAlly);
    }

    // 3
    public void AddComponent(GameObject go)
    {
        // 4
        go.transform.SetParent(parent.transform);
        components.Add(go);
```

```
    // 5
    Debug.Log($"{go.name} component added!");
}

public string GetBlueprint()
{
    if (components.Count == 0)
    {
        return "No components listed, use the Director class!";
    }

    var blueprintLog = $"Support type: {allyType}\n\n";

    // 6
    foreach (GameObject component in components)
    {
        blueprintLog += $" - {component.name} --- installed\n";
    }

    return blueprintLog;
    }
}
```

Let's break down the code:

1.  Changes the component list to store GameObjects instead of strings.
2.  Adds a parent GameObject and instantiates an empty parent in the constructor.
3.  Updates the AddComponent method to take in a GameObject instead of a string.
4.  Parents the new component and adds it to the list of stored components.
5.  Prints the new parts GameObject name to the console when added to the components list.
6.  Updates the blueprint log to use the name of each component GameObject.

Before we test, the concrete builder classes need to be updated to actually create each component before it's added to the SupportAlly components list. Update the Builder.cs script to match the following snippet, which uses the Utilities class (included in the starter project) with a static helper method that takes in a component name and returns a configured GameObject from a ScriptableObject (also included in the **Resources** folder of the starter project):

The Utility class functionality isn't part of the Builder pattern itself, but it helps streamline component creation and separates the component data into easily modifiable data containers. You can use Prefabs, raw data, or any kind of GameObject creation pipeline you feel comfortable with!

```
public class TankBuilder : IBuilder
{
    private SupportAlly _ally;

    public TankBuilder()
    {
        _ally = new SupportAlly("Tank");
    }

    public void BuildFrame()
    {
        // 1
        GameObject go = Utilities.CreateFromSO("Steel Frame");
        _ally.AddComponent(go);
    }

    public void BuildMotor()
    {
        // 2
        GameObject go = Utilities.CreateFromSO("Heavy Treads");
        _ally.AddComponent(go);
    }

    public void BuildWeapon()
    {
        // 3
        GameObject go = Utilities.CreateFromSO("Mortar");
        _ally.AddComponent(go);
    }

    public SupportAlly GetAlly()
```

```
    {
        return _ally;
    }
}

public class DroneBuilder : IBuilder
{
    private SupportAlly _ally;

    public DroneBuilder()
    {
        _ally = new SupportAlly("Drone");
    }

    public void BuildFrame()
    {
        // 4

        GameObject go = Utilities.CreateFromSO("Titanium Hull");
        _ally.AddComponent(go);
    }

    public void BuildMotor()
    {
        // 5
        GameObject go = Utilities.CreateFromSO("Fiberglass Wings");
        _ally.AddComponent(go);
    }

    public void BuildWeapon()
    {
        // 6
        GameObject go = Utilities.CreateFromSO("Missiles");
        _ally.AddComponent(go);
    }

    public SupportAlly GetAlly()
```

```
    {
        return _ally;
    }
}
}
```

 You'll notice that we're repeating the same creation code in each builder interface method. While this approach isn't the cleanest, it allows each component to potentially have different creation logic, which is one of the pattern's strengths. For instance, you could add a component color as an input parameter to the BuildFrame method without having to change the other component implementations. Again, since levels of complexity are stacked on top of one another, you can customize each piece of the LEGO build however you want.

Nothing needs to change in the Client.cs script, which is great for maintenance and reusability. Run the scene again and you'll see a simple 3D drone next to the blueprint UI, fully assembled from its component parts, as shown here:

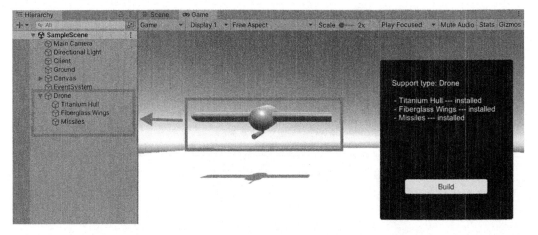

*Figure 6.8: Assembled drone object with component parts shown in the Hierarchy*

If you change the IBuilder instance in Client.cs back to a TankBuilder and run it, you'll see a primitive tank instead:

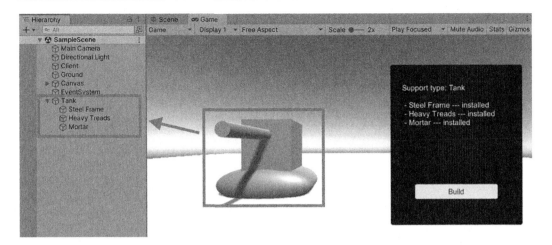

*Figure 6.9: Assembled tank object with component parts shown in the Hierarchy*

While the construction looks instantaneous when you click **Build**, behind the scenes each component is being created and added by the concrete builder and assembled in a sequential order by the Director class. Interchanging concrete builders in the client code doesn't break the construction process if everyone is following the IBuilder interface rules. The end result is a robust assembly line process in exchange for a small upfront architecting cost.

That wraps up the basic Builder pattern implementation, but there's still an important structure variation to cover called the fluent builder, which we'll do in the following section.

## Transitioning to a Fluent Builder structure

As you're digesting the code we've written so far, your spidey senses might have pointed out that the Builder pattern feels kind of static. That's not to say it's not useful as-is, but having each component hardcoded in its respective concrete builder doesn't allow for much customization, which makes the basic pattern only useful in rigid scenarios. You'll be able to do away with the director (which isn't a bad thing), allowing you to create objects in a more reusable way. You've likely run into fluent builders in your C# travels without knowing it; the StringBuilder class is usually the most recognizable example, which lets you chain method calls together in a desired sequence without line breaks, which is the structure we'll copy in the last section here.

Transforming the `IBuilder` interface and concrete builders into fluent builders only requires a slight syntax tweak to let the compiler know our interface methods can be chained together. In the `Builder.cs` script, update the `IBuilder` interface to match the following code snippet, which changes the return type of the assembly methods from void to `IBuilder`. This way, when we use dot notation on any concrete builder instance, the compiler knows we're allowed to tack on additional methods in the same line:

```
public interface IBuilder
{
    // 1
    IBuilder BuildFrame();
    IBuilder BuildMotor();
    IBuilder BuildWeapon();

    SupportAlly GetAlly();
}
```

Now, we need to update each concrete builder with the new interface changes. In the `Builder.cs` script, update the `TankBuilder` class to match the following code, which creates the fluent chain and returns the builder object from each interface method:

```
...

public class TankBuilder : IBuilder
{
    private SupportAlly _ally;

    public TankBuilder()
    {
        _ally = new SupportAlly("Tank");
    }

    // 1
    public IBuilder BuildFrame()
    {
        GameObject go = Utilities.CreateFromSO("Steel Frame");
        _ally.AddComponent(go);
        return this;
```

```
    }

    // 2
    public IBuilder BuildMotor()
    {
        GameObject go = Utilities.CreateFromSO("Heavy Treads");
        _ally.AddComponent(go);
        return this;
    }

    // 3
    public IBuilder BuildWeapon()
    {
        GameObject go = Utilities.CreateFromSO("Mortar");
        _ally.AddComponent(go);
        return this;
    }

    public SupportAlly GetAlly()
    {
        return _ally;
    }
}
```

Let's break down the updated code:

1.  Updates the BuildFrame method to return an IBuilder instance and return the current object.

2.  Updates the BuildMotor method to return an IBuilder instance and return the current object.

3.  Updates the BuildWeapon method to return an IBuilder instance and return the current object.

In the Builder.cs script, update the DroneBuilder class to match the following code block, which modifies the IBuilder interface methods to mirror what we just did with the TankBuilder script:

```
...

public class DroneBuilder : IBuilder
```

```
{
    private SupportAlly _ally;

    public DroneBuilder()
    {
        _ally = new SupportAlly("Drone");
    }

    // 1
    public IBuilder BuildFrame()
    {
        GameObject go = Utilities.CreateFromSO("Titanium Hull");
        _ally.AddComponent(go);
        return this;
    }


    // 2
    public IBuilder BuildMotor()
    {
        GameObject go = Utilities.CreateFromSO("Fiberglass Wings");
        _ally.AddComponent(go);
        return this;
    }
    // 3
    public IBuilder BuildWeapon()
    {
        GameObject go = Utilities.CreateFromSO("Missiles");
        _ally.AddComponent(go);
        return this;
    }

    public SupportAlly GetAlly()
    {
        return _ally;
    }
}
```

To test the code, update the `Client` script to match the following snippet, which replaces the director instance with a fluent builder chain. Notice that without the director class, you're not automatically locked into a set sequence for the build methods or forced to use all of them for every object assembly:

```
public class Client : MonoBehaviour
{
    public Text BlueprintLog;

    public void Build()
    {
        IBuilder builder = new DroneBuilder();

        // 1
        var fluentAlly = builder
                            // 2
                            .BuildFrame()
                            .BuildMotor()
                            .BuildWeapon()
                            .GetAlly();

        // 3
        BlueprintLog.text = fluentAlly.GetBlueprint();
    }
}
```

Let's break down the code:

1. Creates a new variable to hold the final ally product and starts the fluent build chain.
2. Calls the `IBuilder` interface methods in a sequence, ending with `GetAlly` to return the finished object.
3. Sets the UI Text using the `GetBlueprint` method on the configured `fluentAlly` object.

Run the scene again and build the Drone (or Tank), and you'll see that the system works the same, but the client is more straightforward. Sometimes, less architecture overhead is the right move, especially when you need to customize the properties of your object component without passing values down several method levels.

**Customizing object components**

One of the main complaints about the Builder pattern is how hardcoded and static it can be, which begs the question of why we're using it in the first place. This is especially true in Unity, as Prefabs are more UI-friendly to designers and programmers. However, that is only true if the Prefabs are themselves static and your scenarios only need to instantiate them. In those cases, the Prototype or Abstract Factory patterns would be a better fit.

However, when you need to create customizable objects made of different and interchangeable parts, the Builder pattern comes in as a strong contender. I would even argue the Builder pattern is more useful in Unity in these situations, as you can build component parts out of `ScriptableObjects` or Prefabs, configure them however you want, and then assemble them into complex objects in a scene.

As for scaling and flexibility, you can easily add customization parameters to your `IBuilder` interface methods on a component-by-component basis. There's also nothing that says you can't implement the Builder interface as an abstract class, meaning you could add optional overloaded builder methods with different parameter sets. In some sense, the Builder pattern is only as static as you make it – the structure itself doesn't require too much architecting upfront for what you get!

With our fluent builder variation up and running, that's going to bring our chapter to a close. While the Builder pattern isn't widely seen out in the wild of Unity projects, it's a solution you should absolutely keep in your back pocket for assembling and customizing complex objects – you might even convert a Unity team member or two!

## Summary

The Builder pattern isn't something you'll commonly run into with Unity because the Editor makes object construction so intuitive and visual. However, when your project runs into scenarios where objects need to be created or updated at runtime, or while the player actively modifies some aspect of the object in real time, programmatic construction is going to be your best friend.

Remember, the Builder pattern assembles complex objects while separating the construction process from the object's representation. Each of your products has a reference to all its component parts and can add new components whenever you need, while the Builder interface defines the common methods to build each part of the product. Concrete Builder (or Builders) are the corresponding builder classes for each different product representation, which leaves the Director class to initiate and manage all object creation using the builder interface method. The construction process for each component of a complex object can be customized separately while still being a part of the assembly process, and the fluent Builder variation removes the need for a Director and makes the client calling code much cleaner and more easily customizable.

How you go about laying the foundations for these LEGO-building mechanics is entirely up to you, but just because we're doing things in code doesn't mean you should forget about the Unity features we all know and love (they actually work together pretty seamlessly in these situations).

In the next chapter, we'll explore the Object Pool pattern, which gives us fine-grain control over the efficiency and memory management of objects we create.

## Further reading

- Interfaces are a great way to create groups of related functionalities (with or without default implementations) that can be adopted by any class or struct. These are especially handy when you want to have a class inherit from multiple groups of functionalities, which is called object composition. For more, check out the documentation at `https://learn.microsoft.com/en-us/dotnet/csharp/fundamentals/types/interfaces`.

- `ScriptableObjects` are the perfect way to create data containers in your Unity projects (and we'll use them in almost every chapter going forward), but I'd also recommend checking out the documentation at `https://docs.unity3d.com/Manual/class-ScriptableObject.html`.

- Resources is a Unity-specific class that lets you find and load objects and assets placed in a **Resources** folder no matter where that folder is located in your project. We won't use this all the time to fetch the objects we're looking for, but it is helpful in certain situations. You can find more information in the documentation at `https://docs.unity3d.com/ScriptReference/Resources.html`.

# Leave a review!

Enjoying this book? Help readers like you by leaving an Amazon review. Scan the QR code below to get a free eBook of your choice.

# 7

# Managing Performance and Memory with Object Pooling

In the last chapter, we created a pipeline for assembling tanks and drones using the Builder pattern and Unity's ScriptableObjects. In this chapter, we'll switch gears and focus on increasing performance and managing memory allocation when creating new objects with the Object Pool pattern. This approach is twofold; first, you get to control when batches of objects are instantiated, and second, you control how they are stored in a reusable pool that you can grab from whenever you want (without any additional CPU overhead).

By default, Unity already does a great job of allocating, managing, and cleaning up memory usage during object instantiation. So, why would we spend our time reinventing the wheel here? Well, even though Unity has our backs on this topic, you'll find that pooling and reusing objects instead of creating and destroying them over and over has a marked performance impact. So, just because object creation is already covered by Unity, that doesn't mean it's streamlined for all purposes (especially when you're dealing with large amounts of objects being put into the scene). You never want to be throwing out hundreds (or thousands) of enemies during an already computationally expensive boss battle and mess up your player experience!

We'll use this chapter to focus on the following topics:

- The pros and cons of the Object Pool design pattern
- Writing an ObjectPool class
- Object Pool customizations and thread-safety
- Leveraging Unity's generic ObjectPool class

While the basis of the Object Pool pattern is managing how items are taken out of and returned to the pool, we'll complete the chapter with useful pattern variations and how to use Unity's own generic `ObjectPool` class and `IObjectPool` interface.

# Technical requirements

Before you start:

1. Download or clone the GitHub repository at `https://github.com/PacktPublishing/C-Design-Patterns-with-Unity-First-Edition`

2. Open the **Ch_07_Starter** project folder in Unity Hub

3. In **Assets | Scenes**, double-click on **SampleScene**

The project for this chapter is a fun little shooter where you control a player strafing from left to right, trying to destroy all targets in sight. I've configured the player, targets, and projectile mechanics for you, so you can focus all your energy on controlling how projectiles are created and recycled for best performance.

As for the scripts:

- `ObjectPool.cs` is attached to an `Object Pool` object in the **Hierarchy**, which is where you'll do the majority of your work.

- `Projectile.cs` is attached to the **Bullet** Prefabs and handles collisions with targets and a boundary collider at the far end of the level, which is where you'll be implementing Object Pooling.

- `PlayerController.cs` is attached to the `Player` object in the **Hierarchy** and handles side-to-side movement and the shooting mechanic (you won't be updating this, so don't pay it any mind).

We'll also be using some Unity and C# language features to take our code the extra mile. Don't worry if you're not familiar with these; I've included links for the basics, and I'll explain how they apply to our use cases as we go:

- Queues (`https://learn.microsoft.com/en-us/dotnet/api/system.collections.generic.queue-1?view=net-8.0`)

- Multithreading (`https://learn.microsoft.com/en-us/dotnet/standard/threading/using-threads-and-threading`)

- Generics (`https://learn.microsoft.com/en-us/dotnet/csharp/fundamentals/types/generics`)

Our job is to manage the potentially alarming rate of projectiles we can shoot by putting them into a communal pool of accessible objects, which lets us limit how many can be onscreen at a time (and opens up a number of interesting possibilities for player mechanics!).

# Breaking down the Object Pool pattern

While the Object Pool pattern wasn't included in the original Gang of Four content, we're still counting it as part of the Creational family of design patterns because, well, its area of expertise is literally object creation. Because the Object Pool pattern is about pooling shared objects rather than creating and destroying objects one at a time, you'll find it most useful when:

- You have objects that are instantiated and destroyed at a high rate and/or are computationally expensive to instantiate (think about how many bullets a first-person shooter has to put onscreen when you're really in the thick of it).
- You want to keep track of and control memory allocation when creating objects.
- You want to improve performance by allocating and reusing objects with a predictable memory footprint and timeframe.

If you've been to a library, you're intimately familiar with how Object Pooling works. The library receives a certain number of copies of a given book and keeps them in a communal pool of books that are available to the public. Anyone can come in and request a copy of the book they're looking for – if there's one available, you're in luck; if not, you're stuck waiting for someone to return a copy before you can take it home with you, as shown in the following figure. Moreover, libraries can have multiple books, each with multiple copies, which is a scenario we'll cover in the *Managing different pooled objects* subsection.

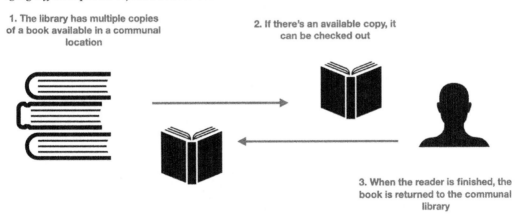

**1. The library has multiple copies of a book available in a communal location**

**2. If there's an available copy, it can be checked out**

**3. When the reader is finished, the book is returned to the communal library**

*Figure 7.1: Example scenario showing checking out and returning books to a communal library*

In the library scenario (as in programming), it would be expensive to create a new book (or object) every time someone wanted to request one but found that none were available. While a library might find it hard to conjure up a new book from thin air, a program can do just that, which makes object instantiation a dangerous game if you're not careful. In a program, there's no natural limit to how many times you can use the new keyword and create a new object instance. You won't find out anything is wrong until you run your game and either a user's hardware can't take it and crashes or they stop playing because it's so unbelievably slow. We discussed this scenario with the Prototype pattern in *Chapter 3, Spawning Enemies with the Prototype Pattern*, where memory starts to be a factor when objects are created and destroyed at a high frequency, as shown in the following figure. Pay special attention to objects that come with resource dependencies like database connections or network sockets, which makes them costly to instantiate even once, let alone in multiples.

**Client can create new objects anytime**

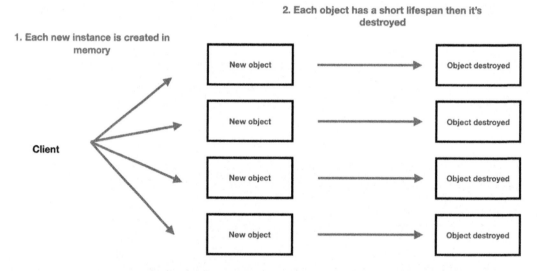

*Figure 7.2: Example of creating and destroying objects with short lifespans at high frequencies*

Looking at the preceding figure, you'll see that each time an object is created, the CPU will show a small spike as the object is instantiated in memory. A few objects won't slow anything down with today's hardware and Unity's default optimizations, but imagine doing this hundreds of times per frame. This can quickly become a playability issue if your game frequently starts to glitch or freeze during crucial interactions (unless your game is called *Frustrated*, then by all means leave Object Pooling by the side of the road).

If you want to see information that's specific to the performance of your project in Unity, the Profiler tool has everything you need. Not only can you get first-hand data on your CPU usage, memory allocation, rendering, and audio costs, but it's delivered in a wonderfully visual display so you can see exactly where you can improve. For more information, check out Unity's documentation at `https://docs.unity3d.com/Manual/Profiler.html`.

In a gaming scenario, you might want to shoot tens of projectiles per second, or spawn massive waves of various enemy units to attack the player, or even a set of database connections that you need to keep accessible throughout the entire application lifecycle. In all cases, creating new objects will produce a significant spike in CPU usage and garbage collection, resulting in slower frame rates and possible crashes. The solution is to create a set number of objects at the beginning of your program or script (or anywhere that it won't negatively affect the CPU), then check out objects when requested and return them when they're no longer needed, as shown in the following figure:

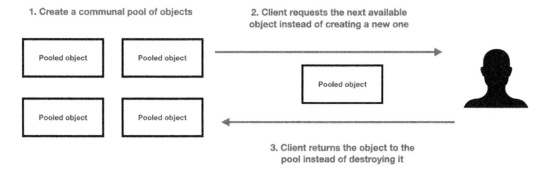

*Figure 7.3: Simplified Object Pooling example for creating, reusing, and returning objects*

An Object Pool also naturally sets an upper limit on how many new objects can be created, forcing the client to wait for the next available object rather than creating new ones. This is kind of like a programmatic sleight of hand, because from the outside it looks like new objects are being created, while the code is managing and reusing the same objects behind the scenes. And because we're reusing objects, we have to reset their initial state before returning them to the communal pool, but we'll talk about that in the *Resetting pooled objects* section.

While it's not always necessary to start out with Object Pools in your projects, it's something to consider as you begin to scale your systems and optimize for different hardware platforms.

## Diagramming the pattern

*Figure 7.4* shows the UML structure of the basic Object Pool design pattern with its three components:

- The **Client** is only concerned with the Object Pool, asking for a reusable object anytime it needs one.
- The Object Pool then checks if one is available and returns it if there's one free.
  - If the list of pooled objects is empty, or all of them are in use, the Object Pool can create and return a new one.
  - If all objects are in use, the client will need to wait for one to become available.
- The reusable `Pooled Object` class holds any object methods or interaction logic.

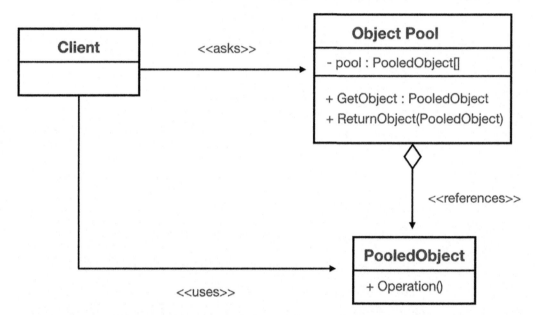

Figure 7.4: UML diagram of the Object Pool pattern components

From the client's perspective, the Object Pool encapsulates all the pool management logic and only exposes a way to get and return objects to the pool on demand.

## Pros and cons

Like all design patterns, there are pros and cons to the Object Pool pattern, but let's keep things positive and look at the benefits first:

- **Performance boost** when the memory and resource cost of instantiating the object is pricey and the rate of creation (and destruction) is high. Reuse is the name of the game in this pattern, so if you find yourself with objects that are popping up again and again at a rapid pace, consider pooling them.

- **Predictability** when object creation depends on resources that might take a varied length of time to access. For example, if you're pulling information from a database or graphical resources, it makes sense that you'd only want to initialize these once and then reuse them rather than destroy and re-instantiate them again and again.

However, be careful of the following pitfalls:

- **Stale state** happens when you don't reset your pooled objects when returning them to the communal pool. If you're old enough to remember VHS, you've probably popped in a movie and sat down to watch it only to realize that the previous person who watched it (maybe you) didn't rewind it to the beginning.

  Stale state can lead to all sorts of problematic and unanticipated behavior, especially when the stale objects are used and added back to the pool over and over – stale state compounds!

- **Threading issues** can spring up if an Object Pool is being used by more than one thread, but this can be nipped in the bud by making the pool mechanics thread-safe, which we'll talk about in the *Thread-safe pools* section.

Now that we've covered the structure, benefits, and limitations of the Object Pool pattern, let's start writing our own object creation code!

## Writing an Object Pool class

Imagine you're building a turret defense game where players fire projectiles from a tower at oncoming enemies, like a 3D version of Asteroids (super fun). The current system creates a new Bullet Prefab every time the player pushes the *Spacebar*, but the bullets stay alive in the scene (not super fun), as shown in *Figure 7.5*. You need a system for improving performance when instantiating projectile objects and limiting the number of projectiles that can be created.

If your players exceed the number of projectiles they're allowed to shoot, they'll need to wait until a new projectile becomes available instead of creating new projectiles indefinitely.

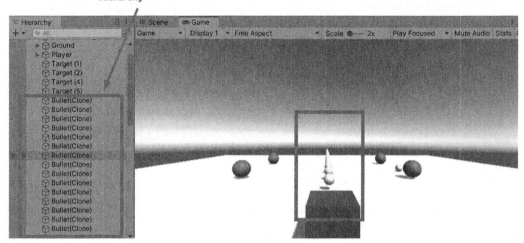

*Figure 7.5: In-game scene showing the player turret creating bullets every time the player fires*

 Even if you added a timed delay for each bullet to destroy itself, the core problem and cost of instantiating and destroying bullets each time the player fires still exists. The goal is to find a solution that limits the instantiation calls to the bare minimum.

If your players exceed the number of projectiles they're allowed to shoot, they'll need to wait until a new projectile becomes available instead of creating new projectiles indefinitely!

## Creating objects and filling the pool

Our ObjectPool class will have four main functional parts – creating, getting, returning, and resetting the pooled objects. I've already included a Projectile class script in the starter project, so the first component of the Object Pool pattern we need to build is an Object Pool class. This class will manage the twin pools of available and in-use objects, as well as how they are retrieved and returned to the pools.

In the **Scripts** folder, open ObjectPool.cs and update its code to match the following code block, which lays out the basic pooling structure we'll start building on:

```
using System.Collections;
```

```
using System.Collections.Generic;
using UnityEngine;

public class ObjectPool : MonoBehaviour
{
    // 1
    public static ObjectPool Shared;

    // 2
    public Projectile pooledObject;

    // 3
    public int poolSize;

    // 4
    private List<Projectile> _available = new List<Projectile>();

    // 5
    private List<Projectile> _inUse = new List<Projectile>();

    // 6
    void Awake()
    {
        Shared = this;
    }
}
```

Let's break down the code:

1. Declares a static shared instance of the ObjectPool class, which creates a basic Singleton

2. Adds a public field to store a pooled object prefab with a Projectile script attached

3. Adds a public field to store the pool size

4. Adds and initializes a private list to store available pooled objects

5. Adds and initializes a private list to store in-use pooled objects

6. Sets the Shared instance to this script instance in the Awake method

The first of four Object Pooling functions is creating an instance of the object we want to pool, which in our example is Projectile objects. Update ObjectPool.cs to match the snippet below, which sets each new projectile as a child of the Object Pooler GameObject in the scene, adds the projectile to the list of available pooled objects, and sets the initial state as inactive.

```
...


// 1
void CreatePooledObject()
{
    Projectile bullet = Instantiate(pooledObject);

    // 2
    _available.Add(bullet);

    // 3
    bullet.gameObject.transform.SetParent(this.transform);

    // 4
    bullet.gameObject.SetActive(false);
}
```

Let's break down the new projectile code:

1.  Declares a private method for creating pooled objects and instantiates a new Prefab instance
2.  Adds the new projectile to the list of available pooled objects
3.  Sets the new projectile as a child of the Object Pool  GameObject in the **Hierarchy**
4.  Sets the new projectile as inactive in the **Hierarchy**

Now that we can create our bullets, update ObjectPool.cs to match the following code, which fills the pool of available objects when the script becomes active and puts all the CPU strain of instantiating the objects at the beginning of the scene. Yes, it can be a lot of work upfront, but with a good loading screen, you won't set unrealistic performance expectations for your players:

```
using System.Collections;
using System.Collections.Generic;
using UnityEngine;
```

```
public class ObjectPool : MonoBehaviour
{
    public static ObjectPool Shared;

    public Projectile pooledObject;
    public int poolSize;

    private List<Projectile> _available = new List<Projectile>();
    private List<Projectile> _inUse = new List<Projectile>();

    void Awake()
    {
        Shared = this;

        // 1
        FillPool();
    }

    void CreatePooledObject()
    {
        //… No changes needed …
    }

    // 2
    void FillPool()
    {
        // 3
        for(int i = 0; i < poolSize; i++)
        {
            CreatePooledObject();
        }
    }
}
```

Let's break down the code:

1. Calls the FillPool method when the script is enabled in the scene
2. Declares a private method for initializing the ObjectPool

3.   Uses a `for` loop to create the desired amount of pooled objects based on the pool size

In the **Hierarchy**, select **Object Pool** and configure it to match *Figure 7.6*:

1.   Drag the `Bullet` Prefab from the **Prefabs** folder into the **Pooled Object** field

2.   Set **Pool Size** to 5

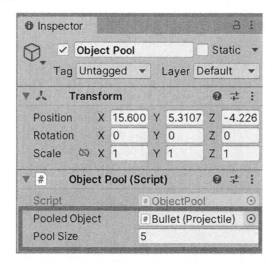

*Figure 7.6: Object Pool in the Inspector showing the Prefab and default pool size*

When you hit **Play**, you'll see five inactive **Bullet** Prefabs instantiated and parented to the **Object Pool** in the **Hierarchy**, as shown in *Figure 7.7*. The shooting mechanic is still using the starter project code for instantiating and firing bullets, which we'll update once our Object Pool is functional.

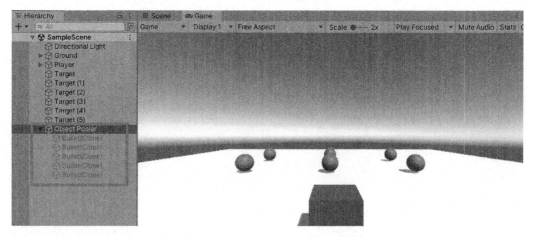

*Figure 7.7: The initial Object Pool being created with a set number of objects*

With our pool full, we can move on to scripting a way to retrieve the next available object in the pool and activating it in the scene, which we'll do in the next section.

## Retrieving pooled objects

The next feature the Object Pool needs is a way to retrieve a pooled object; otherwise, we'll just have a pool of bullets no one can use against the terrifying hordes of red targets. Update ObjectPool.cs to match the following code block, which checks if there's a pooled object in the list of available objects, sets the object state to active, and moves it to the in-use list. If all the objects are being used, the method returns null:

```csharp
...

// 1
public Projectile GetObject()
{
    // 2
    if(_available.Count == 0)
    {
        return null;
    }

    // 3
    Projectile bullet = _available[0];

    // 4
    _available.Remove(bullet);
    _inUse.Add(bullet);

    // 5
    bullet.gameObject.SetActive(true);
    return bullet;
}
```

Let's break down the code:

1. Declares a public method with a Projectile return type
2. Returns null if the available list of objects is empty
3. Stores the first available object in the available list

4.   Removes the pooled object from the available list and adds it to the in-use list

5.   Sets the pooled object state to active and returns the projectile

You can also check if the pool isn't full yet and add a new object if there's still room, which is common if you don't want to fill the pool manually. We're going to stick to filling the pool when the script is enabled for simplicity, but there's no shortage of customizations you can add to the retrieving method.

Before we test, open `PlayerController.cs` and update the `CreateBullet` method to match the following snippet, which uses `ObjectPool` to try and grab an available projectile when the player shoots. If the pool returns a `null` value, we print out a debug message to give the player feedback:

```
...

void CreateBullet()
{
    // 1
    Projectile newBullet = ObjectPool.Shared.GetObject();

    // 2
    if(newBullet != null)
    {
        newBullet.transform.position = this.transform.position;
        Rigidbody bulletRB = newBullet.GetComponent<Rigidbody>();
        bulletRB.velocity = this.transform.forward * bulletSpeed;
    }
    // 3
    else
    {
        Debug.Log("Your cannon is overheated...");
    }
}
```

Let's break down the code:

1.   Uses the shared `ObjectPool` instance to retrieve a projectile when the player shoots

2.   Checks if the projectile is `null`; if it's not, it sets the projectile's position to the player's position

3.  Prints a debug log if `ObjectPool` returns a `null` value

Run the game and click (or hold down) the *Spacebar* and you'll see the **Bullet** Prefabs in the **Hierarchy** turn active and shoot from the player's position, as shown in the following screenshot:

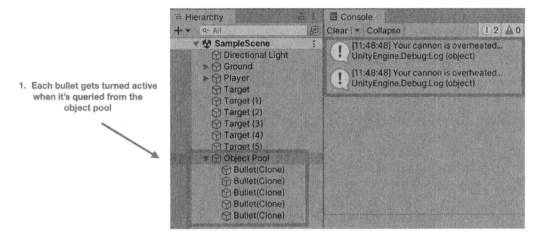

*Figure 7.8: All pooled objects being in use and with no new objects created*

Depending on how many objects are initially pooled, when you run out of bullets the console message appears every time you try and fire a bullet. To refill the pool when projectiles are destroyed, we need to write a method that reverses the `GetObject` functionality, which is our next job!

## Releasing pooled objects

Update `ObjectPool.cs` to match the following code block, which adds a new method to take in a projectile, move it from the in-use list to the available list of pooled objects, and set its state to inactive:

```
…

// 1
public void ReturnObject(Projectile bullet)
{
    // 2
    _inUse.Remove(bullet);
    _available.Add(bullet);
```

```
        // 3
        bullet.gameObject.SetActive(false);
    }
}
```

Let's break down our new code:

1.   Declares a `public` method with a `Projectile` parameter
2.   Removes the pooled object from the in-use list and adds it back to the available list
3.   Sets the objects' state to inactive

To test, update `Projectile.cs` to match the following snippet, which returns the bullets to the Object Pool when they either hit the invisible boundary at the far edge of the platform or successfully hit a target:

```
using System.Collections;
using System.Collections.Generic;
using UnityEngine;

public class Projectile : MonoBehaviour
{
    void OnTriggerEnter(Collider other)
    {
        if (other.gameObject.name == "Boundary")
        {
            // 1
            ObjectPool.Shared.ReturnObject(this);
        }
    }

    void OnCollisionEnter(Collision collision)
    {
        if (collision.gameObject.tag == "Target")
        {
            Destroy(collision.gameObject);

            // 2
            ObjectPool.Shared.ReturnObject(this);
```

```
            }
        }
    }
```

Let's break down the code:

1.  Returns the projectile object to the pool when it hits the boundary box collider
2.  Returns the projectile object to the pool when it hits a target collider

When you hit **Play** and start shooting, you'll see the **Bullet** Prefabs in the **Hierarchy** switch from inactive to active as they are pulled out of the pool and returned, as shown in the following screenshot:

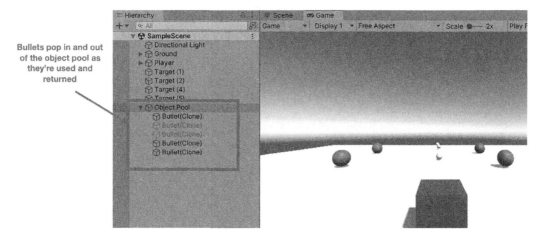

*Figure 7.9: Pooled objects being taken out and returned to the pool for reuse*

Notice the gameplay is largely the same, but there are breaks in the constant shooting during the brief periods when the Object Pool is empty, which can be a fun side-effect of using an Object Pool for shooting mechanics!

The final piece of the Object Pool puzzle is making sure objects get returned to the pool in their default state, which we'll tackle next.

## Resetting pooled objects

Since our projectiles don't have any fields that get updated during their lifetime, we're going to add a contrived example to show the resetting process when returning objects to the pool in new (or slightly used) condition. In our example, each projectile will track the time it's active in the scene, then reset that value when it's returned to the Object Pool.

Update Projectile.cs to match the following code, which adds a float value to track the lifespan of each projectile, increment it with each frame, and finally reset the value to 0 whenever called.

 We could also have put the resetting logic in the OnDisable call because the projectile is a MonoBehaviour, but this way you know how to handle this important scenario inside *and* outside of the Unity environment!

```csharp
using System.Collections;
using System.Collections.Generic;
using UnityEngine;

public class Projectile : MonoBehaviour
{
    // 1
    public int lifespan;

    // 2
    void Update()
    {
        lifespan += 1;
    }

    // 3
    public void Reset()
    {
        Debug.Log($"Projectile lifespan -> {lifespan} frames");
        lifespan = 0;
    }

    void OnTriggerEnter(Collider other)
```

```
    {
        //... No changes needed ...
    }

    void OnCollisionEnter(Collision collision)
    {
        //... No changes needed ...
    }
}
```

Let's break down the code:

1. Adds an int property to track the lifespan time of each projectile

2. Increments the lifespan value by 1 at each frame in the Update method

3. Prints and resets the lifespan value to 0 when called

Now all we need to do is call our new Reset method when pooled objects are returned to the pool and we're off and running! Update ObjectPool.cs to match the following snippet:

```
...

public void ReturnObject(Projectile bullet)
{
    lock(_available)
    {
        // 1
        bullet.Reset();

        _inUse.Remove(bullet);
        _available.Add(bullet);
        bullet.gameObject.SetActive(false);
    }
}
```

Play the game again and look at the console, which is now full of debug messages with the lifespan times of each projectile after it's been shot and destroyed, as shown in *Figure 7.10*. If you select one of the **Bullet** Prefabs in the Hierarchy and watch **Lifespan** while you're shooting, you'll see its value increment while the object is active, reset to 0 when it's returned to the pool and disabled, then increment again when it's taken out.

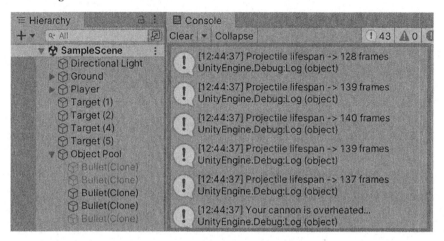

*Figure 7.10: Console showing each pooled object's lifespan before being reset*

Resetting objects is a crucial part of managing your pooled objects, as things will get messy if you're updating objects while they're active and then returning them in various state configurations. Be sure to double-check that you're handling this case if your Object Pool isn't behaving as expected. For example, if you were pooling enemies in an Asteroids-like game and they had zero health when destroyed and returned to the pool without being reset, the next time they're pulled out of the pool, they would instantly be destroyed again because they would come into the scene with their HP already spent!

That's it for our basic Object Pool, but there are a few different customizations to cover in the next section before ending the chapter with a Unity-specific `ObjectPool` class implementation.

## Object Pooling customizations

The basic Object Pool we've written so far works perfectly fine, but it's not as optimized as it could be. We're using multiple lists to store and manage our pooled objects, Object Pool access isn't thread-safe, and we can only handle a single type of pooled object at a time. We'll cover each of these areas in the next few subsections, but let's start by updating our lists to a single queue.

## Queues over lists

Because we need to continually update and track which pooled objects are available or in use, a queue is a more efficient choice. Queues are **first-in, first-out (FIFO)** collections, meaning elements are inserted at one end and removed from the other, creating a circular array, which is exactly what we need.

Update `ObjectPool.cs` to match the following code, which replaces the available and in-use `GameObject` lists with a single queue, then updates `CreateObject`, `GetObject`, and `ReturnObject` to use the `Enqueue` and `Dequeue` methods to add and remove objects, respectively:

```
public class ObjectPool : MonoBehaviour
{
    public static ObjectPool Shared;

    public Projectile pooledObject;
    public int poolSize;

    // 1
    private Queue<Projectile> _available = new Queue<Projectile>();

    void Awake()
    {
        //... No changes needed ...
    }

    public Projectile GetObject()
    {
        if(_available.Count == 0)
        {
            return null;
        }

        // 2
        Projectile bullet = _available.Dequeue();

        bullet.gameObject.SetActive(true);
        return bullet;
```

```
    }

    public void ReturnObject(Projectile bullet)
    {
        bullet.Reset();

        // 3
        _available.Enqueue(bullet);

        bullet.gameObject.SetActive(false);
    }

    void CreatePooledObject()
    {
        Projectile bullet = Instantiate(pooledObject);

        // 4
        _available.Enqueue(bullet);

        bullet.gameObject.transform.SetParent(this.transform);
        bullet.gameObject.SetActive(false);
    }

    void FillPool()
    {
        //… No changes needed …
    }
}
```

Let's break down the code:

1. Adds and initializes a queue to store all available pooled objects
2. Dequeues the first available object when GetObject is called and the queue isn't empty
3. Enqueues the object when it's returned to the pool
4. Enqueues the object when it's initially created

Everything works the same, but your Object Pool code is cleaner and the performance may even be a bit faster, depending on how many pooled objects you're managing in the scene. With our pool using queues instead of lists, we can move on to adding a little thread safety to keep our Object Pool safe from race conditions and deadlocks.

## Thread-safe pools

We covered the basics of thread safety during our Singleton implementation in *Chapter 2, Managing Access with the Singleton Pattern*, which you can reference if you need a refresher. Our example only has two points where the object queue is accessed, which makes it straightforward to safeguard.

Update `ObjectPool.cs` to match the following snippet, which locks the available queue field when it's being updated and unlocks the queue when the modifications are finished. We won't lock the `CreateObject` method because it's private and only gets called in the `Awake` function:

```
...

public Projectile GetObject()
{
    if(_available.Count == 0)
    {
        return null;
    }

    // 1
    lock(_available)
    {
        Projectile bullet = _available.Dequeue();
        bullet.gameObject.SetActive(true);

        return bullet;
    }
}

public void ReturnObject(Projectile bullet)
{
    // 2
    lock(_available)
```

```
    {
        bullet.Reset()
        _available.Enqueue(go);
        bullet.gameObject.SetActive(false);
    }
}
```

Let's break down the code:

1.  Locks the available queue when objects are queried from the pool
2.  Locks the available queue when objects are being returned to the pool

C# doesn't allow null objects to be locked, but luckily, we already initialized the available object queue to an empty queue. Run the game again and you'll see everything still works the same, but now any scripts competing for access to the shared ObjectPool instance will be thread-safe.

> As I've mentioned before, Unity itself is not thread-safe and most of Unity's APIs can't be called from threads other than the main thread (although Unity's job system is an exception, being multithreaded, but that's for another book and another time). However, the concepts (and scenarios) behind thread safety are so critical to software development that I've been including them throughout the book so you can go out into the C# world and feel secure.

## Managing different pooled objects

Suppose each tower can equip different projectile types and each one needs its own ammunition limit. Further, you need a way to create and manage groups of projectiles from a single manager class.

The following code is one example of how to implement multiple pooled objects in the same pool. First, we have a serializable data container class to hold the information for each type of pooled object, then we use procedural programming to fill the dictionary of pools in the Start method. The CreateObject method takes in specific pooled object data, parents each item to an empty game object to keep the Hierarchy clean, and uses the same logic we've already covered to manage a queue. While this code isn't a full implementation, you can use it as a jumping-off point and add your own projectile creation, return, and resetting logic!

> PoolData is also a great fit for using Unity's ScriptableObjects. Revisit previous chapters for the in-depth implementations we've already covered.

```csharp
using System.Collections;
using System.Collections.Generic;
using UnityEngine;

[System.Serializable]
public class PoolData
{
    public string tag;
    public GameObject obj;
    public int size;
}

public class MultiPool : MonoBehaviour
{
    public List<PoolData> pools = new List<PoolData>();
    public Dictionary<string, Queue<GameObject>> poolCollection;

    void Start()
    {
        poolCollection = new Dictionary<string, Queue<GameObject>>();
        foreach (PoolData data in pools)
        {
            CreateObject(data);
        }
    }

    void CreateObject(PoolData data)
    {
        var parent = new GameObject($"{data.tag}'s");
        parent.transform.SetParent(this.transform);
        Queue<GameObject> newPool = new Queue<GameObject>();

        for (int i = 0; i < data.size; i++)
        {
            GameObject newObject = Instantiate(data.obj);
            newObject.SetActive(false);
            newObject.transform.SetParent(parent.transform);
```

```
        newPool.Enqueue(newObject);
    }


    poolCollection.Add(data.tag, newPool);
  }
}
```

Using a dictionary to manage multiple pools allows you to update how you get and return pooled objects by using the `TryGetValue` method, which you can find at `https://docs.microsoft.com/en-us/dotnet/api/system.collections.generic.dictionary-2.trygetvalue`. This can speed up your dictionary look up and makes modifying the dictionary itself more efficient by using an out parameter.

To see this script in action:

1. Right-click in the **Hierarchy** | **Create Empty** and name it `Multi Pool`
2. Create the `MultiPool.cs` script from the code above
3. Drag the `MultiPool.cs` script onto the `Multi Pool` object and fill in the list of Pools with **Bullet** and **Target** Prefabs, as shown on the right side of *Figure 7.11*

Hit **Play** to see the sub-parent objects created for each pooled object type and their inactive children on the left side of *Figure 7.11*.

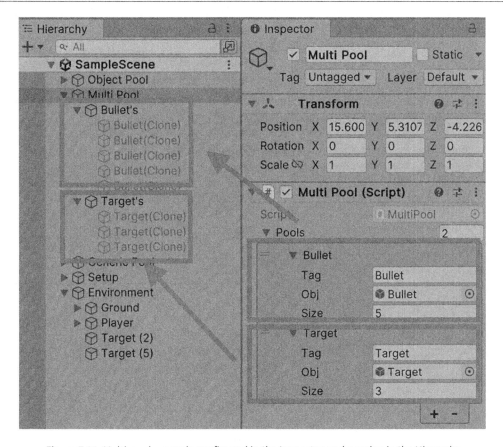

*Figure 7.11: Multi-pool example configured in the Inspector and running in the Hierarchy*

Again, this optimization is not complete, but that's as far as we're going to take it here (that shouldn't stop you from exploring your own solutions or approaches you see out in the programming wild). Go ahead and disable the **Multi Pool** GameObject in the **Hierarchy** before you move forward, just so we have a clean slate. In the last section, we'll transfer everything we've learned about writing Object Pools from scratch into a solution using Unity's IObjectPool interface.

# Leveraging Unity's ObjectPool class

If you're using Unity 2021 or later, you have access to a host of new classes that take out some of the boilerplate code we had to write ourselves in the previous sections. Unity's `ObjectPool<T0>` class is a stack of pooled objects that are optimized and managed for reusability – your job is to fill out the pooling actions and Unity takes care of the rest.

Since we're already familiar with the Object Pool structure, let's focus on the parameters of the `ObjectPool` constructor:

- `createFunc` is used to create a new instance of the pooled object.
- `actionOnGet` is called when a pooled object is taken out of the pool.
- `actionOnRelease` is called when a pooled object is returned to the pool and can contain resetting or cleanup logic.
- `actionOnDestroy` is called when the pool has reached the maximum size and a pooled object can't be returned.

 Each of these parameters is generic – `createFunc` has a generic `Func<T>` signature while `actionOnGet`, `actionOnGet`, `actionOnRelease`, and `actionOnDestroy` all have the same `Action<T>` signature. If you've never used a C# `Action<T>` delegate, it's a way to encapsulate a method with a single parameter and no return value. You can find more information at `https://docs.microsoft.com/en-us/dotnet/api/system.action-1?view=net-6.0`.

Unity also provides parameters for setting default pool values:

- `collectionCheck` is a Boolean value for checking if a pooled object is already in the pool when it's trying to be returned (and only run in the Editor).
- `defaultCapacity` is the initial size of the Object Pool.
- `maxSize` acts as a cap for the Object Pool size, which can be used to create an expandable buffer in situations where you want the pool size to be a value between `defaultCapacity` and `maxSize`.

Now that we've covered the structure of Unity's `ObjectPool` class, we can implement our shooting system in a new script to compare the end results.

In the **Scripts** folder, create a new C# script named GenericPool and update its code to match the following code block. This hefty bit of code establishes all the Object Pool properties we need, sets up a private pool and a lazily initialized public pool, and then finishes by declaring each of the pool functions that we use in the ObjectPool constructor:

```csharp
using System.Collections;
using System.Collections.Generic;
using UnityEngine;

// 1
using UnityEngine.Pool;

public class GenericPool : MonoBehaviour
{
    // 2
    public Projectile pooledObject;
    public int defaultCapacity = 5;
    public int maxCapacity = 10;
    public bool collectionChecks = true;

    // 3
    private IObjectPool<Projectile> _pool;
    public IObjectPool<Projectile> pool
    {
        // 4
        get
        {
            if(_pool == null)
            {
                // 5
                _pool = new ObjectPool<Projectile>
                    (
                        CreatePooledObject,
                        TakeFromPool,
                        ReturnToPool,
                        DestroyPooledObject,
                        collectionChecks,
                        defaultCapacity,
```

```
                    maxCapacity
            );
        }

        // 6
        return _pool;
    }
}

// 7
private Projectile CreatePooledObject()
{
    Projectile bullet = Instantiate(pooledObject);
    bullet.gameObject.SetActive(false);
    bullet.transform.SetParent(this.transform);

    return bullet;
}

// 8
private void TakeFromPool(Projectile bullet)
{
    bullet.gameObject.SetActive(true);
}

// 9
private void ReturnToPool(Projectile bullet)
{
    bullet.gameObject.SetActive(false);
    bullet.Reset();
}

// 10
private void DestroyPooledObject(Projectile bullet)
{
    Destroy(bullet.gameObject);
}
}
```

Let's break down this new script:

1. Adds the Object Pooling namespace to the top of the script
2. Adds fields for the pooled object Prefab, collection checks, default size, and max size
3. Declares a `public` Object Pool with a private backing variable
4. Adds a `public` getter property and checks if the pool is null
5. Creates a new Object Pool using all constructor methods, actions, and variables
6. Returns either the existing or the newly created Object Pool
7. Declares a function to create and configure a pooled object instance
8. Declares a function for taking a pooled object out of the pool and setting it to active
9. Declares a function for returning pooled objects and setting them as inactive
10. Declares a function for destroying extra pooled objects

 You can find more information on the `ObjectPool` class in the Unity documentation at `https://docs.unity3d.com/2021.2/Documentation/ScriptReference/Pool.ObjectPool_1.html`.

The biggest difference between our custom Object Pool and Unity's implementation is not having to manually manage objects being taken and returned to the pool. Our only responsibility inside the pooling methods is handling the projectile `GameObject`'s state or any other game-related logic. Note that holding down the *Spacebar* produces a smooth, steady stream of bullets just like the beginning state of the starter project, which means Unity's implementation is extremely optimized under the hood.

Before we test, update `GenericPool.cs` to match the following changes, which makes `GenericPool` accessible using a public static instance and adds a thread-safety lock to the public Object Pool getter property since Unity's Object Pools aren't thread-safe by default:

```
using System.Collections;
using System.Collections.Generic;
using UnityEngine;
using UnityEngine.Pool;

public class GenericPool : MonoBehaviour
{
    // 1
    public static GenericPool Shared;
```

```csharp
//… No other public variable changes needed …

// 2
private object _poolLock = new object();

private IObjectPool<Projectile> _pool;
public IObjectPool<Projectile> Pool
{
    get
    {
        if(_pool == null)
        {
            // 3
            lock(_poolLock)
            {
                _pool = new ObjectPool<Projectile>
                    (
                        CreatePooledObject,
                        TakeFromPool,
                        ReturnToPool,
                        DestroyPooledObject,
                        collectionChecks,
                        defaultCapacity,
                        maxCapacity
                    );
            }
        }

        return _pool;
    }
}

// 4
void Awake()
{
    Shared = this;
```

```
    }

    //... No method changes needed ...
}
```

Let's break down the updated code:

1.  Adds a `public static` instance of `GenericPool` for Singleton access from other scripts
2.  Adds a `public` object variable to act as a thread-lock
3.  Locks the thread when a new Object Pool is being created
4.  Sets the `Shared` script instance in the `Awake` method

> We're making `GenericPool` a simplified Singleton to make the example easier to follow and implement, but this isn't part of the Object Pool design pattern. Another solution might be to add an `ObjectPool` field to `Projectile.cs` and set its value inside the `CreatePooledObject` function. However, we'd have to do something similar for `Player.cs` to have access to the Object Pool. It's up to you to decide the best way to share pool access with your other scripts!

Update `PlayerController.cs` to match the following snippet to retrieve projectiles from the new `GenericPool` instead of our previous custom `ObjectPool`:

```
...

void CreateBullet()
{
    // 1
    Projectile newBullet = GenericPool.Shared.Pool.Get();

    newBullet.transform.position = this.transform.position;
    Rigidbody bulletRB = newBullet.GetComponent<Rigidbody>();
    bulletRB.velocity = this.transform.forward * bulletSpeed;
}
```

Finally, update `Projectile.cs` to match the following code, which replaces both calls to `ObjectPool` with `GenericPool` when a bullet collides with the scene boundary or hits a target:

```
using System.Collections;
using System.Collections.Generic;
```

```
using UnityEngine;

public class Projectile : MonoBehaviour
{
    public float lifespan;

    //... No changes to Awake, Update, or OnDisable ...

    void OnTriggerEnter(Collider other)
    {
        if(other.gameObject.name == "Boundary")
        {
            // 1
            GenericPool.Shared.Pool.Release(this);
        }
    }

    void OnCollisionEnter(Collision collision)
    {
        if(collision.gameObject.tag == "Target")
        {
            Destroy(collision.gameObject);

            // 2
            GenericPool.Shared.Pool.Release(this);
        }
    }
}
```

To get this to work, create a new empty GameObject in the **Hierarchy** named Generic Pool and attach the GenericPool.cs script (and don't forget to disable the **Multi Pool** object if you haven't already).

Hit **Play** one last time and you'll see the shooting mechanism use Object Pooling just like before, but with slightly better performance and a smoother flow of bullets from the player's turret.

**Different pooling classes in Unity**

In addition to the `ObjectPool<T0>` class, the Unity API has a generic `LinkedPool<T0>` class that uses a linked list instead of a stack. A `LinkedPool` only allocates memory for objects stored in the pool, while an `ObjectPool`'s stack uses an underlying array, which might lead to unused space being reserved in memory.

Unity also has generic options for pooling object collection, including `ListPool<T0>`, `DictionaryPool<T0,T1>`, `HashSetPool<T0>`, and `CollectionPool<T0,T1>` classes. However, Unity's collection pools are all static pool variables under the hood, which could lead to pooled objects persisting across different runs of the Editor. You also can't disable domain reloads, a feature that improves iteration times in the Editor.

Finally, Unity has two classes for using Object Pools without having to create them first – `GenericPool<T0>` and `UnsafeGenericPool<T0>`. These are also static Object Pools behind the scenes, so disabling domain reloads isn't possible but comes with less initialization overhead.

While discussing each of these classes and their respective use cases is outside the scope of this chapter, you can find more information and examples under the *UnityEngine.Pool* heading in the scripting reference documentation at `https://docs.unity3d.com/2021.2/Documentation/ScriptReference/Pool.CollectionPool_2.html`.

For any topic dealing with performance or optimization, I highly recommend using the Unity **Profiler** window to test different scenarios and implementations for yourself. There's no better way to know if you truly need a design pattern like Object Pooling than to look at the stats first-hand. You can find more information on using the Profiler window at `https://docs.unity3d.com/Manual/Profiler.html`.

We've come a long way from our first humble Object Pool class, but my hope is that all the options and variations we've worked through in this chapter have left you with more ideas than headaches. I've said it before in this book and I'll say it again: design patterns are tools, and it's always best to choose the right tool for the job at hand. Don't feel pressured to jump right into Unity's `ObjectPool` class when a simpler one will do (and vice versa)!

# Summary

With computers nowadays being so fast and powerful (and modern programming languages having such advanced and efficient garbage collection), it's not uncommon for the Object Pool pattern to come under scrutiny for its usefulness. However, just because you *can* get away with creating hundreds, thousands, or millions of objects without setting your rig on fire, doesn't mean you *should*. Who knows, using communal pools of reusable objects could save your players from unnecessary rage quitting.

Remember, the Object Pooling pattern allocates, stores, and reuses objects from a communal pool, while the pooled object is reusable and holds any object methods or interaction logic. Your Object Pools can hold GameObjects, Prefabs, C# objects, or collections, and a single pool can manage sub-pools of different pooled object types. The Unity API has a built-in generic ObjectPool class that stores pooled objects in a stack data structure.

In the next chapter, we'll explore how the Command pattern can help us bundle actions and behaviors into self-contained objects, which can then be executed, undone, or redone (on command)!

# Further reading

- Queues are a first-in, first-out collection of objects, which makes them perfect for storing and retrieving elements in the order they were added (just like a line at the bank). If these are new to you, check out the documentation at https://learn.microsoft.com/en-us/dotnet/api/system.collections.generic.queue-1?view=net-8.0.

- Multithreading is a bit of an advanced topic outside the scope of this book, but being able to perform multiple operations at the same time is a useful tool in your toolbox. If you want to know more about this topic, head over to the documentation at https://learn.microsoft.com/en-us/dotnet/standard/threading/using-threads-and-threading.

- Generics open up a whole new world of programming possibilities (which is why I included a generic solution in this chapter), but I'd recommend reading up on the topic at https://learn.microsoft.com/en-us/dotnet/csharp/fundamentals/types/generics.

- Unity **Profiler** is your one-stop shop for all things performance related. You can connect it to networked devices or devices right on your computer or run it straight from the Editor. For more information, check out the documentation at https://docs.unity3d.com/Manual/Profiler.html.

# Join our community on Discord

Join our community's Discord space for discussions with the author and other readers:

`https://packt.link/gamedevelopment_packt`

# 8

# Binding Actions with the Command Pattern

In the last chapter, we learned how to manage and optimize memory usage when creating massive amounts of objects with the Object Pool design pattern. In this chapter, we'll dive into creating actionable requests that can be customized, queued, and undone with the Command pattern. When I say *actionable requests*, what we're really talking about are commands that come pre-packaged with all the information they need to be executed. This way, when we need the requests to do their work, they already have everything they need to get their job done!

The power behind the Command pattern (other than being encapsulated as its own object) is the ability to deal with abstractions. Like other patterns we've covered, the Command pattern uses underlying interfaces, so the client or system doesn't need to know the exact details of the command or even how it's supposed to be fired (no how or why, just the when).

Think of a car – when you press the gas pedal, you expect the car to move. You don't necessarily care how the gas pedal *makes* the car move, just that it goes vroom. The car has everything it needs to perform the action – gas, a motor, a cooling system, and so on – and the car can be moved at any time by pressing the gas pedal.

We'll use this chapter to focus on the following topics:

- The pros and cons of the Command design pattern
- Building a basic command structure
- Creating coupled commands
- Implementing an undo/redo system

By the end of this chapter, you'll have a strong working foundation of the Command pattern structure, but more importantly, you'll learn how to look at data and behavior from a highly abstract perspective (which comes in handy in many of our other design pattern topics)!

# Technical requirements

Before you start, follow these steps:

1.  Download or clone the GitHub repository at `https://github.com/PacktPublishing/C-Design-Patterns-with-Unity-First-Edition`.

2.  Open the **Ch_08_Starter** project folder in Unity Hub.

3.  In **Assets | Scenes**, double-click on **SampleScene**.

The sample project for this chapter is a simple strategy RPG game where you control a player and two allies using key presses (bound to reusable commands). These reusable commands are also interchangeable, so we can configure key bindings any way we want and which character they affect. In the latter sections, we'll add non-reusable movement commands, which can be applied to any of the characters in the scene but can also be undone or redone at any time!

As for the scripts:

*   `Client.cs` holds a reference to the `UIManager` and requires `InputListener.cs`, `UnitController.cs`, and `Invoker.cs` components

*   `InputListener.cs` holds references to the `UIManager` and `UnitManager`

*   `Invoker.cs` is empty to start with (we'll do a ton of work in here)

*   `SelfDestruct.cs` is a `MonoBehaviour` for destroying `GameObjects` after a certain time

*   `UIManager.cs` holds a `Text` reference so we can print out key bindings in the UI

*   `UnitController.cs` holds a list of units and the code for shooting, melee, and blocking game mechanics

*   `Utilities.cs` provides utility functions for object rotation and returning a `Vector3` based on a direction

We'll also be using some Unity and C# language features to take our code the extra mile. Don't worry if you're not familiar with these; I've included links for the basics, and I'll explain how they apply to our use cases as we go:

- Abstract classes (`https://learn.microsoft.com/en-us/dotnet/csharp/language-reference/keywords/abstract`)

- Stacks (`https://learn.microsoft.com/en-us/dotnet/api/system.collections.stack?view=net-8.0`)

There's a lot going on in this starter project, so don't be shy about taking time to get a handle on how things work (I try to keep these as simple as possible to highlight the design pattern we're learning, but this one required a little extra). Our job is to connect the actionable commands to each unit and get our RPG running! As usual, let's start by breaking down the pattern into consumable (some might even say learnable) bites and see what it has to offer.

# Breaking down the Command pattern

If you've been reading the book sequentially, you're braver than I am; if not, that's OK, too! I'm only pausing here because we're leaving the Creational patterns behind and diving into the Behavioral category with the Command pattern, which is all about communication and connection. The Command pattern lets you create actions as objects, meaning you can customize them during instantiation, execute them immediately, store them for later, and even undo or redo them, which is useful when:

- You want to create actions as self-contained objects with all the information needed to execute the action.

- You want interchangeable actions that can work on any receiving object.

- You want to store or queue sequences of actions to be triggered later.

- You want to avoid hard-wiring requests to the client making the request.

- You want to support undo and redo functionality.

Commands shouldn't be anything new – they're all around us. We already talked about how a car's gas pedal works but think about all the other actions in your everyday life that are possible through the connection, communication, and interaction of different moving parts (a helpful way I like to think of commands is as transactions or promises).

Let's take a scenario that happens every month – paying bills. Most bills nowadays can be paid by setting up an automatic payment with your bank, either through an app or online. When you set up the auto-payment, you're giving your bank permission to use the financial information it *already* has to pay a bill.

This data might include your billing address, bank account, and available funds, as shown in the following figure:

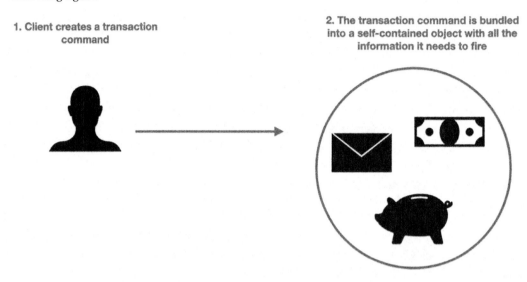

*Figure 8.1: Simplified example of how auto-payments work*

When the bill becomes due, the bank triggers the auto-payment transaction you set up, whether you created it that day or last year. Now, think of yourself as the bank: you have millions of potential transactions to handle every month, so you store them in a list or queue and execute them according to each of their individual due dates, as shown in the following figure:

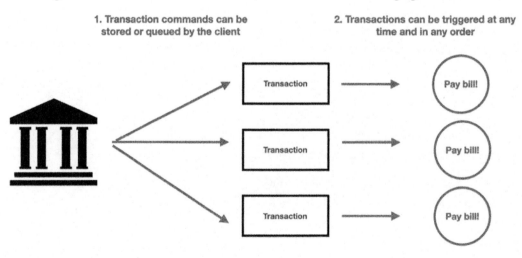

*Figure 8.2: An example of transaction queues and triggering stored actions*

With any transaction, there needs to be some sort of undo feature in case you or your bank make a mistake. Since each auto-payment has a timestamp and transaction data, the bank can look it up and reverse the charge. The entire system works on delegation and deferment – once each transaction, or command, is created, it has everything it needs to be triggered at any time and undone if needed. You and your bank don't need to know the underlying details to pay the bill, just that it needs to be paid on a certain day or the water gets turned off.

## Diagramming the pattern

*Figure 8.3* shows the UML structure of the Command design pattern with its five components:

- The **Abstract Command** class is an interface for handling operation execution
- A **Concrete Command** is responsible for executing the command on a given receiver. Commands can either be bound to a dedicated receiver or get the receiver through the Execute method. We'll talk more about coupled and decoupled commands in the following section, *Reusable versus single-use commands.*
- The **Client** creates the actual command objects and passes them in their respective receivers. The example in this chapter uses a middle-man class called InputListener, which handles the input received from the player (via the keyboard) and returns a pre-bundled command to the client.
- The **Invoker** tells the command to execute, which means we have the freedom to decide when the command is fired.

- The **Receiver** only knows how to perform the logic behind each command, so any class can realistically be a receiver if it has the code for the corresponding command action.

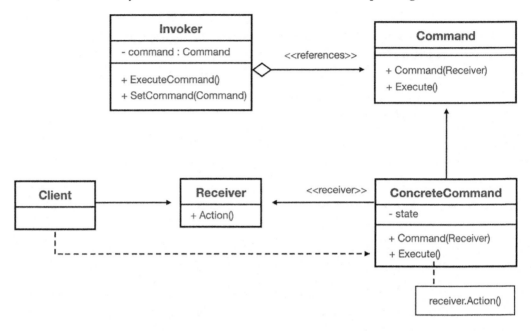

*Figure 8.3: UML diagram of the Command pattern components*

The Invoker class can trigger or undo commands without knowing which Concrete Command it's using since each Concrete Command either inherits or implements the Command base class or interface. Each Concrete Command has a receiver to perform the desired action and optional parameters, while the client doesn't need to know anything other than the Invoker and Receiver for each command.

The encapsulation of information into a standalone transaction is the core of the Command pattern because each command can then be treated as an object. Since each command object has its own set of instructions and data, the client never needs to know how or what the command is tasked with accomplishing, only triggering the task it has.

## Reusable versus single-use commands

Before we dive into any pros and cons, we need to clarify that there are two kinds of commands you can use with the Command pattern (extremely important because they tend to get mashed together out in the wild). First, you can have reusable commands, which have no state and can be passed around at will. A common example of reusable commands would be key bindings (you know them as hotkeys).

For example, the underlying mechanics for shooting, running, and jumping don't usually change, but what keys trigger them and which player or unit performs the action can be interchanged. We can reuse these types of commands because each instance doesn't have any coupled data or relationship with the object receiving and performing the command (some would call this extremely disloyal, but I don't judge), as shown in the following figure:

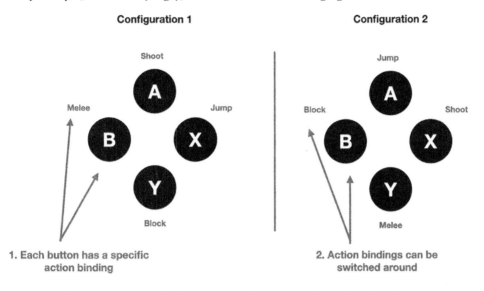

*Figure 8.4: An example of game controller buttons with configured actions*

Second, you can have coupled commands, which store state information and are bound to the object receiving and performing the action. These are unique command objects, which means they can only be used once instead of being passed around at will (and are extremely loyal to their receivers). However, *because* they're unique objects, they can be stored in command sequences, which means they can be undone and redone – hurray for stateful data! You'll see RPG and tactical games use coupled commands to track player movement, especially if the player has a movement limit and wants to be able to undo or redo moves before committing to them. We'll tackle both scenarios in this chapter, but we'll start with the easier of the two – reusable commands.

## Pros and cons

Like all design patterns, there are pros and cons to the Command pattern, but let's keep things positive and look at the benefits first:

- **Decoupling** the invoker from the actor provides an intermediate level of abstraction and control. Not only is this structure less likely to break when actions or inputs are added or changed, but it also allows you to add code to keep track of commands and their order (or sequence).

- **Queued inputs** let you store, track, and control the execution of commands like an undo/redo system, macro key bindings, and command sequences.
- Commands are treated as **first-class objects** meaning they can be extended just like any other class object in our projects.

As for consequences, the Command pattern only has one really concerning pitfall:

- **Code complexity**: Setting up the Command pattern structure requires a lot of work upfront, which can be daunting and counterproductive if you're not intentional with what you're trying to accomplish. We've already discussed using design patterns for the sake of using them (which I actively discourage), but the Command pattern is especially susceptible. However, as long as you're clear about why you're using the pattern, you're all good.

Now that we've covered the structure, benefits, and limitations of the Command pattern, we can get our hands on our own bindable actions!

# Building a basic Command structure

The first piece of any Command pattern structure is the common interface all our commands need to implement. This can be an `interface` or `abstract` class, but I'm going to use abstract classes so we can add default logic later. The base abstract class for all commands is simple – they all need an `Execute` method. We'll start with building out commands that can be reused (i.e., don't have a reference to a specific receiver when concrete subclasses are instantiated), and then move on to coupled commands with internal state information.

## Creating reusable commands

In the **Scripts** folder, create a new C# script named `ReusableCommand`, and update its code to match the following code. All we've done here is declared `ReusableCommand` as abstract to make sure we're forced to create concrete commands and added an abstract `Execute` method that doesn't return anything. This is the basis for how we encapsulate the command information *inside* the command itself. This comes in handy later when we want to pass commands around as self-contained objects:

```
using System.Collections;
using System.Collections.Generic;
using UnityEngine;

// 1
public abstract class ReusableCommand
```

```
    {
        // 2
        public abstract void Execute();
    }
```

Let's break down the code:

1.  It declares a public abstract class called ReusableCommand.

2.  It adds an abstract Execute method that returns void.

We can create concrete commands for a few actions we want our units to be able to take. The starter project already has features for shooting, melee, and blocking actions, so we'll mirror those with the concrete classes (this should look familiar to you from our work with the Abstract Factory pattern in *Chapter 4*).

Add the following code to the bottom of ReusableCommand.cs *outside* of the abstract class (or in a new script if you want to be awesome). All this code does right now is add a concrete command for each action that inherits from ReusableCommand, implements the required Execute method, and prints out a debug log so we know when it's fired:

```
    ...

    // 1
    public class ShootCommand : ReusableCommand
    {
        // 2
        public override void Execute()
        {
            Debug.Log("Shoot command executed...");
        }
    }

    // 3
    public class MeleeCommand : ReusableCommand
    {
        // 4
        public override void Execute()
        {
            Debug.Log("Melee command executed...");
```

```
    }
}

// 5
public class BlockCommand : ReusableCommand
{
    // 6
    public override void Execute()
    {
        Debug.Log("Block command executed...");
    }
}
```

Let's break down the code:

1.   It declares a ShootCommand as a subclass of ReusableCommand.

2.   It implements the Execute method and prints out a debug log.

3.   It declares a MeleeCommand as a subclass of ReusableCommand.

4.   It implements the Execute method and prints out a debug log.

5.   It declares a BlockCommand as a subclass of ReusableCommand.

6.   It implements the Execute method and prints out a debug log.

Now that we have the commands, how do we get them hooked up to a receiver so the actual in-game feature can be activated? The answer is the subject of the next subsection, where we add a receiver to the abstract and concrete classes.

## Adding a receiver

A receiver is any class that does the actual command work. In our game example, the receiver is the UnitController component that's attached to the Player, Ally 1, and Ally 2 objects in the **Hierarchy**. UnitController.cs has publicly accessible methods for shooting, melee, and blocking logic, so we can make any unit do any action.

In ReusableCommand.cs, update the abstract class's Execute method to match the following snippet, which now takes in a UnitController parameter:

```
using System.Collections;
using System.Collections.Generic;
using UnityEngine;
```

```
public abstract class ReusableCommand
{
    // 1
    public abstract void Execute(UnitController receiver);
}
```

Now that the base ReusableCommand class has changed, we need to sync all our concrete classes
to use the new receiver parameter. Update each concrete command class in ReusableCommand.
cs with the following code block:

```
...

public class ShootCommand : ReusableCommand
{
    // 1
    public override void Execute(UnitController receiver)
    {
        Debug.Log("Shoot command executed...");

        // 2
        receiver.Shoot();
    }
}

public class MeleeCommand : ReusableCommand
{
    // 3
    public override void Execute(UnitController receiver)
    {
        Debug.Log("Melee command executed...");

        // 4
        receiver.Melee();
    }
}

public class BlockCommand : ReusableCommand
```

```
    {
        // 5
        public override void Execute(UnitController receiver)
        {
            Debug.Log("Block command executed...");

            // 6
            receiver.Block();
        }
    }
}
```

Let's break down the code:

1. It updates the Execute method in ShootCommand to take a UnitController parameter as the receiver.

2. It calls the Shoot method using the receiver parameter.

3. It updates the Execute method in MeleeCommand to take a UnitController parameter as the receiver.

4. It calls the Melee method using the receiver parameter.

5. It updates the Execute method in BlockCommand to take a UnitController parameter as the receiver.

6. It calls the Block method using the receiver parameter.

**Any class can be a receiver**

Since we only need one receiver for this scenario, I didn't include a receiver interface for UnitController to adopt. However, if you wanted any class to receive command actions, you could create a simple Receiver interface for other classes to adopt. In our example, that would mean the Receiver interface would have methods for Shoot, Melee, and Block actions, as shown in the following example code:

```
public interface IReceiver
{
    void Shoot();
    void Melee();
    void Block();
}
```

Then, `UnitController` would be marked as a Receiver interface adapter and implement the receiver methods, which it already does in our example:

```
public class UnitController : MonoBehaviour, IReceiver {…}
```

You could even break out sub-receiver actions into separate interfaces and compose your receiver classes that way for more flexibility. These scenarios aren't part of the core Command pattern, but there's no reason you can't adopt it to meet your needs.

Again, it's important to understand that our reusable commands are reusable *because* the receiver is passed into the `Execute` method instead of the class constructor. Reusable commands hold no state and can be used on any receiver passed into the `Execute` method and don't need to be reset when you want to use a different receiver. This gives us greater flexibility in not only *when* we call the command, but in *where* we call it and using *what* receiver. In a later section, on single-use commands, you'll see how storing command state (i.e., a receiver and other data) binds actions to specific receivers, which is what we'll need to add an undo/redo system.

With the command groundwork in place, let's move on to setting up an invoker to do the actual command execution.

## Adding an invoker class

At this early stage, the invoker class is dead simple – it takes in a command and a receiver, pairs them up on a blind date, and executes the command. You might be asking why we can't do this directly in the client – we could, but having an invoker means the client doesn't need to know how a command is executed. This kind of abstract is worth it with a design pattern like Command: there's already so much going on behind the scenes, especially when you scale your command infrastructure, the less the client needs to know and the more generic its actions can be, the better.

In the **Scripts** folder, open the `Invoker.cs` script that comes with the starter project and update its code to match the following snippet. This new code adds an `Execute` method to the `Invoker` with arguments for a reusable command and receiver, then initiates the command execution from here:

I included this class in the starter project because I wanted to make sure the client always had an `Invoker` component attached, which I did using Unity's `RequireComponent` attribute at the top of `Client.cs`.

```
using System.Collections;
using System.Collections.Generic;
using UnityEngine;

public class Invoker : MonoBehaviour
{
    // 1
    public void Execute(ReusableCommand command, UnitController receiver)
    {
        // 2
        Debug.Log($"{command.ToString()} invoked...");

        // 3
        command.Execute(receiver);
    }
}
```

Let's break down the code:

1.  It adds a `public` method with parameters for a command and a receiver.
2.  It uses a debug log to print out the command class name to the console.
3.  It fires the command using its `Execute` method and passes in the receiver parameter.

Because we put each of the receiver's actions in their respective concrete classes, all the invoker needs to know about is the abstract `ReusableCommand` class. This separation of concerns makes the Command pattern especially powerful when you want to add, modify, or switch around commands (in all those situations, the invoker doesn't care and keeps trucking along).

The last piece of our Command pattern is an input listener class, which isn't an official part of the design pattern, but nevertheless is super handy when abstracting out the player input.

## Using an input listener

The concept of an input listener class isn't part of the Command pattern in the original Gang of Four material, but it's a useful layer of abstraction in situations where you might be handling a variety of inputs from a game engine like Unity. The input listeners' job is to catch the input system notifications, like key presses and mouse movements, and translate them into commands. These commands are passed to the client, which should already have an invoker that can simply fire them off whenever the player wants. Remember, commands are self-contained objects – we want the currency of this system to be commands, not inputs.

With any new abstraction layer, there's a trade-off between more code to manage and usefulness. While you could put all the input handling code directly in the client class, it makes it crowded, and a crowded client can quickly get out of hand when it's managing more than one system.

Open the InputListener.cs script and update its code to match the following code block. Here, we're adding three command variables to represent different key presses the input listener is going to handle. Notice that we didn't define the commands as the actions we wanted, like shooting or blocking. We want the commands to be the key presses so we can *switch* the action bindings whenever we want:

```
using System.Collections;
using System.Collections.Generic;
using UnityEngine;

public class InputListener : MonoBehaviour
{
    //… No other variable changes needed …

    // 1
    private ReusableCommand _spacebar, _mKey, _bKey;

    void Start()
    {
        // 2
        _spacebar = new ShootCommand();
        _mKey = new MeleeCommand();
        _bKey = new BlockCommand();

        // 3
        UI.AddKeyBinding("Space", _spacebar.ToString());
        UI.AddKeyBinding("M", _mKey.ToString());
        UI.AddKeyBinding("B", _bKey.ToString());

        _unitController = this.GetComponent<UnitController>();
    }
}
```

Let's break down the code:

1.  It adds ReusableCommand variables for three different key presses.

2.  It binds each key press variable to a new command instance.

3.  It updates the UI with the key press and command bindings.

Run the game and you'll see that the UI has been updated to show the current action key bindings we have in place in *Figure 8.5*. This doesn't do anything just yet, but we'll be adding that functionality in the next section.

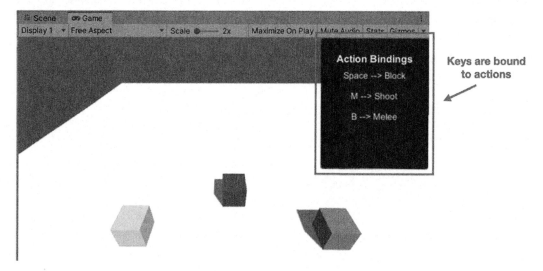

*Figure 8.5: Commands shown in the UI panel*

Now that we have command objects to work with, add the following method to the bottom of the InputListener class. This new code listens for the specific key presses we want (*M*, *B*, and *Spacebar*) and returns the appropriate commands. It's important that we return null if there's no player input, as we'll be checking this method for actionable commands at every frame in the client's Update loop:

```
...

// 1
public ReusableCommand GetActionCommands()
{
    // 2
    if (Input.GetKeyUp(KeyCode.M))
    {
```

```
        return _mKey;
    }

    // 3
    if (Input.GetKeyDown(KeyCode.B))
    {
        return _bKey;
    }

    // 4
    if (Input.GetKeyDown(KeyCode.Space))
    {
        return _spacebar;
    }

    // 5
    return null;
}
```

Let's break down the action binding code:

1.  It declares a new method that returns a ReusableCommand when certain keys are pressed.
2.  It checks whether the *M* key is pressed and returns the respective key-action binding.
3.  It checks whether the *B* key is pressed and returns the respective key-action binding.
4.  It checks whether the *Spacebar* is pressed and returns the respective key-action binding.
5.  It returns null if none of the inputs we're listening for are detected.

 So far, our proposed code solutions have only dealt with single key presses to fire off actions in the game. If you're worried about your players possibly pressing multiple keys at the same time (which we all know can happen), consider adding a cooldown time between potential key presses or checking whether a keypress hasn't been executed in some number of frames.

It's also important to note that separating the input system from the client gives us more freedom to encapsulate *how* we configure the game's input, whether it's with Unity's legacy or new input system. The last piece of our basic command structure is having the client use the input listener to get commands and pass them to the invoker to perform the action, which we'll tackle next.

# Updating the client

Now that we can listen for commands, our client has everything it needs to receive commands and invoke them on any given receiver. Update Client.cs to match the following snippet, which uses the input listener to retrieve commands at every frame, check whether they're null – meaning the inputs we're listening for aren't detected – and finally pass the command and receiver to the invoker to do the execution work:

```csharp
using System.Collections;
using System.Collections.Generic;
using UnityEngine;

[RequireComponent(typeof(InputListener))]
[RequireComponent(typeof(Invoker))]
[RequireComponent(typeof(UnitController))]
public class Client : MonoBehaviour
{
    //… No variable changes needed …

    void Awake()
    {
        //… No changes needed …
    }

    void Update()
    {
        // 1
        var reusableCommand = _inputListener.GetActionCommands();

        // 2
        if (reusableCommand != null)
        {
            Debug.Log("Reusable command input received...");

            // 3
            _invoker.Execute(reusableCommand, _unitController.unit);
        }
    }
}
```

Let's break down the code:

1.  It uses the GetActionCommands method from the input listener and stores it in a local variable.

2.  It checks whether the reusable command is null, and if it isn't, it prints out a debug log.

3.  It passes the reusable command and current unit to the invoker, which executes the command.

 For simplicity, we're lumping actions like Melee and Block together with physics code for the Shoot command. However, all code that uses Unity Physics would ideally go in FixedUpdate, which is a task I leave to you.

Play the game to shoot, melee, and block with the player character – blocking is shown in the following figure:

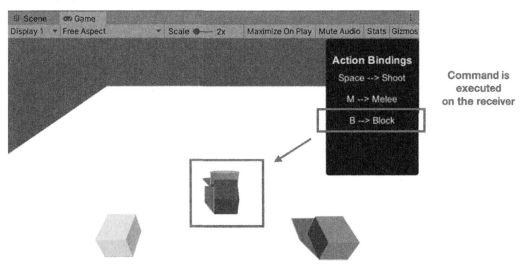

*Figure 8.6: Block command being executed on the player object*

You'll also see our debug tracking messages in the console every time you push one of the designated action keys, as shown in the following figure.

You'll want to collapse the console messages when you're testing so you don't get buried by the waterfall of logs.

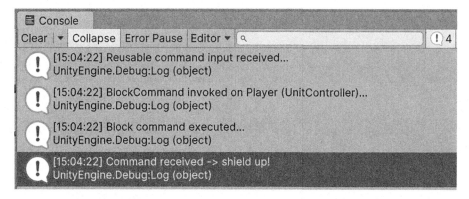

*Figure 8.7: Console output from a melee command being executed*

The console logs here are perhaps the most important learning tool with the Command pattern, so let's break down the sequence of events before moving on:

1.  First, input is received, and a reusable command is returned to the client

2.  The client passes the command and receiver to the invoker

3.  The command itself is executed, which calls the respective receiver method

4.  The receiver gets the call from the command and activates the command logic

For some added razzle-dazzle, update InputListener to match the following code or play around with your own key-command bindings to get a feel for the possibilities:

```
public class InputListener : MonoBehaviour
{
    public UIManager UI;

    private UnitController _unitController;
    private ReusableCommand _spacebar, _mKey, _bKey;

    void Start()
    {
        // 1
        _spacebar = new BlockCommand();
        _mKey = new ShootCommand();
        _bKey = new MeleeCommand();
```

```
        UI.AddKeyBinding("Space", _spacebar.ToString());
        UI.AddKeyBinding("M", _mKey.ToString());
        UI.AddKeyBinding("B", _bKey.ToString());

        _unitController = this.GetComponent<UnitController>();
    }

    public ReusableCommand GetActionCommands()
    {
        //… No changes needed …
    }
}
```

Here's the fun bit – switching around the command bindings in the InputListener doesn't break the client, as shown in the following image. In fact, it's one of the main reasons we put the client-invoker-input trifecta into place. Play the game again and use the new key bindings!

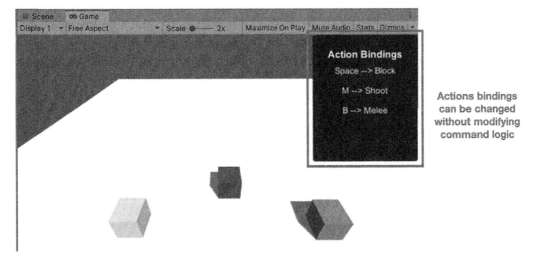

*Figure 8.8: Input commands being re-configured and shown in the UI*

For an even greater dose of awesome, while you're still in **Play Mode**, select the **Unit Manager** in the **Hierarchy**, change the **Unit Index** field to 1, and click back into the **Game View**. When you hit any of the key bindings, you'll see the newly selected unit perform the actions without any hiccups, as shown in the following figure with the Ally 1 object blocking.

Not only can we now switch action bindings, but we can also change receivers as well!

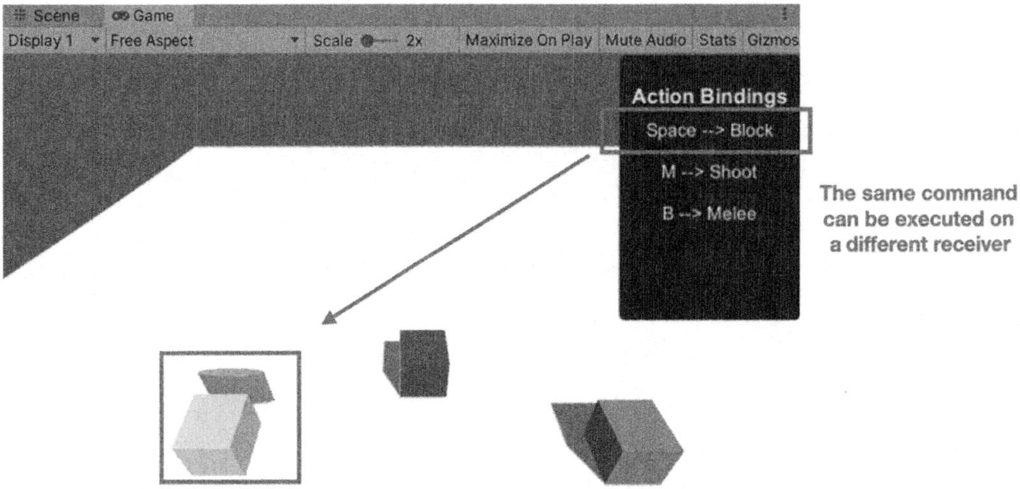

*Figure 8.9: Commands executing on a different receiver*

Now that we've covered reusable and interchangeable commands, it's time to build out a single-use command structure that can store state information and eventually be undone.

## Creating coupled commands

Before we dive into writing commands with state data, let's talk about why they're necessary. Our reusable commands seem wonderful so far (and well suited to their job), but imagine if you needed to be able to record a sequence of commands and either undo or redo them. Since each reusable command is just a wrapper for its Execute method, and we pass in a receiver *every* time we use it, the receiver and the command aren't bound together. Likewise, if we were to store some values inside the reusable commands, we'd be reusing those values because we'd be reusing the same command instance. You're seeing the problem, right? To undo a command, we need to know its state before the command is executed. To redo a command, we need to know its starting state.

For our example, we'll create a new abstract class for movement commands so we can store the unit's starting and ending positions every time it's moved. In the **Scripts** folder, create a new C# script named CoupledCommand and update its code to match the following code block. This new abstract command class needs a receiver when it's initialized as well as an Execute method. This ensures we know what receiver is performing the action so it can later be undone or redone:

I've created two different abstract classes to draw a big line in the sand between re-usable and single-use commands because it's an important distinction. This doesn't mean you have to – if you're feeling fancy, you can combine both Command types into a single abstract class with more abstract inheritance, virtual method overloading, and maybe even some generics. However, I've found that splitting up reusable and single-use commands is more declarative and makes the code clearer.

```
using System.Collections;
using System.Collections.Generic;
using UnityEngine;

// 1
public abstract class CoupledCommand
{
    // 2
    protected UnitController receiver;

    // 3
    public CoupledCommand(UnitController receiver)
    {
        this.receiver = receiver;
    }

    // 4
    public abstract void Execute();
}
```

Let's break down the code:

1. It declares a new abstract class called CoupledCommand.
2. It adds a protected Receiver variable to hold the constructor parameter
3. It adds a class constructor that takes a receiver parameter and stores it in the protected field.
4. It adds an abstract Execute method with no parameters since we always have a receiver.

Just like with our reusable commands, we need a concrete coupled command to do some work. Continuing the tactical RPG example, let's create a Move command that stores some state data so it can be undone and redone when stored in a movement sequence.

At the bottom of CoupledCommand.cs, but outside the abstract class declaration, add the code from the following code snippet. This new code declares a MoveCommand concrete class with private starting and ending position fields and requires a receiver and ending position as class construc-tor parameters. The idea is to store the unit's end position, bind the unit to its receiver during initialization, and cache its starting position when it executes the movement:

```
...

// 1
public class MoveCommand : CoupledCommand
{
    // 2
    private Vector3 _startingPos;
    private Vector3 _endingPos;

    // 3
    public MoveCommand(UnitController receiver, Direction direction) :
base(receiver)
    {
        this._endingPos = Utilities.TargetPosition(direction, receiver.
transform);
    }

    // 4
    public override void Execute()
    {
        // 5
        _startingPos = receiver.transform.position;
        receiver.Move(_endingPos);
    }
}
```

Let's break down the code:

1.  It declares a new MoveCommand class that inherits from CoupledCommand.

2.  It adds two private variables for storing the start and end positions of the unit being moved.

3.  It uses a class constructor to take the receiver and movement direction parameters and sets their values.

4.  It overrides the `CoupledCommand`'s abstract `Execute` method.

5.  It stores the unit's starting position and then moves the unit to its destination.

Now that each `Move` command oversees its own state, we can store moves as unique objects instead of interchangeable actions, as we did earlier with the reusable input commands. This will help us later with the undo/redo feature, but before we get to that, we need to update the `Invoker`. `cs` to match the following code. This new code adds a different overloaded `Execute` method that only takes in a command parameter, as all the other information it needs when triggered is in the command itself:

```
public class Invoker : MonoBehaviour
{
    public void Execute(ReusableCommand command, UnitController receiver)
    {
        Debug.Log($"{command.ToString()} invoked...");
        command.Execute(receiver);
    }

    // 1
    public void Execute(CoupledCommand command)
    {
        // /2
        Debug.Log($"{command.ToString()} invoked...");
        command.Execute();
    }
}
```

Let's break down the code:

1.  It declares a new `public` `Execute` method with a `CoupledCommand` parameter.

2.  It prints the command name to the console and triggers the command.

The next step is to update the `InputListener` to match the following code snippet, which we use to handle key presses for conventional WASD (up, left, back and right) movement and return a *new* `MoveCommand` instance each time one of those keys is pressed. We're also using a helper method I included in the starter project called `TargetDirection`, which returns a new `Vector3` based on the direction we want the unit to be moved.

This isn't the only way to implement your basic tactical RPG unit movement, but I think the code reads better this way:

```
using System.Collections;
using System.Collections.Generic;
using UnityEngine;

public class InputListener : MonoBehaviour
{
    //… No variable changes needed …

    void Start()
    {
        //… No changes needed …
    }

    // 1
    public CoupledCommand GetMoveComamands()
    {
        // 2
        if (Input.GetKeyDown(KeyCode.W))
        {
            return new MoveCommand(_unitController.unit, Direction.Up);
        }

        // 3
        if (Input.GetKeyDown(KeyCode.S))
        {
            return new MoveCommand(_unitController.unit, Direction.Down);
        }

        // 4
        if (Input.GetKeyDown(KeyCode.A))
        {
            return new MoveCommand(_unitController.unit, Direction.Left);
        }

        // 5
```

```
        if (Input.GetKeyDown(KeyCode.D))
        {
            return new MoveCommand(_unitController.unit, Direction.Right);
        }


        // 6
        return null;
    }

    public ReusableCommand GetActionCommands()
    {
        //... No changes needed ...
    }
}
```

Let's break down the code:

1.  It adds a new public method to return a CoupledCommand object based on input.

2.  It checks for *W* key presses and returns a new CoupledCommand instance using the Up direction.

3.  It checks for *S* key presses and returns a new CoupledCommand instance using the Down direction.

4.  It checks for *A* key presses and returns a new CoupledCommand instance using the Left direction.

5.  It checks for *D* key presses and returns a new CoupledCommand instance using the Right direction.

6.  It returns null if none of the WASD keys are being pressed.

Now that we can retrieve new instances of movement commands every time we hit the WASD keys, update Client.cs to match the following code to execute the commands using the invoker. This is the same implementation we used for the reusable commands, except we're calling GetMoveCommands instead of GetActionCommands and listening for the input responses:

```
public class Client : MonoBehaviour
{
    //... No variable changes ...

    void Awake()
```

```
    {
        //… No changes needed …
    }

    void Update()
    {
        var reusableCommand = _inputListener.GetActionCommands();
        if (reusableCommand != null)
        {
            Debug.Log("Reusable command input received...");
            _invoker.Execute(reusableCommand, unitManager.unit);
        }

        // 1
        var coupledCommand = _inputListener.GetMoveComamands();

        // 2
        if (coupledCommand != null)
        {
            Debug.Log("Coupled command input received...");

            // 3
            _invoker.Execute(coupledCommand);
        }
    }
}
```

Let's break down the code:

1.  It uses the GetMoveCommands method from the input listener and stores it in a local variable.

2.  It checks whether the coupled command is null, and if it isn't, it prints out a debug log.

3.  It passes the command to the invoker and uses the commands stored receiver to perform the action.

Play the game now and move the current unit anywhere you want, as shown with the Player unit being moved to the left of the arena in the following figure:

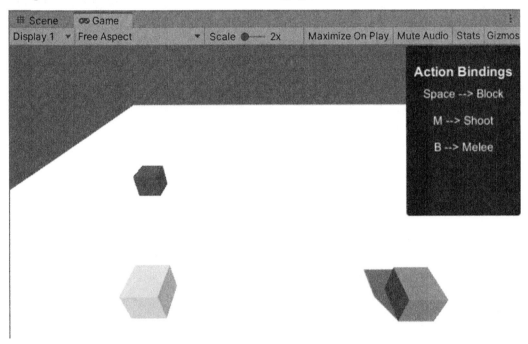

*Figure 8.10: Player being moved with coupled commands*

You can also change the selected unit by going to the **Unit Manager** in the **Hierarchy** and changing the Unit Index value to either 1 or 2, as shown in *Figure 8.11* with the Ally 1 unit moving to the right side of the arena.

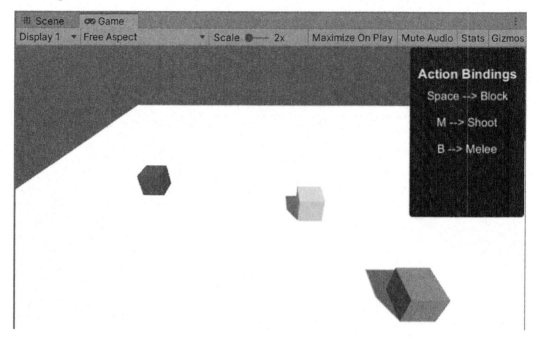

*Figure 8.11: Ally being moved with coupled commands*

The two key takeaways from our coupled command structure are (1) each move command stores its own state as a starting and ending position for movement, and (2) each movement command is a unique instance that's bound to the receiving unit it moves. I wonder what we could do with that…

I'll give you a hint – not all first decisions are the best, and your players deserve the benefit of the doubt (and the ability to undo their mistakes), which is what we'll cover in the next section.

## Implementing an undo/redo system

Now that we have unique movement commands, we can keep track of them as move sequences. This feature is ideal for letting players undo mistakes or redo past moves if they're undone in error, and it is common in strategy games and editor tools.

The undo/redo system we're going to build out in this section works with the Stack type, which is a C# collection type that follows the *Last-In-First-Out* rule, meaning the item on top of the stack is always the last one we added, like a deck of cards. This is perfect since we only want to undo or redo the most recent command in the player move sequence.

You might be asking yourself, "Why not just use the `List` type?" Well, you absolutely can, but it's messier. Lists work off indexes, which means you would have to manually keep track of the current move in the list of moves when you want to undo or redo that move. Further, having to increment and decrement your list index while you're working with command actions is just not efficient or ideal, especially when `Stacks` are built for this scenario.

## Stacking commands

We'll need a stack for storing our move sequence, so your first task is to update `Invoker.cs` to match the following code block. This new code adds a private empty `Stack` and a maximum move limit variable so players can't infinitely move around the game area. When we execute commands, we check whether the player has any moves left; if they do, we add the new command onto the commands stack. This way, we build our move sequence one command at a time when each one is triggered:

```
public class Invoker : MonoBehaviour
{
    // 1
    private Stack<CoupledCommand> _commands = new Stack<CoupledCommand>();

    // 2
    private int _maxMoves = 4;

    public void Execute(ReusableCommand command, UnitController receiver)
    {
        //... No changes needed ...
    }

    public void Execute(CoupledCommand command)
    {
        // 3
        if(_commands.Count < _maxMoves)
        {
            Debug.Log($"{command.ToString()} invoked...");

            // 4
            _commands.Push(command);
```

```
          command.Execute();
      }
      // 5
      else
      {
          Debug.Log("Out of moves...");
      }
    }
}
```

Let's break down the code:

1. It adds an empty `private` `Stack` of type `CoupledCommand`.
2. It adds a `private` integer to set an upper move limit for the player.
3. It checks whether the command stack count is less than the move limit.
4. It adds the new command to the move sequence using the `Push` method.
5. It prints a console message if the player is out of moves and doesn't execute the command.

Play the game now and you'll see that, once you're out of moves, the selected unit can't execute any more commands no matter what, as shown in the following screenshot:

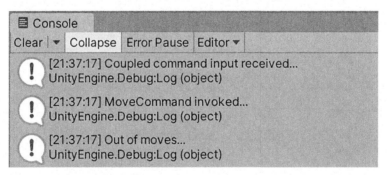

*Figure 8.12: Console output from a coupled move command being fired*

With a stack of commands to work with, we can get down to the business of undoing the last move action the player took!

# Adding an undo feature

Before we can reverse the move command, we need to update the abstract and concrete CoupledCommand classes we've already built. Open CoupledCommand.cs and update its code to match the following snippet, which adds an Undo method to the abstract class and overrides it in the concrete MoveCommand class:

```
public abstract class CoupledCommand
{
    protected UnitController receiver;

    public CoupledCommand(UnitController receiver)
    {
        this.receiver = receiver;
    }

    public abstract void Execute();

    // 1
    public abstract void Undo();
}

public class MoveCommand : CoupledCommand
{
    private Vector3 _startingPos;
    private Vector3 _endingPos;

    public MoveCommand(UnitController receiver, Vector3 endPos) :
base(receiver)
    {
        //… No changes needed …
    }

    public override void Execute()
    {
        //… No changes needed …
    }
```

```
// 2
public override void Undo()
{
    // 3
    receiver.Move(_startingPos);
}
}
```

Let's break down the code:

1.  It adds a `public` abstract Undo method to the `CoupledCommand` abstract class.
2.  It overrides the Undo method in the concrete `MoveCommand` class.
3.  It passes the move's starting position to the receiver to reverse the movement action.

Notice that the undo feature wouldn't be possible without the command knowing its own starting position, which is why we store state information in each coupled command and create new instances each time the player presses a movement key instead of reusing them.

To execute the undo command, update `Invoker.cs` to match the following snippet, which checks whether there are any commands to undo and grabs the most recent command off the stack using the Pop method:

```
...

// 1
public void Undo()
{
    if(_commands.Count > 0)
    {
        // 2
        var lastCommand = _commands.Pop();

        // 3
        lastCommand.Undo();
        Debug.Log("Command undone...");
    }
}
```

Let's break down the code:

1. It declares an Undo method and checks whether the number of commands is greater than 0.

2. It retrieves the last command off the stack using the Pop method.

3. It calls Undo on the most recent command and prints out a console message.

Update Client.cs to match the following code to expose the undo feature to our player. For simplicity, we're not using the input listener for this case because the invoker is already on the client, but you could restructure the code if you want to keep all the inputs together in one handler script:

```
...

void Update()
{
    //... No other changes needed ...

    // 1
    if(Input.GetKeyDown(KeyCode.U))
    {
        _invoker.Undo();
    }
}
```

Play the game, move as many times as you can, then hit the *U* key to undo the last move! You'll see the selected unit move back to its previous starting position and a console message appears, as shown in the following screenshot:

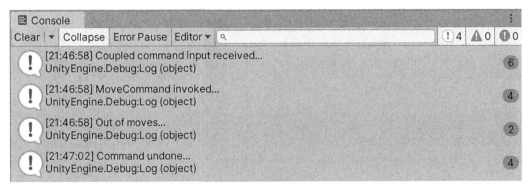

*Figure 8.13: Console output from coupled commands being executed and undone*

Common sense (and player morale) dictates that if moves can be undone, they should be able to be redone as well, which is your next task.

## Adding a redo feature

Redoing commands gets slightly trickier than undoing them because it requires us to manage not one, but two stacks – one for executed commands and one for redo-able commands. This might sound complicated, but we can break the whole process down into three steps:

1.  When a move is triggered, we're already putting it onto the command stack, but we also need to clear any stored moves that were previously undone.

2.  When a move is undone, we're going to remove it from the command stack and add it to the redo stack for easy access.

3.  When a move is redone, it will be added back to the command stack.

This way, we can create move sequences that can be undone or redone as many times as you want, provided there are moves in the command stack to work with. Update Invoker.cs to match the following code, which adds a new stack to track moves that have been undone and can be redone and adds a redo method to execute the last undone move and add it back to the command sequence:

```csharp
public class Invoker : MonoBehaviour
{
    private Stack<CoupledCommand> _commands = new Stack<CoupledCommand>();
    private int _maxMoves = 4;

    // 1
    private Stack<CoupledCommand> _redo = new Stack<CoupledCommand>();

    public void Execute(ReusableCommand command, UnitController receiver)
    {
        // ... No changes needed ...
    }

    public void Execute(CoupledCommand command)
    {
        if (_commands.Count < _maxMoves)
        {
            Debug.Log($"{command.ToString()} invoked...");
```

```
            _commands.Push(command);

            // 2
            _redo.Clear();

            newCommand.Execute();
        }
        else
        {
            Debug.Log("Out of moves…");
        }
    }


    public void Undo()
    {
        if (_commands.Count > 0)
        {
            var lastCommand = _commands.Pop();
            lastCommand.Undo();

            // 3
            _redo.Push(lastCommand);

            Debug.Log("Command undone...");
        }
    }

    // 4
    public void Redo()
    {
        if (_redo.Count > 0)
        {
            // 5
            var lastCommand = _redo.Pop();
            lastCommand.Execute();
```

```
            // 6
            _commands.Push(lastCommand);
            Debug.Log("Command redone...");
        }
    }
}
```

Let's break down the code:

1. It adds a new empty stack to store moves that have been undone.

2. It clears the redo stack whenever a new move command is executed.

3. It adds any commands to the redo stack when they are undone.

4. It declares a redo method and checks whether there are redo commands to work with.

5. It retrieves the most recently undone move and executes it.

6. It adds the redone move back to the command stack and prints a console message.

Add the code from the following snippet to the Update method in Client.cs to redo moves with the *R* key press, then play the game and give the new feature a try:

```
...

void Update()
{
    //... No other changes needed ...

    if(Input.GetKeyDown(KeyCode.U))
    {
        _invoker.Undo();
    }

    // 1
    if(Input.GetKeyDown(KeyCode.R))
    {
        _invoker.Redo();
    }
}
```

Now, you can undo and redo move commands whenever you want as long as you have moves left, as shown in the following screenshot:

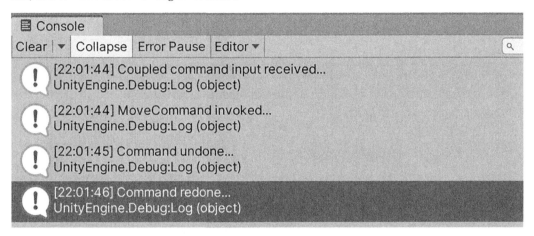

*Figure 8.14: Console output of coupled commands being executed, undone, and redone*

The final part of any undo/redo feature is committing your changes so you can continue with new command sequences, which is what you'll do in the next section.

## Confirming and clearing commands

The nice thing about using stacks is they have a host of methods that can help us manage the elements we're storing. When we commit a sequence of moves, we need to reset the command and redo stacks, so we have a clean slate for the next set of commands or another player's turn.

Update Invoker.cs to match the following snippet, which uses the Clear method to empty both stacks and print out a console message:

```
....

// 1
public void Confirm()
{
    _commands.Clear();
    _redo.Clear();

    Debug.Log("Moves confirmed!");
}
```

For the final time, modify the Update method in Client.cs to match the following code block, which listens for the *Return* key being pressed to commit the current move sequence and clear the command stacks:

```
...

void Update()
{
    //... No changes needed ...

    if(Input.GetKeyDown(KeyCode.U))
    {
        _invoker.Undo();
    }

    if(Input.GetKeyDown(KeyCode.R))
    {
        _invoker.Redo();
    }

    // 1
    if(Input.GetKeyDown(KeyCode.Return))
    {
        _invoker.Confirm();
    }
}
```

If you play the game now, you can still move the player and undo/redo a previous move. However, when you run out of moves now, hitting the *Return* key will confirm the current move sequence, create a clean slate for the invoker's movement tracking, and let you perform four more moves in a new sequence, as shown in the console messages in the following screenshot:

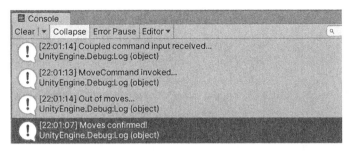

*Figure 8.15: Console output showing coupled commands being executed and confirmed*

### Callbacks and closures

The idea of encapsulating commands, or actions, into their own self-contained objects is often considered a workaround for languages that don't natively support closures. Closures are what's called "first-class functions," meaning you can treat them just like any other data type – you can assign them to a variable and pass them around like an object while still being able to trigger them like a method. A closure can also have "free variables," which aren't method parameters or local variables, but values that are bound *inside* the closure, almost like they're closed over (it's named that for a reason).

I'm bringing up closures at the end of this chapter because you might run into Command patterns in the wild that are fully implemented with closures, which are also referred to as callbacks. Instead of passing around command objects, these implementations will deal in closures by passing the execution methods as objects rather than the command itself.

In C#, closures are created using a combination of `delegate` and `event` types or `Actions` and can accomplish wonders in certain situations. However, I didn't include a complete solution using closures in this chapter because they add a lot of complexity and advanced syntax without a commensurate bump in efficiency. I might even argue that using closures in the Command pattern obscures rather than illuminates the purpose of the system.

However, in the spirit of completeness, I recommend looking at the C# documentation if you're interested in taking your C# syntax to the next level. You can find information on delegates here: `https://docs.microsoft.com/en-us/dotnet/csharp/programming-guide/delegates` and Actions here: `https://docs.microsoft.com/en-us/dotnet/api/system.action-1`.

With that last bit of code, our undo/redo system additions are all wrapped up. Since this functionality is paired so much with the Command pattern, it's a good idea to get comfortable with thinking about the action-tracking solutions that best fit your project!

## Summary

Phew! That was a lot to cover, but we made it through the Command pattern with flying colors! This one takes a little while to digest, especially if you've come across examples in the wild that didn't distinguish between reusable and coupled commands (i.e., commands with and without state information). However, knowing how to implement the pattern correctly for different scenarios is key not just to the Command pattern, but to all design patterns (as we progress through the book, you'll hear me bang on that over and over).

Remember, the Command pattern is useful when you want to create actions that are treated like objects. There are two types of commands, reusable and coupled: reusable commands are interchangeable actions that can work on any receiving object while coupled commands are unique actions that store state information and are bound to their receiving object. Commands can be stored or queued to be triggered later or in sequence and are perfectly suited to support undo and redo functionality.

In the next chapter, we'll explore the Observer pattern and how it can massively increase the efficiency of object communication and keep data in sync across entire projects without having to worry about incorrect (or outdated) information.

## Further reading

- Abstract classes can't be created on their own, but they are excellent solutions when you want a consistent base class blueprint that other classes can inherit from. Many of our solutions in this book rely heavily on abstract classes to provide an abstraction layer between class blueprints and their concrete implementations. You can find more information at https://learn.microsoft.com/en-us/dotnet/csharp/language-reference/keywords/abstract.

- Stacks are a last-in first-out collection of objects, which makes them ideal for storing and retrieving the most recent elements in any given set of data. If these are new to you, check out the documentation at https://learn.microsoft.com/en-us/dotnet/api/system.collections.stack?view=net-8.0.

# Join our community on Discord

Join our community's Discord space for discussions with the author and other readers:

https://packt.link/gamedevelopment_packt

# 9

# Decoupling Systems with the Observer Pattern

In the last chapter, we encapsulated actions into objects and implemented an undo/redo system using the Command pattern. In this chapter, we'll create an event handling system to separate the object sending information from the object, or objects, receiving that information. You've likely encountered the Observer pattern without even knowing it, as most languages use event systems under the hood to facilitate communication between objects. You shouldn't be starting from ground zero for the theory on this one (and even if you are, we'll get you on track in no time).

At its core, the Observer pattern is a syncing machine – when data changes in one object, you want to keep any objects relying on that information up to date. If you've ever wrestled with keeping data in tune with how it's displayed in a UI, you've already figured out the Observer pattern's most popular use case! This structure creates a one-to-many relationship between the subject sending out notifications and the list of observers listening for those notifications.

The nice part is that the object sending out the bat signal that some data has changed doesn't care who's listening, or even if there *is* anyone listening. The message gets sent out just the same and the listeners are responsible for keeping action (or not) on the information they receive.

We'll use this chapter to focus on the following topics:

- The pros and cons of the Observer design pattern
- Creating a basic Observer structure
- Pattern strategies and optimization
- Using native C# event types

- Using native Unity event types
- Upgrading to `ScriptableObject` events

By the end of the chapter, you'll have a great little notification system that can handle a variety of communication scenarios, customizations, and above all, different options for performance. Let's start with the starter project, then move on to the pattern breakdown and get into code of our own!

# Technical requirements

Before you start:

1. Download or clone the GitHub repository at `https://github.com/PacktPublishing/C-Design-Patterns-with-Unity-First-Edition`.

2. Open the **Ch_09_Starter** project folder in Unity Hub.

3. In **Assets | Scenes**, double-click on **SampleScene**.

The project for this chapter is a bare-bones infinite runner where your job is to move the player left and right to avoid the randomly generated objects being thrown at you (red for enemies, green for health). The UI panel in the upper left of the screen will eventually keep track of how good (or bad) you are at this game of white-boxed dodgeball, but for now, it's keeping you at a steady 10 health.

As for the scripts:

- `BasePrefab.cs` is attached to both the `Target` and `Health` prefabs to move them forward when they are instantiated and destroy them when they hit the boundary collider behind the player.
- `Player.cs` is attached to the `Player` GameObject in the **Hierarchy** and handles horizontal movement, player health, and collision logic.
- `Spawner.cs` is attached to the `Spawner` GameObject in the **Hierarchy** and handles the random creation of either enemy or health objects.
- `TrophyManager.cs` is attached to the `Managers` GameObject in the **Hierarchy** and will eventually hold our notification code for specific achievements.
- `UIManager.cs` is attached to the `Managers` GameObject in the **Hierarchy** and is only concerned with showing the real-time health of the player.

We'll also be using some Unity and C# language features to take our code the extra mile. Don't worry if you're not familiar with these as I've included links for the basics, and I'll explain how they apply to our use cases as we go:

- Abstract classes (`https://learn.microsoft.com/en-us/dotnet/csharp/language-reference/keywords/abstract`)

- Interfaces (`https://learn.microsoft.com/en-us/dotnet/csharp/fundamentals/types/interfaces`)

- Delegates (`https://learn.microsoft.com/en-us/dotnet/csharp/programming-guide/delegates/`)

- Events (`https://learn.microsoft.com/en-us/dotnet/csharp/programming-guide/events/`)

- Actions (`https://learn.microsoft.com/en-us/dotnet/api/system.action-1?view=net-8.0`)

- UnityEvents (`https://docs.unity3d.com/Manual/UnityEvents.html`)

- ScriptableObjects (`https://docs.unity3d.com/Manual/class-ScriptableObject.html`)

Our job is to create a decentralized notifications system that lets decoupled objects know about the key events that a primary subject is sending out, but first, we need to understand a little more about what the Observer pattern is and what it can do for us.

# Breaking down the Observer pattern

As part of the behavioral family of design patterns, the Observer pattern is all about communication between objects while keeping the objects sending information decoupled from the receiving objects. The Observer pattern lets you notify any listeners of specific state changes (changing values) or events (the player enters a battle) without tightly coupled references between those objects. I'm sure you can think of at least five situations where this would be an awesome boost to your code, but the Observer pattern is most useful when:

- You have an object that needs to broadcast information or changes to a variety of other objects.

- You have an object with a changing state and don't know how many other objects need to stay up to date.

- You want to avoid tight coupling between objects that share a dependency.

I like to think of this as a downstream operation, with the start of a river branching off into multiple tributaries, streams, and rivulets as gravity pulls its water toward the ocean, as shown in the following figure:

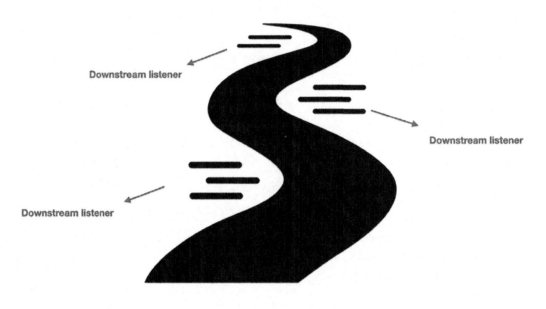

**1. The subject is upstream, broadcasting changes down it's chain of offshoots**

Downstream listener

Downstream listener

Downstream listener

**2. Listeners are paying attention to the changes and reacting**

*Figure 9.1: Example of downstream notification systems*

Subjects hold the data we want to broadcast, and listeners are *listening* for any changes so they can act accordingly. The subject isn't in charge of anything other than signaling that a change has occurred; it's up to the listeners to decide what to do with that information on their own. This moves the information downhill from the subject to any and all listeners, leaving them aware of each other without being shackled to anything or anyone upstream!

Let's take a common scenario in life – waiting for a product that's currently unavailable. Imagine there's a book you've been waiting to buy but it's always sold out. In this example, the subject is the bookstore or online marketplace that sells the book and you're the listener. Most sellers have a way for you to watch or "wishlist" an item that registers you for notifications about the item you want. When new copies of the book come in, you get a text or email, but it's up to you to decide what to do – buy, wait, ask Santa, and so on, as shown here:

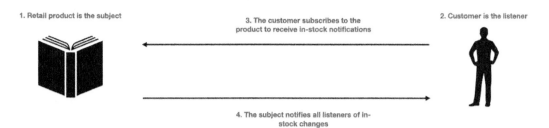

*Figure 9.2: Customer wish list example of subjects and listeners*

The important piece of this relationship is how independent you and the bookstore/online retailer are; there's nothing that says you *must* do something specific when you receive the notification. They can't *make* you buy a product if you don't want to (at least, I don't think they can). The only thing that's guaranteed is that the subject sends out the notifications and you receive it. The great thing is that a book can have an open-ended number of people subscribed for notifications and a customer can be listening for updates on as many books as they want.

In an application or gaming scenario, you may want to notify different UI scripts of value changes so the display is synced with the data or sends out notifications when a player is hit or an enemy is destroyed. Whatever the case, having a distributed system with components that aren't coupled together makes your job much easier. However, we do need to pay attention to the most efficient implementations and performance optimizations in Unity and C#, which we'll build out during this chapter.

## Diagramming the pattern

*Figure 9.3* shows the UML structure of the Observer pattern with its four components:

- The **abstract subject** keeps track of all its observers and provides methods for adding and removing those observing objects.

- A **concrete subject** stores state information and notifies all observers whenever the subject's state changes.

- The **abstract observer** has a single method for receiving and handling state changes sent from a subject.

- The **concrete observer** keeps its own state in sync with the subject it's observing and may sometimes store a reference to the subject.

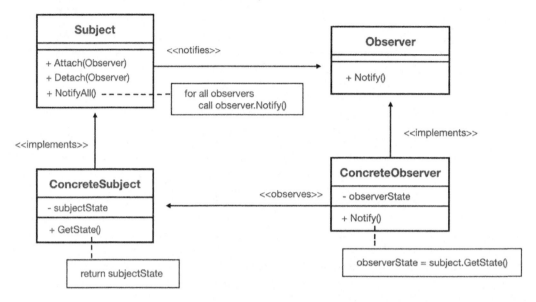

*Figure 9.3: UML diagram of the State pattern components*

The one-to-many relationship between a subject and its observers decouples the sending object from the receiver, or receivers, which creates a clear separation of responsibility for both sides of the system while ensuring that state information is consistent between related and interested objects.

## Pros and cons

Like all design patterns, there are pros and cons. Let's start with the benefits of the Observer pattern:

- **One-to-many relationships** between a subject and its list of observers allow you to create an efficient notification system while keeping the actions of each component separate and independent.

- **Light coupling** between subjects and observers is a key component of the pattern. Subjects only need a list of observers instead of specific information on the observer objects themselves, so both parts can exist in different layers or systems of your code.

  Decoupling subjects and observers also makes the components more **reusable**.

- **Automatic broadcasting** between subjects and their observers allows you to add and remove as *many* observers as you want *anytime* you want.

However, be careful of the following pitfalls when using the pattern in your projects:

- **Unexpected changes** can cascade down a subject's list of observers if the observers are not aware of what exactly is changing. These can be hard to track down in a distributed system like the Observer pattern, but they can be fixed by passing information to the observers about which changes are taking place, which we'll implement later in the chapter.

- **Notification order** can be tricky with this pattern because it's so decoupled. Traditionally, there's no centralized hub for the subject notifications to pass through, so controlling when and in what order they are executed isn't possible. However, the Event Queue pattern addresses this problem, which we'll cover in *Chapter 18*.

- **Memory leaks and ghost objects** are a problem because each subject holds a list of strong references to their observers. When an observer is destroyed, it needs to be removed from the subject to free up the computing resources and avoid null references. It's also a good idea to let observers know whether their subject has been destroyed so they can stop expecting notifications.

Now that we've covered the structure, benefits, and limitations of the Observer pattern, we can start laying out our basic Observer pattern structure in the next section.

## Creating a basic Observer structure

Imagine you're building an infinite runner game like Temple Run or a classic Sonic the Hedgehog entry. You can move the playable character left or right within the bounds of the track to dodge incoming enemies or collect health pickups. As we follow along, we'll be implementing the traditional version of the Observer pattern to track and sync the player's health with the UI. In the latter sections, we'll use native C# events to build a more streamlined Observer structure to handle a simplified trophy system to keep track of the different achievements we've managed to unlock.

## Writing the abstract base objects

In the **Scripts** folder, create two new C# scripts named IObserver and Subject, respectively. It's important to create these two scripts before writing any code because the classes rely on each other in their implementations (and it's hard to lay out a sequential teaching structure when this happens, believe me).

Update `IObserver.cs` to match the following code block, which declares a common interface that all our observing objects will share with a method that subjects can use to notify the observer of any state changes. Notice the `NotifiedBy` method includes a parameter so the subject is passed to the observer, allowing the observer to keep any state information in sync:

```
using System.Collections;
using System.Collections.Generic;
using UnityEngine;

// 1
public interface IObserver
{
    // 2
    void NotifiedBy(Subject subject);
}
```

Let's break down the code:

1.  It declares a `public` `IObserver` interface.

2.  It adds a `public` method for receiving notifications along with the sending subject.

Now that we have an observer interface, we need an abstract subject class that can be inherited by any `MonoBehaviour`. Update `Subject.cs` to match the code following block, which keeps a list of all observing objects, `public` methods for adding and removing observers, and most importantly, a method to notify all those observers in bulk whenever the subject's state changes.

 Notice the subject gets passed to each observer when notified so the observer can grab the latest state directly from the source. We mentioned this earlier in the chapter, but it's important to understand the light coupling between subject and observer, as they are aware of and reference each other.

```
using System.Collections;
using System.Collections.Generic;
using UnityEngine;

// 1
public abstract class Subject : MonoBehaviour
{
```

```
// 2
private List<IObserver> _observers = new List<IObserver>();

// 3
public void AddObserver(IObserver observer)
{
    _observers.Add(observer);
}

// 4
public void RemoveObserver(IObserver observer)
{
    _observers.Remove(observer);
}

// 5
public void NotifyAll()
{
    foreach(var observer in _observers)
    {
        observer.NotifiedBy(this);
    }
}
}
```

Let's break down the code:

1.  It declares an abstract subject class that inherits from MonoBehaviour.
2.  It adds a private list to keep track of all registered observers.
3.  It adds a public method with an IObserver parameter to add new observers to the list.
4.  It adds a public method with an IObserver parameter to remove existing observers from the list.
5.  It adds a public method that loops through all observers and notifies them of state changes.

With the interface and abstract class finished, your next task is to turn the Player script into a subject and the UIManager into one of its observers to track and display your player's health.

# Making the UI an observer

Our first try at implementing the Observer pattern is the simplest – updating the UIManager.cs script to implement the IObserver interface and declaring the NotifiedBy method. This approach is relatively lightweight in terms of added code, but it allows any observer to make decisions about what to do with a subject's state change. Since the Observer pattern is designed to work with a one-to-many relationship between a single subject and multiple observers, it makes sense to store the subject the first time the observer is notified. We'll talk about using the subject reference in the *Cleaning up hanging resources* section when observers are disabled or destroyed, but for now, let's focus on the basics.

Update UIManager.cs to match the following snippet, which replaces the Start method health initialization with the observer interface NotifiedBy method:

```csharp
// 1
public class UIManager : MonoBehaviour, IObserver
{
    public Text health;

    // 2
    private Player _subject;

    // 3
    public void NotifiedBy(Subject subject)
    {
        // 4
        if(!_subject)
        {
            _subject = subject.GetComponent<Player>();
        }

        // 5
        health.text = $"Health: {_subject.health}";
    }
}
```

Let's break down the code:

1.  It updates the UIManager class to implement the IObserver interface.

2. It adds a private variable to store the subject.

3. It declares the NotifiedBy method from the IObserver interface.

4. It checks whether the subject has already been saved, and if it hasn't, then it's saved.

5. It sets the health text in the UI to the subject's current health value.

 The GetComponent call may be a red flag for some developers out there looking at this code. Performance-wise, it's not going to make a dent here, especially since we're only calling it on the first notification, but you're always free to optimize the pattern in your own projects.

Our first observer is fully configured, but we still need to tackle the subject implementation and the sending out of the actual notification events when the player's health changes, which you'll do in the next section.

## Subscribing observers and publishing events

Turning any MonoBehaviour into a subject is almost as easy as creating observers. Update Player. cs to match the following code, which updates the class inheritance, notifies any observers when the player's health changes, and registers observers when the object is enabled in the scene:

```csharp
// 1
public class Player : Subject
{
    public UIManager uiManager;
    public int Health
    {
        get { return _health; }
        set
        {
            _health = value;

            // 2
            NotifyAll();
        }
    }

    //... No other variable changes needed ...
```

```
// 3
void OnEnable()
{
    AddObserver(uiManager);
}

//... No other method changes needed ...
}
```

Let's break down the code:

1.  It updates Player to subclass from the abstract Subject class, which is a MonoBehaviour.

2.  It calls NotifyAll whenever the health value changes.

3.  It declares the OnEnable method and adds the UIManager as an observer.

Adding observers in the OnEnable method may set off some scalability alarm bells in your head, but it's a small price to pay for the benefits of the Observer pattern. You can always fine-tune this part of the pattern to fit your needs as projects become more complex.

Play the game and test out the subject-to-observer relationship. Whenever you get hit by a target, the Player sends out a signal whenever the player is damaged and the UIManager takes care of updating the display, as shown in the following screenshot:

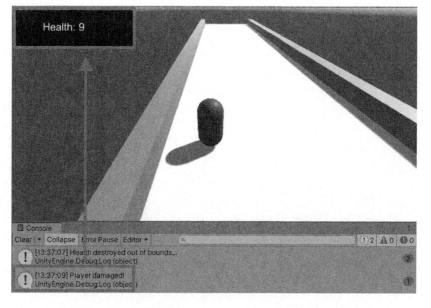

*Figure 9.4: Player damage is synced with the UI text display*

While you probably have several use cases in your own projects for the code we've just written, don't rush off and implement it just yet! There are a few caveats we haven't talked about yet, namely, how to choose the information you send along with the notification, listening for specific events, and safeguarding against memory leaks and ghost objects when subjects and observers are destroyed, all of which are covered in the next section.

# Pattern strategies and optimizations

If you decide the original Observer pattern is right for a portion, or the entirety, of your project, you'll need more clarity in three key areas:

- Choosing the kind of information the subject sends to observers, which is commonly referred to as the communication strategy
- Specifying different events that subjects can send out and choosing which events your observers listen for and act on
- Managing object references and memory leaks when subjects or observers are destroyed or disabled

While I've marked this section as pattern variations and optimizations, incorporating these three topics into your design pattern code is mandatory if you want an efficient, scalable, and safe project.

 I can't stress this enough, especially the object cleanup; ghost objects and memory leaks are no joke and are extremely hard to debug in the decoupled subject-listener structure.

# Choosing a communication strategy

There is a spectrum of communication strategies that apply to the Observer pattern, but the extreme ends are simple – push or pull. The hard part is identifying the perfect sweet spot for your project because there's no *right* or *canon* answer to this question:

- The **push** strategy is just like it sounds – the subject is responsible for pushing any additional data to the observer, but this can get complicated if a lot of information is passed without being used. Your first instinct might be to create different data parameters for each type of observer, but this significantly decreases the usefulness of the Observer pattern because it increases the coupling between the subject and observer objects.

- The **pull** strategy is the opposite – observers are in charge of grabbing whatever data they need from the subject once they are notified of a change. This scenario is completely decoupled, but it requires additional steps before the observer can execute any actions related to the subject's notification.

Again, the strategy you use is up to you and your project. It can be a lot of push, a little pulling, or a mix of the two, but we're going to use the push strategy in the next section because it's the easiest to set up and manage for a simple project like ours.

## Listening for different state changes

A subject that can only send out one notification has limited usefulness; a subject that can choose from a list of notifications for different events is not only useful, but it also lets each observer decide which notifications to pay attention to while executing different actions.

Update `IObserver.cs` to match the following code, which adds an event name parameter to the `NotifiedBy` method, which can be filled in by the subject depending on the notification being sent:

```
public interface IObserver
{
    // 1
    void NotifiedBy(Subject subject, string eventName);
}
```

This update is going to break our existing code but it's an easy fix; just update `Subject.cs` to match the following snippet before playing the game again. This new code adds an event name parameter to the `NotifyAll` method and passes the event name to each observer. Now, the subject can specify which event is being fired, coupled with each observer being able to check and react to specific notifications:

```
public abstract class Subject : MonoBehaviour
{
    //... No other changes needed ...

    // 1
    public void NotifyAll(string eventName)
    {
        foreach(var observer in _observers)
        {
            // 2
            observer.NotifiedBy(this, eventName);
```

```
        }
    }
}
```

Let's break down the updated code:

1. It adds a `string` event name parameter to the `NotifyAll` method.

2. It passes the event name parameter to each observer through the `NotifiedBy` method.

Your next task is to differentiate events in the concrete subject and observer classes, meaning what gets done when and how. Update `Player.cs` to match the following code, which adds an event name to the existing event when the player is damaged and fires off a completely new event when the player's health drops to 0:

```
public class Player : Subject
{
    public UIManager uiManager;
    public int Health
    {
        get { return _health; }
        set
        {
            // 1
            if(value == 0)
            {
                NotifyAll("PlayerKO");
            }
            // 2
            else if(value <= 10)
            {
                _health = value;
                NotifyAll("HealthUpdated");
            }
            // 3
            else
            {
                Debug.Log("Health already full!");
            }
        }
```

```
    }


    //... No other changes needed ...
}
```

Let's break down the code:

1.  It checks the health value, and if it's less than 0, a new `PlayerKO` notification is sent out.
2.  It checks the health value, and if it's less than or equal to 10, a new `HealthUpdated` notification is sent out.
3.  If the health is already full, it doesn't send out an event.

Now that the subject is sending out two different notifications, the UI needs to process them differently. Update `UIManager.cs` to match the following code block, which updates the `NotifiedBy` method to accept the event name parameter and uses a `switch` statement to perform different actions based on the event being received:

 I'm using Unity's `SceneManagement` API to restart the current scene, but if you're not familiar with scene management, take a look at the documentation at `https://docs.unity3d.com/ScriptReference/SceneManagement.SceneManager.html`.

```
public class UIManager : MonoBehaviour, IObserver
{
    public Text health;
    public Text score;

    private Player _subject;

    // 1
    public void NotifiedBy(Subject subject, string eventName)
    {
        if(!_subject)
        {
            _subject = subject.GetComponent<Player>();
        }
```

```
// 2
switch(eventName)
{
    // 3
    case "HealthUpdated":
        health.text = $"Health: {_subject.Health}";
        break;
    // 4
    case "PlayerKO":
        var scene = SceneManager.GetActiveScene().buildIndex;
        SceneManager.LoadScene(scene);
    Debug.Log("Level restarted...");
        break;
}
    }
}
```

Let's break down the code:

1.  It updates the NotifiedBy method to take in the event name parameter from the IObserver interface.

2.  It adds a switch statement based on the event name received from the subject.

3.  It moves the player-damaged code into a new case.

4.  It adds a new case for the player KO event and reloads the current scene.

> Specifying which event is being sent out to observers is also useful when you have several observers on the same subject – each observer can listen to the events they care about and ignore all the others. However, your code can quickly get messy with this type of control flow, especially in a monster switch statement. If your subject is sending out a variety of notifications, the delegate and event structure in the *Using C# event types* section is easier to manage.

Run the game again and purposefully get hit by the red targets until your health drops to 0 and you'll see the game restart. If you collect any green orbs, you'll see the health value still increases but only up to a maximum of 10, meaning the UI manager is handling multiple notifications, as shown in the following screenshot:

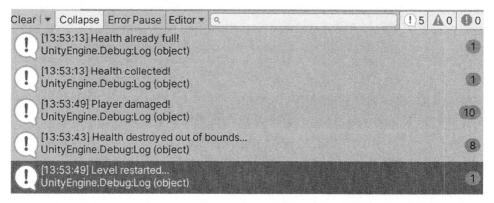

*Figure 9.5: Debug logs showing multiple events being received and different logic execution*

Your final task for this section is to make sure no hanging references or memory leaks occur when a subject or observer is disabled or destroyed in the scene, which we'll cover next.

## Cleaning up hanging resources

The main problem with coupling components together is they rely on each other, and when objects rely on each other, there's always a risk of interdependency and brittleness. In our case, any class implementing the IObserver interface expects to receive event notifications, and every Subject subclass expects its observers to exist anytime it calls NotifyAll. But what happens when a subject or observer is destroyed or disabled?

Since the Subject subclass is the top of the waterfall, all we need to do is send out a final notification when it's destroyed – that way any observer can decide on their next steps individually.

 The scenario described previously is called the lapsed-listener problem, which is super common when objects are dependently coupled together in a notification system. You can read more about the lapsed-listener problem at https://en.wikipedia.org/wiki/Lapsed_listener_problem.

Update Subject.cs script to match the following snippet, which declares the OnDisable method and sends out a final message when it's fired:

```
public abstract class Subject : MonoBehaviour
```

```
{
    //... No other changes needed ...

    // 1
    void OnDisable()
    {
        NotifyAll("SubjectDestroyed");
    }
}
```

The next step is handling things from the observer's perspective, which requires two steps:

1. Handle the "SubjectDestroyed" event that our Subject classes can now broadcast.
2. They remove themselves from the subjects list of observers when they are destroyed or disabled.

Update UIManager.cs to match the following code, which adds a new case statement to NotifyAll and unsubscribes itself as an observer from the subject in OnDisable:

```
public class UIManager : MonoBehaviour, IObserver
{
    public Text health;
    public Text score;

    private Player _subject;

    public void NotifiedBy(Subject subject, string eventName)
    {
        if (!_subject)
        {
            _subject = subject.GetComponent<Player>();
        }

        switch (eventName)
        {
            case "PlayerDamaged":
                health.text = $"Health: {_subject.Health}";
                break;
            case "PlayerKO":
                var scene = SceneManager.GetActiveScene().buildIndex;
```

```
                SceneManager.LoadScene(scene);
                break;
        // 1
        case "SubjectDestroyed":
            Debug.Log("Subject has been destroyed...");
            break;


    }
}


// 2
void OnDisable()
{
    // 3
    if(_subject)
    {
        _subject.RemoveObserver(this);
        Debug.Log("Observer removed from subject...");
    }
}
}
```

Let's break down the code:

1.  It adds a new event case for when the subject is destroyed.

2.  It adds the OnDisable method.

3.  It checks whether there is a stored subject – if there is, remove this observer when it's disabled or destroyed.

Whenever a subject is destroyed, every observer can decide what it wants to do with that information. Likewise, when an observer is destroyed, it updates the subject's observer list, removing any chance that an event notification will be sent out to a nonexistent object. Not only does this make our Observer pattern implementation more thorough, but it'll also save you hours of headaches while trying to chase down ghost objects in your system.

To test the new code, run the game:

1. Get hit by either an enemy or collect a green orb while the player has less than 10 health.

2. Disable the Managers GameObject in the **Hierarchy** and the Player.cs script on the Player object.

3. Look at the debug logs as shown in the following screenshot:

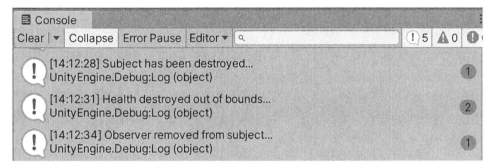

*Figure 9.6: Debug logs showing subject and observers being decoupled when they are disabled*

You won't get a connection between subject and observer with full health because we're not sending any notifications for that scenario. You'll also see the decoupling debug logs when you stop running the game, as the objects are disabled then as well. If you're not seeing both debug logs when you stop running the game, it's due to how Unity is disabling the objects, not your code.

In the next section, we'll dive into C# types that natively support the Observer pattern and consider different scenarios where these types are more useful and efficient than the traditional system we've already written.

# Using C# event types

Before we dive into this section, let's remember that the *Gang of Four* text covered the original Observer pattern in 1994. Many languages back then didn't have built-in events, closures, or systems to easily decouple components. This left programmers to figure out efficient and scalable solutions on their own, with the Observer pattern coming out on top. This doesn't mean the original Observer pattern structure should be thrown out if your language has these built-in tools, which C# and Unity both have.

The original pattern is still very useful for a one-to-many relationship between subject and observers (the waterfall analogy where you want observers to know everything happening downstream), but there are many common scenarios where that's not enough, where observers may need to observe more than one subject at a time (we'll call this the buffet scenario). In those many-to-many cases, we're lucky enough to have the option of moving to native C# objects like events and Actions, which is the smart play, while the UnityEvent type plays better in the Unity **Inspector**.

## Delegates and events

In C#, the delegate type allows you to assign an entire method (with parameters, if it has any) to a variable, which in turn lets you pass the method to other methods or simply call the method programmatically. When paired with the event type, you have a built-in publisher-subscriber model ready to go, which is perfect for the Observer pattern; the subject is the publisher, and the observer is the subscribers. Not only that, but subscribers can also listen for as many events as they want. Unlike the waterfall model, events and delegates create a more buffet-style scenario, which is a more efficient solution when you want a more distributed Observer pattern implementation.

> Delegates and events are broad subjects on their own, so we won't cover the details here. If you're not as comfortable with these topics as you want to be, you can find great resources in the Microsoft documentation at https://learn.microsoft.com/en-us/dotnet/csharp/programming-guide/delegates and https://learn.microsoft.com/en-us/dotnet/csharp/programming-guide/events.

For example, our health and enemy objects both get destroyed when they hit the boundary collider behind the player. This is a perfect place for a trophy or achievement system to take notice. Update BasePrefab.cs to match the following code, which adds a delegate type for when health objects are destroyed and an event to broadcast when the delegate is called. You'll notice the event is marked as static, which makes it easier to reference from other scripts without needing to retrieve or store an instance of the publishing class:

> We're going to use static events in our example, which may set off red flags for you depending on your experience with globally accessible fields and methods. Like Singletons, there's a time and place for static data and events are one of them (not only because subscribing and unsubscribing is efficient, but also because the Unity documentation structures code this way with events). If you'd like to put up more defenses against unauthorized scripts referencing your static events, you can absolutely do that, but we're going to stick with static events for the rest of the chapter.

```
using System.Collections;
using System.Collections.Generic;
using UnityEngine;

// 1
using System;

public class BasePrefab : MonoBehaviour
{
    public float moveSpeed;

    // 2
    public delegate void HealthDestroyed();

    // 3
    public static event HealthDestroyed OnHealthDestroyed;

    void Awake()
    {
        //… No changes needed …
    }

    void OnCollisionEnter(Collision collision)
    {
        if (collision.gameObject.tag == "Boundary")
        {
            // 4
            if(gameObject.tag == "Health")
            {
                OnHealthDestroyed?.Invoke();
            }

            Debug.Log($"{gameObject.tag} destroyed out of bounds...");
            Destroy(this.gameObject);
        }
    }
}
```

Let's break down the code:

1.  It adds the System using directive for access to delegate and event types.

2.  It declares a delegate with a void return type signature.

3.  It declares a static event of type HealthDestroyed.

4.  It checks whether the base prefab is a health pickup, and if it is, the event is raised.

 We use the ? character before we Invoke the event to check that the delegate isn't empty (or null). This prevents our code from throwing a null reference error when an empty delegate is called.

Now, when a health item hits the boundary collider and gets destroyed, our event sends out a notification to anyone who's listening! It's also important to understand that using delegates and events makes it much easier to manage multiple subjects sending out notifications as well as observers listening for multiple subjects (buffet-style more than waterfall).

Since the trophy manager script isn't subscribed yet, we need to subscribe and handle each destroyed health object as needed. Update TrophyManager.cs to match the following code, which subscribes to our new event using the += syntax, stores a counter for how many times a health item has been destroyed, and unlocks an achievement when the player has missed three times. We're also unsubscribing from the event using the -= syntax after the achievement is unlocked because the trophy wouldn't be meaningful if it kept showing up, but you'll also see events be unsubscribed in the OnDisable method (so, we've done both to cover our bases and prevent our own ghost objects from haunting our code):

```
public class TrophyManager : MonoBehaviour
{
    // 1
    public int HealthMissed = 0;

    // 2
    void OnEnable()
    {
        BasePrefab.OnHealthDestroyed += HealthDestroyed;
    }

    // 3
    void HealthDestroyed()
```

```
    {
        HealthMissed++;

        // 4
        if(HealthMissed == 3)
        {
            Debug.Log("Achievement unlocked: Living on the edge!");
            BasePrefab.OnHealthDestroyed -= HealthDestroyed;
        }

        // 5
        void OnDisable()
        {
            BasePrefab.OnHealthDestroyed -= HealthDestroyed;
        }
    }
}
```

Let's break down the code:

1. It adds a counter variable to keep track of how many health objects have been destroyed.

2. It declares the OnEnable method and subscribes to the OnHealthDestroyed event.

3. It declares a method matching the OnHealthDestroyed delegate type to handle the event logic.

4. It checks whether three health objects have been missed – if so, prints a debug log and unsubscribes from the event.

5. It unsubscribes from the OnHealthDestroyed event in the OnDisable method to avoid ghost objects.

Run the game and miss three health orbs coming your way and you'll see the achievement debug logs shown in the following screenshot:

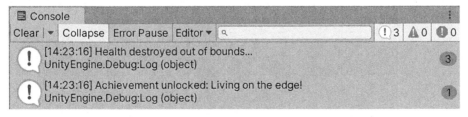

*Figure 9.7: Debug logs after delegate and event are invoked*

**Passing custom data**

You can push data from subject to observers through a `delegate` by specifying a parameter type (or multiple parameter types) in the declaration:

```
public delegate void HealthDestroyed(int health);
public static event HealthDestroyed OnHealthDestroyed;
```

With the updated `delegate`, you'll need to pass in a valid parameter when you invoke the event:

```
if(gameObject.tag == "Health")
{
    OnHealthDestroyed?.Invoke(5);
}
```

Finally, the subscribing method needs to match the new delegate signature when receiving the notification:

```
void HealthDestroyed(int health) {}
```

You may not need anything more complicated than this in your own code, but if you want to efficiently pass more complex event data, C# has an `EventHandler` type built just for this situation. You can find the documentation at `https://learn.microsoft.com/en-us/dotnet/api/system.eventhandler`.

While delegates and event types work just fine, C# has a ready-made type called `Action` that conveniently bundles a `delegate` and `event` into a nice little container, which we'll look at in the next section.

# Updating to Action types

`Action` types are a `delegate` and event package with a `void` return type; there's just less code involved in the declaration. Calling, subscribing, and unsubscribing from an `Action` uses the same exact syntax we've already learned.

> We could have just gone straight to `Action` types, but I've found it's more useful to understand the basics of a system before diving into more complex implementations – even if the complex syntax ends up being the one you go with. You can read more about `Action`s at `https://learn.microsoft.com/en-us/dotnet/api/system.action`.

Update `BasePrefab.cs` to match the following snippet, which adds an `Action` type and invokes it whenever an enemy hits the boundary and is destroyed:

```
using System;

public class BasePrefab : MonoBehaviour
{
    public float moveSpeed;

    public delegate void HealthDestroyed();
    public static event HealthDestroyed OnHealthDestroyed;

    // 1
    public static event Action OnEnemyDestroyed;

    void Awake()
    {
        //… No changes needed …
    }
```

```
void OnCollisionEnter(Collision collision)
{
    if (collision.gameObject.tag == "Boundary")
    {
        if(gameObject.tag == "Health")
        {
            OnHealthDestroyed?.Invoke();
        }
        // 2
        else
        {
            OnEnemyDestroyed?.Invoke();
        }

        Debug.Log($"{gameObject.tag} destroyed out of bounds...");
        Destroy(this.gameObject);
    }
}
```

Let's break down the new code:

1.  It adds a static event of type Action named OnEnemyDestroyed.

2.  It invokes the Action when an enemy object hits the boundary collider in the scene.

Just like any event, we need to subscribe any scripts that are listening for the notification. Update TrophyManager.cs to match the following code block, which subscribes to the new event in OnEnable and executes trophy logic in a new method with a matching signature:

```
public class TrophyManager : MonoBehaviour
{
    public int HealthMissed = 0;

    void OnEnable()
    {
        BasePrefab.OnHealthDestroyed += HealthDestroyed;
```

```
        // 1
        BasePrefab.OnEnemyDestroyed += EnemyDestroyed;
    }

    void HealthDestroyed()
    {
        //… No changes needed …
    }

    // 2
    void EnemyDestroyed()
    {
        // 3
        Debug.Log("Achievement unlocked: Close encounters!");
        BasePrefab.OnEnemyDestroyed -= EnemyDestroyed;
    }

        void OnDisable()
        {
            BasePrefab.OnHealthDestroyed -= HealthDestroyed;

            // 4
            BasePrefab.OnEnemyDestroyed -= EnemyDestroyed;
        }
}
```

Let's break down the code:

1. It subscribes to the OnEnemyDestroyed event when the script is enabled.

2. It declares a new method with a matching signature to fire when the event is received.

3. It debugs a trophy message and unsubscribes from the event after it fires once.

4. It unsubscribes from the OnEnemyDestroyed event when the script is disabled.

The following screenshot shows the new achievement firing when the first enemy is successfully dodged and destroyed by the boundary collider:

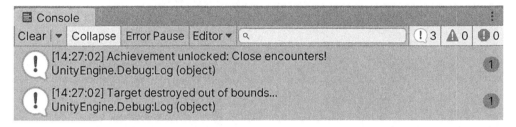

*Figure 9.8: Debug logs after the Action type is invoked*

**Passing event data with Actions**

You can pass your own custom data through your `Action` types as we did earlier with our `delegate` example:

```
public static event Action<int> OnEnemyDestroyed;
```

We can include the new parameter value when we invoke the following action:

```
OnEnemyDestroyed?.Invoke(5);
```

Then, update the subscribed method signature to account for the new parameter:

```
void EnemyDestroyed(int bonus) {}
```

Like delegates, your actions are not limited to a single parameter, so passing complex data or structures isn't a problem.

That brings us to the end of the tour on C# types that work well with the Observer pattern, but we'll continue to build out our game using Unity types for the rest of the chapter.

For completeness, I'm including a link to a tutorial on coding the Observer pattern using the IObservable, IObserver, and IDisposable types at https://learn. microsoft.com/en-us/dotnet/standard/events/observer-design-pattern. However, these aren't Unity types, so there could be serialization problems and unexpected behavior, which you can read more about at https://docs.unity3d. com/Manual/script-Serialization.html.

# UnityEvents and the Inspector

Now that we've exhausted ourselves with native C# types, let's turn to the UnityEvent type. A UnityEvent works just like a C# event/delegate or action, meaning they subscribe, unsubscribe, and store a reference to a desired response when something happens. The big difference is that they can be configured in the Unity Editor, which opens a whole new world of possibilities, especially if your team has non-programmer members who need to access and test these features.

## Adding Unity events

The code that goes with a UnityEvent will look familiar to everything we've done previously – namely declaring an event and then invoking it when the time is right. Update Player.cs to match the following code, which declares a new event for when the player is damaged and fires it every time an enemy collides with the player:

```
// 1
using UnityEngine.Events;

public class Player : Subject
{
    // 2
    public UnityEvent OnPlayerDamaged;

    //… No other variables changes needed …

    void OnCollisionEnter(Collision collision)
    {
        if(collision.gameObject.tag == "Target")
        {
            Health--;
```

```
                    Debug.Log("Player damaged!");

                    // 3
                    OnPlayerDamaged?.Invoke();

                    Destroy(collision.gameObject);
                }
                else if(collision.gameObject.tag == "Health")
                {
                    Health++;
                    Debug.Log("Health collected!");
                    Destroy(collision.gameObject);
                }
            }

            //... No other method changes needed ...
        }
```

Let's break down the code:

1.  It adds the UnityEngine.Events using directive to access the UnityEvent class.

2.  It declares a new UnityEvent for when the player is damaged.

3.  It checks whether the player collides with an enemy, and if the collision happens, then UnityEvent is invoked.

Now, we need the logic we want to execute when the player is hit by an enemy. Open TrophyManager. cs and update its code to match the following snippet, which stores how many times the player has been hit and unlocks an achievement on the first hit:

```
public class TrophyManager : MonoBehaviour
{
    public int HealthMissed = 0;

    // 1
    public int PlayerHits = 0;

    public void OnEnable()
    {
        BasePrefab.OnHealthDestroyed += HealthDestroyed;
```

```
        BasePrefab.OnEnemyDestroyed += EnemyDestroyed;
    }


    //... No other method changes needed ...


    // 2
    public void PlayerDamaged()
    {
        // 3
        PlayerHits++;

        if(PlayerHits == 1)
        {
            Debug.Log("Achievement unlocked: First blood!");
        }
    }
}
```

Let's break down the code:

1.  It adds an integer value to track how many times the player has been hit.

2.  It declares a new public method that can be connected to the UnityEvent in the **Editor**.

3.  It increments PlayerHits when the event is invoked and fires a debug log on the first call.

To set up the event connections:

1.  In the **Inspector**, select **Player**, scroll to the Player component, and click the + button under the OnPlayerDamaged section, as shown here:

*Figure 9.9: New UnityEvent added to the Player script component*

2. Drag **Managers** into the object field, then use the function dropdown to choose **Trophy-Manager | PlayerDamaged**, as shown here:

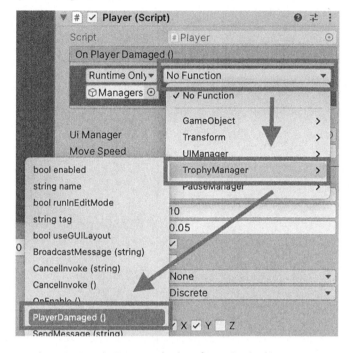

*Figure 9.10: UnityEvent method configuration in the Inspector*

Our event is a powerful tool, but it's not super flexible if it can't accept parameters or be customized in any way. We'll spend the next section updating our OnPlayerDamaged event to take in a string message so we can see what's going on in the console when the game plays!

## Adding UnityEvent parameters

Incorporating parameters with a UnityEvent requires a new extra step that we haven't seen yet – custom serializable objects. Any time you want a new UnityEvent with a parameter (or parameters), you need to create a new UnityEvent subclass. This can add a bit of overhead to your code, but if your project needs access to events in the Editor, it's a small price to pay. It's important to note that UnityEvent parameters can either be passed as **dynamic values** in code or **static values** in the Editor.

Update Player.cs to match the following code block, which adds a new UnityEvent subclass with a string type parameter, updates the OnPlayerDamaged event declaration to use the new subclass, and passes in a dynamic string value when the event is invoked:

```csharp
// 1
using System;

// 2
[Serializable]
public class CustomStringEvent : UnityEvent<string> { }

public class Player : Subject
{
    // 3
    public CustomStringEvent OnPlayerDamaged;

    //… No other variables changes needed …

    void OnCollisionEnter(Collision collision)
    {
        if(collision.gameObject.tag == "Target")
        {
            Health--;
            Debug.Log("Player damaged!");

            // 4
            OnPlayerDamaged?.Invoke("Got ya!");

            Destroy(collision.gameObject);
        }
        else if(collision.gameObject.tag == "Health")
        {
            Health++;
            Debug.Log("Health collected!");
            Destroy(collision.gameObject);
        }
    }

    //… No other method changes needed …
}
```

Let's break down the code:

1.  It adds the System using directive to access the Serializable attribute.

2.  It declares a serializable UnityEvent with a string parameter.

3.  It updates the OnPlayerDamaged type from UnityEvent to CustomStringEvent.

4.  It passes a string value to the event when it's invoked.

Now that the OnPlayerDamaged has a different parameter signature, we need to update TrophyManager.cs to match the following snippet:

```
...


// 1
public void PlayerDamaged(string message)
{
    PlayerHits++;

    if(PlayerHits == 1)
    {
        Debug.Log("Achievement unlocked: First blood!");

        // 2
        Debug.Log(message);
    }
}
```

Let's break down the code:

1.  It adds a string parameter to the PlayerDamaged method to match the OnPlayerDamaged event signature.

2.  It prints out the message we pass in using code or the **Inspector**.

Reconnect the OnPlayerDamaged event in the **Inspector** because we're using a dynamic parameter value, as shown in the following screenshot:

*Figure 9.11: Dynamic parameter set with a UnityEvent in the Inspector*

Run the game again, get hit for the first time, and you'll see the console messages like so:

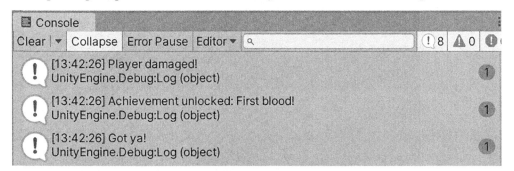

*Figure 9.12: Debug logs after the dynamic UnityEvent parameter is passed*

If you'd rather pass in a `static` parameter value in the **Editor**, reconnect the `OnPlayerDamaged` event in the **Inspector** to the static version of the `PlayerDamaged` method, as shown in the following figure:

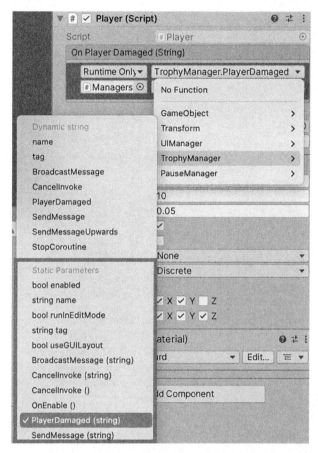

*Figure 9.13: Reconnecting the UnityEvent method to a static parameter*

Then, set the `string` value directly in the `UnityEvent` section, as shown in the following figure:

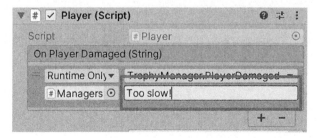

*Figure 9.14: Setting a static parameter value for the UnityEvent*

Run the game one last time for this section, get hit by an enemy, and you'll see the new static debug message printed, as shown here:

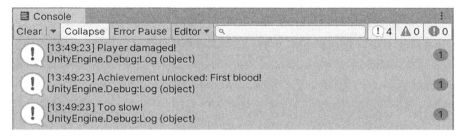

*Figure 9.15: Debug logs after the static UnityEvent parameter is passed*

**Important**

Notice that our dynamic string value in Player.cs will always be overridden by the static value set in the Editor. For safety, it's a good idea to use an empty value in code to remind yourself that the value is being set in the Inspector.

With our UnityEvent system set up and working, it's important that we talk about persistence (and not in the way I persistently collect foreign comics against the advice of my wallet) so we don't end up in situations where our events are not editable in code or the **Inspector**.

## Persistent versus non-persistent events

You may have noticed that we didn't manually unsubscribe (or remove) any listeners in code when working with UnityEvents, which brings up an interesting and not-so-well-documented persistence problem. In Unity, any events that are added in the Inspector are considered persistent and can't be removed in code. This can be confusing because the UnityEvent class *does* have public RemoveAllListeners and RemoveListener methods, but these only work if you add the listener in a script with the AddListner method. Since the big benefit of using UnityEvents is working in the Inspector, this poses a problem if we want to control our subscriptions.

To summarize:

- Events added in the **Inspector** are persistent and can't be removed from the code
- Events added in code are non-persistent and can be removed like event or Action types

However, if you encapsulate the event into its own object, you could remove listeners by disabling the listener component entirely, which is a problem we'll tackle in the last section of the chapter.

# The final boss — drag-and-drop system

Back at the 2017 Unite conference, there was a wonderful talk about building out your game architecture using scriptable objects. Unity has come a long way since then, but scriptable objects are still one of the most useful programming tools for encapsulating data in your games. In this last section, we'll implement the drag-and-drop Observer pattern structure from the Unite conference to give you a starting point for more advanced Unity configurations.

 You can find the Unite talk at https://www.youtube.com/watch?v=raQ3iHhE_Kk&t=0s&ab_channel=Unity and a brief write-up by Ryan Hipple at https://unity.com/how-to/architect-game-code-scriptable-objects.

## Writing a ScriptableObject event

The strategy behind this implementation is to encapsulate a subject into a ScriptableObject, which should look familiar because it's almost exactly what we did at the beginning of the chapter with our traditional hand-rolled Observer pattern (see, it did pay off to start with the basics). Each event will have a list of observers, or listeners, each with its own UnityEvent that we want to execute when the subject sends out a change notification.

 One thing to note about ScriptableObject events in production is that they are not easily referenced in code (because they are project assets). This is something you'll run into when working with any kind of ScriptableObject type, and a full solution is outside the scope of this book. A little Google or Stack Overflow kung fu may be in order to find the best solution for your projects.

In the **Scripts** folder, create a new C# script named SOEvent and update its code to match the following code block. This script sets up the listener pool, listener subscribing and unsubscribing, and automatic notifications when the subject changes.

```
using System.Collections;
using System.Collections.Generic;
using UnityEngine;


// 1
[CreateAssetMenu(menuName = "Events/SO Event")]
```

```
// 2
public class SOEvent : ScriptableObject
{
    private List<SOListener> _subscribers = new List<SOListener>();

    // 3
    public void NotifyAll()
    {
        for (int i = _subscribers.Count - 1; i >= 0; i--)
        {
            _subscribers[i].OnEventInvoked();
        }
    }

    // 4
    public void Subscribe(SOListener listener)
    {
        if (!_subscribers.Contains(listener))
        {
            _subscribers.Add(listener);
        }
    }

    // 5
    public void Unsubscribe(SOListener listener)
    {
        if(_subscribers.Contains(listener))
        {
            _subscribers.Remove(listener);
        }
    }
}
```

Let's break down the code:

1.  It adds the CreateAssetMenu attribute to create ScriptableObjects from the Unity menu.
2.  It declares a new class that inherits from ScriptableObject and adds a private list to store listeners.

3.  It adds a `public` method for notifying all subscribed listeners of a state change and invoking their events.

4.  It adds a `public` method for adding `SOListener` objects to the `private` subscribers list.

5.  It adds a `public` method for removing `SOListener` objects from the `private` subscribers list.

Now for the observers, we need a `MonoBehaviour` class we can attach to any listening objects in our scene. This observer needs a reference to the specific `SOEvent` (or multiple `SOEvents`), a `UnityEvent` type, so we can configure the response in the Editor, and the connection logic to hook it all together.

## Creating listeners

The console says there's an error because we don't have a `SOListener` script, so let's create one. In the **Scripts** folder, create a new C# script named `SOListener` and update its code to match the following code block, which takes care of event subscriptions and calls:

```csharp
using System.Collections;
using System.Collections.Generic;
using UnityEngine;

// 1
using UnityEngine.Events;

public class SOListener : MonoBehaviour
{
    // 2
    public SOEvent subjectEvent;
    public UnityEvent response;

    // 3
    public void OnEnable()
    {
        if(subjectEvent != null)
        {
            subjectEvent.Subscribe(this);
        }
```

```
        }

        // 4
        public void OnEventInvoked()
        {
            response?.Invoke();
        }

        // 5
        public void OnDisable()
        {
            subjectEvent.Unsubscribe(this);
        }
    }
}
```

Let's break down the code:

1.  It adds the `UnityEngine.Events` using directive to access `UnityEvent` types.
2.  It declares an `SOEvent` subject and `UnityEvent` response variables.
3.  It adds the `OnEnable` method and checks whether the subject has been assigned before subscribing the listener.
4.  It adds a `public` method for invoking the response event so it can be called in `SOEvent` objects.
5.  It adds the `OnDisable` method and removes the listener when this script is destroyed or disabled.

Now, all that's left is to create a `ScriptableObject` event in our project assets and connect the pieces in the Editor.

## Creating ScriptableObject event assets

Let's dive right in, shall we?

1.  Select the **ScriptableObjects** folder in the project's **Assets** folder.

2. From the menu, select **Assets | Create | Events | SOEvent**, as shown in the following screenshot (you can also right-click inside any of the **Assets** folders and use **Create | Events | SOEvent**):

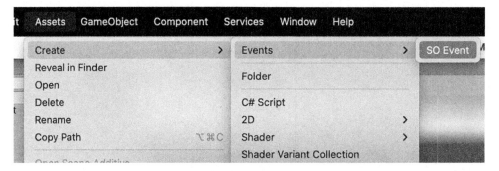

*Figure 9.16: Creating a ScriptableObject from the Assets menu*

3. Name the event `OnPlayerHit`, as shown here:

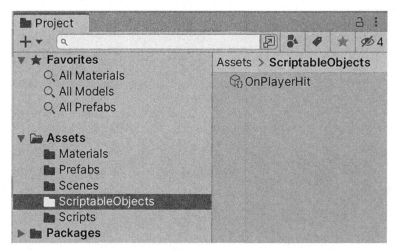

*Figure 9.17: ScriptableObject renamed and stored in the project's Assets folder*

Now that we have a way to create `ScriptableObejct` events in our project's `Assets` folder, we can spend the next section on the last part of our scripting work, which is to manually fire the events when needed!

## Invoking the SOEvent

We've now come full circle back to our first implementation of the Observer pattern, but this time, a subject and its listeners share a reference to the same `ScriptableObject` event.

When the subject sends out its batch notification to all its listeners, the listeners should be able to execute their own UnityEvent no matter what GameObject they're a part of in the scene. In our example, we're going to update OnPlayerDamaged to an SOEvent and send out a notification whenever a player is hit by an enemy object. We'll let any observers determine what to do with that information, but from the Editor.

Update Player.cs to match the following code block, which changes the OnPlayerDamaged event to our new SOEvent type and notifies all listeners when an enemy GameObject collides with the player:

```
using System.Collections;
using System.Collections.Generic;
using UnityEngine;
using UnityEngine.Events;
using System;

public class Player : Subject
{
    // 1
    public SOEvent OnPlayerDamaged;

    //… No other variable changes …

    void OnCollisionEnter(Collision collision)
    {
        if(collision.gameObject.tag == "Target")
        {
            Health--;

            // 2
            OnPlayerDamaged.NotifyAll();

            Debug.Log("Player damaged!");
            Destroy(collision.gameObject);

        }
        else if(collision.gameObject.tag == "Health")
        {
```

```
        Health++;
        Debug.Log("Health collected!");
        Destroy(collision.gameObject);
    }
  }
}
```

Let's break down the code:

1. It updates the OnPlayerDamaged type to SOEvent.

2. It uses the event to notify all listeners of a state change.

With that final bit of work done, we can completely connect up the event system in the **Inspector** and get things rolling!

## Connecting the system

To hook up all the moving parts:

1. Drag the OnPlayerHit ScriptableObject onto the OnPlayerDamaged field on the Player component in the **Inspector**, as shown in the following screenshot:

*Figure 9.18: Setting the ScriptableObject asset in the Inspector*

2. Select Managers in the **Hierarchy** and add an SOListener component, as shown in the following screenshot:

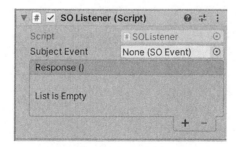

*Figure 9.19: Adding a ScriptableObject listener in the Inspector*

3. Drag the `OnPlayerHit` `ScriptableObject` onto the `Subject Event` field and press the +
   button twice to add two response events, as shown here:

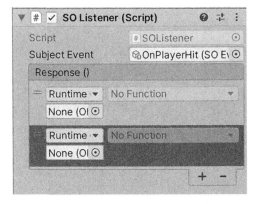

*Figure 9.20: Configuring the ScriptableObject listener with a shared event and re-
sponses*

4. Drag the `TrophyManager` component onto the first response field and select **TrophyMan-
   ager | PlayerDamaged(string),** as shown in the following screenshot, and set its `string`
   parameter to **There can be only one!:**

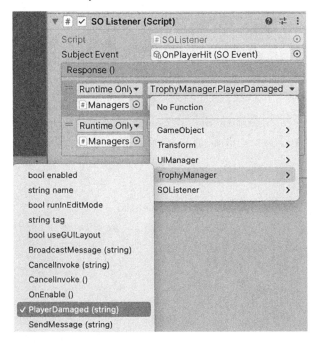

*Figure 9.21: Connecting the SOEvent listener to a response*

5.  Drag the SOListener component onto the second response and select **SOListener | On-Disable**, as shown here:

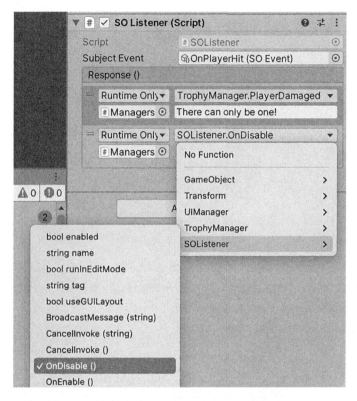

*Figure 9.22: Connecting the SOListener to second response*

With the **Inspector** configurations handling our unsubscribe logic after the first hit, we can delete the extra code we had in TrophyManager.cs to match the following snippet:

```
...

public void PlayerDamaged(string message)
{
    Debug.Log("Achievement unlocked: First blood!");
    Debug.Log(message);
}
```

Run the game one last time, let an evil enemy hit you, and look for the new logs on the first collision, as shown in the following screenshot. Notice that we don't get repeated achievements because the listener is disabled – all from the **Inspector**!

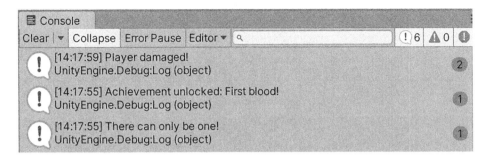

*Figure 9.23: Debug logs for the ScriptableObject event system in action*

We covered a ton in this chapter and I don't want to leave you feeling confused or like there are too many paths to choose from, so I'll leave you with a few subsections to round out our topic discussion with high-level points on performance and implementation options.

## Performance considerations

Performance is an important consideration with the Observer pattern because of its distributed and decoupled structure, so you need to pay attention to how many subjects and observers you're going to have running around your game. Before diving into your code, run through the following list and ask yourself which solution is going to work best for your particular scenario:

- When adding listeners, a C# event allocates less memory than a UnityEvent for a single listener. However, with two or more listeners, C# events create exponentially more garbage than UnityEvents.

- When dispatching a single event, C# events create no garbage while UnityEvents generate garbage but only the first time it's invoked.

- When dispatching tons of events (and I mean tons), C# events considerably outperform UnityEvents. Even in the best-case scenario, UnityEvents are likely to be at least 2x slower than C# events. When you add event arguments into the mix, the disparity is even greater.

 You can find a wonderful data-based breakdown comparing the performance of UnityEvent and C# event types at https://www.jacksondunstan.com/articles/3335.

## Picking the right implementation

Before we close this out, I'm going to lay out the criteria and scenarios that best fit each implementation path I've laid out over the last 41 pages:

- The **traditional** implementation is a great starting point, especially for scenarios with limited subjects and observers. However, this solution doesn't add any benefits over event and Action types, so I would recommend upgrading.

- The **delegate/event or Action** implementation is a perfect way to structure your Observer pattern if you're working primarily in code. Not only is it easier to set up and manage, but it's also the most performant option.

- The **UnityEvent** implementation is a good fit when you need to work in the **Editor**, but this solution puts a strain on your game's performance if you're running a big, distributed network of subjects and listeners. However, be aware of the persistent versus non-persistent problem from the *UnityEvents and the Inspector* section. If you need to work in the **Editor**, I recommend upgrading to the ScriptableObject solution.

- The **ScriptableObject** implementation is the best fit for in-editor work. Period. Not only does it separate listeners into self-contained assets, but you can also modify non-persistent listener subscriptions in the **Editor**. However, keep in mind that ScriptableObject events aren't always the easiest to organize and find in code, so you'll need to adapt the chapter content to fit your needs.

Finding the "perfect" or "ideal" solution isn't always so straightforward as running your finger down a list and picking the prettiest option. I've tried my best to simplify the main breaking points between each option for you, but again, like all design patterns, the reality is always going to be customized for your project. Don't be afraid to take the content here and start down your own path.

## Summary

There you have it – the Observer pattern simplified! (I'm only sort of joking). This was another big content dump, but running with the easiest plug-and-play solution without understanding the underlying foundation is a dangerous game. Luckily, you now have the necessary information to make the best decision for your own projects.

Remember, the Observer pattern sends change notifications from subjects to all subscribed observers. Subjects and observers are decoupled, meaning each observer decides how to react to subject changes. C# has built-in types specific to the Observer pattern – delegate, event, EventHandler, and Action, while Unity has built-in types specific to the Observer pattern – UnityEvent and UnityAction. As we've seen, C# types are exponentially more performant than Unity types.

In the next chapter, we'll tackle object behavior with the State pattern – specifically, how to create objects that can alter their behavior based on internal state and handle transitions between those different states to create complex decision chains!

# Further reading

- Abstract classes can't be created on their own, but they are excellent solutions when you want a consistent base class blueprint that other classes can inherit from. Many of our solutions in this book rely heavily on abstract classes to provide an abstraction layer between class blueprints and their concrete implementations. You can find more information at https://learn.microsoft.com/en-us/dotnet/csharp/language-reference/keywords/abstract.

- Interfaces are a great way to create groups of related functionality (with or without default implementations) that can be adopted by any class or struct. These are especially handy when you want to have a class inherit from multiple groups of functionality, which is called object composition. For more information, check out the documentation at https://learn.microsoft.com/en-us/dotnet/csharp/fundamentals/types/interfaces.

- Delegates are a way of assigning methods to their own references (methods as variables), which means you can call a method right from the delegate. You can find more information on delegates at https://learn.microsoft.com/en-us/dotnet/csharp/programming-guide/delegates/.

- Events enable your objects and classes to notify other objects and classes when something happens in one that the other should be aware of. If events are new for you, I'd highly recommend reading the documentation at https://learn.microsoft.com/en-us/dotnet/csharp/programming-guide/events/.

- Actions are delegate types in C# that don't return any values and are generally easier to set up. Actions let you work with functions in more concise syntax, but they also provide additional functionality under the hood. For more information, check out the documentation at https://learn.microsoft.com/en-us/dotnet/api/system.action-1?view=net-8.0.

- UnityEvents allow you to work with events directly in the **Editor**, which can help in a variety of situations when developing games. For more information, check out the documentation at https://docs.unity3d.com/Manual/UnityEvents.html.

- ScriptableObjects are the perfect way to create data containers in your Unity projects (and we'll use them in almost every chapter going forward), but I'd also recommend checking out the documentation at https://docs.unity3d.com/Manual/class-ScriptableObject.html.

# Join our community on Discord

Join our community's Discord space for discussions with the author and other readers:

`https://packt.link/gamedevelopment_packt`

# 10

# Controlling Behavior with the State Pattern

In the last chapter, we built a decoupled notification system using the Observer pattern. In this chapter, we'll jump into more game mechanic territory with the State pattern to create an object that can change its behavior based on an internal state value. While the State pattern is a mainstay of AI programming, you're intimately familiar with *state* in everyday life – when you're tired, you sleep; when you're hungry, you eat; and when you're happy, you smile. Each internal *state* triggers a different behavior in the same underlying object, you. Likewise, when you do a load of laundry, the machine goes through different states before finishing the cycle – rinse, wash, spin dry, and drain; same old washing machine, different states. Applied in code, the object appears to change its class when its behavior changes, when it's really the underlying state that's updated!

Like the Command pattern, the State pattern is all about encapsulating behavior to hide the inner workings of the system from the client (don't hide things from your actual business clients). The difference is how transitions between behaviors are handled. Each state is responsible for deciding when to switch states and what the next state needs to be. This works well for sequential states that go from beginning to end, like a washing machine, but also for constantly running systems like character controllers that handle non-sequential inputs per frame.

You can use the State pattern in a variety of ways, but they all need a system for storing and managing the states in your game or application. We'll start with a basic **finite-state machine (FSM)**, branch out into hierarchical and concurrent implementations, and end with a look at the importance and usability of tracking state history. Don't worry if this all sounds new; we'll go into greater detail on each of these new topics before touching any code.

We'll use this chapter to focus on the following topics:

- The pros and cons of the State design pattern
- Creating an FSM
- Using a hierarchical state machine
- Adapting for concurrent state machines
- Tracking state history

By the end of the chapter, you'll have hands-on experience with creating versatile, customizable, and scalable states and state machines – all with good decoupled responsibility and enough theory to springboard into more advanced scenarios! As always, let's start with the technical requirements, then move on to the pattern breakdown, and jump into code of our own!

# Technical requirements

Before you start:

1. Download or clone the GitHub repository at `https://github.com/PacktPublishing/C-Design-Patterns-with-Unity-First-Edition`.

2. Open the **Ch_10_Starter** project folder in Unity Hub.

3. In **Assets | Scenes**, double-click on **SampleScene**.

Unity's animation and visual scripting systems already use the State pattern to make your life easier, so kudos if you were thinking along those same lines! Since we're concerned with how to implement the State pattern in C#, we won't be using these ready-made features. However, that doesn't mean you can't use them separately or together. In fact, using code to trigger the animation system works well with our programmatic approach. You can read more about animation state machines at `https://docs.unity3d.com/Manual/StateMachineBasics.html` and Unity's visual scripting at `https://unity.com/features/unity-visual-scripting`.

The project for this chapter is a simple turn-based battle game (hopefully, you have some of the same nostalgia for Pokemon as I do). I've set up the scene to have a player character (you) and an automated enemy (not you) that are locked in a back-and-forth struggle until one of them falls.

As for the scripts:

- `BattleClient.cs` is attached to the **Client** in the **Hierarchy** and will eventually delegate the game behaviors to the current state the game is in.

- `Manager.cs` is attached to the **Client** in the **Hierarchy** and keeps track of all our UI needs and utility functions that aren't state specific.

- `UnitStats.cs` is attached to both the `Player` and `Enemy` in the **Hierarchy** and has the main action methods you and your opponent can choose from.

We'll also be using some Unity and C# language features to take our code the extra mile. Don't worry if you're not familiar with these; I've included links for the basics, and I'll explain how they apply to our use cases as we go.

- Abstract classes (`https://learn.microsoft.com/en-us/dotnet/csharp/language-reference/keywords/abstract`)

- Coroutines (`https://docs.unity3d.com/Manual/Coroutines.html`)

- Stacks (`https://learn.microsoft.com/en-us/dotnet/api/system.collections.stack?view=net-8.0`)

I chose a turn-based example over the traditional character controller tutorial example because it offers the most diverse real-world applications for the State pattern (and the character controller examples have been done to death at this point). This isn't to say a character controller isn't a good usage of the State pattern – it absolutely is, but I've found that building a game system gives more depth and context to this pattern and its applications.

# Breaking down the State pattern

As part of the behavioral family of design patterns, the State pattern allows an object to change its internal behavior based on an internally tracked state. The internal state can be switched to any other concrete `state` object, which are self-contained classes that implement a common set of rules and customized logic. This means the State pattern is most useful when:

- You want an object's behavior to change (either at runtime or at every frame) based on an internal state.

- You want to refactor an object's long conditional statements into separate classes so it can be treated independently.

- You want to add new behavior to an object without changing or breaking existing code.

Going back to the analogy a few pages ago, think of yourself as a state machine. You (as a person) have specific needs that change and depend on various internal and external factors. If you're hungry, you eat; if you're tired, you sleep; if you're full of manic energy, you might go for a run. The problem is that all these states and triggers exist in our body at once, which can make things very confusing for our nervous system to manage, as shown in the following figure:

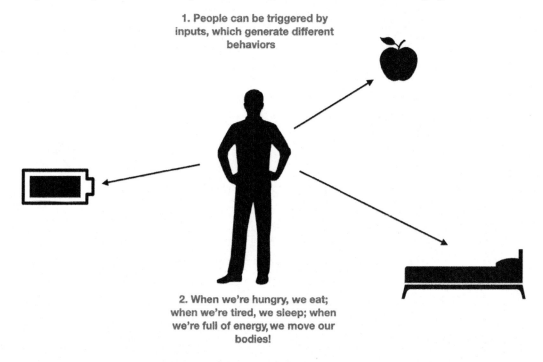

**1. People can be triggered by inputs, which generate different behaviors**

**2. When we're hungry, we eat; when we're tired, we sleep; when we're full of energy, we move our bodies!**

*Figure 10.1: Human state machines and transitions*

 I know it's possible to be hungry *and* tired, but the State pattern only allows one active state, so keep that in mind.

Managing objects in your application or game is no different – there are going to be times when you need an object to *act* in different ways, which appears like it's changing its underlying class. But you also want these behaviors to be reusable components that can be chained together and easily maintained. Luckily, we can decide to break out each set of behaviors into different states and have the object simply track its own internal state. When the internal state changes, we defer the logic to the new state, leaving the object largely unaware of the work being done! In our human example, this would look something like the following figure:

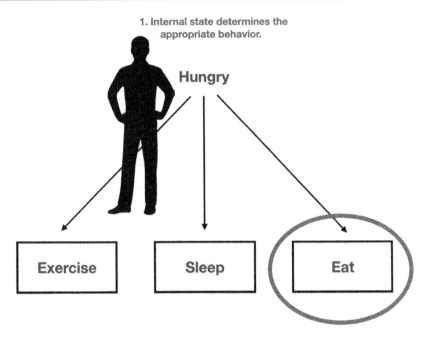

*Figure 10.2: Changing internal state when you're hungry*

In the traditional State pattern, we're more concerned with breaking different behaviors into their own self-contained states so the object can:

- Defer state-specific logic to each state.
- Allow the application to react differently depending on an object's current state.

However, there's always a little more below the surface with most design patterns, and State is no different. So, let's talk about something fun before we get going – automata theory.

## A little automata theory

State pattern implementations come in different flavors, but the most common one you'll see in the wild is the FSM (even if the example or programmer doesn't know they've written an FSM). In contrast to the State pattern, FSMs are concerned with the states and transitions *between* states rather than the state behaviors themselves. This focus creates a fluid sequential or cyclical chain of events that almost seems tailor-made for programming scenarios, as shown in *Figure 10.3*.

The good news is that these two concepts are not mutually exclusive (they're actually more interlinked than some would like to admit) since the State pattern can absolutely be used to build an FSM, and we'll do just that in this chapter.

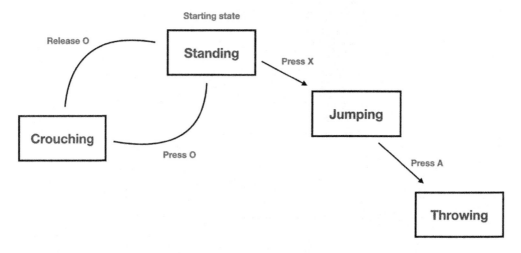

*Figure 10.3: FSM gaming example*

So, how can you identify an FSM? Well, FSMs are studied in computer science as part of **automata theory**, are popular with AI programmers, and have the following traits:

- There are a fixed number of states our context (or state machine) can be in (i.e., running, jumping, swimming, and sitting on the couch).
- There can only be one state active at any given time (so you can't be sitting on the couch and running a marathon).
- Events (which are generally inputs from the user) are sent to the state machine, which triggers a transition to the next state. For example, you're on the couch hanging out (current state), you have a cup of coffee (input), and suddenly you get up and go for a run (transition to a different state).

It's important to understand that the State pattern and FSMs aren't the same thing; one is a structure for encapsulating and managing behaviors into separate objects, and the other is a common implementation of that structure. If you can wrestle these two concepts apart in your head, you're already way ahead of the curve.

Topics in automata theory often use states and state machines to get their work done – if you're interested in exploring more, visit `https://en.wikipedia.org/wiki/Automata_theory` and `https://cs.stanford.edu/people/eroberts/courses/soco/projects/2004-05/automata-theory/basics.html`.

FSMs also have useful extensions for creating hierarchies of shared behavior to avoid repeating yourself using classic object-oriented programming inheritance (called hierarchical state machines), behaviors that run at the same time (called concurrent state machines), and a handy way of storing state history for easier redo/undo actions (called pushdown automaton). These extensions aren't part of the original State pattern but they do provide wonderful concrete benefits when you're dealing with complex real-time behaviors (which makes them super handy and explains why they each have dedicated sections in this chapter).

## Diagramming the pattern

*Figure 10.4* shows the UML structure of the State pattern with its three components:

- The **Context** stores the current state instance and defines the interface for clients to communicate with
- The **State** provides a common interface for all the expected state behaviors

- Each **Concrete State** is responsible for its own logic associated with each behavior or action and you can have as many **Concrete States** as you need.

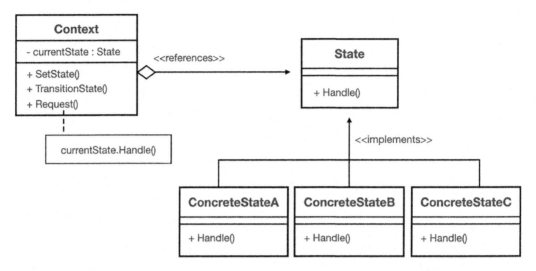

*Figure 10.4: UML diagram of the State pattern components*

In the pattern structure, the context delegates responsibility to the current state, which executes its customized behavior. Since each state determines how and when to transition to the next state, the context is a constant clearinghouse for the changing current state. Like other behavioral patterns we've used, this system lets the client use the context wherever necessary without any knowledge of the current state or how states manage themselves and their transitions.

## Pros and cons

Like all design patterns, there are pros and cons. Let's start with the benefits of the State pattern:

- **Encapsulated object behavior** is a massive part of the State pattern and its biggest asset. Not only does this allow you to separate monolithic conditional statements into their own respective objects, but adding new states into the mix is much simpler and safer.
- **Because each state contains its own behavior**, it also controls its transitions to and from other states without having to query other objects. This makes each state completely self-sufficient and changes your job from herding a giant class to doing what you want, and then to defining states and transitions to form a bigger behavior picture.

- **Adding new states is easy** and doesn't require the pattern structure or client code to change. Since states are their own masters, our job is to simply create a new state, define whatever behavior seems appropriate, and add in transitions (states can even be shared if you feel like it).

However, be careful of the following pitfall when using the State pattern in your projects:

- **Complexity** is the biggest drawback of the State pattern (as we've often seen with other patterns). While a system with a small number of states can be easily managed, things can quickly get out of hand the more states (and state transitions) you need to create and manage. However, this shouldn't scare you away from using the State pattern – it's extremely useful when building complex behavior systems that need to be self-sufficient.

Now that we've covered the structure, benefits, and limitations of the State pattern, we can start laying out the traditional implementation in code.

# Creating a turn-based battle system

Conventionally, a state is only required to have a method for handling state-specific logic, but a more complete implementation will have `Enter` and `Exit` methods and separate methods for handling input and checking for state changes. This is especially useful in Unity when you need to separate physics logic that needs to be fired in `FixedUpdate` versus other state logic that can go in the regular `Update` function in your client script.

For our example, we'll be using the whole bundle – enter, exit, input-handling, and state transition methods, which are going to help us write a more robust (and customizable) state-handling system.

## Defining abstract and base states

In the **Scripts** folder, create a new C# script named `State` and update its code to match the following code block. This class will serve as our blueprint for all states in the game, even if they are used in different state machines. We'll be using coroutines a fair bit in this chapter to simulate wait times between steps in the turn order, which is why our `Enter` and `Exit` methods return an `IEnumerator` type.

Coroutines in Unity are a way of running asynchronous code (work that operates independently of other processes being executed). They also allow you to pause executing code, wait for some other code to run, and then hand back control to the calling method, which is extremely useful in turn-based systems where we need to wait for each turn to finish before moving on to the next one. Coroutines, asynchronous operations, and multithreading aren't small topics, so if you're interested in diving deeper, start with the documentation at `https://docs.unity3d.com/Manual/Coroutines.html`.

If you're using the State pattern in plain C#, you can produce the same effects with the `async` and `await` features, which you can find at `https://learn.microsoft.com/en-us/dotnet/csharp/asynchronous-programming`.

```csharp
using System.Collections;
using System.Collections.Generic;
using UnityEngine;

// 1
public abstract class State
{
    // 2
    public virtual IEnumerator Enter()
    {
        yield break;
    }

    // 3
    public virtual void HandleInput() { }
    public virtual void CheckState() { }

    // 4
    public virtual IEnumerator Exit()
    {
        yield break;
    }
}
```

Let's break down our code:

1. It declares an `abstract` class for all states.

2. It adds a virtual `Enter` method with an `IEnumerator` return type.

3. It adds two virtual methods for input handling and checking state transitions.

4. It adds a virtual `Exit` method with an `IEnumerator` return type.

 You'll commonly see state blueprints written as either an `interface` or `abstract` class; the decision between inheritance and composition is up to you. For this chapter, we'll make every `State` method `virtual`, so each concrete state isn't required to implement all four. This gives us a bit of flexibility and keeps boilerplate code to a minimum, but an `abstract` class is also a place to enforce any hard-and-fast rules you want each state to abide by.

The `Enter` and `Exit` methods will be used when a new state becomes the current state, while the `HandleInput` and `CheckState` methods will be fired in the client `Update` method. You can combine these two steps, but it's easier to manage more complex state logic if they're separated (not to mention more readable code).

 You could also add another method for physics updates that need to run in the client's `FixedUpdate` method, or, even further, encapsulate your logic into methods for handling animations, audio, or anything else really. This pattern is super extensible (especially in Unity) when you get your head around the moving parts!

Now, we can take our state blueprint and write the foundation of the state management system, which in the State pattern is called the **context**.

## Creating a state machine

The context, or state machine, is responsible for two things: keeping track of the current state and transitioning to new states when asked. Every state will have a reference to its context, which allows them to simply ask for the state to be changed whenever necessary. Think of it as a clearing house for any rules and state change timing you might need.

In the **Scripts** folder, create a new C# script named `SMContext` and update its code to match the following code. This code will make sure our `CurrentState` can only be set from this script and provide a public method for initializing and changing states.

Notice that when changing states, we wait for the current state to finish its Exit logic before changing the state and calling Enter on the new one (very important and just good manners). This avoids conflicts or broken dependencies between states when they're updated.

```csharp
using System.Collections;
using System.Collections.Generic;
using UnityEngine;

public class SMContext : MonoBehaviour
{
    // 1
    public State CurrentState { get; private set; }

    // 2
    public void HandleInput()
    {
        CurrentState.HandleInput();
    }

    // 3
    public void CheckState()
    {
        CurrentState.CheckState();
    }

    // 4
    public void ChangeStateTo(State newState)
    {
        StartCoroutine(StateTransition(newState));
    }

    // 5
    private IEnumerator StateTransition(State newState)
    {
        if (CurrentState == newState)
        {
            yield break;
        }
```

```
        // 6
        if(CurrentState != null)
        {
            yield return StartCoroutine(CurrentState.Exit());
        }

        CurrentState = newState;
        StartCoroutine(CurrentState.Enter());
    }
}
```

Let's break down the code:

1. It adds a public State variable to store the current state that can only be set privately.

2. It declares a public method that delegates input handling to the current state.

3. It declares a public method that delegates state transition checks to the current state.

4. It declares a ChangeStateTo method that starts the transition coroutine.

5. It declares a ChangeTo method that checks whether the current state is different from the new state parameter.

6. It checks whether there is a previous state and calls the Exit method if true, waits for it to complete, and then sets the new state and calls its Enter method.

This is all the code we need to successfully manage our states, but it would be nice if we could also make it impossible for states to update if there's already a transition in progress, which we'll tackle next.

## Protecting transitioning states

In a turn-based scenario, overlapping transitioning states may not be a huge issue but it can wreak havoc on your code in a more fluid system like a character controller where states are changing at a rapid pace and could crash into each other mid-transition.

Forward-thinking as we are, let's update SMContext.cs to match the following code, which guards against this happening with a boolean flag inside our ChangeTo method and an initial check at the beginning of every state change to make sure we're not interrupting anything in progress.

```
public class SMContext : MonoBehaviour
{
```

```csharp
    public State CurrentState;

    // 1
    private bool _isTransitioning;

    public void HandleInput() { //… No changes needed… }
    public void CheckState() { //… No changes needed… }
    public void ChangeStateTo(State state) { //… No changes needed… }

    private IEnumerator StateTransition(State newState)
    {
        // 2
        if (_isTransitioning || CurrentState == newState)
        {
            yield break;
        }

        // 3
        _isTransitioning = true;

        if(CurrentState != null)
        {
            yield return StartCoroutine(CurrentState.Exit());
        }

        CurrentState = newState;
        StartCoroutine(CurrentState.Enter());

        // 4
        _isTransitioning = false;
    }
}
```

Let's break down the code:

1. It declares a new `boolean` variable to track the transition state.
2. It checks whether there's already a state transition in progress before continuing.
3. It sets the transition to `true` before the state is updated.
4. It sets the transition to `false` when the state update is finished.

 If you want to be extra safe, you can check whether `newState` is not null before calling `Enter` on the new state. It's a little overkill for our project, but it never hurts to guard against missing states, especially if you're connecting them in the Editor.

Now that we have a base `MonoBehaviour` to work with, we can start subclassing concrete state machines without any boilerplate code, which we'll do in the next section.

## Subclassing state machines

In the **Scripts** folder, create a new C# script named `BattleSM` and update it to match the following code block. This makes things more manageable for the rest of the chapter examples and gives us useful storage space for our state instances. This isn't strictly necessary in all cases, but it will allow you to distinguish the base logic of all state machine contexts with custom behavior you may want to add later.

 If you're wondering why we don't just work entirely in the `SMContext.cs` script, you have a valid point. Since we'll be creating multiple state machine contexts at the end of the chapter, we want an efficient way of creating different context components. For scenarios where you only need a single context running in your project, feel free to do all the work in a single, original context class!

```
public class BattleSM : SMContext
{
    // 1
    public State Setup;
    public State PlayerTurn;
    public State EnemyTurn;
    public State EndBattle;
}
```

Deciding where to store your state objects can be tricky, but it comes down to where you need to access them. Again, since we're going to use multiple state machines by the end of the chapter, we have different state machine classes inheriting from SMContext. However, if you're running a single state machine, you can store your concrete states directly in the SMContext class or wherever works best for your project. You can also experiment with ScriptableObject states or attach State script components to your GameObjects in the Editor.

With an abstract state class and a state management system all finished, it's time to make our concrete states and add in their respective game logic.

## Creating concrete states

Our turn-based game needs four states to make things interesting: Setup, Player, Enemy, and End. The Setup and End states will only happen once per session, but our Player Turn and Enemy Turn states can ping-pong back and forth for as long as either one has health left, as shown in the following figure.

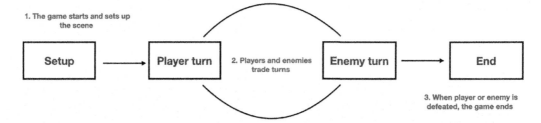

*Figure 10.5: Flowchart of example game states*

Remember that we set all our abstract state methods as virtual, which lets us off the hook for boilerplate code in smaller states like **Setup** or **End** but with the option of expanding into full-featured states for **Player** and **Enemy**.

## Base state

Having a base or parent state comes in handy when you need to differentiate different families of states. In our example, the base state will help us distinguish between turn-based states and weather states (later on), and handle inherited behavior when we get to the *Using a hierarchical state machine* section.

In the **Scripts** folder, create a new C# script named BaseBattleState and update it to match the following code. For now, BaseBattleState inherits from State and only has a protected reference in its state machine context, which gets injected into each State using a constructor.

> We're initializing and storing the protected reference to each state's SMContext (or any subclass) in a base state because we'll be working with multiple state machines later in the chapter. For projects with a single state machine, put this code directly in the abstract State class to avoid repetitive constructors.

```csharp
using System.Collections;
using System.Collections.Generic;
using UnityEngine;

// 1
public class BaseBattleState : State
{
    // 2
    protected BattleSM _stateMachine;

    // 3
    public BaseBattleState(BattleSM sm)
    {
        _stateMachine = sm;
    }
}
```

Let's break down the code:

1. It inherits from the abstract State class.
2. It stores a protected instance of a state machine context.
3. It sets the state machine context variable in the class constructor.

That's all we need for the base state, so we can move on to building our four main battle states for the game.

## Setup state

The first state our battle system starts with is the setup phase, where any initial configurations will be done. In the **Scripts** folder, create a new C# script named SetupState and update it to match the following code.

For our simple example, we're going to use a subclass from BaseBattleState, use the base constructor, and print out a debug log when we enter the state. Next, we'll wait for two seconds to add pacing to the game and switch right into the player turn state. When we exit SetupState, we'll print another debug log, but the Exit method is a great place for any cleanup logic you may have before the next state is called. There's no need to include the HandleInput or CheckState methods because we don't have any code executing in real time, but that will change with our player and enemy turn states later.

```csharp
using System.Collections;
using System.Collections.Generic;
using UnityEngine;

// 1
public class SetupState : BaseBattleState
{
    public SetupState(BattleSM sm) : base(sm) { }

    // 2
    public override IEnumerator Enter()
    {
        Debug.Log("Setting up the arena...");

        yield return new WaitForSeconds(2);
        _stateMachine.ChangeStateTo(_stateMachine.PlayerTurn);
    }

    // 3
    public override IEnumerator Exit()
    {
        Debug.Log("Battle engaged!");
        yield break;
    }
}
```

Let's break down the code:

1. It inherits from `BaseBattleState` and uses the parent class constructor to set the state machine context.

2. It overrides the `Enter` method, waits for two seconds, and then transitions to the player turn state.

3. It overrides the `Exit` method and prints out a debug log.

When you're thinking about state transitions, it helps to visualize a chain of interconnected links. The fun part is you get to decide which links get placed in what order – they can be sequential, cyclical, or a mix of both like our game. Once you start thinking about each state as a self-contained link in the chain, it's a small jump to seeing the potential in a completely modifiable system where you can add new behaviors without breaking the current code; all it takes is updating the flow of state transitions.

## Player state

The player turn is the first meaty state that requires specific logic to be executed in a sequential flow. In the **Scripts** folder, create a new C# script named `PlayerState` and update it to match the following code block.

When we enter the player's turn, their capsule will turn green to signal they can act and their internal variables will be reset to defaults. `HandleInput` tracks whether the user presses the *A* key; they attack and the enemy takes a predetermined amount of damage. If the user presses the *H* key, they are healed by one HP. In our example, the user can only use one action per turn, which means `CheckState` will execute if the player has run out of actions or is defeated, and transition to either the end state or to the enemy turn state. When the player turn is over, the `Exit` method will change the player's capsule back to its original color.

```
using System.Collections;
using System.Collections.Generic;
using UnityEngine;

// 1
public class PlayerState : BaseBattleState
{
    private bool isKO;
    private int movesRemaining;
```

```csharp
    public PlayerState(BattleSM sm) : base(sm) {}


    // 2
    public override IEnumerator Enter()
    {
        Debug.Log("Finally, my turn!");
        Manager.Instance.Player.ChangeColor(Color.green);
        movesRemaining = 1;


        yield break;
    }


    // 3
    public override void HandleInput()
    {
        if (Input.GetKeyDown(KeyCode.A) && movesRemaining > 0)
        {
            movesRemaining--;
            isKO = Manager.Instance.Enemy.TakeDamage(1);
        }
        else if (Input.GetKeyDown(KeyCode.H) && movesRemaining > 0)
        {
            movesRemaining--;
            Manager.Instance.Player.Heal();
        }
    }


    // 4
    public override void CheckState()
    {
        if (isKO)
        {
            _stateMachine.ChangeStateTo(_stateMachine.EndBattle);
        }
        else if(movesRemaining == 0)
        {
            _stateMachine.ChangeStateTo(_stateMachine.EnemyTurn);
```

```
            }
        }

        // 5
        public override IEnumerator Exit()
        {
            yield return new WaitForSeconds(1);

            Debug.Log("I'm out of energy...");
            Manager.Instance.Player.ChangeColor(Color.blue);
        }
    }
}
```

Let's break down the code:

1.   It inherits from BaseBattleState, adds internal variables, and uses the parent constructor to set the context.

2.   It overrides the Enter method, prints a debug log, changes the player capsule color, and sets internal values.

3.   It overrides the HandleInput method to listen for key presses for attacking or healing and decrements player moves.

4.   It overrides the CheckState method to check conditions for transitioning to either the enemy or end states.

5.   It overrides the Exit method, prints out a debug log, and changes the player capsule back to its original color.

This might look overwhelming, but it's the same kind of code we'd otherwise put into a player or game manager class. Instead, everything related to the specific turn (the state) is neatly encapsulated in a separate object. Breaking down each state's responsibilities into clearly defined steps also lets us coordinate complex logic that might need to fire at certain times, like animations, physics logic, or audio.

 You can also inject data into a state's constructor and set internal values as we did with movesRemaining and isKO in PlayerState. Make good use of both strategies for giving your concrete states everything they need to perform logic and make the right choices.

## Enemy state

The enemy turn will be very similar to the player turn, except we're taking the input handling portion out and making the enemy perform a predetermined action. If you're thinking this is a good place for AI programming, you're absolutely right. Our enemy is not super versatile, but this system could accommodate a much smarter AI enemy if you wanted to use behavior trees or other approaches for controlling NPCs (you could even have the enemy use the Strategy pattern to dish out different tactics).

In the **Scripts** folder, create a new C# script named EnemyState and update it to match the following code block. When we enter the enemy's turn, their capsule will change color and their internal values will be reset to defaults. Instead of checking for input, we'll wait for one second and then attack the player and decrease the enemy's moves. CheckState will be looking for whether the player has been knocked out or whether there are no moves left, which triggers a transition to either the end state or back to the player state, respectively. When the Exit method is called, we change the enemy capsule's material back to its original color and print out a debug log.

```csharp
using System.Collections;
using System.Collections.Generic;
using UnityEngine;

// 1
public class EnemyState : BaseBattleState
{
    private bool isKO;
    private int movesRemaining;

    public EnemyState(BattleSM sm) : base(sm) {}

    // 2
    public override IEnumerator Enter()
    {
        Debug.Log("You don't stand a chance!");
        Manager.Instance.Enemy.ChangeColor(Color.green);
        movesRemaining = 1;

        yield return new WaitForSeconds(1);
```

```
        isKO = Manager.Instance.Player.TakeDamage(1);
        movesRemaining--;
    }

    // 3
    public override void CheckState()
    {
        if (isKO)
        {
            _stateMachine.ChangeStateTo(_stateMachine.EndBattle);
        }
        else if(movesRemaining == 0)
        {
            _stateMachine.ChangeStateTo(_stateMachine.PlayerTurn);
        }
    }

    // 4
    public override IEnumerator Exit()
    {
        yield return new WaitForSeconds(1);

        Debug.Log("I'll get you next time...");
        Manager.Instance.Enemy.ChangeColor(Color.magenta);
    }
}
```

Let's break down the code:

1. It inherits from BaseBattleState, adds internal variables, and uses the parent constructor to set the context.

2. It overrides the Enter method, prints a debug log, changes the enemy capsule color, and attacks the player.

3. It overrides the CheckState method to check conditions for transitioning to either the player or end states.

4. It overrides the Exit method, prints out a debug log, and changes the enemy capsule back to its original color.

We've put in a lot of state code and we're almost done – all that's left is the ending state, which we'll finish in the next section.

## Ending state

When the player or enemy has been defeated, the game will stop ping-ponging between their turns and switch to the ending battle state. Like SetupState, ending the battle is simple – print out a debug log and quit the application. In the **Scripts** folder, create a new C# script named EndState and update it to match the following code.

```
using System.Collections;
using System.Collections.Generic;
using UnityEngine;

// 1
public class EndState : BaseBattleState
{
    public EndState(BattleSM sm) : base(sm) { }

    // 2
    public override IEnumerator Enter()
    {
        Debug.Log("Saving game data...");
        Application.Quit();

        yield break;
    }
}
```

Let's break down the code:

1.  It inherits from BaseBattleState and uses the parent class constructor to set the state machine context.

2.  It overrides the Enter method, prints out a debug log, and quits the application.

That was a lot of state game logic, but more important than the game mechanics is how the state methods are executed, encapsulate their own sub-logic, and manage their transitions. Each concrete state is your own personal playground, and adding more states is as simple as creating a new concrete BaseBattleState class and adding your desired transition.

# Putting it all together

Getting the state machine set up isn't as difficult as you might think; all our logic is predetermined in each state and the state machine handles the transitions and delegates behaviors of the current state. The only pieces we don't have are concrete state instances and a running state machine in our client script, which we'll tackle next.

## Initializing concrete states

Open BattleSM.cs and update it to match the following code block, which initializes each state object with a reference to the corresponding state machine and sets the current state to the setup phase. Again, if you're only using a single state machine in your project, then this step would fit better in the SMContext script, but since we're going to use multiple state machines, it's better to explicitly subclass each state machine.

```
public class BattleSM : SMContext
{
    public State Setup;
    public State PlayerTurn;
    public State EnemyTurn;
    public State EndBattle;

    // 1
    void Start()
    {
        Setup = new SetupState(this);
        PlayerTurn = new PlayerState(this);
        EnemyTurn = new EnemyState(this);
        EndBattle = new EndState(this);

        // 2
        ChangeStateTo(Setup);
    }
}
```

Let's break down the code:

1. Add the Start method and initialize each state object with the BattleSM reference.
2. It changes the current state to the setup phase to begin the game.

**Creating states at startup versus on-demand**

In some cases, you may need to pass information from the current state to the next state and the SMContext doesn't have access to that data. A possible solution is to create new state instances when calling ChangeStateTo instead of initializing and storing state instances in SMContext:

```
    _stateMachine.ChangeStateTo(new PlayerState(_
    stateMachine));
```

You could also refactor the CheckState method to return a new optional state when needed and execute the state transitions in SMContext. However, both approaches are more CPU intensive than creating your state instances up front, so be careful to factor that into your optimization if your state machine is creating a ton of states in a rapid sequence (for instance, a character controller).

## Updating the client

Update BattleClient.cs to match the following code, which declares and assigns a state machine instance and delegates the state machine behaviors to the current state in the Update method. Now, the current state behaviors are constantly running, and any state transitions will take place uninterrupted.

```
using System.Collections;
using System.Collections.Generic;
using UnityEngine;

[RequireComponent(typeof(Manager))]
public class BattleClient : MonoBehaviour
{
    // 1
    private BattleSM Battle;

    void Start()
    {
        // 2
        Battle = GetComponent<BattleSM>();
    }
```

```
    void Update()
    {
        // 3
        Battle.HandleInput();
        Battle.CheckState();
    }
}
```

Let's break down the code:

1.  It declares a private BattleSM variable.

2.  It sets the BattleSM value on Start.

3.  It calls HandleInput and CheckState in the Update method.

 If you're looking for a more UI-based solution, the way we've set up the State pattern code will still work. With a little refactoring to the abstract State class to handle and bind specific inputs to actions, you could hook up the client code to UI button clicks or UnityEvents in the Editor. It all depends on the problem you're solving and what outcomes you're trying to achieve; you have enough experience with the State pattern to configure it any way you want.

Run the game and you'll see SetupState initialize in the console, followed by the PlayerState turn, as shown in *Figure 10.6*.

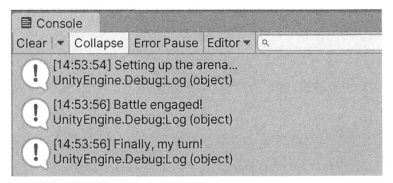

*Figure 10.6: Console logs for setup and player states*

You can choose either to attack (*A* key) or heal (*H* key), which will apply damage or extra health and then transition to the EnemyState turn.

If you or the enemy ever get to 0 health, the game will transition into the EndState and quit.

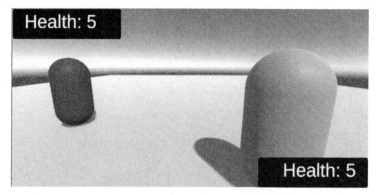

*Figure 10.7: In-game screenshot of player state*

Have some fun experimenting with the different gameplay possibilities, and when you're done, let's talk about how to efficiently account for shared behavior across multiple states!

# Using a hierarchical state machine

Now that our FSM is working, it's only natural to start thinking about sharing behavior across states. Luckily, OOP already provides the answer: just use the existing class hierarchy!

Since all our battle states inherit from BaseBattleState, we can add the logic we want every subclass to have access to without duplicating it in each state script. Then, we can call the base class from each state whenever we want to defer the action. In our example, imagine we want to be able to pause and unpause the game at any time, but also prevent the player state from listening for key presses when the game is paused.

Open BaseBattleState and update it to match the following code block, which overrides the HandleInput method, listens for the *spacebar* key press, and toggles the pause state using the Manager script.

```
public class BaseBattleState : State
{
    protected BattleSM _stateMachine;

    public BaseBattleState(BattleSM sm)
    {
        _stateMachine = sm;
    }
```

```
// 1
public override void HandleInput()
{
    base.HandleInput();

    // 2
    if(Input.GetKeyDown(KeyCode.Space))
    {
        Manager.Instance.Pause();
    }
}
```

Let's break down the code:

1. It overrides the `HandleInput` method and calls the base `HandleInput` method before adding new logic.

2. It listens for a key press and toggles the pause state.

Open `PlayerState.cs` and update the `HandleInput` method to match the following code, which allows the player to pause and unpause the game using the `BaseBattleState` class's `HandleInput` method and restricts player actions when the game is paused.

```
...

public override void HandleInput()
{
    // 1
    if(!Manager.Instance.isPaused)
    {
        if (Input.GetKeyDown(KeyCode.A) && movesRemaining > 0)
        {
            movesRemaining--;
            isKO = Manager.Instance.Enemy.TakeDamage(1);
        }
        else if (Input.GetKeyDown(KeyCode.H) && movesRemaining > 0)
        {
            movesRemaining--;
```

```
                Manager.Instance.Player.Heal();
        }
        // 2
        else
        {
            base.HandleInput();
        }
    }
    // 3
    else
    {
        base.HandleInput();
    }
}
```

Let's break down the code:

1.  It checks whether the game is already paused before allowing player actions.

2.  If the game is paused, the input handling is passed to the base class.

3.  If the game is not paused, the input handling is passed to the base class.

**Overriding base behavior**

HandleInput is the only method we're concerned with in this hierarchical state machine example, but if you have shared code in other State methods, you need to repeat this process for each respective method. For example, if BaseBattleState had a fully implemented hierarchy, it would override the Enter, Exit, and CheckState methods and call the base methods first before adding new logic. The same would go for each substate, just like we did with the pause functionality in PlayerState. With this OOP approach, you're allowed to set default behavior or even basic debugging from the abstract State class all the way to each concrete state.

Run the game again and test how the pause feature works and notice how player actions are turned off when the game is paused when in PlayerState, as shown in the following figure:

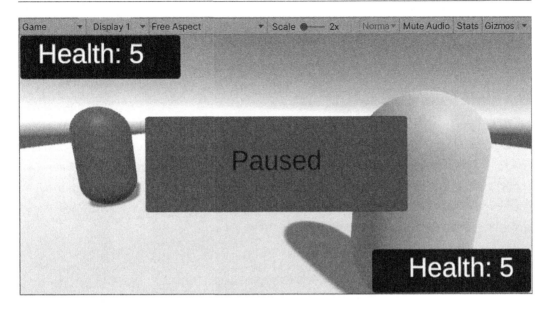

*Figure 10.8: In-game screenshot of pause mechanic*

With the hierarchical states up and running, it's time to tackle another common scenario – multiple state machines running at the same time!

## Adapting for concurrent state machines

Other than prototypes or extremely simple games, you'll likely run into situations where you need to keep track of multiple objects with their own internal states. This problem can quickly become a rabbit hole of concurrency and interdependence, but it boils down to whether the current states are related or not. We'll start by updating our example to deal with unrelated state machines and end the section with recommendations for handling dependent scenarios.

Imagine we wanted to add states for weather conditions – one for sunny days and one for cloudy days. If we used a single state machine context to manage two sets of states, we would need concrete states for each combination (battle states x weather states) to keep tracking a single internal state. In our example, four battle states quickly turn into eight battle/weather combination states, and that's just with two weather options. What if we wanted a third weather state? Now, we're tripling the number of battle states. You get the idea – it's an exponentially scaling nightmare.

Because the battle system and weather are unrelated in our example, the solution to our problems is already in our existing code – create another SMContext subclass to manage the weather states and have the client run the two state machines at the same time!

## Unrelated concurrent states

In the **Scripts** folder, create a new C# script named SunnyState and update it to match the following code block. This state will look a lot like our battle state but it takes in a WeatherSM state machine class instead of a BattleSM class. SunnyState will use a coroutine from the Manager script to adjust the Directional Light in the scene from light to dark to simulate a day-to-night transition and transition to the cloudy state when it's done. We haven't created the WeatherSM or Cloudy scripts yet, so ignore the warnings for now.

```csharp
using System.Collections;
using System.Collections.Generic;
using UnityEngine;

// 1
public class SunnyState : State
{
    protected WeatherSM _stateMachine;

    public SunnyState(WeatherSM sm)
    {
        _stateMachine = sm;
    }

    // 2
    public override IEnumerator Enter()
    {
        Manager.Instance.DayToNight();
        yield break;
    }

    // 3
    public override void CheckState()
    {
        if(Manager.Instance.daylight.intensity == 0.25f)
```

```
        {
            _stateMachine.ChangeStateTo(_stateMachine.Cloudy);
        }
    }
}
```

Let's break down the code:

1. It inherits from the State class, declares a protected state machine variable, and sets it in the class constructor.

2. It overrides the Enter method and starts the day-to-night coroutine using the Manager class.

3. It overrides the CheckState method and transitions to the next state when the Directional Light intensity hits a certain value.

Back in the **Scripts** folder, create a new C# script named CloudyState and update its code to match the following code block, which is almost identical to SunnyState except the Enter method triggers a night-to-day cycle and CheckState transitions back to SunnyState when the Directional Light intensity is back at its original value of 1.

```csharp
using System.Collections;
using System.Collections.Generic;
using UnityEngine;

// 1
public class CloudyState : State
{
    protected WeatherSM _stateMachine;

    public CloudyState(WeatherSM sm)
    {
        _stateMachine = sm;
    }

    // 2
    public override IEnumerator Enter()
    {
        Manager.Instance.NightToDay();
        yield break;
```

```
    }

    // 3
    public override void CheckState()
    {
        if (Manager.Instance.daylight.intensity == 1.0f)
        {
            _stateMachine.ChangeStateTo(_stateMachine.Sunny);
        }
    }
}
```

Let's break down the code:

1. It inherits from the State class, declares a protected state machine variable, and sets it in the class constructor.

2. It overrides the Enter method and starts the night-to-day coroutine using the Manager class.

3. It overrides the CheckState method and transitions to the next state when the Directional Light intensity hits a certain value.

Lastly, we need another state machine subclass to initialize the concrete weather states. In the **Scripts** folder, create a new C# script named WeatherSM and update its code to match the following code. WeatherSM subclasses SMContext, declares the two weather states we just created, and sets the first weather state.

```
using System.Collections;
using System.Collections.Generic;
using UnityEngine;

// 1
public class WeatherSM : SMContext
{
    public State Sunny;
    public State Cloudy;

    void Start()
    {
        // 2
```

```
    Sunny = new SunnyState(this);
    Cloudy = new CloudyState(this);

    // 3
    ChangeStateTo(Sunny);
  }
}
```

Let's break down the code:

1. It inherits from SMContext and declares two weather state variables.

2. It initializes the weather state variables and passes in the WeatherSM to each class constructor.

3. It sets the first weather state to Sunny.

This script takes care of the last of our console errors, so our next step is to attach WeatherSM.cs to the Client in the **Hierarchy** and update BattleClient.cs to match the following code, which runs WeatherSM alongside BattleSM.

```
[RequireComponent(typeof(Manager))]
public class BattleClient : MonoBehaviour
{
    private BattleSM Battle;

    // 1
    private WeatherSM Weather;

    void Start()
    {
        Battle = GetComponent<BattleSM>();

        // 2
        Weather = GetComponent<WeatherSM>();
    }

    void Update()
    {
        Battle.HandleInput();
        Battle.CheckState();
```

```
        // 3
        Weather.HandleInput();
        Weather.CheckState();
    }
}
```

Let's break down the code:

1.   It adds a `private` weather state machine variable.

2.   It initializes the weather state machine variable with the attached component.

3.   It calls `HandleInput` and `CheckState` every frame in the `Update` method.

Run the game and watch as the scene slowly gets darker and lighter as the weather states run concurrently with the battle system. Nothing we've done has affected the turn-based system, so you can still play the game.

## Related concurrent states

As promised, let's talk about concurrent but related states. Imagine our player has a light-based attack that works better when the sun is out versus when it's cloudy. Whenever you have internal states that are dependent on each other, you have a couple of options:

*   Have the `SMContext` try and manage two or more internal current states – in this example, one for the current battle state and one for the current weather state. However, this can be tricky for two reasons:

    *   The different internal states may have different transitions, so you may have to either spend time developing a generic transition method or handle each of the concurrent state transitions in their own method.

    *   Determining combinations of state actions (or dependent behaviors) could lead to messy `if-else` statements in the `HandleInput` method, which is the exact problem we're trying to solve with the State pattern in the first place.

*   Pass in a set or list of state machines to each concrete state so they are aware of each other and can act accordingly. This would create a strong coupling between state machines and concrete states, but it might be worth it if you need to perform logic checks for one state against another.

Fully implementing a concurrent state machine with related behaviors could go in a variety of different directions, so this is one area where it's going to be up to you to decide what works best for your project.

# Storing state history

Before we end the chapter, we should talk about how to keep track of your state machine's history. This feature isn't strictly part of the State pattern, but it's a handy way of automatically assigning the correct next state rather than hardcoding them in each concrete state.

Like the Command pattern undo/redo system from *Chapter 8, Binding Actions with the Command Pattern*, the Stack type is going to save us a lot of trouble with this problem. Using Stack's **last-in-first-out (LIFO)** functionality, we can push new states onto the stack, which always makes the current state the one on top. This doesn't do much for the first state, but when we move through state transitions, the stack will continue storing all the previous states underneath the current state. When we want to revert to the previous state or states, we pop the current state off the top and reference the new state that was next in line!

 In automata theory, the history mechanic we're going to create is called a pushdown automaton. The inner workings and history are outside the scope of this chapter, but you can read more about this classification at https://en.wikipedia.org/wiki/Pushdown_automaton.

## Pushing new states

In our example, we don't re-enter the setup or end states, but tracking the history would be helpful with the transitions between player and enemy turns. Before we touch any concrete states, we need to make sure that duplicate states aren't pushed onto the stack. This keeps the stack relatively small and removes any clutter we would amass if we left out this step.

Open SMContext.cs and update it to match the following code, which adds a Stack variable to store and manage our state history and pushes new states onto the stack during transitions if they're not already present.

```
public class SMContext : MonoBehaviour
{
    public State CurrentState { get; private set; }
```

```
    private bool _isTransitioning;

    // 1
    public Stack<State> history = new Stack<State>();

    public void HandleInput() { //... No changes needed... }
    public void CheckState() { //... No changes needed... }
    public void ChangeStateTo(State state) { //... No changes needed... }

    private IEnumerator StateTransition(State newState)
    {
        if (CurrentState == newState || _isTransitioning)
        {
            yield break;
        }

        _isTransitioning = true;

        // 2
        if(!history.Contains(newState))
        {
            history.Push(newState);
        }

        if(CurrentState != null)
        {
            yield return StartCoroutine(CurrentState.Exit());
        }

        CurrentState = newState;
        StartCoroutine(CurrentState.Enter());

        _isTransitioning = false;
    }
}
```

Let's break down the updated code:

1. It adds a Stack variable to store the state history.

2. It checks whether the new state is already in the history stack and adds it to the stack if it isn't present already.

Now, when we go through the turn-based battle, the setup, player, enemy, and ending states will be added to the history stack during their transitions. The next step is to pop off the enemy state when the enemy state is finished and revert to the player state automatically.

## Reverting to previous states

Since EnemyState is the last in the chain of battle states (the end state only happens once at the end, so it doesn't matter in the history scheme), we can pop it off the top of the history stack, which can be a lifesaver if you're referencing states by name – in this scenario, there's no chance of misspelling anything; the last state is always used. Then, the state transition can reference the new top state in the history stack in CheckState.

Update EnemyState.cs to match the following code, which removes EnemyState as the current state after doing damage to the player and sets PlayerState as the new current state without having to pass UpdateStateTo a hardcoded state instance.

```
public class EnemyState : BaseBattleState
{
    private bool isKO;
    private int movesRemaining;

    public EnemyState(BattleSM sm) : base(sm) {}

    public override IEnumerator Enter()
    {
        Debug.Log("You don't stand a chance!");
        Manager.Instance.Enemy.ChangeColor(Color.green);
        movesRemaining = 1;

        yield return new WaitForSeconds(1);

        isKO = Manager.Instance.Player.TakeDamage();
        movesRemaining--;
```

```
        // 1
        _stateMachine.history.Pop();
    }


    public override void CheckState()
    {
        if (isKO)
        {
            _stateMachine.ChangeStateTo(_stateMachine.EndBattle);
        }
        else if(movesRemaining == 0)
        {
            // 2
            _stateMachine.ChangeStateTo(_stateMachine.history.Peek());
        }
    }


    public override IEnumerator Exit()
    {
        //… No changes needed …
    }
}
```

Let's break down the code:

1.  It removes the most recent state from the history stack.

2.  It uses the Peek method to return the item currently at the top of the history stack.

Play the game one final time and notice that nothing has changed, but the code is much less brittle and prone to human error (which is always a worthwhile goal).

> This has already been a dense chapter, so we're not going to add to it by retreading the ground we've covered in detail in previous chapters. That being said, you can absolutely improve the structure, usability, and performance of the State pattern in Unity with generics, events, and ScriptableObjects on your own journey.

# Summary

We've covered a lot in this chapter and, at this point, you might be wondering whether the State pattern and FSMs have become too tangled up together to be of any real use. Just know that I used FSMs in this chapter not to confuse you, but to show you that the State pattern can be used in situations where your states are largely static (meaning the transitions don't play a major part, like a network connection being active or closed) and when your states are dependent on their transitions (like in a character controller or turn-based battle system). Both implementations are correct and useful, especially when combined to fit your project!

Remember, the State pattern is best suited for breaking bloated decision trees into standalone behaviors with each concrete state determining how it behaves when it's activated, while it's running, and when it ends. Hierarchical state machines can share common behaviors across different states while concurrent state machines can let you run related and unrelated states at the same time, but this scenario isn't the easiest to handle. Storing a state machine's history can make it easier to automate transitions and eliminate hardcoding state sequences, which makes your chain of possible states safer and easier to manage.

In the next chapter, we'll dive into the Visitor pattern, which allows you to effectively add new behavior to existing objects without changing their underlying code!

# Further reading

- Abstract classes can't be created on their own, but they are excellent solutions when you want a consistent base class blueprint that other classes can inherit from. Many of our solutions in this book rely heavily on abstract classes to provide an abstraction layer between class blueprints and their concrete implementations. You can find more information at `https://learn.microsoft.com/en-us/dotnet/csharp/language-reference/keywords/abstract`.

- Coroutines are a specific type of method in Unity that allows you to spread tasks across several frames instead of running them all at once like a normal C# method. For more information, check out the documentation at `https://docs.unity3d.com/Manual/Coroutines.html`.

- Stacks are a last-in first-out collection of objects, which makes them ideal for storing and retrieving the most recent elements in any given set of data. If these are new to you, check out the documentation at `https://learn.microsoft.com/en-us/dotnet/api/system.collections.stack?view=net-8.0`.

# Leave a review!

Enjoying this book? Help readers like you by leaving an Amazon review. Scan the QR code below to get a free eBook of your choice.

# 11

# Adding Features with the Visitor Pattern

In the last chapter, we tackled the mountain that is the State design pattern, finite state machines, and a little automata theory to boot. In this chapter, we'll work with the Visitor pattern, which lets you effectively tack on sets of related operations (or behaviors) to existing objects without changing the underlying object(s) in any way – look but don't touch!

Essentially, new sets of behaviors become the visitors, and the objects you want to modify become the visitable elements; each visitor is applied to a list of visitable elements, new operations are executed, and the original code remains unharmed. The important bit is that each element gets its own custom implementation of the new behavior based on its own type and the visitor doing the visiting, so the entire system is customizable from the ground up.

If this sounds like a job for plain OOP, just wait because there's one key difference that sets the Visitor pattern apart – class hierarchies don't matter in this pattern! Any class or interface can be expanded if it is visitable (we'll get to that soon). It's like a shortcut to new behavior without the OOP overhead or restrictions.

Think of the Visitor pattern like going to a party at a friend's house (I hope you have all been to a party or this analogy won't work) – the address and guests don't change, but you can modify the party-going experience if you set a theme and ask every guest to bring something different that matches the theme. Everything depends on the party theme and what your guests are bringing to the party – visitor and visitable objects are both necessary parts of the decision-making process and can't have the desired impact without each other.

We'll focus on the following topics in this chapter:

- The pros and cons of the Visitor design pattern
- Creating a save system
- Working with composite elements
- Selective visitation with ScriptableObjects

By the end of the chapter, you'll have a whole new set of tools for adding new features without changing existing code, updating legacy projects, and all-around freedom from class hierarchies! Let's start off with the starter project's technical requirements and look at the pattern breakdown, and then we can move on to code of our own!

# Technical requirements

Before you start:

1.  Download or clone the GitHub repository at `https://github.com/PacktPublishing/C-Design-Patterns-with-Unity-First-Edition`.
2.  Open the **Ch_11_Starter** project folder in Unity Hub.
3.  In **Assets | Scenes**, double-click on **SampleScene**.

The project for this chapter doesn't have any flashy mechanics, just a playable character that you can move around the scene and the ability to save your progress and eventually collect different upgrades (for now, we can only ineffectively bump into the little red orbs). The power of the Visitor pattern isn't flashy, but it's definitely one of the most valuable, and practical, design patterns to have in your toolbox.

As for the scripts:

- `Client.cs` stores a `Player` variable and an empty method hooked up to the **Save** button in the scene.
- `Movement.cs` lets you control the character in the scene.
- `Player.cs` has the required component attributes for `Movement`, `Stats`, and `Weapon` components.
- `Stats.cs` has two variables, one for a player's intelligence and another for strength.
- `UIManager.cs` stores references to the `Stats` and `Weapon` components attached to the `Player` and shows their data in the UI at every frame.

- `Utilities.cs` has a single for fetching `PlayerPrefs` by key and formatting them into a readable debug log.
- `Weapon.cs` has variables for the weapon's name, damage, critical multiplier, and a list of modifications.

We'll also be using some Unity and C# language features to take our code the extra mile. Don't worry if you're not familiar with these; I've included links to learn the basics, and I'll explain how they apply to our use cases as we go:

- Interfaces (`https://learn.microsoft.com/en-us/dotnet/csharp/fundamentals/types/interfaces`)
- PlayerPrefs (`https://docs.unity3d.com/ScriptReference/PlayerPrefs.html`)
- ScriptableObjects (`https://docs.unity3d.com/Manual/class-ScriptableObject.html`)

Our task is to build a saving system using the `PlayerPrefs` API to store the player's stats and weapon data, as well as create configurable upgrades as `ScriptableObjects` later in the chapter. This design pattern takes a bit more code to set up than most, so stick with the explanations until we get the structure in place to see some output!

# Breaking down the Visitor pattern

As part of the Behavioral family of design patterns, the Visitor pattern is all about adding new features without changing existing structures or class hierarchies. This approach is ideal when you want to apply new requirements to pre-existing objects or when dealing with legacy code (or systems) that can't be directly modified for one reason or another. The Visitor pattern is useful when:

- You need to add new behaviors (i.e., operations or algorithms) to existing objects without changing the object's class.
- You want to perform operations on a set of unrelated objects that don't share the same interfaces or parent classes.
- You want to group related sets of behaviors or algorithms that can be applied to a set of objects without adding unrelated behaviors to classes that don't need them.

Sometimes, the party-guest-visiting analogy isn't concrete enough to visualize, even though the pattern is called **Visitor** (and wouldn't it be wonderful if things all aligned?) but there are other examples we can pull from our everyday lives that illustrate the idea.

For instance, we've all been to a restaurant with a group of people. Let's say there's a group of three adults and two kids sitting at a table looking at menus; when enough time has passed, a server approaches the group and asks them what they'd all like to drink. In this scenario, the server is the visitor and ordering is the new functionality being added, but the diners themselves aren't being modified. The server is simply going around the table taking orders, while each individual diner gets to decide what they want, as shown in *Figure 11.1*.

 "But what about the kids?" you shout. Well, depending on the age of the kids, either they will order for themselves or the parent will order for them. Either way, we'll get to component (child) objects in the *Working with composite elements* section, don't worry!

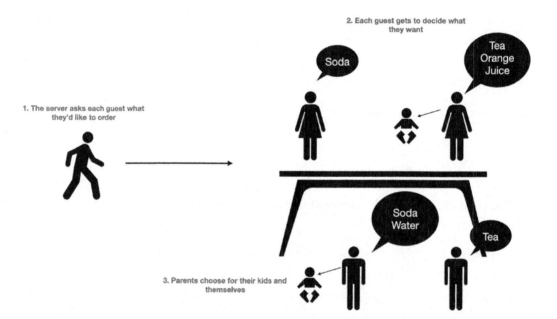

*Figure 11.1: Restaurant example of real-life Visitor pattern application*

The nice thing about the Visitor pattern is how decoupled the visitor is from each visited item (or diner in our restaurant example). The server can come up to the same table for all sorts of reasons, and each diner is still in charge of their response; the diners don't even have to be the same (men, women, children, pet hamsters, etc. – it doesn't matter as long as they all agree that they're at the restaurant for the same reason).

For instance, the server can ask if anyone has any food allergies, if someone needs a vegetarian menu, or how everyone would like to pay at the end of the meal. Again, the table of guests doesn't change when the server adds new behavior, as shown in the following figure:

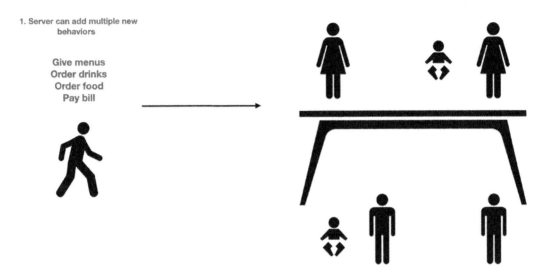

*Figure 11.2: Decoupling the visitor from visited elements*

However, it's important to use the Visitor pattern in the right context. In the restaurant, the number of diners is mostly set when they sit down, so that's not likely to change. The server can be confident that they know how many people they are responsible for at a given table (and can add in as many new behaviors as they want). But if the diners are constantly leaving or arriving, this doesn't work so well. The server may have to repeat the ordering process from scratch with each new guest, which is a red flag that the Visitor pattern isn't a good fit for your project. This shouldn't scare you off if you need *a little* flexibility in your visitable elements (that's totally fine); I just wouldn't recommend this pattern if your visitable elements are in constant flux.

## Diagramming the pattern

*Figure 11.3* shows the UML structure of the Visitor pattern with its five component elements:

- The **Visitor** interface has methods for each concrete element that will be visited in the object structure: Each method passes in the **concrete Element** type being visited as a parameter, which lets each visitor access the element and do whatever work is required.

- **Concrete visitors** implement each method of the `Visitor` interface and add specific logic depending on which **Element** is being visited: This allows a custom approach for each element being visited while allowing you to store the local state.

- The **element** interface has a single method called `Accept` with a `Visitor` interface parameter.

- **Concrete elements** implement the `Accept` method required by the `Element` interface and use the `Visitor` parameter to call the appropriate Visitor method.

- **Object structure** stores and enumerates its elements so a concrete `Visitor` can sequentially visit each **element** one by one.

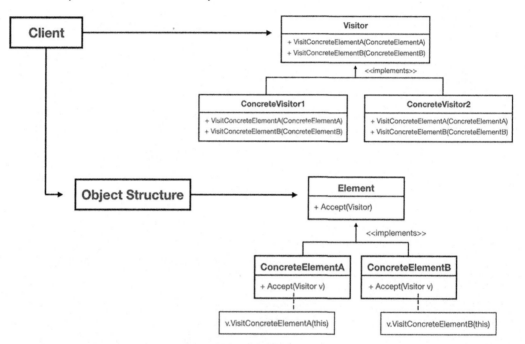

*Figure 11.3: UML diagram of the Visitor pattern components*

Again, it's important to really understand the dual hierarchy implications of the Visitor pattern before implementing it in your projects. Since each concrete visitor will need a method for visiting each concrete element, the pattern is most efficient when the number of concrete elements in an object structure is fairly static. You can have as many new visitor as you want, but adding new concrete elements means updating each concrete visitor you may have.

However, that's not to say you can't have more than one object structure; in that case, you'll need a visitor interface for each object structure to keep things in sync.

## Pros and cons

Like all design patterns, there are pros and cons. Let's start with the benefits of the Visitor pattern:

- **The open/closed principle** is a huge benefit of visiting objects – each concrete element is open to extension but not modification.

- **Concrete element class hierarchies don't matter!** Each concrete element just needs to be able to accept a visitor, nothing more in common is necessary, which frees us from OOP restrictions and bloated inheritance.

- **Each visitor is responsible for its own behavior.** This keeps responsibilities nicely encapsulated and away from the concrete elements being visited (they can largely act as data containers).

However, be careful of the following pitfalls when using the pattern in your projects:

- **Adding new concrete elements is a hassle** – your first job is always to assess if the problem you're facing is a good fit for the design pattern solution you're considering.

- **Concrete elements** are more exposed than might be comfortable since the visitor may need access to fields and information that you may want to keep private (which can break your class encapsulation).

- **Code complexity** is a big factor with the Visitor pattern (as you'll see); there's a lot of work upfront before the pattern starts earning its keep.

Now that we've covered the structure, benefits, and limitations of the Visitor pattern, we can start laying out the traditional implementation by creating a save system.

## Creating a save system

Imagine you're coming into a game project as a new developer and your first assignment is to create a system for saving user data, which includes the player's stats, weapon, and weapon modifications (if they've collected any). Development is already pretty far along, so you're not allowed to mess with any of the existing classes that manage all the fun stuff, but you have access to the player and, therefore, indirect access to its stats, weapon, and mods.

Since the Player object has a set structure, you know exactly what needs to be done – implement the Visitor pattern and create a data-saving visitor that can be applied to each of the player component elements without changing the underlying objects.

We'll do this with a combination of interfaces, concrete elements, and, of course, a `Visitor` class, all of which are covered in the following subsections.

## Structuring the interfaces

One of the things I appreciate most about the Visitor pattern is that defining the visitor and visitable element interfaces is straightforward – all the information already exists in your code (otherwise this pattern wouldn't be the best fit). In our example, the player (our object structure) has components for its stats and weapon, and each weapon has a list of modifications to track what the player is equipped with or has picked up. This translates directly into what elements our visitor interface needs to account for – stats, weapons, and weapon mods.

In the **Scripts** folder, create a new C# script named `IVisitor` and update its code to match the following code block. Our new interface declares three visiting methods, one for each element in the `Player` object structure, and passes in an argument matching each element we're visiting. Like the Observer pattern, this dependency injection approach lets us work with the object we're modifying without having to waste time in each concrete visitor class finding the element we're trying to work with.

```
using System.Collections;
using System.Collections.Generic;
using UnityEngine;

// 1
public interface IVisitor
{
    // 2
    void VisitStats(Stats stats);
    void VisitWeapon(Weapon weapon);
    void VisitWeaponMod(WeaponMod mod);
}
```

Let's break down the visitor interface:

1.  It declares a `public interface` for all visitor classes to implement.
2.  It declares methods for each concrete element that can be visited.

Each object structure needs its own corresponding visitor interface or abstract class – you can change the guests who come to your party and what they bring, but if they visit a stranger's house, things aren't going to go as expected. We're only dealing with the Player object structure in the examples for this chapter, but keep in mind that you might have more than one visitor and visitable element interface for a more complex project.

If you want to simplify the IVisitor methods into a single method that takes in an IElement type parameter, you can, but it's less declarative and hides the underlying object structure components.

We need a way for elements being visited to accept their guests, which means going to the **Scripts** folder again, creating a new C# script named IElement, and updating its code to match the code snippet below. This new interface says that every element we want to visit must have an Accept method that takes in an IVisitor parameter, with each concrete element implementing their own accept logic.

```
using System.Collections;
using System.Collections.Generic;
using UnityEngine;

// 1
public interface IElement
{
    // 2
    void Accept(IVisitor visitor);
}
```

Let's break down the Element interface:

1.  It declares a public interface for all elements that can be visited.

2.  It adds an Accept method with an IVisitor parameter.

Now that we have the blueprints for our visitors and visitable elements, let's create some concrete versions of each and start putting our save system together.

## Adding a concrete visitors

Each concrete visitors you write should have a clear objective – apply related operations to different elements in the object structure. In our example, we want a visitors to go through each `Player` component and decide what (and how) specific game data is saved. We're going to use `PlayerPrefs` to save simple data, but this is an example of related behavior. For example, we wouldn't want to put `PlayerPrefs` saving logic with JSON or XML exporting logic in the same visitors – while these are all ways to save data, they are different implementations and need their own visitors classes.

 OK, yes, I see you raising your hand and saying, "But we could totally put all the different saving format logic into a single Visitor." And yes, you could. But would it be the best solution? No. Keeping responsibilities separate (even if they are related at a high level) ensures each `Visitors` class only has one set of responsibilities and doesn't have to make decisions about what it's supposed to do every time it is called.

In the **Scripts** folder, create a new C# script named `PlayerPrefVisitor` and update its code to match the following code. This new concrete visitors has methods for visiting each `Player` element and saving the necessary property values.

```
using System.Collections;
using System.Collections.Generic;
using UnityEngine;

// 1
public class PlayerPrefVisitor : IVisitor
{
    // 2
    public void VisitStats(Stats stats)
    {
        PlayerPrefs.SetInt("_intelligence", stats.Intelligence);
        PlayerPrefs.SetInt("_strength", stats.Strength);
    }

    // 3
    public void VisitWeapon(Weapon weapon)
    {
        PlayerPrefs.SetString("_weaponName", weapon.Name);
        PlayerPrefs.SetInt("_weaponDamage", weapon.Damage);
```

```
        PlayerPrefs.SetInt("_weaponCritical", weapon.Critical);
    }

    // 4
    public void VisitWeaponMod(WeaponMod mod)
    {
        PlayerPrefs.SetString("_weaponMod" + mod.Slot, mod.Name);
    }
}
```

Let's break down our first concrete visitor:

1. It declares a new public class that implements the IVisitor interface.
2. It adds a method for visiting the Stats element and saves data to PlayerPrefs.
3. It adds a method for visiting the Weapon element and saves data to PlayerPrefs.
4. It adds a method for visiting WeaponMod elements and saves data to PlayerPrefs.

> It's OK if you're not familiar with the PlayerPrefs API. It's not a core feature of the Visitor pattern, but it *is* a nice way of saving data between game sessions and is a good fit for our example (building out a JSON or XML parser/saver doesn't add to the design pattern content). However, I should point out that using PlayerPrefs to store massive amounts of game data is not a recommended approach (and not what the API is for), but there are several tools available on the Unity Store if you find yourself in need. You can find more information on PlayerPrefs in the Unity docs at https://docs.unity3d.com/2022.2/Documentation/ScriptReference/PlayerPrefs.html.

Notice that we've encapsulated the PlayerPrefs saving feature into its own class but implemented the logic for each element independently (and each element has the necessary information to do the required work). With a concrete visitor established, we need party guests for it to visit, which we'll tackle in the next section!

## Adding concrete elements

The starter project already has existing Player components, which makes turning them into visitable objects that much easier.

Open Stats.cs and update its code to match the following code block, which implements the IVisitor interface, declares the Accept method, and uses the visitor parameter to determine which visiting method needs to be executed.

```
using System.Collections;
using System.Collections.Generic;
using UnityEngine;

// 1
public class Stats : MonoBehaviour, IElement
{
    public int Intelligence;
    public int Strength;

    // 2
    public void Accept(IVisitor visitor)
    {
        // 3
        visitor.VisitStats(this);
    }
}
```

Let's break down the code:

1. Updates the Stats class to implement the IElement interface
2. Adds the required Accept method with an IVisitor parameter
3. Uses the IVisitor parameter to call VisitStats and pass in the Stats object

The wonderful part of this step in the pattern is that any object can be a visitable element, no matter its existing class hierarchy (something that OOP can't accomplish without a *lot* of extra work). Stats knows itself (the lock) and what visiting method to call (the key), which means there's no ambiguity when it comes to accepting a visitor (they both know their roles and how they fit together to open the door).

Before we test, open Weapon.cs and update its code to match the code block below, which turns the class into a visitable element, adds the Accept method, and calls the appropriate visiting method (this step needs to be repeated with any and all elements you want to be visitable, but it's virtually the only repetitive overhead this pattern has).

```
using System.Collections;
using System.Collections.Generic;
using UnityEngine;

// 1
public class Weapon : MonoBehaviour, IElement
{
    public string Name;
    public int Damage;
    public int Critical;

    public List<WeaponMod> _modifications = new List<WeaponMod>()
    {
        new WeaponMod("Critical buff", 1),
        new WeaponMod("Stamina recovery", 2)
    };

    // 2
    public void Accept(IVisitor visitor)
    {
        // 3
        visitor.VisitWeapon(this);
    }
}
```

Let's break down the code:

1.  Updates the Weapon class to implement the IElement interface
2.  Adds the required Accept method with an IVisitor parameter
3.  Uses the IVisitor parameter to call VisitWeapon and pass in the Weapon object

 Don't worry about the list of WeaponMod objects in the Weapon class; we'll get to that code when we tackle composite objects (objects that have child objects of their own) in the *Working with composite elements* section.

Both of our main visitable elements are now configured. We can put together our Player object structure and test out the save functionality in the next section.

# Adding an object structure

An object structure is a managing entity with no real logic of its own – its one and only job is to put together a list of elements with related needs, iterate through each element when a visitor comes calling, and pass in a concrete visitor to each element's Accept method. Again, it's important to recognize that these elements don't have to be related by type but rather by need. Our Player class is an object structure by default, so we'll use that to store our Stats and Weapon elements and visit them when needed.

Open Player.cs and update its code to match the following code block, which adds a private list of IElement objects, initializes the list with the Stats and Weapon components in the Start method, and declares a new method to loop through and visit each element.

```
using System.Collections;
using System.Collections.Generic;
using UnityEngine;

[RequireComponent(typeof(Movement))]
[RequireComponent(typeof(Stats))]
[RequireComponent(typeof(Weapon))]
public class Player : MonoBehaviour
{
    // 1
    private List<IElement> _elements = new List<IElement>();

    void Start()
    {
        // 2
        _elements.Add(this.gameObject.GetComponent<Stats>());
        _elements.Add(this.gameObject.GetComponent<Weapon>());
    }

    // 3
    public void Accept(IVisitor visitor)
    {
        // 4
        foreach (var element in _elements)
```

```
        {
            element.Accept(visitor);
        }
    }
}
```

Let's break down the object structure code:

1.  Creates an empty list of IElement objects

2.  Adds the Stats and Weapon components to the object structure list

3.  Declares an Accept method with an IVisitor parameter

4.  Iterates through each IElement in the object structure list, calls the Accept method on each element, and passes in the IVisitor parameter

To test our Visitor pattern in action, open Client.cs and update its code to match the following code snippet, which adds a concrete visitor and passes it to the Player in a public method we'll connect to the **Save** button in the scene. All the work is nicely hidden from the client by the object structure (Player), the visitor (PlayerPrefVisitor), and the visitable elements (Stats and Weapon components). Therefore, anytime we want to change or run multiple visitor on the Player, all we need to do is swap out the concrete visitor class!

```
using System.Collections;
using System.Collections.Generic;
using UnityEngine;

public class Client : MonoBehaviour
{
    public Player Player;

    // 1
    private IVisitor _visitor;

    void Start()
    {
        // 2
        _visitor = new PlayerPrefVisitor();
    }
```

```
    public void SaveData()
    {
        // 3
        Player.Accept(_visitor);

        // 4
        Utilities.PrintPlayerPrefs();
    }
}
```

Let's break down the updated client code:

1.  Adds a private `IVisitor` variable

2.  Sets the `IVisitor` variable to a new instance of `PlayerPrefVisitor` in `Start`

3.  Calls `Accept` on the `Player` object and passes in the concrete visitor

4.  Prints out the saved data from `PlayerPrefs` after they've been saved

Hit **Play,** click the **Save** button, and select the console log to see our saved `Stats` and `Weapon` data printed nicely, as shown in the following screenshot. If you can't see the entire output message, adjust the bottom of the **Console** window. Don't worry that the weapon mods are empty; we haven't actually visited those elements yet (more on that in the next section).

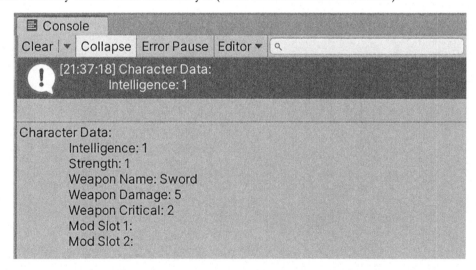

*Figure 11.4: Visitor code executing on character stats*

You may have already figured this out, but while swapping out concrete visiting classes is encouraged (that's the whole point of the Visitor pattern), swapping object structures will break your code – if you're dealing with more than one object structure, you'll need corresponding visitor interfaces for each one. Going back to our first example of inviting people to a party, you can change the guests and what they're bringing to your party because it's at *your* house – but if your guests showed up at a random stranger's door, there would be a drastically different outcome.

Before we wrap up this portion of the Visitor pattern, there's still the matter of our weapon modifications that needs to be visited, which we'll work on in the next section.

# Working with composite elements

There are going to be times when your object structure isn't the only thing with visitable child elements, and that's absolutely fine. In our case, each `Weapon` has a list of modifications that can also be expanded with a concrete visitor on demand. The solution for this scenario isn't scary or undiscovered, it's just a good-old inheritance question mixed with a little added iteration!

Open `Weapon.cs` and update the `WeaponMod` class code at the bottom of the file to match the following snippet, which implements the `IElement` interface, adds the required `Accept` method, and uses the concrete visitor parameter to call the corresponding visiting method just like we've done with our other visitable elements.

```
// 1
public class WeaponMod : IElement
{
    public string Name;
    public int Slot;
    public int Level = 1;

    public WeaponMod(string name, int slot)
    {
        this.Name = name;
        this.Slot = slot;
    }

    // 2
    public void Accept(IVisitor visitor)
```

```
    {
        // 3
        visitor.VisitWeaponMod(this);
    }

}
```

Let's break down the code:

1. Updates WeaponMod to implement the IElement interface

2. Adds the required Accept method with an Ivisitor parameter

3. Uses the Ivisitor parameter to call VisitWeaponMod and pass in the WeaponMod instance

Update Weapon.cs to match the following code, which changes the modifications list type to Ielement, but more importantly, iterates through the modifications and calls Accept on each Ielement before calling Accept on the Weapon itself.

```
public class Weapon : MonoBehaviour, Ielement
{
    public string Name;
    public int Damage;
    public int Critical;

    // 1
    public List<Ielement> _modifications = new List<Ielement>()
    {
        new WeaponMod("Critical buff", 1),
        new WeaponMod("Stamina recovery", 2)
    };

    public void Accept(Ivisitor visitor)
    {
        // 2
        foreach(var mod in _modifications)
        {
            // 3
            mod.Accept(visitor);
        }

        visitor.VisitWeapon(this);
    }
```

```
    }
```

Let's break down the code:

1.  Updates the _modifications list to store Ielement objects

2.  Iterates over the _modifications list of WeaponMod items

3.  Calls the Accept method on each item and passes in the WeaponMod instance

 This bottom-up approach on the visitable element hierarchy lets you take care of any logic or scenarios in the child objects before working your way up to the parent (it's easier to eat your own food at a restaurant when your kids are already happily fed).

Our Visitor pattern infrastructure doesn't need any updates to run this new code as the IVisitor interface already has a visiting method; Weapon just didn't know it needed to open the door. Click **Play** again and save your character's data, which will show updated values for each weapon modification, as shown in the following screenshot:

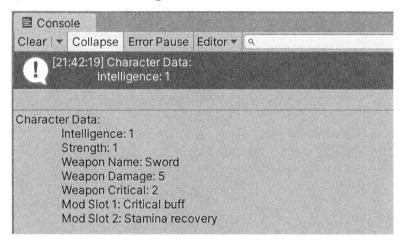

*Figure 11.5: Component elements being visited*

We've covered the basics of the Visitor pattern, but all our code up until now assumes that each element in the object structure needs to be visited whenever a visitor comes knocking. That's all perfectly fine, but what if we want a visitor to only visit *some* elements in an object structure, depending on the visitor? In our example, not every element may need to be saved, but it's more fun to think of this selective visitation in terms of upgrades or buffs – depending on the upgrade, all or some of the elements might need to be visited, which we'll tackle in the last section.

# Accounting for selective visitation

Our concrete PlayerPrefVisitor didn't store any local data (it doesn't have to if it's not necessary), but the Visitor pattern can also account for the context of the visitation; visitors can be set up to apply behaviors and algorithms to specific elements and element combinations. This is a bit of an inversion of how we traditionally think of this pattern, but it's equally as valid and useful. In this section, we'll create visiting ScriptableObjects (because we love them) that deliver upgrades and buffs to elements on our Player depending on each concrete visitor's local state (conditions).

In the **Scripts** folder, create a new C# script named SOVisitor and update its code to match the following code block. Like PlayerPrefsVisitor, SOVisitor has methods for visiting the Stats, Weapon, and WeaponMod components on our Player, but with added variables to determine when a component needs to be visited. How you handle a visitor's local state and selective visitation is entirely up to you, but pay special attention to who you let into each element (and under what conditions).

```
using System.Collections;
using System.Collections.Generic;
using UnityEngine;

// 1
[CreateAssetMenu(fileName = "Upgrade", menuName = "SOVisitor")]

// 2
public class SOVisitor : ScriptableObject, Ivisitor
{
    // 3
    public int StatsBoost;
    public int DamageBoost;
    public int CriticalBoost;
    public bool UpgradeMod;

    // 4
    public void VisitStats(Stats stats)
    {
        if (StatsBoost == 0)
            return;
```

```
        stats.Intelligence += StatsBoost;
        stats.Strength += StatsBoost;

        Debug.LogFormat($"Intelligence -> {stats.Intelligence}, Strength
-> {stats.Strength}");
    }


    // 5
    public void VisitWeapon(Weapon weapon)
    {
        if(DamageBoost > 0)
        {
            weapon.Damage += DamageBoost;
            Debug.LogFormat($"Damage increased -> {weapon.Damage}");
        }

        if(CriticalBoost > 0)
        {
            weapon.Critical *= CriticalBoost;
            Debug.LogFormat($"Critical increased -> {weapon.Critical}");
        }
    }


    // 6
    public void VisitWeaponMod(WeaponMod mod)
    {
        if (UpgradeMod == false)
            return;

        mod.Level++;
        Debug.LogFormat($"{mod.Name} level increased -> {mod.Level}");
    }
}
```

Let's break down the new concrete visitor:

1.  Uses a `CreateAssetMenu` attribute to add the `ScriptableObject` to the Unity menu

2.  Declares a new `ScriptableObject` class that implements the `Ivisitor` interface

3.   Adds multiple variables to track and implement visited class logic

4.   Adds a method for visiting the Stats element and updating class data

5.   Adds a method for visiting the Weapon element and updating class data

6.   Adds a method for visiting the WeaponMod element and updating class data

Now it's time to take our SOVisitor for a spin! I'm going to create and configure three different upgrades for testing so our player can collect more than one upgrade and see the different visitation rules apply. You can either use the values I've supplied in the screenshots below or set up your own – either way, you'll need to follow these steps:

1.   Select the **ScriptableObjects** folder in the **Project** assets.

2.   From the Unity menu, select **Create | SOVisitor**.

3.   Select the new SOVisitor object, hit *Enter,* and rename it to something descriptive.

4.   Set the values for Stats Boost, Damage Boost, Critical Boost, and Upgrade Mod.

5.   Repeat steps 1–4 as many times as you like!

For reference, here is my **Stats Upgrade** with the values I used:

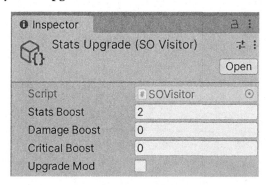

*Figure 11.6: Stats Upgrade ScriptableObject values*

Below is the **Weapon Upgrade** with the values I used:

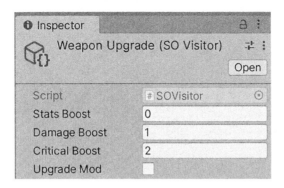

*Figure 11.7: Weapon Upgrade scriptable object values*

Finally, below is the **Mega Upgrade** with the values I used:

| Inspector | |
|---|---|
| **Mega Upgrade (SO Visitor)** | Open |
| Script | # SOVisitor |
| Stats Boost | 1 |
| Damage Boost | 2 |
| Critical Boost | 2 |
| Upgrade Mod | ✓ |

*Figure 11.8: Mega Upgrade scriptable object values*

The starter project already has an Upgrade Prefab ready to go (and three in the scene), so let's write a quick script to connect SOVisitor to the game. In the **Scripts** folder, create a new C# script named UpgradePickup and match its code to the snippet below. The important part of this last bit of code is the SOVisitor variable; we can use it in the **Editor** and pass it to the Accept method when colliding with the Player.

```
using System.Collections;
using System.Collections.Generic;
using UnityEngine;

public class UpgradePickup : MonoBehaviour
```

```
{
    // 1
    public SOVisitor Upgrade;

    // 2
    private void OnCollisionEnter(Collision collision)
    {
        if(collision.gameObject.name == "Player")
        {
            // 3
            Player player = collision.gameObject.GetComponent<Player>();

            // 4
            player.Accept(Upgrade);

            // 5
            Destroy(this.gameObject);
        }
    }
}
```

Let's break down the code:

1.  Adds a public SOVisitor variable to store a ScriptableObject visitor
2.  Declares the OnCollisionEnter method and checks for collisions with the Player
3.  Creates a local Player variable and gets the component from the collision GameObject
4.  Uses the player to call the Accept method and pass in the ScriptableObject visitor
5.  Destroys the GameObject

In the **Prefabs** folder, select **Upgrade**, click **Add Component**, and choose the UpgradePickup script (as shown in the following figure), which will update all three Prefab instances in the scene.

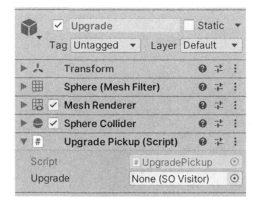

*Figure 11.9: Upgrade Pickup component added to the Upgrade Prefab*

In the **Hierarchy**, select each Upgrade Prefab and drag and drop your SOVisitor into each UpgradePickup component in the **Inspector**, as shown in the following screenshot.

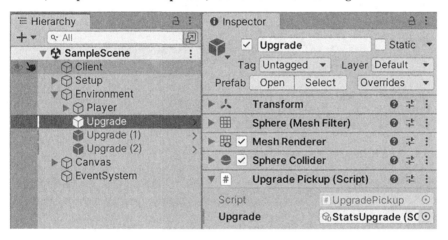

*Figure 11.10: Upgrade components being configured*

Hit **Play** one more time, walk around collecting the available pickups in the scene, and you'll see the UI update with the most recent character data and console logs showing what's going on behind the scenes.

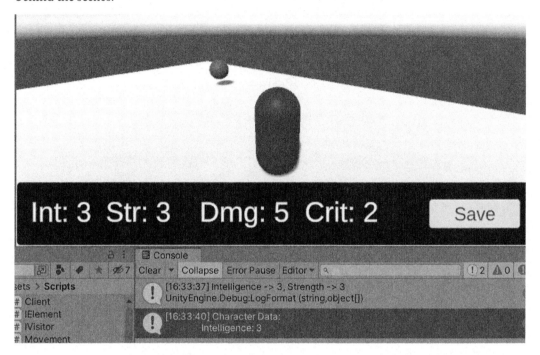

*Figure 11.11: Stat values updating based on Visitor mechanic*

You'll also be able to save your character's data anytime you want, so try and pick up an upgrade and hit the **Save** button to get a new console log showing the updated information!

Once you've played around with the upgrade system a little, you should have a whole host of other scenarios where the Visitor pattern can be effective in your own projects (especially ones with legacy code)!

# Summary

The Visitor design pattern is one of my all-time favorites because it provides an elegant, practical solution to a pervasive problem – how do we update existing classes without changing the class itself or needlessly creating messy class hierarchies? Not only that, but the way concrete visitors seem to naturally help you think about what behaviors should be grouped together and what concrete elements need to be involved is a great boost when thinking through new features.

Remember, the Visitor pattern is ideal for applying new behavior to objects without changing the objects themselves. Concrete elements you want to visit don't have to be related or in the same hierarchy and concrete visitors naturally group sets of related behaviors (or operations) together instead of adding them into unrelated classes. Composite elements (elements with sub-elements) are responsible for applying a visitor to their children, which means you can choose to visit every element in an object structure or selectively visit only the objects that meet certain criteria. As usual with Unity, `ScriptableObjects` can be a great way to work with interchangeable concrete visitors in the Editor.

In the next chapter, we'll dive into the Strategy pattern and creating families of related and interchangeable behaviors (strategies) that can be applied at runtime!

# Further reading

- Interfaces are a great way to create groups of related functionality (with or without default implementations) that can be adopted by any class or struct. These are especially handy when you want to have a class inherit from multiple groups of functionality, which is called object composition. For more information, check out the documentation at https://learn.microsoft.com/en-us/dotnet/csharp/fundamentals/types/interfaces.

- `PlayerPrefs` lets you easily store preference data in string, float, or integer format between game sessions in Unity. However, this system is not encrypted, so it's not recommended for storing sensitive information. I'd encourage you to check out the documentation for a deeper dive at https://docs.unity3d.com/ScriptReference/PlayerPrefs.html.

- `ScriptableObjects` are the perfect way to create data containers in your Unity projects (and we'll use them in almost every chapter going forward), but I'd also recommend checking out the documentation at https://docs.unity3d.com/Manual/class-ScriptableObject.html.

## Join our community on Discord

Join our community's Discord space for discussions with the author and other readers:

`https://packt.link/gamedevelopment_packt`

# 12

# Swapping Algorithms with the Strategy Pattern

In the last chapter, we used the Visitor pattern to apply different behavior to objects without changing the underlying object itself. In this chapter, we're going to explore how the Strategy pattern lets us configure classes with interchangeable algorithms (or behaviors) at runtime. Not only is this a fantastic way to define different variants of a given algorithm but also your client code doesn't need to worry about each algorithm's internal state or data dependencies.

I love this pattern because we use strategies in real life all the time! Think of the moments before you leave the house – it's always a good idea to check the weather to decide whether you need a coat if it's cold, an umbrella if it's going to rain, or extra sunblock if it's scorching hot. Each possibility has its own strategy (cold weather, stormy weather, or hot weather), but you can choose whichever one fits the situation best.

The Strategy pattern is all about doing a specific task in different ways, whether it's sorting a list using different criteria, saving an object to different formats, or configuring an object based on expected behavior. Inputs to the strategy are consistent and always the same (for the same class of strategies), while each strategy does the actual work in different ways.

We'll use this chapter to focus on the following topics:

- The pros and cons of the Strategy design pattern
- Creating a sorting system
- Understanding strategy optimizations
- Upgrading to ScriptableObject strategies

Let's start off with the starter project and then we can move into the pattern breakdown and code of our own!

# Technical requirements

Before you start:

1.  Download or clone the GitHub repository at `https://github.com/PacktPublishing/C-Design-Patterns-with-Unity-First-Edition`.

2.  Open the **Ch_12_Starter** project folder in Unity Hub.

3.  In **Assets > Scenes**, double-click on **SampleScene**.

The project for this chapter is a pared-down **Real-Time Strategy** (**RTS**) example with three playable or bot-controlled characters displayed in the scene and in the leaderboard UI. I've also included `Enemy` and `Item` objects to make things more interesting when we start building different behavior strategies, but for now, it's a pretty static arena.

As for the scripts:

*   `Client.cs` has a list of `Player` objects, a `TMP_Text` reference for the leaderboard, and methods for each type of sorting the project supports (already connected to UI buttons in the **Inspector**).

*   `Player.cs` has logic that can be used from other scripts that can be configured with `Vector3` values for **RigidBody** movement and rotation.

*   `SelfDestruct.cs` simply destroys the object it's attached to when there's any type of collision in the scene.

We'll also be using some Unity and C# language features to take our code the extra mile. Don't worry if you're not familiar with these; I've included links for the basics, and I'll explain how they apply to our use cases as we go:

*   Interfaces (`https://learn.microsoft.com/en-us/dotnet/csharp/fundamentals/types/interfaces`)

*   ScriptableObject (`https://docs.unity3d.com/Manual/class-ScriptableObject.html`)

It's our job to use the traditional Strategy pattern to create different sorting algorithms for the player leaderboard and `ScriptableObject` strategies to add drag-and-drop behavior mechanics to all the characters in the project!

# Breaking down the Strategy pattern

As part of the behavioral family of design patterns, the Strategy pattern is all about decoupling calling classes from how work gets done. Instead, the calling code (or client) chooses *how* it wants something done and delegates the execution to a middleman and an algorithm object with all the required data. Again, this might sound like the Command or State patterns, but using strategies is a different approach to similar problems. The Strategy pattern is useful when:

- You have a hierarchy of related classes that only differ in *how* they get something done.
- You need different variations of the same algorithm (families of behavior) and they should be interchangeable at runtime.
- You need algorithms to be decoupled from the client classes that use them.

Think of any gaming console you've ever had that required a disk or cartridge. The console itself doesn't need to understand the differences between every game, it just needs to know what to do with them – play them! You can choose which game to put in the console but, once you hit the power button, they all play (although you may or may not have to blow in the cartridge first), as shown in *Figure 12.1*. You can even switch them out if you want – the behavior stays the same if you keep the game formats the same (you can't play a PlayStation game on a Nintendo 64).

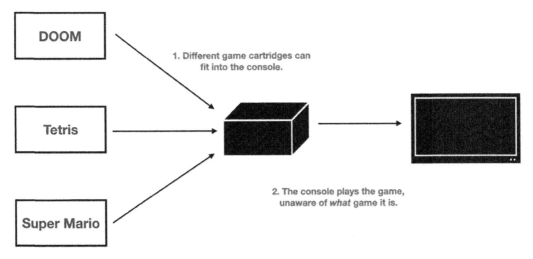

*Figure 12.1: Example of game cartridge systems*

A common way to think of strategies is doing something in different ways. For example, if you want to sort a list of players (like we'll do in the *Creating a sorting system* section), you'll need different sorting strategies to get it done. Sorting is still the main feature, but *how* you sort the list can change (you could use a bubble sort, an alphabetical sort, or something entirely new and unique to your project). The important piece of the puzzle is how the strategies are managed using a context class – the context only knows about the strategy interface (or sorting interface in this case), not each individual sorting algorithm. That way, all the context needs to do is delegate the work to each strategy in a similar way to how the State pattern delegates actions to its current internal state, as shown in *Figure 12.2*.

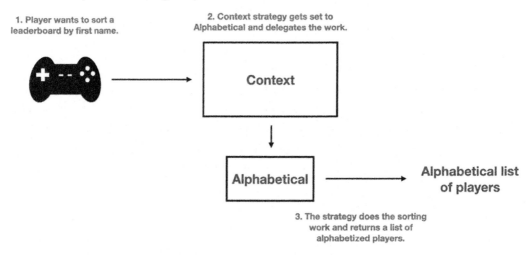

Figure 12.2: Example of contextual strategies being used for a sorting feature

One of the main pain points with this pattern is conceptual – how is it different than the Command or State patterns? On the surface, they all seem to encapsulate behaviors into their own objects, but it's the *way* they solve similar problems that sets them apart. For example, the Command pattern separates behaviors into actions (*what* needs to get done), the State pattern executes different behaviors based on internal state and state transitions, and the Strategy pattern uses different behaviors based on *how* something needs to get done. This might sound academic but you'll see the differences as we go through the example code in this chapter.

## Diagramming the pattern

*Figure 12.3* shows the Strategy pattern with its three component elements:

- The **Strategy** interface is responsible for the algorithms shared by all concrete strategies (different families of concrete strategies need their own strategy interfaces).

- Each ConcreteStrategy is responsible for implementing the strategy interface algorithm (or algorithms) accordingly.

- The **Context** stores a strategy reference passed in through the class constructor or configuration method and determines how information is shared or injected into the strategy object.

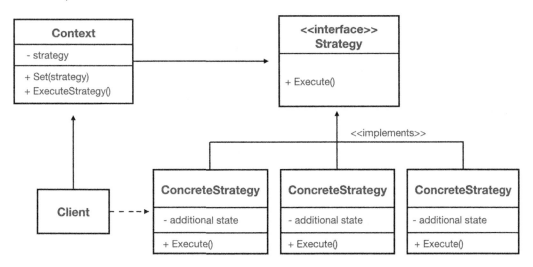

*Figure 12.3: UML diagram of the Strategy pattern components*

The preceding structure allows our clients to delegate operations to a Context object without worrying about how each concrete strategy executes the work being done. While the context is only a thin abstraction layer between the client and concrete strategies, it's an important boundary because it allows you to not only set initial strategies but also dynamically switch them out! We'll cover these topics in the *Optimizing your strategies* section, but before that, let's continue to the pros and cons of the Strategy pattern.

## Pros and cons

Like all design patterns, there are pros and cons. Let's start with the potential benefits the Strategy pattern can add to your project:

- **Encapsulation** separates algorithms (and families of related algorithms) from their context, which boosts **reuse**, **extensions**, and **interchangeability**.

- **Eliminating conditional statements** when choosing behaviors makes your client more efficient and readable.

- **Runtime** strategy selection makes the whole system more dynamic without sacrificing complex choices.

However, be careful of the following pitfalls when using the pattern in your projects:

- **Clients** are forced to know about all the possible strategy choices it can make, which can cause coupling issues if the strategies aren't relevant to the client.

- Every strategy is an **additional object** in your project, so the more strategies you have, the more crowded your codebase gets.

- **Concrete strategies** may end up not using all the information they get passed by the context, which means parameters could be initialized and never be used. This isn't a huge drawback unless you're passing some pretty dense data, but you can always update the context with extra rules for what strategies require which data.

Again, the Strategy pattern has the most impact when you have a unit of work or feature that needs to be executed in different ways but *always* with the same inputs (this goes for families or groupings of work units or features as well). Anywhere you've got large `if-else` or `switch` statements that are doing work with the same input but in slightly different ways is a giant neon sign saying "Use the Strategy pattern!"

Now that we've covered the structure, benefits, and limitations of the Strategy pattern, we can start laying out the traditional implementation in code.

# Creating a sorting system

It's common to use the Strategy pattern to do some kind of work, whether it's processing a string into different data formats or calculating the nearest enemy depending on the weapon currently selected. The first step is to lay out the kind of work our strategies are going to do – in this case, sort a list of `Player` objects using different criteria in each strategy to configure a leaderboard that our users can adjust based on what they're looking for!

## Defining a strategy interface

The first strategy building block we need is a common interface that our strategies will share, as long as they're in the same strategy family. If you're creating more than one strategy group, each family will need its own strategy interface.

In the **Scripts** folder, create a new C# script named `ISortStrategy` and update it to match the following code snippet, which adds a sorting interface with one method that takes in a list of players and returns a new list of players in a different order (we'll leave the sorting work to each concrete strategy):

Adding a strategy interface

```
using System.Collections;
using System.Collections.Generic;
using UnityEngine;

// 1
using System.Linq;

// 2
public interface ISortStrategy
{
    // 3
    List<Player> Sort(List<Player> players);
}
```

Let's break down our strategy interface:

1.  Adds the System.Linq namespace needed for different sorting criteria

2.  Declares a public interface for all strategies

3.  Adds a Sort method that takes and returns a list of Player objects

 Your strategy interface isn't limited to a single method and doesn't require a return type or even method parameters. Where the data is stored, processed in some way, and returned (or not) is a question of scenario, not design pattern. Don't worry, we'll talk about this more in section *12.4*.

Having rules for the work our sorting strategies are going to do means we can create as many concrete strategies as we need, one for each different sorting algorithm we want to be able to use in our game.

## Adding concrete strategies

Our game is so simple that we only need three ways to sort the leaderboard: by default (the order in which they're added in the **Editor**), by rank (based on each player's Rank property), and alphabetically (using the first letter of each player's name).

Update ISortStrategy.cs to match the following code, which adds three concrete strategy classes with unique logic for sorting a list of players.

The sorting isn't really important, it's more about noticing that each one represents the same *kind* of work being done in *different* ways.

```csharp
...


// 1
public class DefaultSort : ISortStrategy
{
    public List<Player> Sort(List<Player> players)
    {
        Debug.Log("Leave sort order as-is...");
        return players;
    }
}


// 2
public class TopRankSort : ISortStrategy
{
    public List<Player> Sort(List<Player> players)
    {
        Debug.Log("Sorted by rank!");
        return players.OrderBy(x => x.Rank).ToList();
    }
}


// 3
public class AlphabeticalSort : ISortStrategy
{
    public List<Player> Sort(List<Player> players)
    {
        Debug.Log("Sorted by first letter!");
        players.Sort((first, second) => string.Compare(first.name, second.
name));
        return players.ToList();
    }
}
```

Let's break down the code:

1.  Declares a default concrete sorting class that inherits from ISortStrategy and returns the players untouched

2.  Declares a ranking concrete sorting class that inherits from ISortStrategy and returns a new list ordered by each player's Rank

3.  Declares an alphabetical concrete sorting class that inherits from ISortStrategy and returns a new list ordered alphabetically by name

The internal sorting logic isn't the focal point in the above code, so don't get too bogged down with that. What you should be noticing is how we've laid out three concrete classes that are doing the same kind of work in different ways (while conforming to a shared interface)!

All that's left to get the sorting strategies off the ground is a way to manage which one is used at runtime, which we'll do in the next section.

## Creating a context

The context is the middleman between the client and the concrete strategy being used – its only job is to keep track of the strategy the client chooses and delegate the actual work to the strategy's interface method (or methods). If you're thinking this sounds eerily familiar to how we track internal state in the State pattern, you'd be right!

In the **Scripts** folder, create a new C# script named LeaderboardContext and update its contents to match the following code, which adds a context for setting, storing, and executing a chosen strategy using the ISortStrategy interface. This means both the client and the context don't need to know anything about how the strategies themselves do the work, which is a huge decoupling advantage.

```
using System.Collections;
using System.Collections.Generic;
using UnityEngine;

// 1
public class LeaderboardContext
{
    // 2
    private ISortStrategy _strategy;

    // 3
```

```
    public LeaderboardContext(ISortStrategy strategy)
    {
        _strategy = strategy;
    }


    // 4
    public List<Player> SortPlayers(List<Player> players)
    {
        // 5
        return _strategy.Sort(players);
    }
}
```

Let's break down the code:

1. Declares a new public class called LeaderboardContext
2. Adds a private variable to store the current ISortStrategy
3. Uses the class constructor to set the initial strategy
4. Adds a public method with the same signature as the ISortStrategy interface method
5. Executes the sorting algorithm using the current strategy and returns a list of players

Now our LeaderboardContext is acting as a clearing house for strategies received from the client, which puts all the sorting effort squarely in each concrete Strategy object and safely away from anything else in our code.

Update Client.cs to match the following code, which creates a new LeaderboardContext instance, sets the initial strategy, and uses the context to sort and return an ordered list of Player objects. Again, notice the delegation power of the client to the context to the current concrete strategy and back again – with the strategy class being the only object aware of the actual algorithmic work being done!

 The client can be any managing class that doesn't know about how the Strategy pattern is implemented as long as it has the data to choose which strategy should be used at runtime.

```
public class Client : MonoBehaviour
{
    public TMP_Text Leaderboard;
    public List<Player> Players;

    void Start()
    {
        // 1
        var _context = new LeaderboardContext(new DefaultSort());

        // 2
        var defaultList = _context.SortPlayers(Players);

        // 3
        UpdateLeaderboard(defaultList);
    }

    public void RankSort()
    {
        // … No changes needed …
    }

    public void AlphabeticalSort()
    {
        // … No changes needed …
    }

    private void UpdateLeaderboard(List<Player> players)
    {
        // … No changes needed …
    }
}
```

Let's break down the code:

1. Initializes a LeaderboardContext instance with the DefaultSort strategy

2. Uses the context to sort the list of players and stores the result

3. Updates the UI with the new ordered list of players

Run the game and you'll see the leaderboard UI updated with a list of all our players sorted by default (the order in which they are added to the Client component in the **Editor**), as shown in *Figure 12.4*:

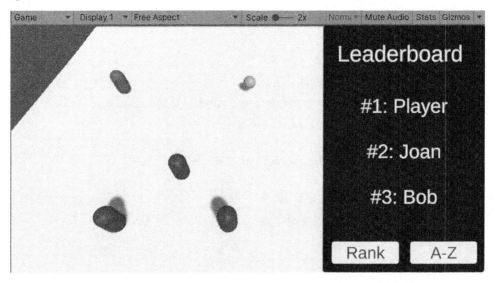

*Figure 12.4: Leaderboard UI sorted in default order*

That's all we need for a working Strategy pattern implementation, but there are optional tweaks we can add to make things more convenient, which we'll tackle in the next section.

# Optimizing your strategies

Our Strategy code is pretty vanilla right now, but we can make the context more efficient and robust by allowing strategies to be swapped out at any time, using a default strategy, and deciding whether to inject or store the information our strategies need to get work done.

## Adding interchangeable strategies

I've mentioned that strategies get chosen at runtime (and that's how it was laid out in the original Gang of Four content), but it's also useful to be able to switch strategies using the same context while the application is running.

Update LeaderboardContext.cs to match the following code, which adds a public method for changing the current strategy to the method parameter. Not only is this approach more flexible (because you're not limited to runtime strategy decisions) but it's also handy if your strategies are components attached to GameObjects in the scene and you want to pass them to your context but don't have a class constructor at your disposal.

```
public class LeaderboardContext
{
    private ISortStrategy _strategy;

    public LeaderboardContext(ISortStrategy strategy)
    {
        _strategy = strategy;
    }

    // 1
    public void SetStrategy(ISortStrategy newStrategy)
    {
        // 2
        _strategy = newStrategy;
    }

    public List<Player> SortPlayers(List<Player> players)
    {
        return _strategy.Sort(players);
    }
}
```

Let's break down the code:

1.  Adds a new public method that takes an ISortStrategy parameter
2.  Sets the private strategy variable with the new strategy value

To test out dynamic strategy switching, update Client.cs to match the code, which adds a class context variable and fills in the existing methods connected to sorting buttons in the scene by switching strategies when our users select different sorting criteria.

```
public class Client : MonoBehaviour
{
    public TMP_Text Leaderboard;
    public List<Player> Players;

    // 1
    private LeaderboardContext _context;
```

```
void Start()
{
    // 2
    _context = new LeaderboardContext(new DefaultSort());

    var defaultList = _context.SortPlayers(Players);
    UpdateLeaderboard(defaultList);
}

public void RankSort()
{
    // 3
    _context.SetStrategy(new TopRankSort());
    var rankedList = _context.SortPlayers(Players);
    UpdateLeaderboard(rankedList);
}

public void AlphabeticalSort()
{
    // 4
    _context.SetStrategy(new AlphabeticalSort());
    var alphabeticalList = _context.SortPlayers(Players);
    UpdateLeaderboard(alphabeticalList);
}

private void UpdateLeaderboard(List<Player> players)
{
    // ... No changes needed ...
}
}
```

Let's break down the code:

1.  Adds a private LeaderboardContext variable to the class scope

2.  Uses the new context instance to set the initial strategy

3.  Sets a new TopRankSort strategy, sorts the list of players, and updates the UI

4.  Sets a new AlphabeticalSort strategy, sorts the list of players, and updates the UI

Having interchangeable strategies on a single context is entirely optional and not part of the original Gang of Four approach, but it's extremely useful when you only need a single context at a time, However, we could have created new `LeaderboardContext` instances in `RankSort` and `AlphabeticalSort` and been just fine.

Play the game again and have fun changing between the different sorting strategies in the leaderboard, as shown in *Figure 12.5*!

*Figure 12.5: Different sorting strategies running in the UI*

## Using default strategies

Another variation that can make your client code even more error-proof is to have your context use a default strategy. How you implement a default strategy is largely up to you, but we're going to update the `LeaderboardContext` constructor for this example.

Update `LeaderboardContext.cs` to match the following code, which makes the class constructor parameter optional and sets the strategy based on whether the parameter is null or not. When working with `MonoBehaviour` components, you could accomplish the same thing in the `SetStrategy` or `SortPlayers` methods.

```
...

public class LeaderboardContext
{
    private ISortStrategy _strategy;

    // 1
    public LeaderboardContext(ISortStrategy strategy = null)
```

```
{
    // 2
    if (strategy == null)
        _strategy = new DefaultSort();
    // 3
    else
        _strategy = strategy;
}

public void SetStrategy(ISortStrategy newStrategy)
{
    _strategy = newStrategy;
}

public List<Player> SortPlayers(List<Player> players)
{
    return _strategy.Sort(players);
}
}
```

Let's break down the code:

1.  Changes the constructor parameter to an optional value that is null by default

2.  Checks whether the constructor parameter is null – if it is, it uses the DefaultSort strategy

3.  Sets _strategy to the new value if the constructor parameter is not null

Since we use the default sorting strategy when Client.cs is initialized, we can update its code to match the following code and leave out the strategy constructor parameter.

```
public class Client : MonoBehaviour
{
    //… No variable changes needed …

    void Start()
    {
        // 1
        _context = new LeaderboardContext();

        var defaultList = _context.SortPlayers(Players);
```

```
        UpdateLeaderboard(defaultList);
    }


    //…. No method changes needed …
}
```

Run the game again and you'll see the leaderboard start out with the default sorting strategy with the same result as before (but with cleaner code), as shown in *Figure 12.6*.

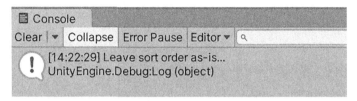

*Figure 12.6: Console log message of the default strategy being used*

**Where should the data live?**

Ideally, you don't want the client to be responsible for injecting strategy-specific data into concrete strategies or the context, but it's not a hard-and-fast rule (just good decoupling). That leaves us with either the context, concrete strategies, or both. The simple (but difficult to implement) answer is that it's up to you and what you need. You could have all the strategy data live in the context and pass it to the strategy when its algorithm is executed; you could also have all the data live in each concrete strategy and use the context as a pure middleman; or you could split the difference and store data where it's most convenient and share or inject as needed.

This also brings up the problem of where the returned data goes once the algorithm is finished with its work. Whether you want the data to stay in the concrete strategy once it's finished processing, return it to the context, or all the way up the chain to the client as we did with the sorting system – again, that's up to you! More often than not, you'll find that the data self-organizes where it's most convenient in this design pattern.

# Strategies the Unity way

When it comes to adapting the Strategy pattern to Unity, your first instinct may very well be to jump right into MonoBehaviours.

While this is perfectly fine for the context class, attaching individual concrete strategies as components on a GameObject and passing them to a context class gets a little messy. That's not to say
you *can't* do it that way, but ScriptableObjects shine in this kind of delegation capacity, especially
when the strategies need data injected into them from the context *and* when the strategies have
specific data they need to store.

Going the ScriptableObject route also opens possibilities for in-game testing, emergent design,
and creating a variety of strategies *as assets* that you can drag and drop in the **Editor**. The starter
project already has three characters in the scene, which makes it a perfect fit for applying different
behavior strategies at runtime.

## Upgrading to ScriptableObjects

In the **Scripts** folder, create a new C# script named SOStrategy and update its code to match the
following snippet. The new abstract ScriptableObject class will be the basis for all concrete
ScriptableObject assets, giving you the freedom to configure a Strategy context with drag-and-
drop magic in the **Editor**.

```csharp
using System.Collections;
using System.Collections.Generic;
using UnityEngine;

// 1
public abstract class SOStrategy : ScriptableObject
{
    // 2
    public abstract void Think();

    // 3
    public abstract void React(BehaviorContext context);
}
```

Let's break down the code:

1.  Declares a public abstract class that inherits from ScriptableObject
2.  Adds an overridable method for all concrete strategies to implement
3.  Adds another overridable method that takes a BehaviorContext parameter

To fix the console error, create a new C# script named BehaviorContext and update its code to match the following code. Our context class is going to be a MonoBehaviour we can attach to each Player object in the scene, which means it'll store an SOStrategy, pass *itself* to the strategy, and execute the strategy methods in Start and Update.

```csharp
using System.Collections;
using System.Collections.Generic;
using UnityEngine;

// 1
[RequireComponent(typeof(Player))]

// 2
public class BehaviorContext : MonoBehaviour
{
    // 3
    public SOStrategy Strategy;

    // 4
    [HideInInspector]
    public Player Player;

    // 5
    void Start()
    {
        Player = GetComponent<Player>();
        Strategy.Think();
    }

    // 6
    void Update()
    {
        Strategy.React(this);
    }
}
```

In the **Prefabs** folder, select Player, add the BehaviorContext component, and save the new changes. To make sure everything is in order, check that the Player, Joan, and Bob objects in the scene all have the new component script attached.

Since we want a few behaviors to choose from when configuring our playable (or bot) characters, we'll create three concrete SOStrategy assets in our project:

- A somewhat useless helper
- Manual control by the player
- Seek and destroy an enemy

Like the State pattern, the implementation of each concrete strategy in this example isn't important (although it *is* fun) – it's about encapsulating these strategies into interchangeable objects that the client and context can manipulate using interfaces or abstract classes.

In the **Scripts** folder, create a new C# script named NoobBehavior and update its code to match the following snippet, which prints a console log when the behavior is in "thinking" mode and moves the GameObject in a continuous circle when in "reacting" mode. Notice the strategy gets all the required data from the context object (in this case, the Player component) but we could have just as easily stored a reference in NoobBehavior and initialized it in the Think method. Again, with the Strategy pattern it's completely up to you and your project to determine how and where data is stored that each strategy depends on.

```
using System.Collections;
using System.Collections.Generic;
using UnityEngine;

// 1
[CreateAssetMenu(fileName = "Noob", menuName = "SOStrategy/Noob")]

// 2
public class NoobBehavior : SOStrategy
{
    // 3
    public override void Think()
    {
        Debug.LogFormat($"Player Behavior -> Complete noob...");
    }
```

```
// 4
public override void React(BehaviorContext context)
{
    Vector3 movement = Vector3.forward * context.Player.MoveSpeed;
    Vector3 turning = Vector3.up * context.Player.TurnSpeed;

    context.Player.ConfigureInput(movement, turning);
}
}
```

Let's break down the code:

1.  Uses the CreateAssetMenu attribute to add the ScriptableObject to the Unity menu

2.  Declares a new class that inherits from SOStrategy

3.  Overrides the abstract Think method and prints out a custom debug log

4.  Overrides the abstract React method and moves the GameObject in a circle

In the **Scripts** folder, create a new C# script named ManualBehavior and update its code to match the following snippet, which has string variables for input axes (to make things easier to run right away, but you could specify these values any way you want), and uses the input values to move the GameObject according to user input.

```
using System.Collections;
using System.Collections.Generic;
using UnityEngine;

// 1
[CreateAssetMenu(fileName = "Manual Control", menuName = "SOStrategy/
Manual")]

// 2
public class ManualBehavior : SOStrategy
{
    // 3
    public string ForwardInput;
    public string TurnInput;

    // 4
    public override void Think()
```

```
    {
        Debug.LogFormat($"Player Behavior -> Manual Control...");
    }


    // 5
    public override void React(BehaviorContext context)
    {
        float horInput = Input.GetAxis(ForwardInput) * context.Player.
MoveSpeed;
        float verInput = Input.GetAxis(TurnInput) * context.Player.
TurnSpeed;

        Vector3 movement = Vector3.forward * horInput;
        Vector3 turn = Vector3.up * verInput;

        context.Player.ConfigureInput(movement, turn);
    }
}
```

Let's break down the code:

1.  Uses the CreateAssetMenu attribute to add the ScriptableObject to the Unity menu
2.  Declares a new class that inherits from SOStrategy
3.  Adds two string variables to set input axes in the **Editor**
4.  Overrides the abstract Think method and prints out a custom debug log
5.  Overrides the abstract React method and moves the GameObject according to the input

In the **Scripts** folder, create a new C# script named SearchBehavior and update its code to match the following snippet, which implements the logic for finding and moving toward the Enemy object in the scene.

```
using System.Collections;
using System.Collections.Generic;
using UnityEngine;


// 1
[CreateAssetMenu(fileName = "Search and Destroy", menuName = "SOStrategy/
S&D")]
```

```
// 2
public class SearchBehavior: SOStrategy
{
    // 3
    public float SpeedMultiplier;

    // 4
    public override void Think()
    {
        Debug.LogFormat($"Player Behavior -> Search & Destroy...");
    }

    // 5
    public override void React(BehaviorContext context)
    {
        GameObject enemy = null;

        if(enemy == null)
        {
            enemy = GameObject.FindGameObjectWithTag("Enemy");
        }

        if (enemy == null)
        {
            context.Player.ConfigureInput(Vector3.zero, Vector3.zero);
            return;
        }

        Vector3 targetVector = (enemy.transform.position - context.
transform.position);
        context.transform.LookAt(enemy.transform);
        context.Player.ConfigureInput(targetVector * SpeedMultiplier,
Vector3.zero);
    }
}
```

The preceding code uses the same structure as our earlier concrete sorting strategies but with the added benefits of being ScriptableObject assets that we can create and configure from the **Editor**.

To create our new strategies, navigate into the **ScriptableObjects** folder and create three SOStrategy assets, as shown in *Figure 12.7*:

1.  Select **Assets > Create > SOStrategy > Noob**

2.  Select **Assets > Create > SOStrategy > Manual Control**

3.  Select **Assets > Create > SOStrategy > Search and Destroy**

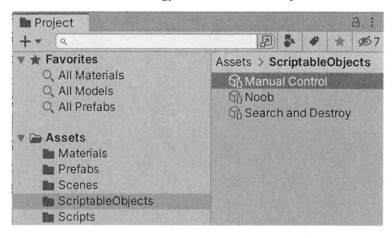

*Figure 12.7: Project window updated with new ScriptableObject assets*

Configure the **Manual Control** and **Search and Destroy** assets however you want or use my settings in *Figure 12.8*, but you can leave **Noob** alone because it doesn't have any additional settings:

*Figure 12.8: ScriptableObject strategy values*

Now comes the fun part! In the **Inspector**, drag and drop whichever ScriptableObject strategies you want onto the BehaviorContext components that Player, Joan, and Bob each have and hit **Play** to watch (or control) them. I'm using Player as my controllable character, Joan as my attacker, and Bob as the noob, as shown in *Figure 12.9*.

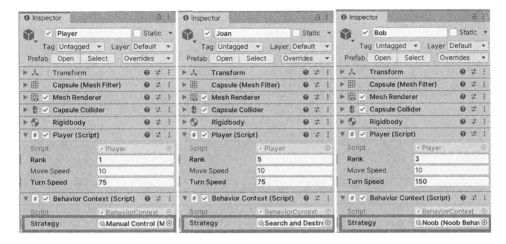

*Figure 12.9: Context classes being updated with ScriptableObject strategies*

When you play the game now, you'll be able to manually control the **Player**, while **Joan** is going to make a beeline for the **Enemy**, and Bob is all about running around in useless circles (it's difficult to see this in action but I attempted to grab a frame in *Figure 12.10*).

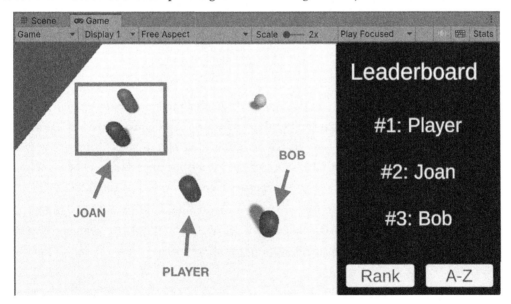

*Figure 12.10: Gameplay with strategies executing in each character context*

With our prototype test running smoothly, we now have a fully configurable and interchangeable Strategy pattern implementation – complete with `ScriptableObject` assets to help us set up our business logic right in the **Editor**.

# Summary

If you're reading this, then you've made it through the Strategy pattern, which should really be called the delegation pattern! We have a working prototype that can do similar work (sorting and behavior actions) in different ways while also allowing us to dynamically switch *how* the work is done at any time. Our system also lets us work with `ScriptableObject` assets instead of hardcoding our concrete strategies, and everything is nicely decoupled using interfaces (not bad for an afternoon of code)!

When using the Strategy pattern, remember that each family or grouping of strategies will need their own strategy interface, concrete strategies, and context. It also pays to think about how your project gets each concrete strategy the data it needs – it can be passed in from the context, stored in the strategy interface, or a mix of both. The only potential coupling downside with this pattern is that the client needs to know about all the available concrete strategies it can choose from to pass to the context, but you can make this less brittle with `ScriptableObject` assets in the **Editor**.

In the next chapter, we're going to take a stab at the Type Object design pattern (one of the few in this book that isn't in the original Gang of Four content). I wanted to include this pattern because it's a wonderfully efficient way of sharing data between similar objects *without* creating a complicated subclassing hierarchy!

# Further reading

- Interfaces are a great way to create groups of related functionality (with or without default implementations) that can be adopted by any class or struct. These are especially handy when you want to have a class inherit from multiple groups of functionality, which is called object composition. For more, check out the documentation at `https://learn.microsoft.com/en-us/dotnet/csharp/fundamentals/types/interfaces`.

- ScriptableObjects are the perfect way to create data containers in your Unity projects (and we'll use them in almost every chapter going forward), but I'd also recommend checking out the documentation at `https://docs.unity3d.com/Manual/class-ScriptableObject.html`.

# Join our community on Discord

Join our community's Discord space for discussions with the author and other readers:

`https://packt.link/gamedevelopment_packt`

# 13

# Making Monsters with the Type Object Pattern

In the last chapter, we worked on a system of interchangeable algorithms (strategies) that could be assigned at runtime or during gameplay without the client knowing the nitty-gritty details. In this chapter, we're going to take a step back from behavior and put our sights on data and the Type Object pattern, which lets you create different configurations of the same object with the least number of classes (because all the cool kids use flat hierarchies).

Specifically, we'll try to find common data that *all* related objects share, separate it out into its own class, and inject it *back* into the object we want to configure. You can create infinite combinations of the same object by giving them different types (shared data templates) without a huge class hierarchy that needs babysitting every time you add or modify the code!

For example, a hero or heroine could be a human, giant, or elf, but they all have hp, stamina, and weaknesses. Rather than thinking of humans, giants, and elves as hero subclasses, we pull out the shared data (hp, stamina, weaknesses) into their own hero *types*, meaning we can initialize a hero or heroine with whatever *type* we want with just two classes (hero and hero type). The same data properties (hp, stamina, weaknesses) can have different configurations (humans will have average hp and stamina, giants will have lots of hp and little stamina, and elves will be naturally awesome and graceful at everything).

Here's the kicker: when we want to offer players the option to be a human mage, human paladin, or human thief, we don't have to start from scratch; they're all human *type* characters with human *type* data.

All we need to do is figure out what additional stuff we want to tack on for mages, paladins, and thieves, and voila: we have a flexible and scalable variety of human characters that don't need to be hardcoded. There's one drawback: this pattern is built for *data*, not *behavior*, but we'll tackle that at the end of the *Optimization, inheritance, and behavior* section, so stick with me until then.

We'll use this chapter to focus on the following topics:

- The pros and cons of the Type Object design pattern
- Building a monster creation system using monster types
- Optimizing for memory allocation and inheritance
- Using `ScriptableObjects` as configurable data containers

Let's start off with the starter project and then we can move into the pattern breakdown and code of our own!

# Technical requirements

Before you start:

1. Download or clone the GitHub repository at `https://github.com/PacktPublishing/C-Design-Patterns-with-Unity-First-Edition`

2. Open the **Ch_13_Starter** project folder in Unity Hub

3. In **Assets > Scenes**, double-click on **SampleScene**

The project for this chapter is a simple scene with three prefab objects in front of the camera and a `Client` ready to print out data to the console. Since this pattern is all about data (and not so much behavior-focused), our debug logs are an important part of learning how the code works before getting into Unity implementations.

As for the scripts:

- `Client.cs` is a blank slate attached to a `Client` object in the scene.
- `Monster.cs` has `private` properties and a `public` method for printing them out – this will be our Typed Object (or Instance Object, as we'll call it, to avoid confusion).
- `Pokemon.cs` is a `MonoBehaviour` attached to the `Pokemon` prefab.
- `Utilities.cs` has an extension method for mixing colors.

We'll also be using some Unity and C# language features to take our code the extra mile. Don't worry if you're not familiar with them; I've included links for the basics, and I'll explain how they apply to our use cases as we go.

- ScriptableObjects (`https://docs.unity3d.com/Manual/class-ScriptableObject.html`).

Our job is two-fold: first, create a strictly C# monster system where we can put together different kinds of enemies with only two classes (leaving bloated class hierarchies in the dust); and second, create a more robust implementation using `ScriptableObjects` and Pokemon!

# Breaking down the Type Object pattern

While the Type Object pattern wasn't included in the original Gang of Four context, it still belongs to the behavioral category because it deals with communication between objects, specifically between the Instance Object (all playable characters are heroes) and its type object (elves are elvish *type* heroes). The Type Object pattern is useful when:

- You don't know the exact number or kind of types you'll need right from the start.
- You want to avoid big class hierarchies that initialize, override, and manage the same shared properties.
- You need to add or change types without breaking existing code.

Let's start from scratch to avoid any assumptions. We have a game that needs lots of monsters; monsters can be trolls, zombies, or dragons, and these trolls, zombies, and dragons can come in strong, average, or weak flavors. On top of that, our monsters can have ice, fire, and lightning elemental properties, as shown in *Figure 13.1*:

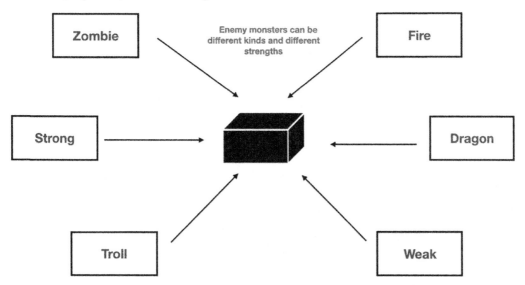

*Figure 13.1: Example of different monster configurations*

Sounds like a job for regular **Object-Oriented Programming (OOP)**, right? Well, yes (that's a perfectly acceptable answer) but here's the rub – the problem we're addressing is how to create different representations of the *same* object (the only thing that's different about each instance is their type information). So, like the good OO programmers we were taught to be, we start a class hierarchy with a base class, add a few subclasses, and pass in or override properties to get the right child configuration: an enemy base class has values for hp, strength, and element, and every different enemy in our game is a separate enemy subclass with the same constructor and overridden properties.

We've got an unwieldy visual for this in *Figure 13.2*, which I purposefully left crowded to make you cringe a little when you think about writing these virtually identical classes over and over again (sometimes you need a visceral reaction to see the full problem):

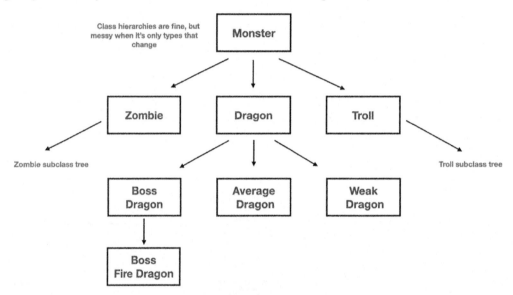

*Figure 13.2: Traditional OOP class hierarchy solution*

To put numbers to the solution in the preceding figure, our OO approach has yielded a class hierarchy containing a whopping 28 classes to account for our simple example (3 breeds x 3 strength levels x 3 elements + 1 base class). That's insane when the only difference between these monsters is their data (hp, strength, and element). And that's the blaring red alarm that should go off in your head – the *enemies* aren't actually different; their enemy *type* is.

Think of it another way – everyone's DNA is made up of the same four base types: A, T, C, and G. But every person is fundamentally different and unique with just four building blocks (or really two pairs because A's are stubborn and only play with T's, while C and G only have eyes for each other). Back to our game analogy, we want a system that can build as many unique combinations of enemies with as few classes as possible – an enemy class and an enemy-type class. Each enemy class has a property for what *type* of enemy it is and pulls all its initial data from that variable in its constructor. We can create any type of monster combination we want by instantiating a monster type and injecting it into said monster – instant and endless easy-bake enemy varieties, as shown in *Figure 13.3*!

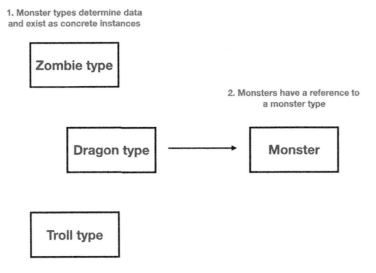

*Figure 13.3: Flat hierarchy solution with separate classes for type and Typed Objects*

Put down your hand because I can guess your next question – why would we want a system like this that can't use inheritance? Well, the Type Object pattern *can* use inheritance, and it's just as adaptive and customizable as a class hierarchy (as long as you spend the time to create good inheritance graphs).

Every monster type can simply have a reference to a parent or base monster type, which creates chains of monster data inheritance instead of coupled class hierarchies, as shown in *Figure 13.4*.

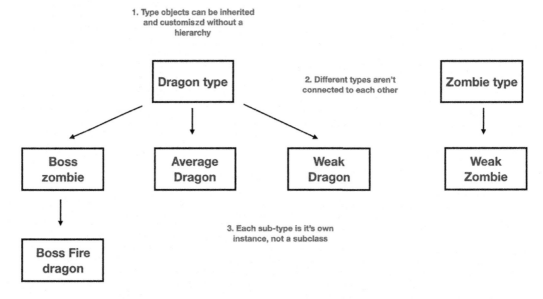

*Figure 13.4: Example of inheritance in the Type Object pattern*

Again, I can't stress this enough – the Type Object pattern is a stellar *data*-sharing solution, not a *behavior*-sharing solution. It's the ultimate programming expression of "work smarter, not harder."

## Diagramming the pattern

*Figure 13.5* shows the UML structure of the Type Object pattern with its two main component elements:

- The **Type Object** represents the data we want to share between similar objects. Each logical type in our code gets its own type object instance, but these can be reused so there only needs to be one per concrete type.
- The **Typed Object** stores all of its instance-specific data, but gets its shared data from a type object instance.

*Figure 13.5: UML diagram of the Strategy pattern components*

 I know the components of this pattern have almost identical names, so I'll try my best to use other descriptors and always provide examples to showcase what's going on. For example, I'll refer to the Typed Object as the Instance Object, while Type Object will stay the same. Onward!

With only two components in this pattern, it's essential to understand that the Typed Object is your monster instance, while the Type Object represents the *type* of monster it is (dragon, troll, or zombie), which holds all the shared data that *all* monsters have in common).

## Pros and cons

Like all design patterns, there are pros and cons. Let's start with the potential benefits the Type Object pattern can add to your project:

- **No class hierarchies** – the two main classes can create an unlimited number of configurations and inheritance is still available with a little extra effort (which provides a ton of creative freedom during object initialization).

- **Classes are not hardcoded** – you can create new types whenever you need and changing or adding new types of objects doesn't affect existing code.

However, be careful of the following pitfalls when using the pattern in your projects:

- **Sharing behavior isn't built in** and adapting for behavior dilutes the power and efficiency of the pattern. However, you can absolutely combine the Type Object pattern with other behavior-specific patterns for great results (Strategy and State spring to mind, hint hint).

- **Not optimized for memory usage** out of the box, but you can adapt for performance (which we'll cover in the *Optimization, inheritance, and behavior* section). This is also a perfect place to pop in the Object Pool, Factory, or Flyweight patterns for peak CPU happiness.

Now that we've covered the structure, benefits, and limitations of the Type Object pattern, we can start laying out the traditional implementation in code.

# Creating monsters

Imagine your game has a wide and varied array of enemy monsters it can throw at your players – trolls, zombies, dragons, accountants – anything that wants to do damage. You could approach this the OOP way by creating a base monster class and adding new subclasses to the hierarchy for every type of monster. But you'll quickly realize that adding a new monster subclass every time a designer decides that demonic squirrels aren't challenging enough is time consuming (demonic rabbits are in fact necessary) and can have ramifications up and down the monster class hierarchy.

Another way to come at this problem is to think about what properties *every* monster has, rather than what each monster subclass *is* (we'll be using this solution in our example code). This approach ends up showing us what categories of monsters we have and what they all have in common. When we start thinking of demonic squirrels and demonic rabbits as the same demonic monster *type* with the same underlying data properties, we eliminate the need for them to exist in a related class hierarchy. Instead, they can *share* their base data and keep their unique quirks!

 Breaking out shared types between objects doesn't mean OOP class hierarchies aren't useful – in fact, they can be great for sharing behavior between monsters while leaving the different monster types to deal with the data.

# Adding a Type Object

The type object in the Type Object pattern is the data template that all our Monster Instance Objects share. In our case, all monsters have values for health, level, toughness, and a war cry when they attack. However, different monster types will have different values for each of these properties that can be shared – fire dragons, ice dragons, and lighting dragons are all *dragons,* so they can all share properties from a dragon type and still do their own elemental dragon-y things.

In the **Scripts** folder, create a C# script named MonsterType and update it to match the following code, which configures the class properties and constructor:

```
using System.Collections;
using System.Collections.Generic;
using UnityEngine;

// 1
```

```
public class MonsterType
{
    // 2
    public int HP { get; private set; }
    public int Level { get; private set; }
    public int Toughness { get; private set; }
    public string WarCry { get; private set; }

    // 3
    public MonsterType(int hp, int level, int toughness, string warCry)
    {
        HP = hp;
        Level = level;
        Toughness = toughness;
        WarCry = warCry;
    }
}
```

Let's break down our strategy interface:

1.  Declares a public MonsterType class
2.  Adds a field for each monster field with public get and private set properties
3.  Uses a class constructor to accept and initialize each monster-type field

**Exposing your type object data**

We're using a public get and private set property for each Type Object field, but that's not the only way to do it. I prefer using properties because it's cleaner and more legible – if you haven't run into these before check out the documentation at https://learn.microsoft.com/en-us/dotnet/csharp/programming-guide/classes-and-structs/properties.

You can also use a combination of public properties with private backing fields:

```
private int _hp;
public int HP { get { return _hp; } }
```

Or keep all properties strictly `private` and add `public` access methods:

```
public class PokemonType
{
    private int _hp;
    public int GetHealth()
    {
        return _hp;
    }
}
```

These are all variations on the same theme – allowing you to control access and optionally computer property values if you need to before requesting them. Use whichever fits your needs best!

We've now separated the shared data requirements for every monster instance, which means we can inject them into our `Monster` objects! Down the line, this decoupling would let us efficiently populate `MonsterType` fields from a backend or JSON file without polluting the main monster class, and if we want to update our monster data, we only need to change `MonsterType` instead of an entire class hierarchy.

## Configuring monsters

Update `Monster.cs` to match the following code, which modifies the class constructor to accept a `MonsterType` parameter and initialize its private data fields according to the type. Notice that a `Monster` can have its own fields completely separate from its type (like `_name`) – it's completely up to you what data comes from a type object and what data is unique to the object itself. This flexibility is the best of both worlds when it comes to assembling your monsters in different configurations:

```
using System.Collections;
using System.Collections.Generic;
using UnityEngine;

public class Monster
```

```
{
    // 1
    private MonsterType _monsterType;

    private string _name;
    private int _level;
    private int _hp;
    private int _toughness;
    private string _warCry;

    // 2
    public Monster(MonsterType type, string name)
    {
        // 3
        _monsterType = type;
        _name = name;

        // 4
        _level = type.Level;
        _hp = type.HP;
        _toughness = type.Toughness;
        _warCry = type.WarCry;
    }

    public void PrintStats()
    {
        //... No changes needed ...
    }
}
```

Let's break down the code:

1.  Adds a private MonsterType variable

2.  Adds a class constructor with MonsterType and string parameters

3.  Sets the type and name of the Monster object using the constructor parameters

4.  Sets the other class properties using the MonsterType parameter

The same data privacy and access decisions that applied to the Type Object apply here as well – however you want to store and expose properties you've initialized using the type object is perfectly fine (this pattern is all about the data)!

Our Monster objects aren't hardcoded to be a single *type* of monster – they can be initialized with their type when created. Or better yet, you could add a SetType method to make them interchangeable in real-time, like what we did with interchangeable strategies in the last chapter (think of a boss fight where the monster changes type at different stages of the battle).

Let's test out our new Monster creation powers by updating Client.cs to match the following code, which creates a base MonsterType for all zombie enemies and initializes two unique zombie-type monsters.

```
using System.Collections;
using System.Collections.Generic;
using UnityEngine;

public class Client : MonoBehaviour
{
    void Start()
    {
        // 1
        var zombieType = new MonsterType(100, 1, 20, "Brains!");

        // 2
        var ghoul = new Monster(zombieType, "Ghoul");
        var undeadMage = new Monster(zombieType, "Undead Mage");

        // 3
        ghoul.PrintStats();
        undeadMage.PrintStats();
    }
}
```

Let's break down the code:

1.  Creates a MonsterType with values for hp, level, toughness, and war cry
2.  Initializes two Monster objects with unique names and the shared MonsterType

3. Prints out the properties for each monster

> It's worth talking about optimization and memory usage here, because we've doubled the number of instantiated objects we need for each monster. This could be a performance problem if you're creating hundreds (or thousands) of enemies.

> This design pattern is all about finding a better way to decouple shared data and give you the freedom to organize (and compose) objects with max flexibility, not necessarily optimize for performance. We'll see how ScriptableObjects can help optimize the pattern a bit more in *Creating ScriptableObject monsters* section, but we'll also look at how this problem can be solved with a performance-first mindset in the Flyweight design pattern chapter.

Notice how clean and simple our Monster constructor becomes when creating new enemies – shared data is decoupled and injected, opening possibilities for designers and programmers to work together without having to refactor a huge class hierarchy every time a demonic mammal needs to be added.

Run the game and check the console, which shows the data of our two zombie-type enemies being virtually identical (except for their names) as shown in *Figure 13.6*:

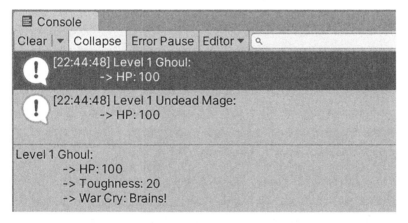

*Figure 13.6: Console logs showing monster values using type objects*

Be aware that changing the MonsterType would trickle down into all Monster objects initialized with that shared type – but that's one of the powerful advantages of the pattern itself. Changing a value in the zombieType would be updated in the ghoul and undeadMage without any extra effort!

If you're worried about shared data updates leaking into some objects and not others, it may be a sign to reevaluate how you're constructing your types and if this pattern is the right fit for your scenario.

That's going to wrap up the basic vanilla implementation of the Type Object pattern! However, there's always more we can do to sharpen our tools, which is what we'll cover in the following sections!

# Optimization, inheritance, and behavior

The Type Object pattern focuses on reusing shared data between objects so we can do away with complicated class hierarchies and adapt for situations when we don't know *all* the different objects we want down the line. With that in mind, let's try and level up our design pattern implementation by:

- Making things safer for ourselves and our team (by controlling access to the type and Typed Object classes)
- Adding optional inheritance (still without class hierarchies)
- Understanding our options for sharing behavior

## Controlling allocation and initialization

There may come a time when an object's allocation and initialization are big players in your performance and player experience. For those occasions, it's ideal for there to be a single point of access where your monsters are being created. Not only is this safer (because it keeps your AudioManager from creating zombie hedgehogs by accident), but you can also make sure any performance-based code is executed *before* you inject types into new monsters (the Object Pool pattern is great for this kind of thing; see *Chapter 7*).

Update Monster.cs to match the following code, which marks the Monster class constructor as private, moves the MonsterType class *into* the Monster class, and puts the monster instantiation logic into the hands of the monster's type. Not only does this safeguard our monster creation from any other classes, but it also gives us a place to handle customized memory allocation if needed.

```
public class Monster
{
    //… No variable changes needed …

    // 1
```

```
    private Monster(MonsterType type, string name)
    {
        //... No changes needed ...
    }

    public void PrintStats()
    {
        //... No changes needed ...
    }

    // 2
    public class MonsterType
    {
        public int HP { get; private set; }
        public int Level { get; private set; }
        public int Toughness { get; private set; }
        public string WarCry { get; private set; }

        public MonsterType(int hp, int level, int toughness, string
warCry)
        {
            HP = hp;
            Level = level;
            Toughness = toughness;
            WarCry = warCry;
        }

        // 3
        public Monster CreateMonster(string name)
        {
            // 4
            return new Monster(this, name);
        }
    }
}
```

After that's done, go ahead and delete `MonsterType.cs` from the project to avoid confusion and duplicate class declaration errors!

Let's break down the code:

1.  Changes the `Monster` constructor's access modifier to `private`

2.  Embeds the `MonsterType` class inside the `Monster` class

3.  Declares a method for creating monsters with a `string` parameter

4.  Returns a new `Monster` using the current `MonsterType` and the name parameter

 If you're familiar with C++, you might be thinking this is a perfect place for a `friend` class (meaning it can access private and protected members of other classes that it's friends with). Unfortunately, C# doesn't come with a simple way to achieve the same behavior, which is why we're just popping the `MonsterType` class *into* the `Monster` class and marking the `Monster` constructor as `private`. However, that's not the only way to make this work – you could use different `Assemblies` and `Reflection` to separate out the `Monster` and `MonsterType` classes from the rest of your code base, or you could split things up into `partial` classes (although that may be more work than it's worth). Since this is more of an academic question in terms of the Type Object pattern, I'll leave you to explore at your leisure.

Our new changes will cause a few errors to pop up in the console, so let's update `Client.cs` to match the following code. Not only do we have to go through the `Monster` class to get to the `MonsterType` class when we create the `zombieType`, but we also create the individual enemies from the `MonsterType` as well. Again, this `Monster` class black boxing helps us control who can make enemies and how they're initialized.

```csharp
public class Client : MonoBehaviour
{
    void Start()
    {
        // 1
        var zombieType = new Monster.MonsterType(100, 1, 20, "Brains!");

        // 2
        var ghoul = zombieType.CreateMonster("Ghoul");
        var undeadMage = zombieType.CreateMonster("Undead Mage");

        ghoul.PrintStats();
        undeadMage.PrintStats();
```

```
        }
    }
```

Let's break this new code down:

1.  Calls the MonsterType constructor from the newly private Monster class

2.  Creates and returns new Monster instances directly from the MonsteryType objects

If you run the game again nothing will change in the console logs, but the code is now much clearer on *where* monster creation happens and *what* classes can access the MonsterType constructor!

## Adding parent type objects

Just because we've gone off the deep end trying to avoid inheritance in this design pattern, doesn't mean we can't make it work for our Type Object paradigm. In fact, it's a powerful variation to this design pattern and can exponentially increase your configuration options when it comes to composing complex objects. The idea for our example is to give each MonsterType the option of inheriting traits from a base (or parent) type object. This can be done in different ways and with a variety of rules for what and how data is inherited or combined, but we're going to stick with the most open-ended approach – every MonsterType property *can* be overridden but doesn't *have* to be.

Update Monster.cs to match the following code, which adds a base MonsterType parameter to the MonsterType class constructor. If we don't want to use a base type object there's no problem, but if we enter default or null values when initializing a MonsterType, the values inherit their data from the base type object.

```
public class Monster
{
    //... No changes needed ...

    public class MonsterType
    {
        public int HP { get; private set; }
        public int Level { get; private set; }
        public int Toughness { get; private set; }
        public string WarCry { get; private set; }

        // 1
        public MonsterType(MonsterType baseType, int hp, int level, int
toughness, string warCry)
```

```
            {
                HP = hp;
                Level = level;
                Toughness = toughness;
                WarCry = warCry;

                // 2
                if(baseType != null)
                {
                    // 3
                    if (hp == 0)
                        HP = baseType.HP;
                    if (level == 0)
                        Level = baseType.Level;
                    if (toughness == 0)
                        Toughness = baseType.Toughness;
                    if (warCry == null)
                        WarCry = baseType.WarCry;
                }
            }

            public Monster CreateMonster(string name)
            {
                //... No changes needed ...
            }
        }
    }
```

Let's break down the code:

1. Adds a MonsterType parameter for an optional base object

2. Checks if baseType is null

3. Checks each property for default or null values and optionally inherits from baseType

> Using ternary operators would be a more readable solution to our long list of if
> statements in the above code, but that's a stretch goal I'll leave to you.
>
> Using default parameter values in the MonsterType constructor is also a valid way of
> controlling how or when data is inherited – there's no shortage of creative freedom to
> this part of the pattern, which is why it's so flexible and fun to use in the right context.

Our new code is going to generate a few more errors in the console, so let's fix them by updating
Client.cs to match the following code. We've added a null value for the zombieType constructor
because it doesn't need to inherit from a base type and created a new stronger zombie MonsterType
using zombieType as its base type. The advantage here is that we can inherit the Toughness and
WarCry values from our base type while choosing not to inherit the HP and Level.

```csharp
public class Client : MonoBehaviour
{
    void Start()
    {
        // 1
        var zombieType = new Monster.MonsterType(null, 100, 1, 20,
"Brains!");

        var ghoul = zombieType.CreateMonster("Ghoul");
        var undeadMage = zombieType.CreateMonster("Undead Mage");
        ghoul.PrintStats();
        undeadMage.PrintStats();

        // 2
        var bossZombieType = new Monster.MonsterType(zombieType, 120, 10,
0, null);

        // 3
        var megaZombie = bossZombieType.CreateMonster("Mega Zombie!");

        // 4
        megaZombie.PrintStats();
    }
}
```

Let's break down the code:

1.  Adds a null value to the zombieType constructor
2.  Creates a new MonsterType that inherits some of its values from a base type
3.  Creates a Monster from the new MonsterType
4.  Prints out the monster's property values

 The more data you want to inherit from a parent the more useful this addition is to the pattern, but it may be overkill (or premature optimization) if inheriting from a parent doesn't bring much to your table.

Run the game again and you'll see the new Boss Zombie stats that we set in the constructor and inherited from the base type object, as shown in *Figure 13.7*:

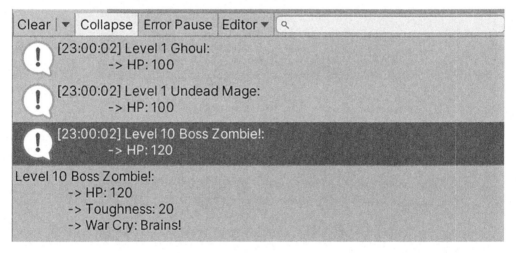

*Figure 13.7: Console logs of type inheritance working*

**Multiple inheritance is possible...but tricky**

While you might be tempted to go nuts and accommodate more than one parent or base type object property in each type object, it's harder than it looks. For example, let's say an enemy is a Zombie Ogre – what does the inheritance look like? What do we inherit from the Zombie type and what gets left to the Ogre type? What if we had more than two parents or base types? All these questions have answers (and honestly, I think this is the most fun you can have with the Type Object pattern), but these decisions are entirely subjective to the project so I'll leave you to explore!

Bottom line: if your game doesn't specifically call for some sort of breeding or combination mechanic, it might be better to stick with single (or no) inheritance. However, if you do end up needing multiple inheritance functionality, invest in good tools so your designers and other developers can understand the inheritance decisions and implications of the system (and learn about inheritance graphs).

# Sharing behavior isn't easy

The Type Object pattern is about data; it's never advertised itself as being a great fit for storing shared behavior. So, what do we do? One, you could go down the rabbit hole of behavior *as* data, which will likely lead you to the Interpreter pattern in the original Gang of Four text (and maybe the more esoteric Bytecode pattern). I'm not saying these aren't valid ways to solve the lack of behavior accountability in the Type Object pattern, but they may end up costing you more time and energy than the efficiency they generate.

Instead, you could add in the Strategy or State patterns to your Typed Objects and build their behavior that way (monsters could have AI strategies or changing states for their behavior), or even store a strategy in each type object. Whatever solution you choose or come up with, if behavior is something that really makes this pattern a mismatch for your scenario then it wasn't the right one in the first place (which is good data in itself).

With that, we've come to the end of our C# implementation, but that doesn't mean there's nothing more to learn. The Type Object pattern is one of my absolute favorites *because* of its flexibility and how well it scales with Unity's ScriptableObject class, which we'll explore for the rest of the chapter.

# Creating ScriptableObject monsters

The great part of our monster configuration scenario is that we can have fun with the inheritance; some values can be pulled right from the base type, and others can be combined (like a monster's color) or added to the existing value (like a monster's weaknesses). The sky is really the limit with this pattern – you make all the rules.

In the **Scripts** folder, create a new C# script named SOType and update its code to match the following code. There's a fair bit going on in this code, but if you look closely, we're applying what we've already learned in a new wrapper. Our type object still has a set of properties we want to inject into another object, and they can either be set in the **Editor** or optionally inherited from a base object of our choice.

I know Pokemon might not be monsters in the strictest sense, but I love them and this design pattern makes it so much fun to mix and match traits to create new Pokemon that I couldn't resist.

If you're reading the paperback, upcoming screenshots will be black and white, so you may not see color changes in the Inspector's **Color** field. These changes will still appear on your screen based on the adjustments made to your Pokémon ScriptableObjects..

```csharp
using System.Collections;
using System.Collections.Generic;
using UnityEngine;

// 1
using Extensions;

// 2
[CreateAssetMenu(fileName = "SOType", menuName = "SO Type")]
public class SOType : ScriptableObject
{
    // 3
    public SOType BaseType;

    // 4
    public int HP;
    public Color Color;
    public Element Element;
    public List<Element> Weaknesses;
```

```
    // 5
    [ContextMenu("Inherit")]
    private void Configure()
    {
        // 6
        if (HP == 0)
            HP = BaseType.HP;
        if (Element == Element.None)
            Element = BaseType.Element;

        Color = Utilities.MixColors(Color, BaseType.Color);

        foreach (var baseWeakness in BaseType.Weaknesses)
        {
            if (!Weaknesses.Contains(baseWeakness))
                Weaknesses.Add(baseWeakness);
        }
    }

    // 7
    [ContextMenu("Inherit", true)]
    bool Validate()
    {
        return BaseType!= null;
    }
}
}
```

Let's break down the code:

1.  Declares an Element enum for all Pokemon to choose from

2.  Declares a new Pokemon class that inherits from ScriptableObject

3.  Adds an optional SOType that can be used for inheritance

4.  Adds properties for data that all Pokemon share

5.  Uses the ContextMenu attribute to add the Configure method in the **Inspector**

6.  Adds a private method to configure inherited properties using the BaseType

7.  Checks that BaseType is not null before showing the Inherit option in the **Inspector**

If you've never seen the ContextMenu attribute before, don't worry – we use it to add commands to the default context menu of a script when it shows up in the **Inspector**. You can access the context menu by selecting the three vertical dots icon at the top-right of any script component in the **Inspector**. For more information on the ContextMenu attribute, check out the documentation at https://docs.unity3d.com/2022.2/Documentation/ScriptReference/ContextMenu.html.

In the **ScriptableObjects** folder:

1. **Right-click | Create | SOType**

2. Name the **SOType** asset

3. Repeat until you have three or more **SOType** assets, as shown in *Figure 13.8*:

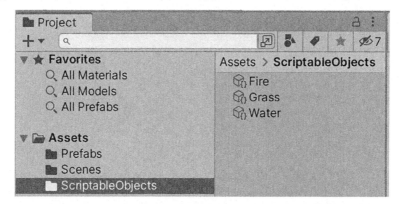

*Figure 13.8: SOType assets in the ScriptableObject project folder*

Feel free to use *Figure 13.9* to configure your type objects with the data I used (or get creative and fill them out yourself):

*Figure 13.9: ScriptableObject configuration in the Editor*

Now that we have type object assets we can configure in the **Editor**, our next step is to initialize each Pokemon prefab with an SOType. Update Pokemon.cs to match the following code, which adds an SOType field and initializes the class properties when the game runs:

```
using System.Collections;
using System.Collections.Generic;
using UnityEngine;

public class Pokemon : MonoBehaviour
{
    // 1
    public SOType PokemonType;
```

```
    public string Name;
    public int Health;
    public Element Element;
    public List<Element> Weaknesses;

    void Start()
    {
        // 2
        Health = PokemonType.HP;
        Element = PokemonType.Element;
        Weaknesses = PokemonType.Weaknesses;

        // 3
        var renderer = GetComponent<Renderer>();
        renderer.material.SetColor("_Color", PokemonType.Color);
    }
}
```

Let's break down the code:

1.  Adds an SOType variable to be set in the **Editor**
2.  Sets the Health, Element, and Weaknesses using the SOType
3.  Sets the GameObject's color using the SOType

In the **Hierarchy**, select each Pokemon prefab and set their Breed in the **Inspector** to whichever **SOType** assets you like! I'm using all three of mine, but the pattern also works well if you want to have multiple objects using the same type, as shown in *Figure 13.10*.

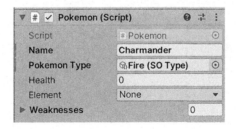

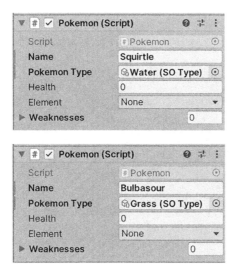

*Figure 13.10: Monster Instance Objects configured with Type Object*

Run the game and you'll see each **Pokemon (Script)** configures its properties using the assigned **Pokemon Type**, as shown in *Figure 13.11*:

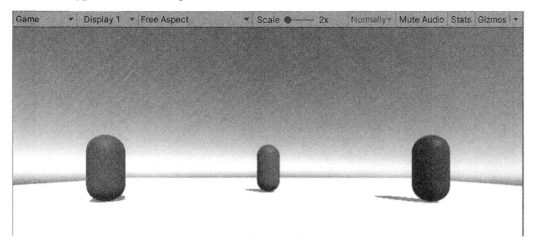

*Figure 13.11: Type Objects properties in action*

The real fun starts when we play with inheritance – mixing and matching Pokemon types to get more complex results. In the **ScriptableObjects** folder, create a new **SOType** asset named `Fire-Ground` and set its values to match *Figure 13.12*:

*Figure 13.12: An SOType using a base type*

To execute the inheritance, select the **three vertical dots** icon in the upper-right of the `ScriptableObject` and click **Inherit**, which will populate the data according to our inheritance rules shown in *Figure 13.13*. If you've got the black and white print edition, I swear the color changed to a deeper orange when mixed with the parent Fire type.

*Figure 13.13: An SOType after inheriting data*

In the Inspector, select a `Pokemon` prefab, switch out the `Fire` breed with the `Fire-Ground` type, and press **Play** to get a glimpse of our mixed type in action!

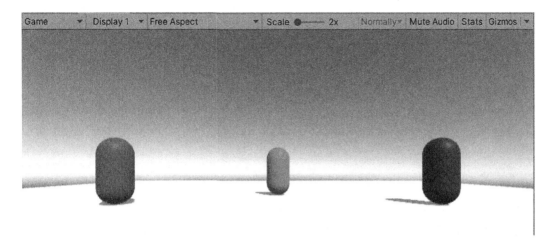

*Figure 13.14: A monster using inherited data*

**Leveling up your types**

It's my duty to put in a good word here for how well the Type Object pattern works with external data, i.e. databases, text files, JSON, whatever floats your backend boat. ScriptableObject creation isn't limited to the **Editor**, there's a perfectly good scripting API for programmatically adding them to your project, which you can find at https://docs.unity3d.com/ScriptReference/ScriptableObject.html.

However, you'll need to be aware of two things:

- You'll need to use the AssetDatabase class to store the ScriptableObject you create, which means you need to be careful of the asset path you use to save the type. I'd suggest looking into using the AssetDatabase. GenerateUniqueAssetpath method to avoid overriding existing ScriptableObjects.

- You'll need to manage how and when the ScriptableObjects get updated from the backend data – it could slow your game down to a crawl if you have hundreds of ScriptableObject types trying to update every time you compile or run the game (you might want to invest in creating your own editor tool for this process).

Don't be put off by the extra work here – `ScriptableObject` types powered by external data is a powerful combo!

With our `ScriptableObject` inheritance is working, that's going to round off our dive into optimizing the Type Object pattern for **Editor**-friendly features and possibilities. Don't worry though: the structure we've built leaves you plenty of room to play around and experiment before moving on to other chapters!

## Summary

Phew, we got through our second non-Gang of Four approved pattern – I hope it flipped your data mindset on its head as much as it did mine! Remember, the Type Object pattern works best when you have mountainous hierarchies that describe different data representations of the same object – super strong fire dragons are still *dragon*-type monsters; everything else is a data decision.

With just two classes, a type object and a Typed Object, we can create endless configurations by changing (and inheriting) shared data. This pattern works especially well with the drag-and-drop functionality of ScriptableObjects, which you should take full advantage of in your teams; putting creativity and testing powers into the hands of your designers is not only efficient, but it also leaves the door wide open for emergent design (Google it, I promise it's worth it).

In the next chapter, we'll explore how the Memento pattern gives us the power to take snapshots of data, state, or whatever information strikes our fancy and restore an object using that saved information later on (almost like how that vacation memento brings back fond memories of getting burned to a crisp on the beach).

## Further reading

- ScriptableObjects are the perfect way to create data containers in your Unity projects (and we'll use them in almost every chapter going forward), but I'd also recommend checking out the documentation at `https://docs.unity3d.com/Manual/class-ScriptableObject.html`.

# Leave a review!

Enjoying this book? Help readers like you by leaving an Amazon review. Scan the QR code below to get a free eBook of your choice.

# 14

# Taking Data Snapshots with the Memento Pattern

In this chapter, we're going to focus on a wonderful way of storing, managing, and restoring data snapshots (the internal state of an object at a given point in time) using the Memento pattern. This should sound familiar because we see this functionality all over the place, like when we cancel transactions, carry out undo or redo actions (like we did in *Chapter 8, Binding Actions with the Command Pattern*), use checkpoint systems, and – most importantly – version control!

Object state can be a tricky subject because we not only have to be aware of how we're tracking and updating the state values, but how we're exposing the stateful information to other objects in our projects. We already covered how to manage internal state transitions in *Chapter 10, Controlling Behavior with the State Pattern*, so instead we'll focus on safely exposing (and saving) snapshots of internal state.

And that's the real power of the Memento pattern – copying data from encapsulated objects *without breaking encapsulation*. This solution not only preserves boundaries between objects (which is always a good thing), it turns your saved data into decoupled objects that can be passed around, substituted, and restored without upsetting the class that created them.

We'll use this chapter to focus on the following topics:

- The pros and cons of the Memento design pattern
- Creating and restoring data snapshots
- Working with `MonoBehaviours`
- Memento pattern variations

Let's start off with the starter project and then we can move into the pattern breakdown and code of our own!

# Technical requirements

To get started:

1. Download or clone the GitHub repository at https://github.com/PacktPublishing/C-Design-Patterns-with-Unity-First-Edition

2. Open the **Ch_14_Starter** project folder in Unity Hub

3. In **Assets | Scenes**, double-click on **SampleScene**

The starter project for this chapter is a simple character design screen, complete with sliders for adjusting initial health, magic power, and intelligence (because it's always good to be smarter than the average orc). You also have UI buttons for saving your work and restoring the sliders to the default of previous configurations.

As for the scripts:

- `Character.cs` has variables for HP, MP, and INT and a SetData method for updating the class information from other classes.

- `Client.cs` has references to the three **Slider** components that are already set up in the UI, and empty Save and Restore methods for us to fill out as we progress through the chapter example.

- `SliderControl.cs` is a helper script that displays the value of each **Slider** component in a corresponding UI text field. Don't worry about this file, we won't be changing it at all (but it makes the UI look nice and responsive).

Our job for this chapter is to create a system for saving and loading snapshots of your avatar data without compromising any class encapsulation. We'll approach this in two steps – first, we'll work with the plain C# Character class (which is included in the starter project that you hopefully downloaded from GitHub), and second, we'll transform Character into a MonoBehavior and wire everything up in the **Inspector**. Once you're done testing out the starter project, it's time to dive into some code of our own.

# Breaking down the Memento pattern

As part of the Behavioral family of design patterns, the Memento pattern is all about saving an object's internal state data at a point in time without breaking the object's encapsulation. The Memento pattern is useful when:

- You need to save a snapshot of an object's internal state (data) so it can be easily restored later.

- You need to keep the target object's internal state and implementation encapsulated.

This sounds a little too computer science-y even for me, so let's break down the Memento pattern into more relatable chunks. Imagine you go on a dream vacation you've been planning for years. While on said fantastic vacation, you take pictures, buy souvenirs, and get a nasty sunburn, thus capturing the all-around good time you're having (current internal state). When you get home, the mail is stacked up to the ceiling, you discover that a pipe burst in your bathroom while you were away, and the new neighbors are *really* into early morning clog dancing (updated internal state). So, what do you do? You put the kitschy souvenirs on your desk, take out your phone (or physical media capturing device), and look at the lovely pictures you took – and bam, you're transported back to the wonderful memories you made (restored internal state) with the help of the nice mementos you brought home, as shown in *Figure 14.1*.

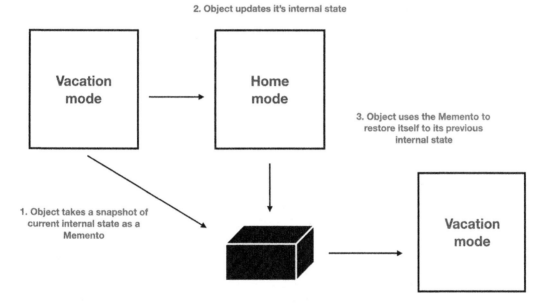

*Figure 14.1: Vacation example showing real-world Memento patterns*

Instead of directly accessing an object's internal data, the object creates a copy of its own data in a separate data structure (a memento class), which is stored and retrieved from another separate class (a caretaker). This structure allows the client to delegate data snapshot creation and restoration to the object we care about (the originator) while keeping the snapshot data safely tucked away in decoupled classes.

When we're thinking about programming scenarios, this sounds a lot like an undo/redo system, which is one of the best use cases for the Memento pattern. If we already have an implementation that supports one Memento snapshot, we can easily store a series of sequential mementos and work our way back down the chain of events. We can even modify the memento chain at any time by inserting a new snapshot, as shown in *Figure 14.2.*

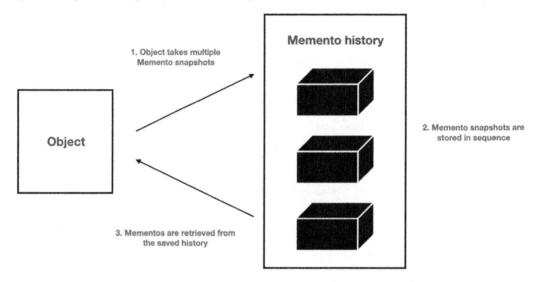

*Figure 14.2: Simplified scenario of storing and retrieving Memento history*

All the client does is coordinate when to create and save a new Memento and when to retrieve from and restore an object's internal state to an existing Memento we previously saved!

## Diagramming the pattern

*Figure 14.3* shows the structure of the Memento pattern with its three component elements:

- The **Originator** has the encapsulated data (internal state) we're trying to save or restore and is responsible for creating a Memento snapshot of its current information as well as restoring that internal state from a saved Memento.

- The **Memento** stores a snapshot of the Originator's internal state data, which can be as much or as little of the Originator's data as needed. In more complex implementations, only the Originator that created the Memento would be able to access its internal state, which effectively locks out access from other objects.

- The **Caretaker** stores, manages, and returns the Memento snapshot (or current snapshot from a list of previous snapshots) and never operates or examines the actual Memento contents.

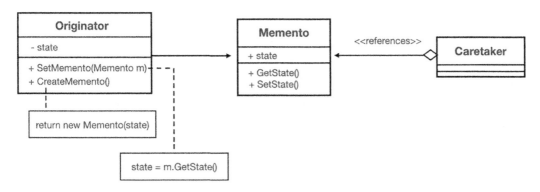

*Figure 14.3: UML diagram of the Flyweight pattern components*

`Originators` create and restore their internal states using `Memento` objects and the `Caretaker` stores these `Memento` objects, but the `Memento` objects themselves are entirely passive; they're just data containers. If you find yourself putting behavior into a `Memento` class, that's a red flag letting you know you might not be using the pattern correctly (or the pattern may not be a good fit for the problem you're facing).

## Pros and cons

Like all design patterns, there are pros and cons. Let's start with the potential benefits the Memento pattern can add to your project:

- Keeps encapsulation boundaries intact by creating external copies of an originator's internal data without exposing any of that internal data to other classes. This is a big plus for complex originator classes because they get to decide what information is included in a `Memento` and how state restoration is handled.
- Simplifies your `Originator` classes by moving any internal state tracking responsibilities to the `Caretaker` class, which frees up the `Originator` from handling requests and events from the `client` class.

However, be careful of the following pitfalls when using the pattern in your projects:

- **Memento storage can be expensive** as your `Originators` are copying big chunks of data to `Memento` snapshots and restoring them at a rapid pace. There are also potential storage costs with `Caretakers` and the `Memento` objects they manage. One possible solution to this scenario is to only update parts of existing mementos to avoid creating new `Memento` objects in memory if they're only being incrementally modified.

- **Memento access is difficult to limit**, especially when you only want to allow access to the Originator. As mentioned in the previous section, the Originator *should be* the only class that can access the Memento state. C# doesn't have a simple answer for this problem, but you can refer to *Chapter 13, Making Monsters with the Type Object Pattern*, for solution ideas.

On paper, it looks like the Memento pattern has more cons than pros, but today's hardware comes with enough storage to offset these concerns in most cases. However, it's always a good idea to actively test your memory consumption to make sure this pattern is delivering a reasonable return on investment.

Now that we've covered the structure, benefits, and limitations of the Memento pattern, we can start laying out the traditional implementation in code.

# Creating and restoring data snapshots

Imagine your game has a complex character-creation process where players can choose every detail of their avatars – hair color, eyebrow thickness, nostril flare (if you're into that). Now imagine that your players aren't happy with the results, and they want to start over, or worse yet, they want to go back to the twenty-third configuration they put together an hour ago. What do you do?

The core solution we're going to build is a data snapshot system where the game (or player) can save and restore their avatar details to default or past states. If you've ever used version control, you'll know how crucial this functionality can be. It's no different in games or applications with modifiable data – users should have the option of saving their work, level checkpoints, or whatever incremental information they want and restore or undo their changes at any time.

## Adding the memento class

In the **Scripts** folder, create a new C# script named Memento and update it to match the following code. The Memento class is the core of the Memento pattern (go figure) because it's effectively a mirror of whatever class we want to snapshot. In this case, the originator is the Character class because it has the values for HP, MP, and INT we want to save, so we'll grab those in our snapshot and print out a console message whenever a new Memento snapshot is created!

```
using System.Collections;
using System.Collections.Generic;
using UnityEngine;

// 1
using System;
```

```
// 2
public class Memento
{
    // 3
    public float HP { get; protected set; }
    public float MP { get; protected set; }
    public float INT { get; protected set; }

    // 4
    private DateTime _date;

    // 5
    public Memento(float hp, float mp, float intel)
    {
        HP = hp;
        MP = mp;
        INT = intel;
        _date = DateTime.Now;

        Debug.Log($"New memento created at {_date}");
    }
}
```

Let's break down the code:

1. Adds the System using directive to access the DateTime class
2. Creates a new public Memento class
3. Adds public variables with protected set properties to match the Character class data
4. Adds a private DateTime variable specific to each Memento instance
5. Declares a constructor for setting the instance values and prints out a debug log to let us know the snapshot was successfully created

You can add snapshot-specific information to the Memento if needed – in our case adding a time-stamp when the Memento instance is created is a handy bit of information. You also have the option of leaving *out* information the memento doesn't need to know, which can simplify your snapshot when you have large data structures.

While our Memento class is small in this example, every memento snapshot we create is more memory our project is using. While we might not see any performance impact at first, it's important to be aware of the size and complexity of the snapshots that we're saving.

 You can absolutely create a memento interface or abstract class if we need to handle multiple memento classes, but since we're only dealing with a single Memento snapshot, we're going to stick with a single concrete Memento class in this chapter.

Now that we have a Memento blueprint, we need some way of storing and retrieving the most recent snapshot, which is where a Caretaker object comes into play.

## Setting up the caretaker

In the **Scripts** folder, create a new C# script named Caretaker and update it to match the following code. The basic Caretaker class is usually a Memento instance – you can decide how you want to set this up, whether it's with a simple public variable or a private variable with a public accessor, or whatever you're comfortable with. Since we don't have anything crazy going on in our project, we'll leave the Memento public and go from there (but we *will* talk about more complex Caretaker functionality in the *Memento pattern variations* section):

```
using System.Collections;
using System.Collections.Generic;
using UnityEngine;

// 1
public class Caretaker
{
    // 2
    public Memento CurrentMemento;
}
```

With our Memento and Caretaker classes all set up, we can go back to the Character class and add in the code needed to create and restore data snapshots.

## Updating the originator

The originator creates a snapshot of itself *and* restores its own state when handed a Memento instance. Like the Prototype and Type Object patterns, we put this functionality in the class to keep the snapshot responsibility as close to the snapshot data as possible.

In a perfect world, only the originator that created a Memento instance would have access to its internal state, but since C# doesn't have the concept of a friend class, we're going to settle for public get and protected set properties on each Character variable (you can see another solution to this problem in *Chapter 13, Making Monsters with the Type Object Pattern*).

Update Character.cs to match the following code, which adds two new public methods – one for creating and returning a new Memento instance with the current HP, MP, and INT values, and another for restoring those values to a previous state:

 I wrote the Character class with a SetData method to update the protected variables for simplicity. You can absolutely use a class constructor (although this won't scale if you want to change Character into a MonoBehaviour), add a public method to update each variable individually, or any other solution you can get working. How you handle updating your encapsulated data is up to you and is not part of the core Memento pattern – *keeping* your data encapsulated is the important part.

```csharp
using System.Collections;
using System.Collections.Generic;
using UnityEngine;
using System;

public class Character
{
    public float HP { get; protected set; }
    public float MP { get; protected set; }
    public float INT { get; protected set; }

    public void SetData(float hp, float mp, float intelligence)
    {
        //... No changes needed ...
    }

    // 1
    public Memento CreateMemento()
    {
        Debug.Log("Creating new memento...");
        return new Memento(HP, MP, INT);
```

```
    }


    // 2
    public void RestoreMemento(Memento memento)
    {
        HP = memento.HP;
        MP = memento.MP;
        INT = memento.INT;


        Debug.Log("Restored to previous memento state...");
    }
}
```

Let's break down the code:

1.  Declares a public method that creates and returns a Memento instance
2.  Declares a public method that takes in a Memento and restores the internal values

 If you have multiple originator objects running around your project that need to be able to create snapshots of themselves, this is a good place for a generic component. Check out the end of *Chapter 3, Spawning Enemies with the Prototype Pattern*, for implementation ideas!

Now that the Character class can create new Memento instances and restore its internal values using an existing Memento object, we can wire up the client code to use the new Caretaker class to manage our avatar data!

## Wiring up the client

Update Client.cs to match the following code, which uses the Originator and Caretaker classes to create and manage our snapshot system. For reference, the Save and Restore methods are hooked up to buttons in the UI so you don't need to do any additional setup.

It's not uncommon for extra state management to come into play while you're saving or restoring Memento snapshots. For instance, you may not want the game to keep running while you're in the middle of saving your Character data because the data may change during the saving process. Likewise, you may not want the game to start running while a snapshot is being used to restore your Character data. In both cases, making the Save and RestoreMemento methods Coroutines would give you the flexibility to wait for these methods to finish running before handing control back to the calling code.

```csharp
using System.Collections;
using System.Collections.Generic;
using UnityEngine;
using UnityEngine.UI;

public class Client : MonoBehaviour
{
    public Slider HPSlider;
    public Slider MPSlider;
    public Slider INTSlider;

    // 1
    private Character _originator;
    private Caretaker _caretaker;

    // 2
    void Awake()
    {
        _originator = new Character();
        _caretaker = new Caretaker();

        Save();
    }
```

```csharp
    public void Save()
    {
        // 3
        _originator.SetData(HPSlider.value, MPSlider.value, INTSlider.
value);

        // 4
        var newMemento = _originator.CreateMemento();

        // 5
        _caretaker.CurrentMemento = newMemento;
    }

    public void Restore()
    {
        // 6
        _originator.RestoreMemento(_caretaker.CurrentMemento);

        // 7
        HPSlider.value = _originator.HP;
        MPSlider.value = _originator.MP;
        INTSlider.value = _originator.INT;
    }
}
```

Let's break down the code:

1.  Declares Caretaker and Character variables to store private references

2.  Initializes new Caretaker and Character instances and saves a default state

3.  Uses the _originator to set its data before a new Memento snapshot is saved

4.  Creates a new Memento snapshot from the current _originator state

5.  Saves the new Memento snapshot in the _caretaker for later restoration

6. Restores the _originator state from the most recent _caretaker snapshot when required

7. Sets the Slider values from the restored _originator state, which completes the memento cycle

When you run the game, you'll see the sliders at zero, the console printing out our initial Character state, and the default Memento that we saved on Awake, as shown in the following figure:

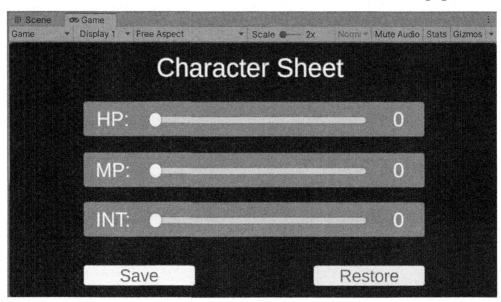

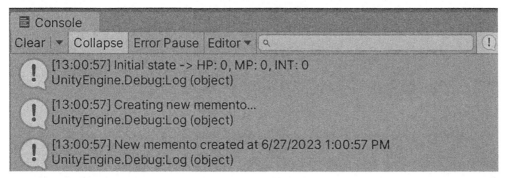

*Figure 14.4: Default Character state and new memento when game starts*

To test that our default snapshot code is working, let's move the **HP** slider to **3**, the **MP** slider to **1**, and the **INT** slider to **5**, as shown in the following figure:

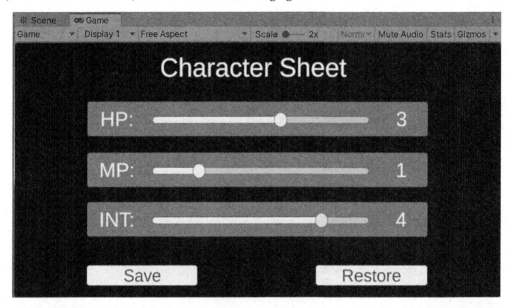

*Figure 14.5: Updated Character data values*

Now let's hit **Restore** to see the values pop back to zero using the initial Memento snapshot we created and saved in the Client.cs Awake method, as shown in the following figure:

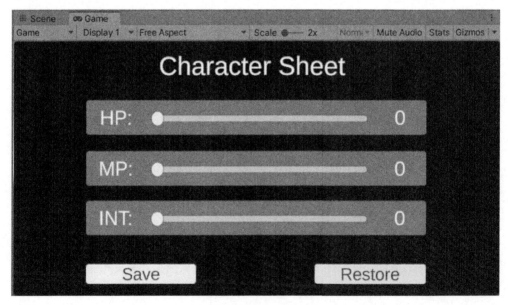

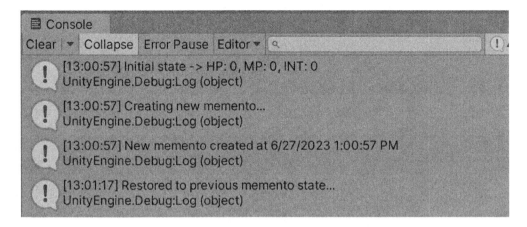

Figure 14.6: Console logs of restored Memento state

For a final test, change the slider values to any numbers you like, then hit **Save**, change the numbers again (I know, it's a chore), then hit **Restore** and see the values pop back to the most recently saved Memento!

 You'll notice that we can only save one Memento at a time, but we'll cover how to implement an undo/redo system in the *Memento pattern variations* section.

Now that we have the basic Memento pattern implemented, let's work on how the system plays with MonoBehaviours.

# Working with MonoBehaviours

Originator classes don't have to be straight C# classes; with a little tweaking, they can also be Unity components. The thing you have to remember is that the Memento pattern is best suited to originators that want to *keep* their encapsulation intact, which means you probably won't have a ton of public variables in an originator Monobehaviour.

Unity does allow you to work with private variables (as you probably know), but it also has the option to serialize fields (which you might not know). But wait, how can we serialize a field if we have a variable with a get and set property, especially one with different access modifiers? Since Unity automatically generates backing fields for all properties, you can use a special attribute to tell Unity to serialize the backing field of any property, giving us the best of both worlds – encapsulation *and* serialization.

Update `Character.cs` to match the following code, which adds the `[field: SerializeField]`
attribute to all our originator variables and updates their value whenever the **Slider** component
fires off its `OnValueChanged` event:

 We could have stayed with our `SetData` method for updating values, but the events
are more interesting since we can see the changes right in the **Inspector**.

```
using System.Collections;
using System.Collections.Generic;
using UnityEngine;
using System;

// 1
public class Character : MonoBehaviour
{
    // 2
    [field: SerializeField]
    public float HP { get; protected set; }

    [field: SerializeField]
    public float MP { get; protected set; }

    [field: SerializeField]
    public float INT { get; protected set; }

    // 3
    public void OnHPChanged(float value) => HP = value;
    public void OnMPChanged(float value) => MP = value;
    public void OnINTChanged(float value) => INT = value;

    public Memento CreateMemento()
    {
        // … No changes needed …
    }

    public void RestoreMemento(Memento memento)
```

```
    {
        // … No changes needed ….
    }
}
```

Let's break down the code:

1.  Changes Character to a MonoBehaviour, so we can attach it to a GameObject in the scene
2.  Adds attributes to serialize backing fields for HP, MP, and INT, making them visible in the **Editor**
3.  Adds public methods for updating the HP, MP, and INT values, which can be accessed from the UI as OnClick events

Update Client.cs to match the following code, which allows us to work with the Character class as a MonoBehaviour in the **Editor**. All the originator value updates are handled through events so our client code is a whole lot simpler to use and manage:

```
using System.Collections;
using System.Collections.Generic;
using UnityEngine;
using UnityEngine.UI;

public class Client : MonoBehaviour
{
    public Slider HPSlider;
    public Slider MPSlider;
    public Slider INTSlider;

    // 1
    public Character _originator;

    private Caretaker _caretaker;

    // 2
    void Awake()
    {
        _caretaker = new Caretaker();
        Save();
    }
```

```
// 3
public void Save()
{
    var newMemento = _originator.CreateMemento();
    _caretaker.CurrentMemento = newMemento;
}

public void Restore()
{
    // … No changes needed …
}
}
```

Let's break down the code:

1. Changes the Character variable access modifier from private to public so its properties can be seen in the **Inspector**

2. Deletes the Character instance initialization from Awake because Character is a MonoBehaviour now

3. Deletes the SetData method because the Character takes care of its own updates

To hook everything up:

1. In the **Inspector**:

    a. Drag Character.cs as a **Component** onto the **Client** GameObject

    b. Drag the **Character** component into the **Originator** field on the **Client**

*Figure 14.7: Originator value being set in the Inspector*

2. In the **Hierarchy**, open the **Canvas | Stats panel | HP**:

    a. Select the **Slider** and add a new OnValueChanged event.

    b. Drag the **Client** GameObject into the Object field.

    c. From the function dropdown, select **Character | OnHPChanged** (the dynamic option).

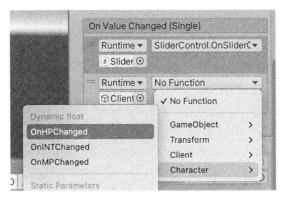

*Figure 14.8: OnValueChanged event being set in the Inspector*

3. Repeat *the previous step* for the **MP** and **INT** objects in **Canvas | Stats panel**, using the respective OnMPChanged and OnINTChanged functions when configuring the OnValueChanged event:

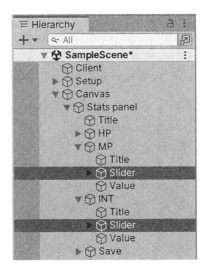

*Figure 14.9: MP and INT slider objects in the Hierarchy*

Run the game again and you'll see the slider values onscreen reflected in the **Character** component on the **Client**. Whenever you restore an old memento, both the UI and the **Character** component values are synced up. Likewise, when you save a new memento and restore, the system behaves exactly like it did when Character.cs was just a wee C# class.

That wraps up the vanilla Memento pattern implementation, but there are a few variations we should look at to make our solution more fully featured, because why wouldn't we want to store multiple snapshots, or bundle our Originator and Caretaker classes together?

# Memento pattern variations

In some cases, the plain Memento pattern is enough to get things rolling, but there will always be situations where more features are needed to make your project the best version of itself. For instance, storing a single Memento object is usable but not ideal for scenarios where you want to have a history of data snapshots that can be undone and redone at your convenience, or injecting an Originator instance into your Caretaker class constructor (yes, it's more coupling, but it also puts all the memento management responsibilities into a single place).

Again, these are optional, but I've found them extremely useful in my own projects (hopefully they spark your creativity when thinking of different ways to apply the Memento pattern in your own code).

## Storing memento history

The Memento pattern is one of the best go-to solutions for creating a robust undo/redo system, so let's write a basic implementation to see how it works (you'll see it bundled with the Command pattern quite a bit out in the programming wilds).

Update Caretaker.cs to match the following code, which manages a private list of Memento snapshots through publicly accessible methods – adding snapshots to the list when they are saved in the game and returning the last snapshot in the list when needed. I've also added a little default code for our example because we always start with the slider values at 0 (but you can customize or remove this if it doesn't work for your situation):

```
using System.Collections;
using System.Collections.Generic;
using UnityEngine;

// 1
using System.Linq;
```

```csharp
public class Caretaker
{
    // 2
    private List<Memento> _mementos = new List<Memento>();

    // 3
    public void Save(Memento newMemento)
    {
        _mementos.Add(newMemento);
    }

    // 4
    public Memento RestoreLast()
    {
        if(_mementos.Count == 0)
        {
            return new Memento(0, 0, 0);
        }

        // 5
        var lastMemento = _mementos.Last();
        _mementos.Remove(lastMemento);

        return lastMemento;
    }
}
```

 Stack and Queue types are also great options when tracking undo and redo operations. If you need ideas on how to implement that solution, check out what we did in *Chapter 8, Binding Actions with the Command Pattern.*

Let's break down the code:

1. Adds the Linq namespace so we can access the Last method on List types
2. Declares and initializes an empty List of Memento objects
3. Adds a Save method with a Memento parameter that adds a new object to _mementos

4.  Adds a `RestoreLast` method that returns a `Memento` object (and a default object if _ mementos is empty)

5.  Removes and returns the last object in _mementos

Update `Client.cs` to match the following code, which reflects the new changes we've made to our `Caretaker`:

```
public class Client : MonoBehaviour
{
    public Slider HPSlider;
    public Slider MPSlider;
    public Slider INTSlider;
    public Character _originator;

    private Caretaker _caretaker;

    void Awake()
    {
        // … No changes needed …
    }

    public void Save()
    {
        _originator.SetData(HPSlider.value, MPSlider.value, INTSlider.
value);
        var newMemento = _originator.CreateMemento();

        // 1
        _caretaker.Save(newMemento);
    }

    public void Restore()
    {
        // 2
        _originator.RestoreMemento(_caretaker.RestoreLast());

        HPSlider.value = _originator.HP;
        MPSlider.value = _originator.MP;
```

```
                    INTSlider.value = _originator.INT;
        }
    }
```

Run the game now, change the slider values around, and **save** multiple snapshots, and then hit **Restore** as many times as you want. You'll see the slider values work their way back down the list of previous states until they finally default to all zeroes.

## Bundling originator and caretaker

We can make things even easier on ourselves by injecting an originator object into the Caretaker, which places all our memento management code together. Be aware that this does increase the coupling between these two classes where before they were separate.

Update Caretaker.cs to match the following code, which stores and initializes a Character (originator) instance using the Caretaker constructor and moves the Memento snapshot responsibilities we had in Client.cs to the Save and RestoreLast methods:

```
using System.Collections;
using System.Collections.Generic;
using UnityEngine;
using System.Linq;

public class Caretaker
{
    private List<Memento> _mementos = new List<Memento>();

    // 1
    private Character _originator;

    // 2
    public Caretaker(Character originator)
    {
        _originator = originator;
    }

    // 3
    public void Save()
    {
```

```
        _mementos.Add(_originator.CreateMemento());
    }

    // 4
    public void RestoreLast()
    {
        if(_mementos.Count == 0)
        {
            _originator.RestoreMemento(new Memento(0, 0, 0));
            return;
        }

        var lastMemento = _mementos.Last();
        _mementos.Remove(lastMemento);

        _originator.RestoreMemento(lastMemento);
    }
}
```

Let's break down the code:

1.  Adds a private `Character` variable to store the originator object
2.  Declares a class constructor with a `Character` parameter and initializes `_originator`
3.  Updates the `Save` method to get a new `Memento` directly from the `_originator` instead of a new object being passed in
4.  Updates the `RestoreLast` method to restore a `Memento` directly from the `_originator`

Update `Client.cs` to match the following code, which takes advantage of our new `Caretaker` functionality:

```
using System.Collections;
using System.Collections.Generic;
using UnityEngine;
using UnityEngine.UI;

public class Client : MonoBehaviour
{
    public Slider HPSlider;
    public Slider MPSlider;
```

```
        public Slider INTSlider;
        public Character _originator;

        private Caretaker _caretaker;

        void Awake()
        {
            // 1
            _caretaker = new Caretaker(_originator);
            Save();
        }

        public void Save()
        {
            // 2
            _caretaker.Save();
        }

        public void Restore()
        {
            // 3
            _caretaker.RestoreLast();

            HPSlider.value = _originator.HP;
            MPSlider.value = _originator.MP;
            INTSlider.value = _originator.INT;
        }
    }
```

Let's break down our variation update:

1.  Passes in the _originator object when the Caretaker class is constructed
2.  Calls the Save method on the _caretaker, which uses the _originator it was constructed with
3.  Calls the RestoreLast method on the _caretaker, which uses the _originator it was constructed with to manage the snapshot history

When you run the game one last time, you won't see any behavior changes, but the Client is a little cleaner and could be built out into its component more easily.

## Managers and ScriptableObject snapshots

We kept this example almost entirely in code (with a little help from the UI and Character component), but that doesn't mean that's your limitation. You could expand what we've done here by making the Caretaker a singleton (or service – see *Chapter 19, Global Access with the Service Locator Pattern*). You could even update your system to work with ScriptableObject mementos, which would make your game configuration and testing much more Editor-friendly!

## Persisting data

This variation is more of a stretch goal for you to implement on your own if your project needs it, but the Memento pattern provides a wonderfully decoupled structure for tying in additional saving and loading functionality. Whether you choose to keep the originator and caretaker classes separate or bundled up together, the point of contact is the same – when a memento is created and stored. From there, you could save and restore your snapshots locally in XML, JSON, or a binary file, pass them off to a database, or a mix of both (if you're feeling fancy). Any way you slice it, Memento plus persistent data is a win-win.

## Summary

And that brings us to the close of our Memento exploration. We've covered a lot of ground here, but it's for a good cause. Saving and restoring state snapshots is not only useful but crucial in almost any meaningful application or game. Without it, your users (and players) may feel like they don't have any agency when it comes to making mistakes or being creative (for fear that they can't spam the back button if they don't like where they end up).

Remember, the Memento pattern works best when you need to save and restore internal state information without breaking an object's encapsulation. The Originator class is responsible for creating and restoring Memento snapshots, your Memento is a storage-only class that mirrors whatever Originator data you want to save, and the Caretaker class stores and provides the current Memento on demand. You're not limited to a single stored snapshot because the Caretaker class can be upgraded to store a list of previous Memento objects (which is perfect for implementing an undo/redo system). You can even bundle your Caretaker and Originator classes together for easier access (but tighter coupling) or add in data persistence with local storage or backend databases.

In the next chapter, we'll dive into the Decorator pattern and its ability to let us dynamically add new behaviors to existing classes without any subclassing!

## Further reading

- Coroutines are a specific type of method in Unity that allows you to spread tasks across several frames instead of running them all at once like a normal C# method. For more information, check out the documentation at `https://docs.unity3d.com/Manual/Coroutines.html`.

## Join our community on Discord

Join our community's Discord space for discussions with the author and other readers:

`https://packt.link/gamedevelopment_packt`

# 15

# Dynamic Upgrades with the Decorator Pattern

In the last chapter, we built a flexible system for saving data snapshots at different moments in our program's lifecycle. In this chapter, we'll move away from data and back to behavior with the Decorator pattern, which lets us *dynamically* add new behaviors to existing objects *without* using traditional subclassing techniques.

Adding responsibilities and behaviors to classes that already exist can be a somewhat prickly decision, especially in object-oriented programming. Inheritance and subclassing are valid solutions when you're attacking this problem, but they can get bloated and aren't the most flexible. I say "not the most flexible" because customizing subclass hierarchies can be quite static; or, if you're feeling brave, you code in a bunch of default subclass properties that give the appearance of flexibility, but really, they're just a maintenance headache waiting to strike the moment you need to make changes.

The Decorator pattern offers a more dynamic solution by sidestepping the question of inheritance altogether by separating the added behaviors into separate decorator classes, which are completely optional! Your existing objects have 100% freedom to choose if they want to opt into the custom behaviors or not, all with a two-class flat hierarchy (and they can even opt into multiple chained behaviors if they want).

We'll use this chapter to focus on the following topics:

- The pros and cons of the Decorator design pattern
- Building a simple decorator structure

- Adding customized behaviors
- Using `ScriptableObject` decorators

Let's start off with the technical requirements for this chapter, then move to the pattern breakdown and get into code of our own!

# Technical requirements

To get started:

1. Download or clone the GitHub repository at `https://github.com/PacktPublishing/C-Design-Patterns-with-Unity-First-Edition`

2. Open the **Ch_15_Starter** project folder in Unity Hub

3. In **Assets > Scenes**, double-click on **SampleScene**

The starter project for this chapter is a simple character screen from your run-of-the-mill role-playing or first-person shooter game (really anything that has a modifiable player). The UI displays your character's current attack power and has buttons for buffing your character, going into battle when you're satisfied, and resetting everything if you want to start over. The Decorator pattern is so widely applicable that I chose a static example like this to highlight the pattern code rather than game mechanics, but once you get the feel for the pattern structure, you'll have tons of ideas for your own projects!

As for the scripts:

- `Client.cs` stores the `Attack` text field in the UI, a reference to a `CharacterBehavior` script that is set in the **Inspector**, and methods hooked up to the UI buttons in the scene.

- `CharacterBehavior.cs` is a blank slate with empty methods matching the UI buttons that we'll fill in as we go (this is where the bulk of our actions will execute).

We'll also be using some Unity and C# language features to take our code the extra mile. Don't worry if you're not familiar with these; I've included links for the basics and I'll explain how they apply to our use cases as we go.

- Interfaces (https://learn.microsoft.com/en-us/dotnet/csharp/fundamentals/types/interfaces)

- Abstract classes (https://learn.microsoft.com/en-us/dotnet/csharp/language-reference/keywords/abstract)

- ScriptableObjects (https://docs.unity3d.com/Manual/class-ScriptableObject.html)

Our job is to create buff items that can modify the character's Attack value at compile time and runtime, and make sure they can be stacked if they're applied in sequence! Along the way, we'll add in some ScriptableObject data and talk about different variations, but for now, let's focus on breaking down the Decorator pattern.

# Breaking down the Decorator pattern

As part of the Structural family of design patterns, the Decorator pattern is all about dynamically adding behaviors to individual objects without subclassing or changing the entire existing class. Instead of creating a subclass for each possible configuration you can think of, customizations are separated into decorator classes that wrap the object you want to modify – think changing an object's skin versus its guts or internal workings (we'll return to this analogy throughout the chapter). The Decorator pattern is useful when:

- You want to dynamically add behaviors to specific objects without affecting other objects or class hierarchies.

- You want the flexibility to add *and* remove additional behaviors.

- You want to avoid large inheritance hierarchies while still keeping your combination options open.

Let's take an everyday example – getting dressed. When you wake up in the morning, you may (like me) check the weather outside and decide whether a jacket or hat is needed. You may also (like me) have more than one person in your household, and they may also need to make a daring clothing choice.

In a classic inheritance solution, we might have an extremely deep subclassing tree or a base class that *must* include the almost endless combinations of stylish additions, as shown in the following figure:

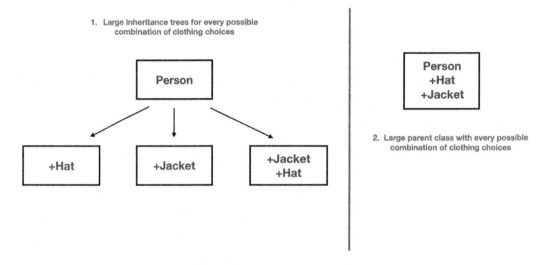

*Figure 15.1: Example solution using inheritance*

Even with only two options (jacket or hat), our class hierarchy quickly becomes unmanageable, and neither of these options gives us flexible, fine-grained control over customization. But what if we decide that all people *can* wear jackets and hats, but only if they want to? That way, I can decide whether my default clothing is good enough (t-shirt and shorts), or put on a jacket, or add thirteen layers before stepping out into a snowstorm. Whatever the case, the underlying person class doesn't change, only the individual instance, as shown in the following figure:

1. Decorators hold the added behaviour

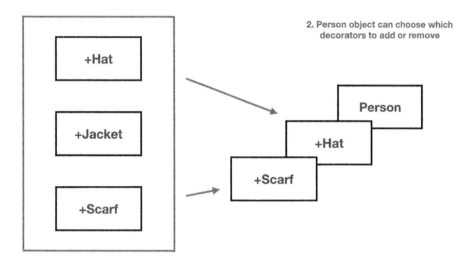

*Figure 15.2: Example solution using separate decorator objects*

Now here's the good part – even though there are multiple people in my household, nobody is *required* to make a clothing decision. We can all decorate ourselves if and when we want (dynamically adding behavior) without breaking our requirements as people, or we can function perfectly fine without any decoration at all (although I wouldn't recommend it). And while this is all going on behind the scenes, our client code only sees people, whether they're wearing extra clothes or not. If you're already thinking of how this pattern would be a flexible solution to creating weapon systems, item upgrades, armor smithing, and anything else that requires "decorating" an object, then you're already ahead of me!

# Diagramming the pattern

*Figure 15.3* shows the UML structure of the Decorator pattern with its four main component elements:

- The **Component** interface holds all the requirements for objects we want to decorate. These can be methods, get/set properties, or a mixture of both.

- **Concrete Components** are the decoratable objects that implement the Component interface. These can have data and behaviors separate from the Decorator pattern structure just like any other class object.

- **Decorator** classes implement the Component interface and are responsible for storing a reference to a Component object they want to decorate. We'll implement all Decorators as abstract classes, but they can also be interfaces if you prefer.

- **Concrete Decorators** have all the data and behaviors that are applied to their underlying Component object.

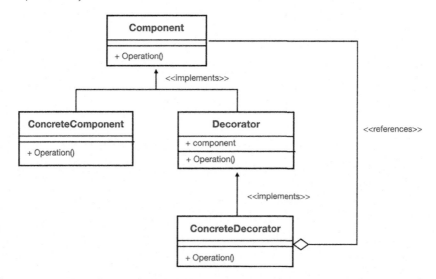

*Figure 15.3: UML diagram of the Decorator pattern components*

Notice that Concrete Components and Decorators both implement the Component interface, which makes it easy for the client to treat them the same without knowing which is which. Like the State pattern and individual states, we're deferring any data and behaviors up the decorator class hierarchy. You can create as many concrete Components or concrete Decorator as you like, all with different values and actions, then use them to build a wide variety of scenarios!

# Pros and cons

Like all design patterns, there are pros and cons. Let's start with the potential benefits the Decorator pattern can add to your project:

- **Adding behaviors is more flexible and dynamic** than with conventional inheritance. These behaviors are completely optional, can be added and removed at runtime, and can be chained multiple times. This scenario avoids deep subclass hierarchies for every new behavior (and it goes without saying, but inheriting from a class more than once should be a no-go).

- **Future-proofs your classes**, so there's no need to build in every conceivable behavior you may want a customizable class to have; instead, you can compose complex functionality from simple decorator classes, mix and match them any way you want, and avoid paying for features before you need them. This approach also avoids unwanted access to information or features that aren't related to the behaviors you want to add.

However, be careful of the following pitfalls when using the pattern in your projects:

- **Components and Decorators aren't always the same**: While Components and Decorators implement the same interface, Decorators are essentially containers that wrap Component objects. While they can be treated the same in terms of their shared interface, they are not the same when it comes to object identity.

- **Pieces all over the floor**: While the Decorator pattern avoids nested and inflexible class hierarchies, it does leave your project with lots of small class objects that all look the same to your client code. This can be hard to debug and use if you're onboarding a new team member with the pattern already implemented, but this can be said of all design patterns and shouldn't be a big deterrent (just something to keep in mind).

Many times, choosing the Decorator pattern over other solutions is a question of what you want to leave up to chance. If you want to change the internal workings of a class, the Strategy pattern is a much better fit; but if you want to change the outer layer or skin of an individual object (and not the entire class), that's where the Decorator really shines.

Now that we've covered the structure, benefits, and limitations of the Decorator pattern, we can start writing our own code.

# Building a simple Decorator

Imagine you're building a loadout screen for an RPG or FPS where players can configure their character with buffs or items before going into battle. The idea here is to make these modifications dynamic (available when the game is running) so your players can play around with different configurations before committing. For our example, we'll assume our in-game characters have an Attack stat and a Battle behavior that gets executed when we're ready to enter the arena.

The flexible part of this scenario is that our players can choose to start the game with the character defaults and applied modifications or reset everything and start all over again! We'll build this structure with a combination of interfaces, abstract classes, and concrete elements, all of which are covered in the following subsections.

## Adding a Component interface

The foundation of the Decorator pattern is the Component interface, which is going to hold all our shared data and behaviors for future concrete Components and Decorators. If you've already powered through *Chapter 11, Adding Features with the Visitor Pattern*, this is very similar to the visitable object structure. Since our example is fairly simple, our Components and Decorators will only need to be able to return a default or decorated Strength value and a default or overridden Battle method, so let's put that into action!

In the **Scripts** folder, create a new C# script named ICharacter and update its code to match the following code snippet, which declares a new public interface with two methods (one for returning the strength value and one for battling).

 You could also use a get property instead of the Strength method if your decorator interface is only dealing with data; I'd actually encourage you to do so, since it clearly separates expectations for data and behavior in your code and makes things more legible in the long run (I'm not using that approach in this chapter to make things easier to understand). On the flip side, with any behavior operations (like Battle), it's recommended to use a regular method.

```
using System.Collections;
using System.Collections.Generic;
using UnityEngine;

// 1
```

```
public interface ICharacter
{
    // 2
    int Strength();

    // 3
    void Battle();
}
```

Let's break down the main Component interface:

1.  It declares a `public` interface for all decorators to implement.

2.  It adds a `Strength` method to return a base value or a decorated value.

3.  It adds a `Battle` method to execute default behavior or decorator operations.

We want to keep the shared `Component` interface in the decorator structure as lightweight as possible – any data or concrete behaviors should exist in concrete implementations. Now that we have a blueprint, we can go ahead and create some concrete Component classes, starting with a base character class that we'll set up in the next section.

## Creating a concrete Component

The base concrete component in the traditional Decorator pattern simply returns default values for the `Component` interface requirements, so let's start with that implementation. In the **Scripts** folder, create a new C# script named `BaseCharacter` and update its code to match the following snippet, which sets the `Strength` method to return a default value and the `Battle` method to print out a debug log when our players are ready to jump into the fray.

 Your concrete Components don't need to be as boring as our example; they can have their own constructor, initial values, or anything you need, as long as you also implement the Component interface (in our case, `ICardComponent`). Class constructors are more flexible if we don't want to automatically assume that all characters inherit from the same base class (for instance, if we wanted different stats for mages, ogres, and barbarian rabbits). This is especially true if you're incorporating `ScriptableObject` assets and want to keep things scalable without bloated class hierarchies – we'll see more of that later in the chapter!

```
using System.Collections;
using System.Collections.Generic;
```

```csharp
using UnityEngine;

// 1
public class BaseCharacter : ICharacter
{
    // 2
    public int Strength()
    {
        return 5;
    }

    // 3
    public void Battle()
    {
        Debug.Log($"Character ready to battle!");
    }
}
```

Let's break down the base character class:

1. It declares a base class that inherits from the ICharacter interface.

2. It implements the required Strength method and returns a default value of 5 without any decoration.

3. It implements the required Battle method and prints a default debug log without any decoration.

Again, you're not limited to a single concrete Component class. We could absolutely have a range of base cards for different categories like creatures, spells, enchantments, etc. But now that we have a base class to work with, we can start building out the decorator code to treat Components and decorator objects the same, which we'll dive into in the next section!

## Using a base Decorator

A base decorator class really has only one job – to wrap a Component object it wants to decorate and delegate any behaviors or data to that underlying object. Similar to other patterns like the Visitor and State, this part of the decorator structure is all about delegation! Making your base decorator an abstract class isn't a necessity (it can be an interface if you'd like), but using an abstract class lets us take care of boilerplate code around the Component we're wrapping (decorating).

In the **Scripts** folder, create a new C# script named Decorator and update its code to match the following snippet, which declares a new abstract class that inherits from ICharacter (very important; in fact, the entire point of this pattern), stores a reference to the Component we want to decorate, and sets the value in the class constructor. Finally, we delegate the Component interface methods to the wrapped (or decorated) Component object and we're all ready to go.

 You don't have to use a base decorator class, but I've found it to be extremely helpful when trying to cut down on boilerplate code. I mention this here so you don't get thrown off if you see this pattern out in the wild and the base decorator class is muddled up with concrete Decorators (it works, but it's not pretty, easy to read, or easy to maintain).

```csharp
using System.Collections;
using System.Collections.Generic;
using UnityEngine;

// 1
public abstract class Decorator : ICharacter
{
    // 2
    protected ICharacter _character;

    // 3
    public Decorator(ICharacter character)
    {
        _character = character;
    }

    // 4
    public virtual int Strength()
    {
        return _character.Strength();
    }

    // 5
    public virtual void Battle()
```

```
    {
        Debug.Log($"Applying decorator => Str: {Strength()}");
        _character.Battle();
    }
}
```

Let's break down the abstract decorator class:

1.  It declares a new abstract class that inherits from ICharacter.
2.  It adds a protected ICharacter reference for the object we want to decorate.
3.  It adds a class constructor with an ICharacter parameter and sets the protected reference value.
4.  It implements the ICharacter Strength method, marks it as virtual, and returns the protected references Strength method value.
5.  It implements the ICharacter Battle method, marks it as virtual, adds a debug log, and calls the protected references Battle method.

Notice that the base decorator is a nice wrapper for the object we want to decorate, but since the class constructor takes in an ICharacter parameter, we also have the ability to chain decorators to our heart's desire – which we'll do in the *Chaining multiple Decorators* section.

Now that we have a blueprint for our all decorators to follow, we can start building out individual concrete decorator classes with custom behaviors, which we'll do in the next section!

## Building a concrete Decorator

Just like with our concrete Component, we need a concrete Decorator to make this all work, so let's add a fun item that bumps the strength of our character by some amount when applied before battle.

In the **Scripts** folder, create a new C# script named StrengthAmulet and update its code to match the following snippet, which passes the class constructor parameter to the parent class, adds a Strength value to the underlying component being decorated, and prints out a debug log before invoking the parent Battle method.

```
using System.Collections;
using System.Collections.Generic;
using UnityEngine;

// 1
```

```
public class StrengthAmulet : Decorator
{
    // 2
    public StrengthAmulet(ICharacter character) : base(character) { }

    // 3
    public override int Strength()
    {
        return base.Strength() + 1;
    }

    // 4
    public override void Battle()
    {
        Debug.Log($"Strength decorator => Str + 1");
        base.Battle();
    }
}
```

Let's break down our new concrete decorator class:

1. It declares a new class that inherits from the abstract Decorator class.
2. It initializes the constructor and passes the ICharacter parameter to the parent class.
3. It overrides the Strength method, adds 1, and returns the result.
4. It overrides the Battle methods, adds a debug log, and executes the base Battle method.

 Like the State pattern, the order of operations matters here (notice where we put the debug logs). If we move around the debug logs, we get different output sequences because we're using abstract classes and interfaces to construct our system. This isn't anything new to OOP, just something to keep in mind when you're dealing with your order of operations.

With our first concrete Decorator class all ready to go, we can finally test to see how our code works! Update CharacterBehavior.cs to match the following code, which adds and initializes an ICharacter reference as our base concrete Component and then Decorates it using the methods I included in the starter project:

```
using System.Collections;
```

```csharp
using System.Collections.Generic;
using UnityEngine;

public class CharacterBehavior : MonoBehaviour
{
    // 1
    public ICharacter Base;

    void Start()
    {
        // 2
        Reset();
    }

    public void Decorate()
    {
        // 3
        Base = new StrengthAmulet(Base);
    }

    public void Battle()
    {
        // 4
        Base.Battle();
    }

    public void Reset()
    {
        // 5
        Base = new BaseCharacter();
        Debug.Log("Card set to default values...");
    }
}
```

Let's break down our new code:

1. It adds an ICharacter reference to hold a base concrete Component..

2. It calls the Reset method on Start to initialize Base with a default BaseCharacter object.

3.  It decorates the `Base` object using the concrete `StrengthAmulet` decorate class.

4.  It executes the `Battle` method from the `Base` object whether it's decorated or not.

5.  It resets the `Base` object to a default `BaseCharacter` object and debugs the output.

The final step is to update `Client.cs` to match the following code snippet, which always keeps the UI in sync with our character `Strength` stats inside the client's `UpdateUI` method:

```csharp
public class Client : MonoBehaviour
{
    //… No other changes needed …

    void UpdateUI()
    {
        attack.text = "Attack: " + Character.Base.Strength();
    }
}
```

Let's run the game to see our default character stats, as shown in the following screenshot:

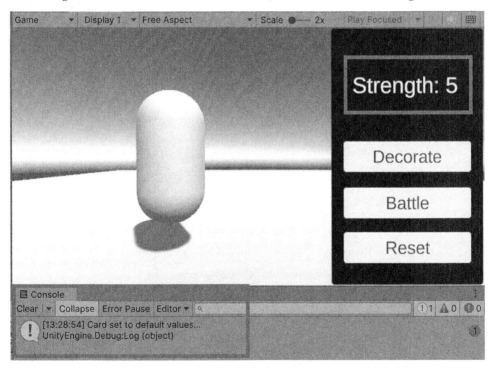

*Figure 15.4: Default Component being initialized*

Now hit **Decorate** to add our StrengthAmulet to the character, then **Battle** to see our applied decorator values, and look at the console output in the following screenshot:

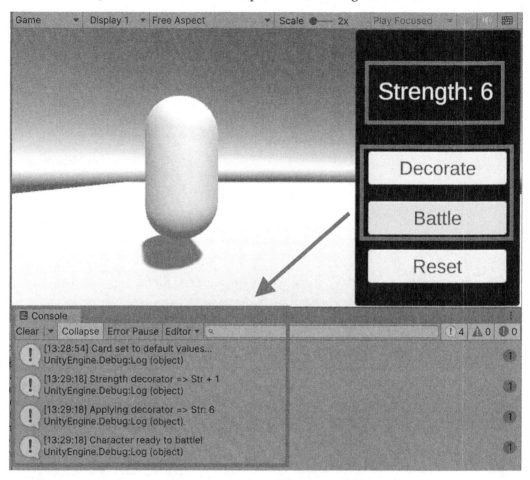

*Figure 15.5: Component being decorated and operations executed*

Since we don't have any mechanics for limiting how many decorators can be applied, you can dynamically stack them by hitting the **Decorator** button several times before selecting **Battle**, which will print out the console logs for each StrengthAmulet you add:

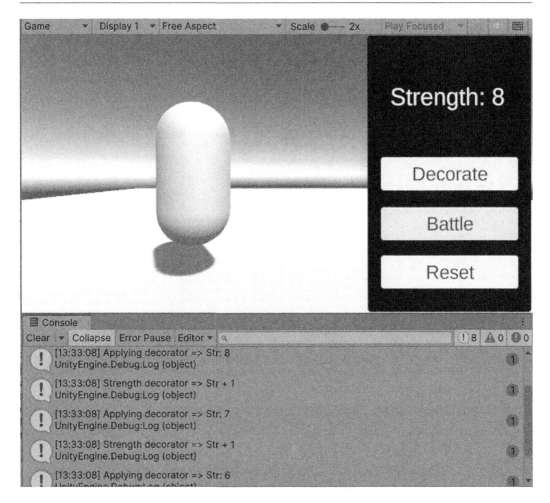

*Figure 15.6: Multiple decorators being applied to the same component*

That wraps up the basic Decorator pattern structure, but there are still a few variations we should talk about before ending the chapter – the first of which is how to chain multiple decorators in code!

## Chaining multiple Decorators

Since we wrote the Decorator class to accept an ICharacter constructor parameter, chaining decorators in code is super simple. Update CharacterBehavior.cs to match the following code snippet, which initializes a StrengthAmulet object with another StrengthAmulet object (because you never know when you'll need a double buff):

```
public class CharacterBehavior : MonoBehaviour
{
    public ICharacter Base;

    void Start()
    {
        //... No changes needed ....
    }

    public void Decorate()
    {
        Base = new StrengthAmulet(new StrengthAmulet(Base));
    }

    //... No other changes needed ...
}
```

This is going to give us the same output as clicking the **Decorate** button in the UI multiple times, but it's nice to be able to duplicate that behavior in our code. Run the game again, hit **Decorate** just once, and see the Strength stat increase by 2!

Now that we can chain multiple decorators in code, we can talk about the Decorator pattern's secret weapon – adding custom decorator behaviors, which we'll cover in the next section.

# Adding customized behaviors

While the Decorator pattern code we've been working with is almost exclusively focused on delegation, this design pattern also gives us the option of adding behaviors *inside* any concrete Decorators – and more importantly, firing off those behaviors whenever we choose!

Looking at this feature from the outside, the possibilities for customized behaviors in game scenarios are almost limitless, so we'll stick to something extremely simple to avoid confusing game mechanics and Unity best practices with the underlying decorator code – we're going to change the player's color (I know, gasp!) when a specific concrete Decorator is applied.

In the **Scripts** folder, create a new C# script named HolyMail and update its code to match the following code block. Our new concrete Decorator is going to take in a GameObject target reference, so we know what object to apply the color change to, and decorate the Strength stat value before going into battle. The crucial addition is the private AddEffect method, which is our customized behavior – this is executed *before* passing the Battle method call through the class hierarchy:

```
using System.Collections;
using System.Collections.Generic;
using UnityEngine;

// 1
public class HolyMail : Decorator
{
    GameObject _target;

    public HolyMail(ICharacter character, GameObject target) :
base(character)
    {
        _target = target;
    }

    // 2
    public override int Strength()
    {
        return base.Strength() + 2;
    }

    // 3
    public override void Battle()
```

```
    {
        Debug.Log($"Strength decorator => Str + 2");
        AddEffect();
        base.Battle();
    }

    // 4
    void AddEffect()
    {
        Renderer rend = _target.GetComponent<Renderer>();
        rend.material.SetColor("_Color", Color.red);
    }
}
```

Let's break down our new concrete Decorator class:

1. It declares a new `Decorator` class, stores a `GameObject` reference, and initializes values inside the class constructor.

2. It overrides the `Strength` interface method and returns a new decorated value.

3. It overrides the `Battle` interface method, executes the additional behavior, and calls the base `Battle` method.

4. It adds a `private` method with custom decorator logic.

This setup gives us the option of adding any customized logic to a concrete Decorator on an as-needed basis, while also giving us control of *when* that behavior is fired!

To test out the new concrete Decorator, update `CharacterBehavior.cs` to match the following code snippet, which chains `StrengthAmulet` and `HolyMail` decorators together when we hit the **Decorate** button in the UI. Notice that we're still using the `Base` concrete Component as the decorated object, but this time we're adding in the `GameObject` parameter so we can access and modify the object in the scene for some decorated visual feedback!

 It's completely up to you how you handle data or objects that your concrete Decorators may need to perform their added behaviors. You can inject them into class constructors as we did, you could use get/set properties, or you could even have the added behavior method(s) live in the target object itself and call them inside the concrete Decorator.

```
public class CharacterBehavior : MonoBehaviour
{
    public ICharacter Character;

    void Start()
    {
        //… No changes needed ….
    }

    public void Decorate()
    {
        Base = new StrengthAmulet(new HolyMail(Base, this.gameObject));
    }

    //… No other changes needed …
}
```

When you play the game, decorate your player then charge into battle and see not only the Strength stat increase by 3 (1 from the StrengthAmulet and 2 from the HolyMail) but also our player character turn bright red out of apparent embarrassment, as shown in the following screenshot.

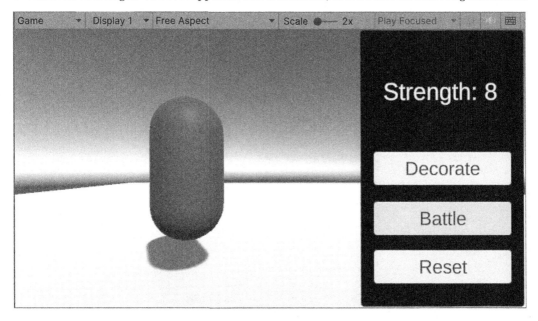

*Figure 15.7: Data and GameObject decoration*

Optional custom behavior in concrete Decorators marks the end of our discussion on the traditional Decorator pattern, but there's still one area we need to implement if we want to get the most out of Unity – and that's ScriptableObjects!

## Using ScriptableObject Decorators

As we've done with many a chapter throughout our design pattern journey, we're going to round off the decorator discussion with a little side trip into ScriptableObject assets (which makes runtime flexibility and scaling exponentially more manageable).

In the **Scripts** folder, create a new C# script (for the 100th time) named SOData and update it to match the following code snippet.

If you read *Chapter 13, Adding Features with the Visitor Pattern*, this should look familiar, because it is! This isn't the only way to do things in Unity, but since our Component interface has both data *and* behavior, we're only splitting out the data into a ScriptableObject (configurable behaviors in ScriptableObjects require a ton of extra work and sort of defeat the purpose in the first place). If your Components only store and decorate data values, your ScriptableObject classes can inherit from the Component interface just fine!

```
using System.Collections;
using System.Collections.Generic;
using UnityEngine;

[CreateAssetMenu(menuName = "SO/Data")]
public class SOData : ScriptableObject
{
    public int Strength = 0;
}
```

All we've done is add a simple ScriptableObject class with one single, solitary property for Strength. Now, from the **Asset** menu, select **Create | SO | Data**, name it BaseCharacter, and set its **Strength** value to **5**, as shown in the following screenshot.

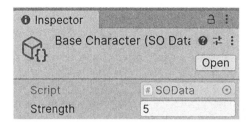

*Figure 15.8: SOData ScriptableObject in the Inspector*

Repeat the same steps to create the StrengthAmulet and HolyMail decorators (with Strength values of 1 and 2, respectively). We'll use this new data asset to inject any configuration values we want into our concrete Components and Decorators, freeing us from the dreaded hardcoding experience. All we need are a few updates to our existing classes and we'll be ready to go.

Update BaseCharacter.cs to match the following code block:

```
public class BaseCharacter : ICharacter
{
    // 1
    private SOData _data;

    // 2
    public BaseCharacter(SOData data)
    {
        _data = data;
    }

    public int Strength()
    {
        // 3
        return _data.Strength;
    }

    public void Battle()
    {
        Debug.Log($"Character ready to battle!");
    }
}
```

This new code adds a private SOData reference, initializes the value in the class constructor, and returns its Strength property inside the Strength method. All that's left is to change the base decorator class to mirror the same logic we added above, so update Decorator.cs to match the following code snippet:

```
public abstract class Decorator : ICharacter
{
    protected ICharacter _character;

    // 1
    protected SOData _data;

    // 2
    public Decorator(ICharacter character, SOData data)
    {
    _character = character;
    _data = data;
    }

    public virtual int Strength()
    {
        // 3
        return _character.Strength() + _data.Strength;
    }

    public virtual void Battle()
    {
        // 4
        Debug.Log($"Strength decorator => Str + {_data.Strength}");

        Debug.Log($"Applying decorator => Str: {Strength()}");
        _character.Battle();
    }
}
```

Let's break down the updates to our abstract Decorator class:

1. It adds a new SOData reference we can set in the **Inspector**.

2. It updates the class constructor parameters and initializes _data in the constructor.

3. It adds and returns the base Strength and the SOData Strength properties together.

4. It adds a debug log to output the decorated Strength value.

Now that our base decorator class does a lot more of the boilerplate work for us, we can update the two concrete Decorators we've already written and start customizing in the Inspector.

Update StrengthAmulet.cs to match the following code snippet, which updates the class constructor to accept a SOData parameter and deletes the Strength and Battle methods we no longer need (since they're in the abstract Decorator class now):

```
public class StrengthAmulet : Decorator
{
    // 1
    public StrengthAmulet(ICharacter character, SOData data) :
base(character, data) { }
}
```

We'll delete the Strength method in our HolyMail.cs script because the abstract Decorator class has us covered, but we still need to keep the overridden Battle method in order to execute our added effects:

```
public class HolyMail : Decorator
{
    GameObject _target;

    // 1
    public HolyMail(ICharacter character, SOData data, GameObject target)
: base(character, data)
    {
        _target = target;
    }

    public override void Battle()
    {
        // 2 … Delete previous debug log …
        AddEffect();
        base.Battle();
    }
}
```

```
        void AddEffect()
        {
            Renderer rend = _target.GetComponent<Renderer>();
            rend.material.SetColor("_Color", Color.red);
        }
    }
```

Now the fun part! Update `CharacterBehavior.cs` to match the following code block:

```
public class CharacterBehavior : MonoBehaviour
{
    public ICharacter Base;

    // 1
    public SOData BaseData;
    public SOData MainDecorator;
    public SOData SecondaryDecorator;

    void Start()
    {
        Reset();
    }

    public void Decorate()
    {
        // 2
        Base = new StrengthAmulet(new HolyMail(Base, MainDecorator, this.
gameObject), SecondaryDecorator);
    }

    public void Battle()
    {
        Base.Battle();
    }

    public void Reset()
    {
        // 3
```

```
        Base = new BaseCharacter(BaseData);
        Debug.Log("Card set to default values...");
    }
  }
```

Let's break down these new updates:

1.  It adds references for our three ScriptableObject assets that we can set in the **Inspector**.

2.  It initializes the concrete Component and Decorator Strength values with the new ScriptableObject assets.

3.  It passes in the BaseData ScriptableObject to the BaseCharacter class constructor.

In the **Hierarchy**, select **Environment | Character** and drag-and-drop our ScriptableObjects into the CharacterBehavior Component, as shown in the following figure:

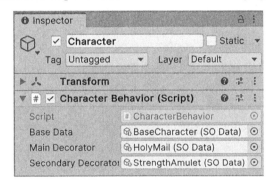

*Figure 15.9: ScriptableObject Decorators and Components in the Inspector*

Like our hardcoded values, the order only matters if you want a specific decoration sequence or custom behavior order of operations (which is super cool, don't get me wrong). Hit play and everything works as before, but now you have full control over initial values from the Inspector.

## Static vs dynamic decoration in action

Our focus has been on statically modifying objects when our game starts, but the Decorator pattern is also perfectly applicable to dynamic use cases. For example, if we built out our character system, we could add buttons or UI icons for each decorator object to give our players the ability to modify their avatars by clicking or dragging and dropping items in different configurations (which would work well paired with the ScriptableObject structure we set up).

You could also build in a tracking system for which decorators are applied and add undo/redo functionality just like we did in *Chapter 8, Binding Actions with the Command Pattern*. This would add a finer level of control over what buffs are applied and let your players move up and down the chain of decorators they create in real time.

Both of these pattern extensions (or combinations of the two) are wonderful tools to have in your pocket!

## Summary

That's going to close out our Decorator pattern discussion, but let's review the key points before you jump to your own projects. First, the Decorator pattern is best used when you want to change the skin of an object instance and not the inner workings of its class. If you want to dynamically change the guts of a class, refer to *Chapter 12, Swapping Algorithms with the Strategy Pattern*. This solution is a wonderful option in lieu of inheritance and large class hierarchies.

The Decorator pattern is made up of the main Component interface, concrete Component classes, the Decorator abstract class, and concrete Decorator classes. Both the concrete Components and concrete Decorators in your projects need to implement the Component interface so the client can treat them the same. Your decorators function as transparent wrappers for the Components you want to decorate, adding or modifying the Component in some way while also calling the Components' base behaviors. You can (and should!) chain concrete Decorators together to take advantage of the built-in additive functionality of the pattern.

Keep in mind that we're trading off large subclass hierarchies for lots of small decorator and Component classes running around our codebase. However, the flexibility to customize individual object instances at runtime (and during gameplay) more than makes up for the extra script files – with the added benefit that you never pay for code you don't use, which you absolutely will if you use inheritance!

## Further reading

- Interfaces are a great way to create groups of related functionality (with or without default implementations) that can be adopted by any class or struct. These are especially handy when you want to have a class inherit from multiple groups of functionality, which is called object composition. For more information, check out the documentation at https://learn.microsoft.com/en-us/dotnet/csharp/fundamentals/types/interfaces.

- ScriptableObjects are the perfect way to create data containers in your Unity projects (and we'll use them in almost every chapter going forward), but I'd also recommend checking out the documentation at https://docs.unity3d.com/Manual/class-ScriptableObject.html.

- Abstract classes can't be created on their own, but they are excellent solutions when you want a consistent base class blueprint that other classes can inherit from. Many of our solutions in this book rely heavily on abstract classes to provide an abstraction layer between class blueprints and their concrete implementations. You can find more information at https://learn.microsoft.com/en-us/dotnet/csharp/language-reference/keywords/abstract.

## Join our community on Discord

Join our community's Discord space for discussions with the author and other readers:

`https://packt.link/gamedevelopment_packt`

# 16

# Converting Incompatible Classes with the Adapter Pattern

In the last chapter, we used the Decorator pattern to dynamically add new behavior to existing classes without using a traditional subclassing approach. In this chapter, we'll stick with the idea of adding new behavior without touching an existing class, but this time, we'll use interfaces to adapt existing incompatible classes to work together using the Adapter pattern (which is perfect when you need to force two unruly systems to play together nicely without overhauling either one).

Now, the Adapter pattern can be used for all kinds of situations, including porting an existing class into an interface your client code already uses, creating reusable classes that work with classes you haven't even built yet, or bypassing a deep subclass hierarchy by adapting a single parent class. You can even use the pattern to converge properties from classes that don't share any common class hierarchies! While these scenarios cover concepts we've tackled before, there's one standout situation where the Adapter really shines: when we can't edit or modify an existing class but need to make it work with some other class or system. If you've ever worked with third-party libraries or legacy code, you'll be intimately familiar with this type of roadblock (and most likely have a few mental scars to prove it).

Like most design patterns, the Adapter structure comes in two distinct flavors – class adapters and object adapters. These two variations have their own pros and cons (as we'll see), but it's important to make a conscious decision between the two *before* tackling any code updates.

Don't worry, most of the time the choice depends on the existing code you've already got running and whether inheritance or composition is better for your project.

We'll use this chapter to focus on the following topics:

- The pros and cons of the Adapter design pattern
- Building a class adapter
- Creating an object adapter
- Mapping properties in mismatched hierarchies

Let's start off with the technical requirements for this chapter, and then move on to the pattern breakdown and get started on our own code!

# Technical requirements

To get started:

1. Download or clone the GitHub repository at `https://github.com/PacktPublishing/C-Design-Patterns-with-Unity-First-Edition`.

2. Open the **Ch_16_Starter** project folder in Unity Hub.

3. In **Assets > Scenes**, double-click on **SampleScene**.

The starter project for this chapter is a top-down arena where you control a simple player capsule and try to collect all the red items in the scene. You can run forward and back using vertical key inputs, rotate using horizontal key inputs, and even jump if the mood strikes you.

As for the scripts:

- `PlayerBehavior.cs` is the client class for this example. Its only job is to hold a reference to a `MovementController` instance (which we'll switch later on) and call its `Move` and `Jump` methods in `FixedUpdate`.
- `MovementController.cs` is responsible for the default player locomotion – moving and rotating smoothly using the *WASD* or arrow keys and jumping using the *Space* key.
- `TeleportController.cs` is the secondary movement control scheme that we're going to pretend is a third-party asset we can't modify, which uses a mouse-follow mechanic instead of key inputs.
- `SelfDestruct.cs` simply destroys a `GameObject` when there's a collision detected (these are attached to the Items in the scene).

We'll also be using some Unity and C# language features to take our code the extra mile. Don't worry if you're not familiar with these; I've included links for the basics, and I'll explain how they apply to our use cases as we go along:

- Interfaces (`https://learn.microsoft.com/en-us/dotnet/csharp/fundamentals/types/interfaces`)
- Get and Set properties (`https://learn.microsoft.com/en-us/dotnet/csharp/programming-guide/classes-and-structs/using-properties`)

For this chapter, we're going to pretend that `TeleportController` is a third-party plugin that we can't modify in any way, which means our main job is going to be creating a unified interface that allows `PlayerBehavior` to use `MovementController` and `TeleportController` interchangeably, *without* modifying `TeleportController` in any way!

# Breaking down the Adapter pattern

As part of the Structural family of design patterns, the Adapter pattern is all about compatibility, turning classes that don't naturally work together because of incompatible interfaces into coworkers that your client code can handle. Think of the charging plug for your phone – if you tried to use a cord with the wrong plug, you couldn't get the phone to connect and charge. But with an adapter acting as a middleman, you could get the electricity running and your phone charged without having to buy a whole new device (or redo the entire electrical system in your home, which is always a plus).

The Adapter pattern is useful when:

- You want to use an existing class with an interface that doesn't match the one your client uses.
- You need to create reusable classes that can work with unrelated (and future) classes that may not have compatible interfaces.
- You have existing subclass hierarchies that would take time and resources to adapt one by one (in which case the object adapter variation would be able to adapt the parent class without any extra work).

Since most programs deal with multiple systems, and those systems don't always share a common interface or parent class, it's common to run into problems when you want these incompatible systems to work together.

Let's imagine we have two systems that deal with application data – one for local storage in XML and one for cloud storage in JSON (these are entirely fictitious and bear no resemblance to real or imagined storage systems). For our example, let's also imagine that the XML system saves and loads data, while the JSON only saves data to the cloud, as shown in the following image:

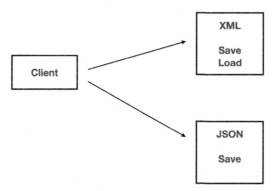

*Figure 16.1: Example of an application using different data-saving systems*

While we could write a method that decides whether the situation calls for the XML or JSON systems right from our client code, that would require our client to know the context in order to make a decision. Our client would also have to know that the JSON system doesn't have a way of loading data like the XML system, which makes even more work. The less context and decision-making our client code has to handle, the better! Instead, what the Adapter pattern lets us do is declare a shared interface that both incompatible classes can agree on while leaving our client none the wiser:

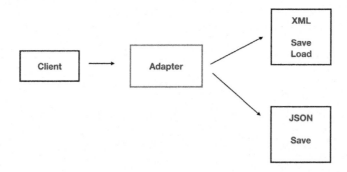

*Figure 16.2: Example of using an adapter to work with incompatible classes*

Again, you might be shouting, "Wait, wait, that's too much code for a situation where we could just reorganize our classes." And you'd be absolutely right; you could do that. Many of our design pattern solutions can be accomplished with brute force, but what happens when you can't modify one or more of the incompatible classes (like third-party libraries or legacy code)?

Well, the next best thing is to have complete control over the intermediary adapter, which not only provides concrete implementations of a shared interface but also allows you to add any missing functionality your incompatible classes may need (such as the JSON load feature in the preceding example).

The Adapter pattern is one of the simplest design patterns to implement, but it also has one of the widest applications, so a little more theoretical groundwork is required before we get into the code!

## Diagramming the pattern

Whichever variation you end up using, the Adapter pattern has four main component elements:

- The **target** defines the interface that your client uses and all **adapter** and **adaptee** classes implement.

- The **client** uses class objects that have implemented your **target** interface – in the starter project, this is PlayerBehavior.cs.

- The **adaptee** is any existing class that you want to convert to the **target** interface –in the starter project, this is MovementController.cs and TeleportController.cs.

- The **adapter** is responsible for converting the **adaptee** interface to the **target** interface (where all the work happens).

As mentioned earlier, you can structure the Adapter pattern one of two ways – as a class adapter or an object adapter. When choosing between these two variations, the decision breaks down into whether you want (or need) to use inheritance or composition in your adapter class. For the class adapter variation, you'll use multiple inheritance to create a concrete adapter that can pass any requests directly to the adaptee class without the client knowing, as shown in the following UML diagram:

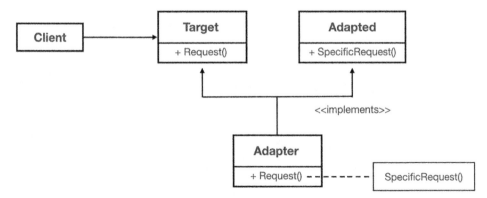

*Figure 16.3: UML diagram of the class adapter variation*

If you're going with the object class variation, you'll use object composition in the concrete adapter to essentially wrap the adaptee object and defer requests, as shown in the following diagram:

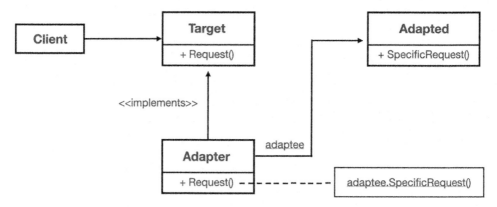

*Figure 16.4: UML diagram of the object adapter variation*

Again, the structure of the classes you're adapting in real-world projects is usually pretty set and may not be modifiable; the choice between class and object adapter solutions is often made for you. Since both of our Adapter pattern variations have different pros and cons, let's cover those before writing any code.

## Pros and cons

Like all design patterns, there are pros and cons. Let's start with the potential benefits that the Adapter pattern can add to your project:

- **Looking but not touching**: The Adapter pattern provides a standardized structure when reconciling incompatible classes that either don't have a shared interface or can't be modified, such as third-party libraries or legacy code.

- **Flexible and reusable classes**: These are a staple of this pattern, especially when dealing with project expansion and maintenance – you already have a structure in place for future classes to adopt without introducing breaking changes.

- **Easily override adaptee behavior with the class adapter**: The adapter class already sub-classes the adaptee class, as well as the target interface, so there's no extra subclassing work required.

- **Class hierarchies aren't an issue with the object adapter**: A single adapter class can work with an adaptee and all its subclasses and, better yet, can add functionality to all adaptees at one time.

However, be careful of the following pitfalls when using the pattern in your projects:

- **Legacy code hangs around**: It may be nice to get things running without rewriting your legacy code, but it still lets the old parts live rent-free. Not only does this take up space in your project; it also keeps outdated systems alive and working, which poses a compatibility threat the longer the legacy code exists.

- **Subclassing can be an issue with the class adapter**: Adapter and adaptee are concrete commitments, so this approach isn't ideal when you want to adapt a class that has subclasses.

- **Overriding adaptees is more work with the object adapter**: The adapter class would need to refer to each adaptee subclass in order to override existing behavior.

Looking at the preceding list, your decision comes down to what you're working with. If the class you're adopting doesn't have any subclasses, the class adapter variation is the way to go (and it's less code because there's no need to wrap the **adaptee** class). If you need to adapt a class with several subclasses, the object adapter variant is a better fit.

Now that we've covered the structure, benefits, and limitations of the Adapter pattern, we can start writing our own code.

# Building a controller adapter

Imagine you're building an old-school top-down adventure game where players can run around an arena collecting items and jump over obstacles, using the traditional *WASD* and arrow keys. Nothing new in the mechanics department.

But now, suppose you wanted to spice things up and give players the ability to upgrade their movement controls, and you found the perfect mouse-follow and teleport script in a third-party library. Ideally, you'd like your existing game code to work with both the standard and mouse-follow movement controls, but you can't modify the third-party script in any way. How would you make this scenario work?

## Defining a target

The first step in our Adapter journey is creating a target interface, which holds all the responsibilities our adapter and adaptee classes are going to share. In the starter project, MovementController. cs and TeleportController.cs both have a way of moving the player, although the methods have different names. The MovementController also has a method for players to jump, and even though TeleportController doesn't come with that feature, the Adapter pattern will let us add it in later.

For now, our target is going to contain two methods that *all* our movement schemes can agree on, one for moving the player and one for a jump mechanic. In the **Scripts** folder, create a new C# script named IController and update it to match the following snippet with our target code:

> You might hear different types of target interfaces referred to as narrow or wide, which means the least and most shared features, respectively. A narrow interface in our example would be just the Move method in the IController interface, but since we want to round out the missing jumping feature in TeleportController, we're going to use a slightly wider approach. This decision is completely scenario-dependent, which means it's a good idea to think about what you're trying to accomplish before deciding on the inner workings of your target interface.

```csharp
using System.Collections;
using System.Collections.Generic;
using UnityEngine;

// 1
public interface IController
{
    // 2
    void Move();
    void Jump();
}
```

Let's break down the new interface:

1.  Declares a new target interface for all adapter and adaptee classes.

2.  Adds Move and Jump methods to be implemented in the adapter and adaptee classes.

Now, because we want to adapt the existing MovementController class to work with the target interface, we need to update MovementController.cs to match the following code snippet. Since MovementController already has methods for Move and Jump, there's no other updates needed once we've implemented the IController interface:

```csharp
// 1
public class MovementController : MonoBehaviour, IController
{
    //… No other changes needed …
}
```

Before we run the game to make sure everything still works, we also need to update PlayerBehavior. cs to use the IController interface instead of the concrete MovementController class, in order to switch out control schemes in the future. Notice that this makes PlayerBehavior independent of whichever control scheme we want to use without breaking any client code!

```
public class PlayerBehavior : MonoBehaviour
{
    // 1
    private IController _controller;

    void Start()
    {
        _controller = this.GetComponent<MovementController>();
    }

    void FixedUpdate()
    {
        _controller.Move();
        _controller.Jump();
    }
}
```

If you play the scene now, you still have the same *WASD* and arrow key movement controls and jump mechanic, but the client code now has the freedom to *not* differentiate between the concrete movement controller classes – it's all done with the IController interface!

Now, we can adapt as many controller schemes as we want, and as long as they implement the IController interface, our client code won't be any the wiser. Since we already have the TeleportController script, let's build a concrete adapter class to make that code work with our new interface.

## Adding the class adapter

For this example, we're going to start with a class adapter, but we'll also build an object adapter so that you can see the difference in the code. Since TeleportController.cs is the existing class we can't touch but want to adapt, we'll start there.

In the **Scripts** folder, create a new C# script named TeleportClassAdapter and update its code to match the following snippet.

Note that the class adapter not only defers the movement logic to the TeleportController but also adds a jump mechanic, according to the IController interface!

```csharp
using System.Collections;
using System.Collections.Generic;
using UnityEngine;

// 1
public class TeleportClassAdapter : TeleportController, IController
{
    // 2
    public float hoverHeight = 3;
    private bool _isLevitating;

    // 3
    void Update()
    {
        _isLevitating = Input.GetKey(KeyCode.Space);
    }

    // 4
    public void Move()
    {
        TeleportPlayer();
        Debug.Log("Using adapted movement behavior from
TeleportController...");
    }

    // 5
    public void Jump()
    {
        if (_isLevitating)
        {
            Vector3 hover = this.transform.position;
            hover.y = (Vector3.up * hoverHeight).y;
            rb.position = hover;
        }
```

```
        Debug.Log("Using new jump behavior from TeleportClassAdapter...");
    }
}
```

We use the GetKey() method to detect if our *Spacebar* is being pushed inside the Update method, but be aware that there is a difference between the execution timing of key presses in the Update and FixedUpdate methods. This approach won't work if you called GetKeyDown in the same scenario, but there are other Unity solutions you can find in the documentation.

Let's break down the new adapter class:

1. It declares a new class that inherits TeleportController and implements IController.
2. It adds adapter-specific variables needed to make the additional behavior work.
3. It stores player input for the additional jump mechanic.
4. It passes the movement logic from the adapter to the underlying TeleportController class.
5. It adds the missing jump mechanic logic to comply with the IController interface.

To test:

1. In the **Hierarchy**, drag and drop TeleportClassAdapter.cs onto the Player GameObject.
2. Update PlayerBehavior.cs to control the character actions from MovementController to TeleportClassAdapter in the following code snippet:

Note that we don't need to change any of the methods that our _controller uses because the adapter shares the same IController interface, which is the adapter pattern at work!

```
public class PlayerBehavior : MonoBehaviour
{
    private IController _controller;

    void Start()
    {
        // 1
        _controller = this.GetComponent<TeleportClassAdapter>();
```

```
    }

    void FixedUpdate()
    {
        _controller.Move();
        _controller.Jump();
    }
}
```

When you run the game now, you'll be able to control the character using your mouse, and when you push and hold the *Spacebar* key, the character will levitate and land wherever you put the mouse!

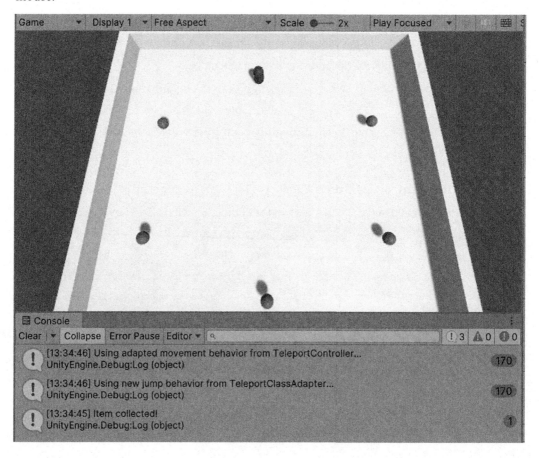

*Figure 16.5: Adapter movement controller working in the scene*

The Adapter pattern is deceptively simple but extremely powerful in the right situations. We didn't set up a huge chunk of structural support code to make the pattern work, but we implemented a meaningful change in the application using a third-party component without introducing breaking changes or copious client rewrites. Abstracting behavior is always a plus when dealing with interchangeable parts because, one, it makes the code less dependent on context, and two, there's only one place where something can go wrong (which makes bug hunting that much easier). We still need to see how an object adapter would work, which is what we'll do in the following section!

# Creating an object adapter class

An object adapter is almost exactly the same as a class adapter, but with the added wrapper around a concrete adaptee reference instead of subclassing – in our case, a private `TeleportController` object instead of inheriting from `TeleportController`. To see this in action, create a new C# script in the **Scripts** folder, name it `TeleportObjectAdapter`, and update its code to match the following snippet, which uses the wrapped adaptee object to execute the underlying adaptee logic:

```
using System.Collections;
using System.Collections.Generic;
using UnityEngine;

// 1
public class TeleportObjectAdapter : MonoBehaviour, IController
{
    public float hoverHeight = 3;
    private bool _isLevitating;

    // 2
    private TeleportController _adaptee;

    // 3
    void Start()
    {
        _adaptee = this.GetComponent<TeleportController>();
    }

    void Update()
    {
```

```
        _isLevitating = Input.GetKey(KeyCode.Space);
    }

    public void Move()
    {
        // 4
        _adaptee.TeleportPlayer();
        Debug.Log("Using adapted movement behavior from
TeleportController...");
    }

    public void Jump()
    {
        if (_isLevitating)
        {
            Vector3 hover = this.transform.position;
            hover.y = (Vector3.up * hoverHeight).y;

            // 5
            _adaptee.rb.position = hover;
        }

        Debug.Log("Using new jump behavior from TeleportClassAdapter...");
    }
}
```

Let's break down the code:

1.  It declares a new class that implements the IController target interface.

2.  It adds a private TeleportController field to provide access to the adaptee.

3.  It calls the teleport movement method from the _adaptee object.

4.  It references the _adaptee Rigidbody component to implement the jump mechanic.

Our testing steps are similar to how we tested the class adapter in the previous section, but let's be double-sure that everything works as expected by following these steps:

1. In the **Hierarchy**, drag and drop `TeleportObjectAdapter.cs` onto the `Player` GameObject.

2. Update `PlayerBehavior.cs` to control the character actions from `TeleportClassAdapter` to `TeleportObjectAdapter` in the following code snippet:

```
public class PlayerBehavior : MonoBehaviour
{
    private IController _controller;

    void Start()
    {
        // 1
        _controller = this.GetComponent<TeleportObjectAdapter>();
    }

    void FixedUpdate()
    {
        _controller.Move();
        _controller.Jump();
    }
}
```

Since there's no difference in playable mechanics, everything works the same, but now you have all the tools you need to decide between class and object adapters (inheritance vs. composition) in your own projects!

Now, normally, this would signal the end of most high-level implementations of the Adapter pattern, but there's one more little scenario where the pattern really shines, and that's consolidating class fields from disparate class hierarchies into something cohesive.

## Mapping properties in separate hierarchies

If you observed the starter project closely, you may have noticed that `MovementController.cs` and `TeleportController.cs` both have a property called `moveSpeed`. However, if we wanted our client to reference this in some way, we couldn't make that happen as-is because the `moveSpeed` property isn't present in their shared interface – which is exactly what we're going to fix in this section.

I'm using this super-simple contrived scenario to showcase how the Adapter pattern could be used to consolidate incompatible class properties, but it's important to think about where this could benefit your codebase. Are there built-in classes that you wish shared a parent class? Are there classes that share a parent class but that parent is so far up the class hierarchy that the property you want to access isn't present? Are there classes for each of these situations that you can't modify for one reason or another? All good questions, and all powerful implementations of the Adapter pattern!

Update `IController.cs` to match the following code snippet, which adds a `public get/set` property to our target interface:

```
public interface IController
{
    // 1
    int mSpeed { get; set; }

    void Move();
    void Jump();
}
```

Because we have several classes that depend on the `IController` interface, we'll need to update them, starting with `MovementController.cs`:

```
[RequireComponent(typeof(Rigidbody))]
public class MovementController : MonoBehaviour, IController
{
    // 1
    public int mSpeed
    {
        get { return moveSpeed; }
        set { moveSpeed = value;}
    }

    //... No other changes needed ...
}
```

We'll do the same modification for `TeleportClassAdapter.cs` in the following snippet so that our class adapter properly implements the `mSpeed` property from the `IController` interface:

```
public class TeleportClassAdapter : TeleportController, IController
{
    // 1
    public int mSpeed
    {
        get { return moveSpeed; }
        set { moveSpeed = value; }
    }

    //... No other changes needed ...
}
```

Finally, we'll add the `mSpeed` property to `TeleportObjectAdapter.cs` to fulfill our `IController` interface contract and complete the update in the following code:

```
public class TeleportObjectAdapter : MonoBehaviour, IController
{
    // 1
    public int mSpeed
    {
        get { return _adaptee.moveSpeed; }
        set { _adaptee.moveSpeed = value; }
    }

    //... No other changes needed ...
}
```

To test, we can simply print out the `mSpeed` value in `PlayerBehavior.cs` (because we don't really have a use for it in this example), but don't let that stop you from thinking of interesting ways to streamline your project with this solution:

```
public class PlayerBehavior : MonoBehaviour
{
    private IController _controller;

    void Start()
```

```
    {
        _controller = this.GetComponent<MovementController>();

        // 1
        Debug.Log(_controller.mSpeed);
    }

    void FixedUpdate()
    {
        _controller.Move();
        _controller.Jump();
    }
}
```

With that bit of code running, we've got all the Adapter pattern tools we need to tackle third-party assets, legacy code, and incompatible class hierarchies!

## Summary

That's going to close out our Adapter pattern discussion, but let's review the key points before you run off and reformat your projects into a variety of target interfaces! First, the Adapter pattern is best for cases where you have existing or third-party classes you want to integrate into a cohesive interface for your client code, but it can also be used to support cross-platform APIs and create common reusable interfaces, and it is a great fit to build test mocks when unit-testing your applications.

The Adapter pattern is made up of the target interface, adapter class (or classes), adaptee class (or classes), and a client. Both the adapter and adaptee classes need to implement the target interface so that your client doesn't need to know which is which when calling their behaviors. As we saw, you can choose to create your adapter classes as either class adapters or object adapters, depending on whether inheritance or composition is a better fit. The only difference is that the class adapter inherits the adaptee class while the object adapter wraps an adaptee reference. Even though our chapter example wasn't too complex, you shouldn't be afraid to create more substantial adapters that combine the approaches we covered.

Keep in mind that decisions between class and object adapters, or narrow and wide target interface features, are design choices you should be making upfront whenever possible. However, because the Adapter pattern is most often used in cases where there's legacy code (or unmodifiable code for one reason or another), these answers should already be apparent in your project structure – look to the existing code!

In the next chapter, we'll use the Façade pattern to build ourselves a little one-way barrier between client code and various subsystems, making complex operations and groupings of functionality easy to fire from anywhere!

## Further reading

- Interfaces are a great way to create groups of related functionality (with or without default implementations) that can be adopted by any class or struct. These are especially handy when you want a class to inherit from multiple groups of functionalities, which is called object composition. For more information, check out the documentation at `https://learn.microsoft.com/en-us/dotnet/csharp/fundamentals/types/interfaces`.

- `Get` and `Set` properties give you access to a code block when a property is read or set, respectively. This allows you to add extra instructions before and after you get or set property values, much like a method. You can find more information at `https://learn.microsoft.com/en-us/dotnet/csharp/programming-guide/classes-and-structs/using-properties`.

## Leave a review!

Enjoying this book? Help readers like you by leaving an Amazon review. Scan the QR code below to get a free eBook of your choice.

# 17

# Simplifying Subsystems with the Façade Pattern

In the last chapter, we used the Adapter pattern to convert incompatible classes into shared interfaces that a client can use interchangeably. In this chapter, we'll stay on the topic of client simplification by using the Façade pattern to build a... well, a façade or decorative wall between the client and your more complex, interdependent systems. Think of unlocking your phone using thumbprint recognition – when you (the client) touch your fingertip to the phone you get a nice interface that tells you the security check is processing (the façade), but underneath, the phone's software is cranking away at the complicated process of verifying that you're a living, breathing human!

The Façade pattern comes in handy quite a bit because all but the simplest of programs have underlying subsystems. You can use it to provide a unified, high-level interface for virtually any block of work that requires interactions between complex, coupled, or dependent classes. However, it's a common misconception that the Façade pattern is just for hiding *bad* or poorly structured code (and the secret is it's not). Like the Singleton pattern, this pattern isn't a silver-bullet solution for spaghetti code; it's an intentional tool for working with projects that you've (hopefully) thought about architecting well.

Now, the Façade pattern doesn't have a host of variations or flavors, but it does allow you the option of creating your façades as abstract or concrete classes (we'll cover that topic in the *Upgrading Façades* section at the end of the chapter). Whether it's icebergs or ducks on a pond, we only see the smallest, simplest information – all the real work happens beneath the surface!

We'll use this chapter to focus on the following topics:

- The pros and cons of the Façade design pattern
- Building a subsystem façade
- Adding multiple façade methods
- Upgrading façades

Let's start off with the technical requirements for this chapter, then move on to the pattern breakdown and get into code of our own!

# Technical requirements

To get started:

1. Download or clone the GitHub repository at `https://github.com/PacktPublishing/C-Design-Patterns-with-Unity-First-Edition`.

2. Open the **Ch_17_Starter** project folder in Unity Hub.

3. In **Assets | Scenes**, double-click on **SampleScene**.

The starter project for this chapter is a fun 3D platformer where the objective is to collect all the items in the scene (if you've gotten this far in the book, you're used to those little red orbs). Each item randomly generates how many points you receive when collected, and you can run, jump, collect, and fall off the tallest platform at your leisure. And so as not to leave out visual feedback, the UI displays a simple score counter at the bottom right of the screen.

As for the scripts:

- `Client.cs` is a `Singleton` class that stores the player's score and the UI text object – we'll be using our Façade class(es) from here during the chapter.

- `DataConverter.cs` is a simplified subsystem class with a single method that accepts a `double` value and returns a `float`.

- `PlayerBehavior.cs` is the movement controller for the playable character, so there's no need to modify this at all.

- `SaveSystem.cs` is another simplified subsystem with a single method that accepts a `float` value and stores it using the PlayerPrefs API.

- `SceneController.cs` is the final simplified subsystem that stores a reference to the pausing UI panel and can pause or unpause the game with its two `public` methods.

- `SelfDestruct.cs` holds the item collection logic and assigns random points to the client's score whenever there's a collision (before self-destructing, of course).

Even though there are perfectly good built-in C# and Unity APIs for these subsystems, we don't want to get lost in creating real-world complexity and lose sight of the Façade intent. The pattern's principles are the same whether you apply them to super simple scenarios like ours or enterprise-level software.

We'll also be using some Unity and C# language features to take our code the extra mile. Don't worry if you're not familiar with them – I've included links for the basics, and I'll explain how they apply to our use cases as we go:

- PlayerPrefs (https://docs.unity3d.com/ScriptReference/PlayerPrefs.html)
- Coroutines (https://docs.unity3d.com/Manual/Coroutines.html)

Our job is to implement an auto-save feature using a façade class between our client and the three subsystems involved in saving player data (DataConverter, SaveSystem, and SceneController). Like most design patterns, our goal is to make the life (and contextual overhead) of our client classes as flexible and context-agnostic as possible – and the Façade pattern is the perfect fit.

# Breaking down the Façade pattern

As part of the Structural family of design patterns, the Façade pattern is all about simplifying communication between a client and the sometimes hectic and complex web of interconnected systems our programs use to do work. We run into façades all over the place, and we've even found them in other design patterns in this book (because anywhere there was a factory in our code, there was a façade standing guard). But even though any intervening layer between a client and a subsystem is a kind of façade, the Façade pattern itself is a much more targeted solution to accessing your complex subsystems.

The Façade pattern is useful when:

- You need a simplified interface when accessing a much more complex subsystem or set of interrelated subsystems. Even when subsystems grow and change, the façade provides the same default set of operations so your client code remains unbroken.
- You want to decouple your client code from your subsystem classes. This solution makes it much easier for subsystems to be reusable and work independently.
- You have several layers of dependent subsystems and need a common entry point to each layer. You can even go so far as creating Façades for each layer, meaning they are decoupled and communicate through their own Façades.

Let's imagine we're at a restaurant ordering food (because everyone needs to eat). Since you and I are the ones requesting food, we'll act as the client. In a busy restaurant, it would be incredibly inefficient for every customer to start yelling their orders at different people in the kitchen (I can personally vouch for this – it's not fun and it doesn't work). Not only would this be utter chaos, but with so many dependent systems working at once there's no telling when, where, or which operations are being executed!

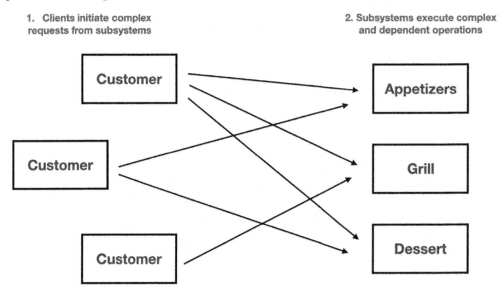

*Figure 17.1: Restaurant example of customers ordering food without servers*

When a server comes up to us and asks for our order, I'll order a hamburger and maybe you'll order a coffee and pie (you could even add special instructions like ice cream on the side). The server acting as the façade between you, me, and the kitchen staff then takes that information and passes it to the kitchen where multiple cooks start preparing our food. At no time do we directly interface with anyone in the kitchen, and even though our food order may be complicated and require different members of kitchen staff working together, we as the clients have absolutely zero idea how the food is being made. We place the order, the server writes it down and bridges the gap between us and the inner workings of the kitchen, and we get a delicious meal.

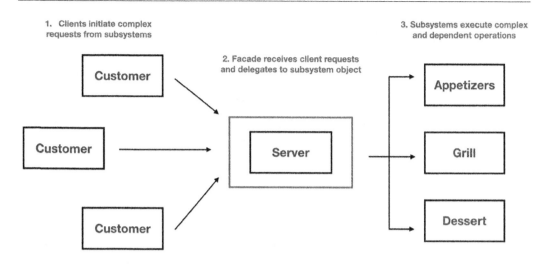

*Figure 17.2: Restaurant example of ordering food through a server*

Now, before we get into more façade theory, there are two important pieces of the puzzle to understand. First, the server knows the different members of the kitchen staff on shift. If we order a hamburger, the server needs to tell whoever is at the grill. If we order dessert, the server likewise knows they may need to ask the pastry chef to get that done. Second, any server would know the same information, so we could place our order with whoever was available. But, if we needed someone with special knowledge of wine (at a much fancier restaurant), the sommelier may come over and mediate between us and an entirely new set of subsystems. In any of these situations, interchangeable servers or concrete specialists all act as an abstraction layer between the client and the operation – leaving you free to enjoy a wonderful meal!

## Diagramming the pattern

The Façade pattern doesn't have a variety of moving parts, but its three component elements are:

- The **Client** is responsible for passing in any complex requests requiring one or more subsystems.

- The **Façade** knows which subsystems exist, stores an object from each subsystem, and delegates the client requests to the correct subsystem object.

The subsystem classes execute the subsystem features without any knowledge of the façade.

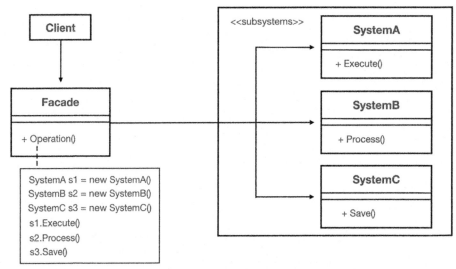

*Figure 17.3: UML diagram of the Façade pattern components*

When looking at the diagram above, notice that each subsystem has no reference to the façade and the client has no direct access to any of the individual subsystems. This isn't to say the client *can't* access subsystems directly when necessary, but that's outside of the Façade pattern. Something else that we need to remember with the structure of this pattern is that information passed from the client to the façade may not directly translate into what the subsystems are expecting, which means the façade class may have to do some translating to adapt the façade interface to its subsystems.

## Pros and cons

Like all design patterns, there are pros and cons. Let's start with the potential benefits the Façade pattern can add to your project:

- Complex operations are decoupled from the client and shielded behind an accessible façade. This not only keeps the inner workings of your subsystems hidden, but it also lowers the number of class objects your client has to keep track of.
- Refactoring subsystems doesn't break the client because the client is only aware of the Façade class, not the underlying classes and implementations.

- It doesn't put subsystems under lock and key, meaning your client and other classes can access subsystems when necessary, which offers you a choice between easy use with a façade or direct requests to subsystems.

However, be careful of the following pitfalls when using the pattern in your projects:

- **The temptation to hide messy code** is one of the main drawbacks to the Façade pattern, which means it's up to you to think about how your subsystems are structured (which in a way is a positive, because you should always be thinking about this).

- **Runaway Façades are a thing**, meaning because they're so easy to implement (and useful), they become overused like the Singleton pattern. This is especially true if you have several globally accessible façade classes in your application or game that depend on each other. Note that the scenario I just described is different from having façades for different layers of related subsystems.

Looking at the drawbacks of this pattern, you can see they are entirely to do with usage, not code structure. It's up to you to thoughtfully manage and implement them where they're most useful, which we'll cover in the rest of the chapter! Now that we've covered the structure, benefits, and limitations of the Façade pattern, we can start writing our own code.

# Building a subsystem Façade

Imagine you're building a 3D platformer game, and like all sensible games (Souls games notwithstanding), you want to provide a handy auto-saving feature that updates the saved score every three points your player scores or collects. However, there are several interconnected subsystem classes that handle different parts of this feature. For example, an auto-save feature might be responsible for pausing the game, converting the current score into a different format, and storing the converted value in a database or PlayerPrefs. Luckily, your team lead suggests you use a façade class to wrap and execute the subsystem details and give your client a simplified interface to call when auto-saving!

## Defining subsystem objects

The first building block we need for our Façade pattern is a Façade class (I didn't see that coming either) to store an instance of each subsystem. In the **Scripts** folder, create a new C# script named `AutosaveFacade.cs` and update it to match the following code block, which declares a new Façade class and `private` subsystem fields so our client doesn't have access to them and can't accidentally do the work the Façade is being created to take over.

You don't have to limit your `Façade` class to just subsystem objects. Our example doesn't require any additional data, but you could absolutely store any extra properties you need that the client doesn't need to be aware of.

```
using System.Collections;
using System.Collections.Generic;
using UnityEngine;

// 1
public class AutosaveFacade: MonoBehaviour
{
    // 2
    private DataConverter _dataConverter;
    private SaveSystem _saveSystem;
    private SceneController _sceneController;
}
```

Let's break down the new interface:

- It declares a new `MonoBehaviour` Façade class to hold all subsystem references.
- It adds `private` variables for each subsystem class in order to call their methods in complex sequences.

Now that we have the subsystems declared, we need to initialize them when `AutosaveFacade` is created. For Unity, we'll do our subsystem initializing in the `Start` or `Awake` methods, but if your Façade class isn't a `MonoBehaviour` (which is absolutely fine), this setup work should be done in the Façade class constructor.

## Initializing subsystems

Since we're using a `MonoBehaviour`, update `AutosaveFacade.cs` to match the following code snippet, which initializes each subsystem object on `Start`.

 Notice that our subsystems don't need any constructor parameters, but if they did, that is also perfectly fine. Also, since `SceneController.cs` is attached to the **Client** GameObject in the project **Hierarchy**, we can initialize it in `AutosaveFacade` with a `GetComponent` call on `Start`. If you're dealing with `MonoBehaviours` that are a little harder to find, you'll need to decide the best approach for your project.

```
public class AutosaveFacade: MonoBehaviour
{
    private DataConverter _dataConverter;
    private SaveSystem _saveSystem;
    private SceneController _sceneController;

    // 1
    void Start()
    {
        _dataConverter = new DataConverter();
        _saveSystem = new SaveSystem();
        _sceneController = this.GetComponent<SceneController>();
    }
}
```

Two points of note here. First, if your subsystems need extra configuration work after initialization, that's not a problem at all – just add in private façade methods to set up what you need and call those private methods in Start or Awake; second, your client should never know about or access your subsystems *through* the façade and your subsystems should not *reference* your Façade class. If either of these is true, you're not creating any decoupling – only the appearance of structured code that doesn't do the intended job.

## Adding a public Façade method

Now that we have our subsystems to work with, we can add a public method for Client.cs to call without knowing any of the complicated logistics involved in the auto-save feature (we're just ordering a burger – we don't need to know who's cooking the meat, who chops the vegetables, or who's off sick that day).

Update AutosaveFacade.cs again to match the following code block, which adds a new Save method with a double parameter for our player score and handles pausing the game, converting the score, saving the score, and finally unpausing the game before handing control back to the player!

```
public class AutosaveFacade: MonoBehaviour
{
    //… No variable changes needed …

    void Start()
```

```csharp
{
    //… No changes needed …
}

// 1
public IEnumerator Save(double score)
{
    // 2
    _sceneController.PauseScene();

    // 3
    float convertedScore = _dataConverter.FormatScore(score);
    _saveSystem.Save(convertedScore);

    // 4
    yield return new WaitForSecondsRealtime(1.5f);
    _sceneController.UnpauseScene();
    Debug.Log("Subsystem work complete!");
}
}
```

Let's break down our subsystem code:

1.  It adds a new `public IEnumerator` method that accepts a `double` parameter value.
2.  It uses the `SceneController` subsystem to pause the game.
3.  It uses the `DataConverter` subsystem to convert the score and `SaveSystem` to save the data.
4.  It waits for 1.5 seconds, then unpauses the game using the `SceneController` subsystem again.

Since our Save method takes in a double, our facade class has everything it needs to use the necessary subsystems. However, in cases where it's easier for the client to pass in more complex (or multiple) façade parameters, the façade methods may need to convert what the client is providing into what the subsystems need. This functionality is part of the pattern and, like with the Adapter pattern, the façade can do more than just provide a boring wrapper.

To test out our new feature, update `Client.cs` to match the following code snippet, which adds and uses an instance of `AutosaveFacade` each time the score goes up by 3 points.

```csharp
using System.Collections;
```

```csharp
using System.Collections.Generic;
using UnityEngine;
using TMPro;

public class Client : MonoBehaviour
{
    // 1
    public AutosaveFacade facade;

    public static Client Instance;
    public TMP_Text scoreUI;

    private int _itemsCollected = 0;
    public int Items
    {
        get { return _itemsCollected; }
        set
        {
            _itemsCollected = value;

            // 2
            if (_itemsCollected % 3 == 0)
            {
                StartCoroutine(facade.Save(_score));
            }
        }
    }

    private double _score = 0.0;
    public double Score
    {
        get { return _score; }
        set
        {
            _score = value;
            scoreUI.text = $"Score: {_score.ToString("0.0")}";
        }
    }
```

```
void Awake()
{
    // 3
    facade = this.gameObject.AddComponent<AutosaveFacade>();

    //… No other changes needed …
}
}
```

Let's break down our new code update:

- It adds an AutosaveFacade variable so we can call our façade Save method.
- It checks when items are collected in increments of 3 and calls the façade Save method.
- It initializes and adds an instance of AutosaveFacade to the **Client** GameObject in the **Hierarchy** on Awake.

Save the new changes to AutosaveFacade.cs, go back into Unity to play the scene, and walk around merrily picking up items. Every third or fourth item you collect will trigger the auto-save feature, which you can see in the screenshot below – the game pauses, the score saves, and the game unpauses for you to continue collecting items!

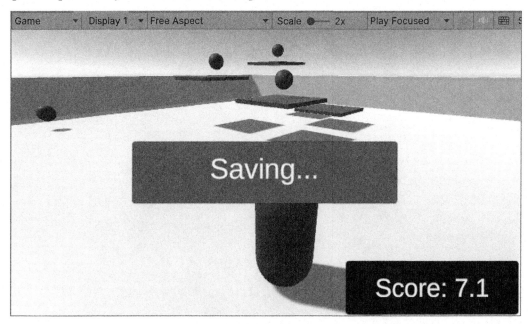

*Figure 17.4: AutoSave façade class executing in 3-point increments*

You can also track the individual steps being executed between the façade and each separate subsystem in the console logs, as shown in the following screenshot:

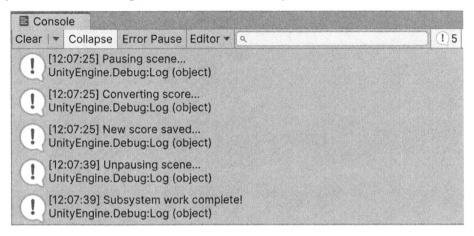

*Figure 17.5: Console logs showing AutoSave façade methods firing*

The client is now completely hands-off with the auto-save feature but still has control over when it's executed and the data needed to make the subsystems work! However, there are a couple of minor topics we'll cover before wrapping up the chapter, so you have everything you need to adapt your own program architecture.

# Adding multiple Façade methods

Even though our auto-save feature only needs one method, that won't always be the case – in most scenarios, your façade will need to handle multiple combinations of subsystem operations. In these situations, you have the freedom to add as many public Façade methods as you want (as long as you follow the same client-subsystem separation)!

For example, we could add another public Façade method that only converts and saves the player's score without pausing and unpausing the game, which you can see in the following code block:

```
public class AutosaveFacade: MonoBehaviour
{
    //… No variable changes needed …

    void Start()
    {
        //… No changes needed …
    }
```

```
public IEnumerator Save(double score)
{
    //… No changes needed …
}


// 1
public void ConvertAndSave(double score)
{
    // 2
    float convertedScore = _dataConverter.FormatScore(score);
    _saveSystem.Save(convertedScore);
}
}
```

Let's break down the shortened façade method:

1.  It adds a new `public` façade method that accepts a `score` parameter for saving.

2.  It converts and saves the `score` parameter without using the `SceneController` subsystem.

Your `public` Façade methods are entirely up to you and what your client class needs – the Façade pattern doesn't have any limitations in this area. With multiple inroads into our subsystems covered, we can talk about our last topic – building upgraded façade variations!

# Upgrading Façades

There's no rule in the Façade pattern that says you can only have a single type of façade, which means you may find yourself in situations where an `abstract` base class comes in handy. While this isn't something new or revolutionary for you object-oriented folks, you could have a `Façade` class like the one in the following code that all other façades must implement:

```
public abstract class AbstractFacade : MonoBehaviour
{
    public abstract IEnumerator Save(double score);
}
```

Then you could derive concrete subclasses any way you like – for example, different auto-save façades dealing with cloud and disk storage, as seen in the following snippet:

```
public class CloudStorageFacade : AbstractFacade
{
    public override IEnumerator Save(double score)
```

```
    {
        yield break;
    }
}

public class LocalStorageFacade : AbstractFacade
{
    public override IEnumerator Save(double score)
    {
        yield break;
    }
}
```

If you're going down this route, you'll need to decide whether or not to include subsystem objects in the abstract class definition or do that in the concrete implementation classes themselves. Either way, you get more flexibility and reusability down the road.

Another option for using multiple façades is simply creating different concrete Façade classes and configuring them with the required subsystem objects. This is a more hardcoded approach if you don't need a common interface for your client code (which you may not, but if you do, see *Chapter 16, Converting Incompatible Classes with the Adapter Pattern*).

Whatever road your project takes you down, it's important to remember that the Façade pattern isn't the closet you stuff all your excess junk in when cleaning the house – eventually, you'll have to open the closet again and everything will come tumbling out. What the Façade pattern *will* do is provide a simplified shortcut to access your more complex operations and subsystems, which is never a bad thing.

## Summary

We've reached the end of our short-and-sweet dive into the Façade pattern, but let's review a few key points before wrapping up. First, the Façade pattern is best when you need a simple interface for a subsystem or set of subsystems that work together on complex operations. This structure creates an easy access point for your client to make complicated requests without knowing how the work is done and decouples any dependencies between your client and those subsystems.

Because the Façade pattern structure is relatively uncomplicated, you only need to be aware of the Façade class and your subsystems.

The Façade class stores object instances of each subsystem and delegates any client requests straight to the subsystem in question, often calling multiple subsystem operations in sequence to stack pieces of functionality into complex features (like we did with our auto-save feature). Keep in mind that you can make your Façade classes abstract or concrete depending on the shape of your subsystems and the types of requests your clients are likely to dish out.

And as always, be mindful and intentional about how you use (or potentially overuse) the Façade pattern – it's *not* a silver bullet, a fix-all, or a place to hide poorly designed code components. It *is* a wonderfully efficient way of turning complex behaviors into easily accessible requests.

In the next chapter, we'll journey into the depths of object creation once again and see how the Flyweight pattern allows us to share certain data between objects without having to start from scratch!

## Further reading

- Coroutines are a specific type of method in Unity that allows you to spread tasks across several frames instead of running them all at once like a normal C# method. For more information, check out the documentation at https://docs.unity3d.com/Manual/Coroutines.html.

- PlayerPrefs lets you easily store preference data in string, float, or integer format between game sessions in Unity. However, this system is not encrypted, so it's not recommended for storing sensitive information. I'd encourage you to check out the documentation for a deeper dive, at https://docs.unity3d.com/ScriptReference/PlayerPrefs.html.

## Join our community on Discord

Join our community's Discord space for discussions with the author and other readers:

https://packt.link/gamedevelopment_packt

# 18

# Generating Terrains with the Flyweight Pattern

In the last chapter, we used the Façade pattern to create a one-wall barrier between our client code and numerous interconnected subsystems doing complex tasks. In this chapter, we'll take a step back from worrying about how our clients communicate with our larger project structures and dive back into the topic of efficiency. This won't be a completely alien topic if you've been working through the previous chapters, but if you haven't, I'd really encourage you to at least take a peek at *Chapter 3, Spawning Enemies with the Prototype Pattern, Chapter 7, Managing Performance and Memory with Object Pooling,* and *Chapter 13, Making Monsters with the Type Object Pattern,* before getting started here. It's important to understand the intent behind patterns that are closely related in how they approach similar problems – intent is everything!

Like the Prototype, Object Pool, and Type Object patterns, the flyweight solution is an answer to an age-old question: how much is object creation going to cost me? In our programs today, memory and processing power are much cheaper than in 1994 when design patterns were first put together, but cheaper doesn't mean infinite (there's always a price). Where Prototypes are copies, Object Pools are reusable storage, and Type Objects offer polymorphism without the inheritance overhead, flyweight objects store shareable state information that can be used over and over without any new objects created in memory. Any additional information or context a flyweight might need to do its work is passed into the object from the calling code or factory when needed.

The separation of an object's information into two separate categories not only gives us a performance boost but also draws a clear line in the sand between data that can be shared between *all* Flyweight objects (this is called intrinsic state) and data that depends on the specific *context* of the Flyweight object (which is called extrinsic state).

We'll drill down into these distinctions before we get to any code, but we have enough to get started for now!

We'll use this chapter to focus on the following topics:

- The pros and cons of the flyweight design pattern
- Creating shareable terrains
- Adding a Flyweight factory
- Working with unshared flyweights
- Upgrading to ScriptableObjects
- Flyweight or Type Object?

Let's start off with the technical requirements for this chapter, then move to the pattern break-down and get into code of our own!

## Technical requirements

To get started:

1. Download or clone the GitHub repository at https://github.com/PacktPublishing/C-Design-Patterns-with-Unity-First-Edition.

2. Open the **Ch_18_Starter** project folder in Unity Hub.

3. In **Assets | Scenes**, double-click on **SampleScene**.

The starter project for this chapter is a completely blank canvas that we're going to diligently (and randomly) draw on with generated terrain tiles to provide our future players with an arena to explore. Any 2D or 3D tactics games you've played in the past (I'm looking at you, *Final Fantasy Tactics*) will be our guiding light. Since this example is heavily dependent on procedurally creating our visuals, you'll have to be a little patient with the UI until we get things running in the scene.

As for the scripts:

- Client.cs is set up to generate our terrain based on a given number of rows, columns, and parent objects we want all the terrain tiles to belong to (we're going to be executing all our flyweight code here).
- Utilities.cs is a helper class that finds the corner tiles of any terrain (given the row and column values) and adjacent tiles, given the position of any tile. We won't be doing any work here (it just keeps the sprinkling of vector math out of our hair).

We'll also be using some Unity and C# language features to take our code the extra mile. Don't worry if you're not familiar with these; I've included links for the basics, and I'll explain how they apply to our use cases as we go:

- Interfaces (https://learn.microsoft.com/en-us/dotnet/csharp/fundamentals/types/interfaces)
- ScriptableObjects (https://docs.unity3d.com/Manual/class-ScriptableObject.html)
- Vector2Int (https://docs.unity3d.com/ScriptReference/Vector2Int.html)

Our job is to fill our terrain grid with random assortments of different tiles (water, ground, grass, and edges) while keeping memory usage to a minimum and object reuse to a maximum using shared flyweight objects!

# Breaking down the Flyweight pattern

As part of the structural family of design patterns, the Flyweight pattern is all about optimization for performance, memory management, and reusability when dealing with vast numbers of objects. Instead of copying or pooling entire objects, the Flyweight pattern focuses on identifying (and separating) an object's data into two categories: context-dependent and context-independent. Context-independent information can be shared between object instances, while context-dependent information can be injected and used without being stored. We call context-independent data *intrinsic* data and context-dependent *extrinsic* data (internal and external).

The Flyweight pattern is useful when:

- Your application uses a large number of objects that eat up considerable storage space.
- You have objects that store lots of extrinsic state, which could be paired down to a few shared objects once that extrinsic state is removed.
- You don't need to identify the large numbers of objects by their identity, leaving them open to sharing resources.

Let's think about flyweights in more concrete terms by considering a forest. This mythical forest is made up of palm trees (I'm not sure why) that all have the same properties – base model, leaves, bark, height, position, and size.

If we were to metaphorically plant a few trees in our code, we'd do fine with a few trees but, at some point, our hardware performance would start to suffer as we kept creating more and more trees (especially if we're doing it on the fly), as shown in the following figure:

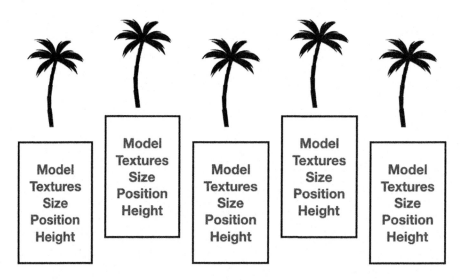

*Figure 18.1: Computationally expensive example for creating objects*

This performance hit is especially true if our trees have any resources that are expensive to create and store, like textures for leaves and bark or the tree model itself. But when we look at each tree, we can start to see that there are really two different sets of data being used – internal data that *every* tree has and external data that *depends* on each individual tree's context. For our example, the intrinsic tree state is the base model and textures for the leaves and bark, which leaves the extrinsic state as the height, position, and size. We can put the intrinsic state into a shareable flyweight object and just pass in the contextual information when we want to plant a new tree!

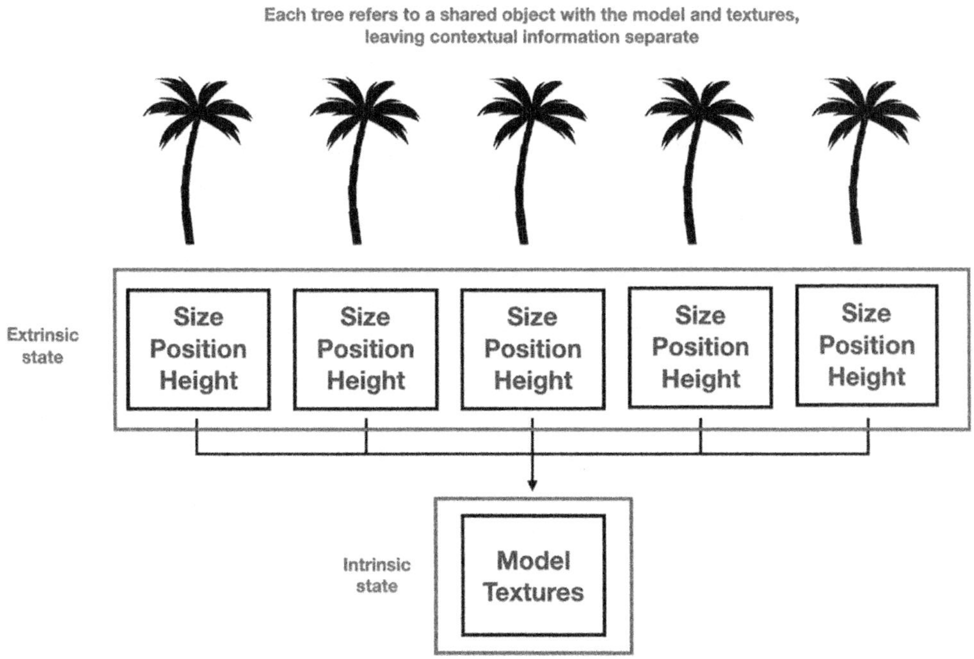

Each tree refers to a shared object with the model and textures, leaving contextual information separate
Extrinsic state
Size
Position
Height
Size
Position
Height
Size
Position
Height
Size
Position
Height
Size
Position
Height
Intrinsic state
Model
Textures

*Figure 18.2: Example of separation between intrinsic and extrinsic state*

Now think of a forest with multiple types of trees (palm, banana, coniferous pines, etc.) – the problem gets even worse without being able to reuse at least some tree data, but in this case, we can create a flyweight for each *type* of tree and manage them with a tree factory!

Tree factory stores and supplies Flyweight objects without creating new instances
Tree planter
Tree factory
Model
Textures
Model
Textures
Model
Textures

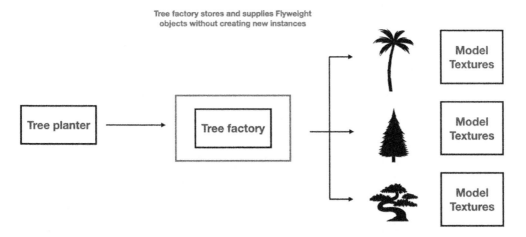

*Figure 18.3: Example of a flyweight factory for better extensibility*

Before we jump in, a word of warning early on – the Flyweight pattern is an optimization pattern that should only be used *when necessary*; it's not something you would normally start your project with. If you aren't facing any performance issues or use cases where an absolute deluge of objects are being created, you don't need flyweights just yet; you'd just end up with extra code to manage that doesn't help you solve a specific optimization issue. However, I'm always a fan of having the right tool for the job, so it's worth your time to learn how the Flyweight pattern could help you in the future and keep it in your back pocket!

## Diagramming the pattern

The Flyweight pattern has five main components that we can break down and identify, including their interactions, as shown in *Figure 18.4*:

- The **Flyweight** is an interface with methods for accepting and acting on extrinsic state. Traditionally, there are no properties or fields specified in the interface to keep things as generic as possible and allow you to create different types of flyweight objects down the line. If you're only working with a single flyweight type, you could add properties and fields, and even make this an abstract class with default implementations.

- **Concrete Flyweights** are classes that implement the flyweight interface and store intrinsic state, which means these objects are one hundred percent context-free and shareable.

- **Unshared Flyweights** are classes that also implement the flyweight interface, but they are not shareable and can store any state, whether it's intrinsic or extrinsic (context-free or context-dependent). Unshared flyweights aren't used as much in the flyweight pattern because they don't add to efficiency and savings when it comes to memory management. However, they are extremely useful when you need a shared interface for a client *and* an object that can manage child flyweight objects.

- A **Flyweight factory** creates and tracks flyweight objects, but also makes sure client requests are receiving shared flyweights without new objects being instantiated.

- The **Client** is responsible for computing or storing whatever extrinsic state your flyweight objects may need.

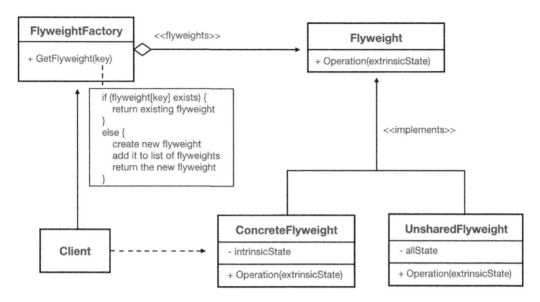

*Figure 18.4: UML diagram of the Flyweight pattern components*

Looking at the UML diagram above, what hopefully jumps out at you right away is the separation between state and operations – this is where flyweights differ from other patterns like Prototype or Type Object. By removing the shareable state, we're splitting our objects in half, making one half reusable and the other half configurable. The client doesn't care that these objects are split or if they need to be queried from a factory – the performance optimization is neatly hidden behind the flyweight interface.

## Pros and cons

Like all design patterns, there are pros and cons. Let's start with a potential benefit the Flyweight pattern can add to your project:

- **Sharing is caring** – Being able to reuse a flyweight object with its intrinsic state is a huge space saver when creating large volumes of objects. The more shared intrinsic state you can separate into a flyweight, the more storage you save. Plus, the more you can compute your extrinsic state, the more storage you save on top of the intrinsic optimization boost!

However, be careful of the following pitfall when using the pattern in your projects:

- **Wrong scenario usage** – It's easy to see the Flyweight pattern as a catch-all for performance, but if you find that you've separated your intrinsic and extrinsic state and are still left with as many kinds of extrinsic state as you had original objects, there's not going to be a net gain in efficiency and performance. The best cases for the flyweight are when there's a core of intrinsic state that can be shared, and extrinsic state can be easily sectioned off and computed rather than stored.

Keep these in mind when deciding whether to implement this pattern.

Now that we've covered the structure, benefits, and limitations of the Flyweight pattern, let's start generating our game terrain!

# Creating shareable terrains

Imagine you're building a 3D tactics game where players explore different locations made of randomized terrain tiles. Each tile may be water (which you can't walk on), ground (which you can), grass (which may contain ninjas), or edges (which keep you boxed in). When you start building your terrain-generating scripts, everything is fine because you're only testing with a 10x10 grid with a maximum of 100 tiles (no big deal with today's hardware). However, during playtesting, you find your players wanting bigger and bigger areas to explore, eventually leading you to consider creating entire tiled worlds. What's more, you may want to create more than three types of tiles (I know I'd like there to be more variety when I'm walking around a game world), making tile management and performance an even bigger issue.

What are your options when performance optimizations and hardware limitations are in the mix? Can you just copy them? No, because some parts of each tile are the same and some are different. Can you just share the same bits over and over? No again, because each tile still needs its own identity. Enter the Flyweight pattern!

## Adding a Flyweight interface

Like many patterns in our rear-view mirror, the first step is to create a shared interface that a client can use without knowing the gritty details of the implementing object. With the Flyweight pattern, we need a flyweight interface with a method (or methods) that accepts some extrinsic state (in our case, an x and z coordinate and a parent object) and can act on that data when combined with the intrinsic state of any concrete flyweight object (tile type, color, height, and size).

In the **Scripts** folder, create a new C# script named IFlyweight and update it to match the following code block:

```
using System.Collections;
using System.Collections.Generic;
using UnityEngine;

// 1
public interface IFlyweight
{
    // 2
    public void Create(int x, int z, Transform parent);
}
```

Let's break down our new interface:

1.  It declares a Flyweight interface for all flyweight objects to implement.

2.  It adds a Create method for accepting and acting on extrinsic data for each terrain tile.

The simpler the interface, the easier it is for us to change future implementations without breaking our client code! At this point, we could continue with our extrinsic state split between three different values. More often than not, a better use of your brainpower and coding time is to combine your extrinsic state into its own object (especially if the extrinsic state computes properties instead of storing them), which we'll cover in the next section.

## Extracting extrinsic state

In the **Scripts** folder, create a new C# script named ExtrinsicState and update its contents to match the following code, which adds properties for the x and z coordinates of each terrain tile and a parent Transform so we can parent those tiles to a GameObject in the **Hierarchy**.

Our example isn't complex enough to warrant computed extrinsic data, which means we'll just store it in an ExtrinsicState instance. But, computing any extrinsic state inside its own object will save you even more memory storage, which, combined with the shared intrinsic state, makes the Flyweight pattern an optimization package deal.

If you can't imagine what computed extrinsic state would look like, imagine a text editor application – each letter is a flyweight object, but its extrinsic state is a map or tree structure of fonts. The extrinsic state object would be responsible for adding and keeping track of fonts as they are applied to each letter, which means almost no data is actually stored (except maybe an index for the font tree structure).

```
using System.Collections;
using System.Collections.Generic;
using UnityEngine;

// 1
public class ExtrinsicState
{
    // 2
    public int xCoord;
    public int zCoord;
    public Transform parent;
}
```

Let's update IFlyweight.cs with the new ExtrinsicState class to match the following code snippet:

```
public interface IFlyweight
{
    // 1
    public void Create(ExtrinsicState context);
}
```

Now we can peacefully move on to building our actual flyweight terrain objects (concrete and unshared), which we'll start in the next section.

## Building a concrete Flyweight

When it comes to concrete flyweight objects, you have two main choices – hardcode each object's intrinsic data in its respective classes or create a configurable class that takes in intrinsic data in the class constructor. The choice comes down to *where* and *how* you want to get intrinsic data into each flyweight. We're going to use the first option because it's more extendable, but it all depends on what your future plans are for your flyweights.

In the **Scripts** folder, create a new C# script named `Tile` and update it to match the following code, which creates a helper enum with cases for each of our terrain tile types and a concrete flyweight class that accepts and sets intrinsic state using the class constructor. We also need to include the `Create` method because we're implementing the `IFlyweight` interface and, in this case, we're going to instantiate, configure, and parent the new tile using a combination of intrinsic and extrinsic information:

```
using System.Collections;
using System.Collections.Generic;
using UnityEngine;

// 1
public enum TerrainType { Ground, Water, Grass, Edge }

// 2
public class Tile : IFlyweight
{
    // 3
    public TerrainType type { get; }
    public Color color { get; }
    public float height { get; }
    public float size { get; }

    // 4
    public Tile(TerrainType type, Color color, float height)
    {
        this.type = type;
        this.color = color;
        this.height = height;
        this.size = 1;
    }

    // 5
    public void Create(ExtrinsicState context)
    {
        Vector3 position = new Vector3(context.xCoord, 0, context.zCoord);
        Vector3 scale = new Vector3(size, height, size);
        GameObject tile = GameObject.CreatePrimitive(PrimitiveType.Cube);
```

```
        Renderer renderer = tile.GetComponent<Renderer>();

        tile.name = $"{type.ToString()} Tile";
        renderer.material.SetColor("_Color", color);
        tile.transform.position = position;
        tile.transform.localScale = scale;
        tile.transform.SetParent(context.parent);
    }
}
```

Let's break down the new concrete Flyweight:

1.  It declares an enum for each type of terrain tile in our project to make selection easier.

2.  It declares a new concrete flyweight class that implements the IFlyweight interface.

3.  It adds properties for each intrinsic state value we want our flyweights to store.

4.  It accepts and sets all intrinsic state properties in the class constructor when the flyweight is created.

5.  It implements the Create method to instantiate new terrain tiles using an extrinsic state parameter passed in by the client.

> Two points about intrinsic data:
>
> - It's up to you where you want to store these declarations. The traditional way is to put any intrinsic data right into the concrete flyweight objects, which keeps the flyweight interface much more reusable. However, you can include intrinsic data in the interface definition, but be aware that the interface ends up not being as flexible.
>
> - Intrinsic state declarations can be get/set properties, private variables with public getter methods, protected or read-only fields, or whatever works best for your project – as long as they are immutable after they are initially set! We don't want other classes to be able to change these values, only reference them.

We can now create concrete flyweight objects whenever we like, but we still want to limit when and where that happens (we can't let the power go to our heads), which is where a flyweight factory comes in, which we'll build in the next section.

# Adding a Flyweight factory

In the **Scripts** folder, create a new C# script named FlyweightFactory and update its contents to match the following code block, which stores a Dictionary of IFlyweight objects (indexed by the TerrainType name) and returns either a newly created or reused tile flyweight when queried by the client:

```
using System.Collections;
using System.Collections.Generic;
using UnityEngine;

// 1
public class FlyweightFactory
{
    // 2
    private static Dictionary<string, IFlyweight> _cache = new
Dictionary<string, IFlyweight>();

    // 3
    public static IFlyweight GetFlyweight(TerrainType type)
    {
        // 4
        var key = type.ToString();

        // 5
        if(!_cache.ContainsKey(key))
        {
            IFlyweight newTile = null;

            switch(type)
            {
                case TerrainType.Ground:
                    newTile = new Tile(type, Color.white, 0.75f);
                    break;
                case TerrainType.Water:
                    newTile = new Tile(type, Color.blue, 0.65f);
                    break;
```

```
        case TerrainType.Grass:
            newTile = new Tile(type, Color.green, 1.0f);
            break;
        case TerrainType.Edge:
            newTile = new Tile(type, Color.black, 1.5f);
            break;
    }

    Debug.Log("New flyweight created…");
    _cache.Add(key, newTile);
    }


    // 6
    Debug.Log("Flyweight returned…");
    return _cache[key];
    }
}
```

Let's break down our new factory class:

1.  It declares a new FlyweightFactory class.

2.  It adds a Dictionary of IFlyweight objects that can be looked up by a string key.

3.  It adds a public method that accepts a TerrainType parameter and returns an IFlyweight object.

4.  It converts the TerrainType parameter to a string for easier lookup.

5.  It checks if the Dictionary already contains the requested IFlyweight, and if not, runs a switch statement to create and store a new instance.

6.  It returns the IFlyweight instance if it already exists in the Dictionary.

 Since we're making heavy use of a factory in this chapter, I'd recommend revisiting *Chapter 4, Creating Items with the Factory Method Pattern*, to brush up on the challenges and solutions that come with using factories. However, you'll notice that we're only using the new keyword in the factory class, which means no new memory is used when we reuse the flyweight objects later in our client code.

Now that we have a working factory that either grabs an existing flyweight object or creates a new one from scratch, let's update `Client.cs` to match the following code and use an `ExtrinsicState` instance and the newly minted `FlyweightFactory` class to fill out the gaps in our procedural terrain generating methods (feel free to add in your own procedural logic)!

```csharp
public class Client : MonoBehaviour
{
    public int gridRows = 10;
    public int gridColumns = 10;
    public Transform parent;

    // 1
    private ExtrinsicState _context = new ExtrinsicState();

    void Start()
    {
        // 2
        _context.parent = parent;

        GenerateCorners();
        GenerateTerrain();
    }

    private void GenerateTerrain()
    {
        for (int x = 0; x < gridRows; x++)
        {
            for (int z = 0; z < gridColumns; z++)
            {
                // 3
                IFlyweight tile = null;
                _context.xCoord = x;
                _context.zCoord = z;

                // 4
                if(Random.Range(0, 5) == 0)
```

```
            {
                tile = FlyweightFactory.GetFlyweight(TerrainType.
Grass);
            }
            else if(Random.Range(0, 10) == 5)
            {
                tile = FlyweightFactory.GetFlyweight(TerrainType.
Water);
            }
            else
            {
                tile = FlyweightFactory.GetFlyweight(TerrainType.
Ground);
            }

            // 5
            tile.Create(_context);
        }
      }
    }

    public void GenerateCorners()
    {
        //… No changes needed …
    }
}
```

Let's break down our new client code:

1.  It adds a private ExtrinsicState variable.
2.  It sets the parent property on the _context object in Start.
3.  It creates a new IFlyweight instance set to null and updates the _context coordinate properties in each loop iteration.
4.  It uses the FlyweightFactory class to request tile instances of a specific type.
5.  It calls the IFlyweight interface Create method on each tile and passes in the current _context.

Notice that we update the _context with each new loop iteration, and while this isn't doing much for us right now, if we decided to add another level of abstraction and have the client keep track of the grid, the _context could take care of computing its current position *within* that grid at any point in time (which is a great use of computed extrinsic state).

Run the game and you'll see a random terrain grid each time you press **Play**!

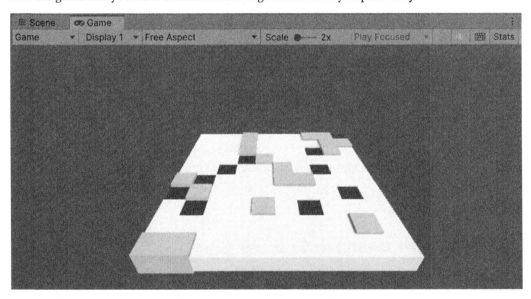

*Figure 18.5: Random terrain generation using flyweight objects*

However, the magic is in the console logs shown in the following image – each time we query a new type of tile, it gets created *once* and then the flyweight is stored and returned for all other client requests!

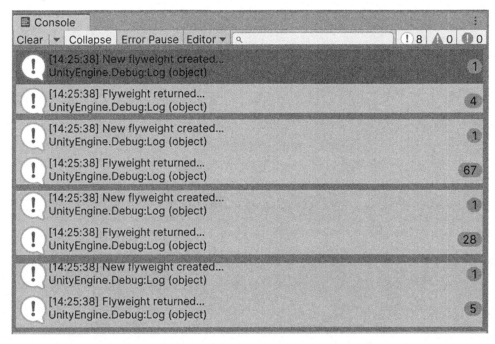

*Figure 18.6: Console logs showing new objects and flyweight objects being created*

This code and testing wraps up the super basic version of the Flyweight pattern structure, but we still need to look at how to incorporate UnsharedFlyweight objects when needed (and maybe how to upgrade our system to use ScriptableObject assets), all of which we'll cover in the following sections.

# Working with unshared Flyweights

Unshared flyweights are the black sheep of the Flyweight pattern because they don't actually help with performance or memory optimization – so why use them? Two reasons: first, they let your client treat unshared and shared flyweight objects under the same interface (which means you could choose to change an unshared object to a concrete flyweight object later without any breaking changes). Second, there are helpful use cases where you need an object or objects that have flyweight children – anytime you run into this situation, these are good candidates for unshared Flyweights.

In the **Scripts** folder, create a new C# script named Corner and update its content to match the following code snippet, which adds a new flyweight class (that will not be shared) and draws a center edge tile plus four additional edge tiles to form a cross shape at each corner of the grid:

```
using System.Collections;
using System.Collections.Generic;
using UnityEngine;

// 1
public class Corner : IFlyweight
{
    // 2
    private IFlyweight _tile;
    private List<Vector2Int> _intersects;
    private ExtrinsicState _context;

    // 3
    public Corner()
    {
        _tile = FlyweightFactory.GetFlyweight(TerrainType.Edge);
    }

    // 4
    public void Create(ExtrinsicState context)
    {
        // 5
        _context = context;
        _intersects = Utilities.GetIntersectTiles(context.xCoord, context.
zCoord);
        _tile.Create(context);

        foreach(Vector2Int position in _intersects)
        {
            // 6
            context.xCoord = position.x;
            context.zCoord = position.y;
```

```
            _tile.Create(context);
        }
    }
}
```

Let's break down our unshared flyweight class:

1.  It declares a new class that implements the `IFlyweight` interface.
2.  It adds all state variables the unshared flyweight will need in the `Create` method.
3.  It requests a tile flyweight from the `FlyweightFactory` in the class constructor to use in the `Create` method.
4.  It implements the `IFlyweight` interface `Create` method with an `ExtrinsicState` parameter.
5.  It sets the `_context` and `_intersects` values and creates a center corner tile.
6.  It updates the `_context` for each intersecting tile position and creates four additional tiles around the central corner tile.

The main point to notice with unshared flyweight objects is that there is no separation between intrinsic and extrinsic state; there's just all the objects' state (because it's all unshared and content-dependent). This setup is why we're allowed to store our `_context` and any other variables we need. There's a great quote from the original Gang of Four text that says "the flyweight interface *enables* sharing; it doesn't enforce it" (something to keep in mind). The added abstraction layer only comes into play if you need it too but I wanted you to have a real-world implementation to refer back to!

Since each `Corner` instance isn't going to be shared, we can update `FlyweightFactory.cs` to simply return a new `Corner` object whenever we want one:

```
public class FlyweightFactory
{
    //... No changes needed ...

    public static IFlyweight GetFlyweight(TerrainType type)
    {
        //... No changes needed...
    }

    // 1
```

```
      public static Corner GetCorner()
      {
          Debug.Log("Unshared flyweight created...");
          return new Corner();
      }
  }
```

I've already included a method for generating corners in the starter project, so let's fill that in by updating Client.cs to match the following code:

```
public class Client : MonoBehaviour
{
    public int gridRows = 10;
    public int gridColumns = 10;
    public Transform parent;

    private ExtrinsicState _context = new ExtrinsicState();

    void Start()
    {
        //… No changes needed …
    }

    private void GenerateTerrain()
    {
        //… No changes needed …
    }

    public void GenerateCorners()
    {
        List<Vector2Int> corners = Utilities.GetCorners(gridRows,
gridColumns);
        foreach(Vector2Int corner in corners)
        {
            // 1
            _context.xCoord = corner.x;
            _context.zCoord = corner.y;
```

```
        // 2
        var cornerTile = FlyweightFactory.GetCorner();
        cornerTile.Create(_context);
    }
  }
}
```

Let's break down this little piece of procedural programming:

1.   It sets the _context coordinates in each iteration of the corners list to provide new corner positions in the scene.

2.   It requests the corner unshared flyweight from the flyweight factory and calls the Create method with the updated _context, which leaves all the extra corner creation to the corner flyweight instead of the client.

When we hit **Play** again, we'll see our random terrain but, this time, we also get four wonderful corner objects to complete the scene!

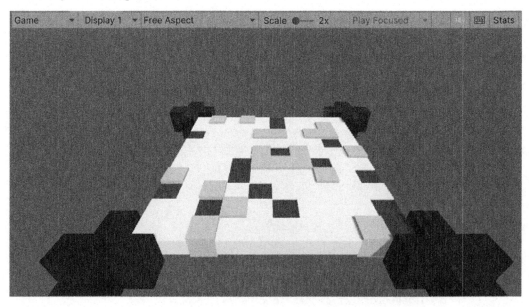

*Figure 18.7: Unshared flyweight corner objects being instantiated*

Looking at the console logs, you'll see that on top of creating and reusing our terrain tiles, we've also created four new corner objects, as shown in the following figure:

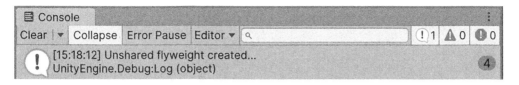

*Figure 18.8: Console log of unshared flyweight corner objects being created*

Again, unshared flyweights are a secondary use case for the pattern, but they absolutely have a place in your code whenever you want to manage child flyweight objects and don't need to differentiate between intrinsic and extrinsic state – all while providing a consistent interface for the client class.

To round out the chapter, let's finish strong with an upgrade to ScriptableObject assets so we can use the **Inspector** a bit more and add a little drag-and-drop efficiency into our lives, which we'll do in the next section.

# Upgrading to ScriptableObjects

Our chapter wouldn't be complete without a little Unity-specific application, so let's transform everything we've learned about the Flyweight pattern into ScriptableObject format so we can use the **Inspector** to wire up some shareable objects and a factory.

In the **Scripts** folder, create a new C# script named SOTile and update its contents to match the following code block, which creates a ScriptableObject tile class with all the same intrinsic data we have in the Tile class:

```
using System.Collections;
using System.Collections.Generic;
using UnityEngine;

// 1
[CreateAssetMenu(fileName = "Tile Data", menuName = "ScriptableObjects/SO
Tile")]

// 2
public class SOTile : ScriptableObject, IFlyweight
{
    // 3
    public TerrainType type;
    public Color color;
```

```
public float height;
public float size;

// 4
public void Create(ExtrinsicState context)
{
    Vector3 position = new Vector3(context.xCoord, 0, context.zCoord);
    Vector3 scale = new Vector3(size, height, size);
    GameObject tile = GameObject.CreatePrimitive(PrimitiveType.Cube);
    Renderer renderer = tile.GetComponent<Renderer>();

    tile.name = $"{type.ToString()} Tile";
    renderer.material.SetColor("_Color", color);
    tile.transform.position = position;
    tile.transform.localScale = scale;
    tile.transform.SetParent(context.parent);
}
}
```

Now let's create ScriptableObject tiles for each of our flyweight objects by going to **Project**:

1.  Select the **ScriptableObject** folder and right-click, then go to **Create | ScriptableObjects | SOTile** and name it Ground.

2.  Set the **Type**, **Color**, **Height**, and **Size** properties to match the values we used in FlyweightFactory.cs, as shown for the **Ground** tile in the following figure:

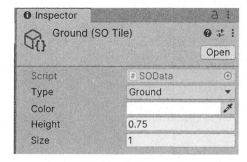

*Figure 18.9: ScriptableObject in the Inspector*

3.  Repeat steps 1 and 2 for the other flyweight tiles we've been using (**Water**, **Grass**, and **Edge**) so your **ScriptableObject** folder looks like the following screenshot:

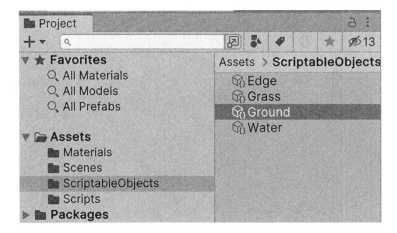

*Figure 18.10: ScriptableObject folder with SOTile objects*

For our factory class, all we need is a list of SOTile objects and methods for requesting Flyweights and Corners. In the **Scripts** folder, create a new C# script named SOFactory and update its content to match the following code block, which procedurally fills a Dictionary of IFlyweight objects in the Awake method indexed by string keys, returns IFlyweight objects when queried without any extra caching code (because they'll be linked in the **Inspector**), and returns new Corner instances on demand:

```
using System.Collections;
using System.Collections.Generic;
using UnityEngine;

public class SOFactory : MonoBehaviour
{
    public List<SOTile> tiles;
    private static Dictionary<string, IFlyweight> _cache = new
Dictionary<string, IFlyweight>();

    void Awake()
    {
        foreach(SOTile tile in tiles)
        {
            var key = tile.type.ToString();
            _cache.Add(key, tile);
        }
```

```
    }

    public static IFlyweight GetFlyweight(TerrainType type)
    {
        var key = type.ToString();
        return _cache[key];
    }

    public static Corner GetCorner()
    {
        return new Corner();
    }
}
```

To test out the new data system, select **Client** in the **Hierarchy**, add the SOFactory script, and drag and drop each of the SOTile assets into their respective variables, as shown in the following image:

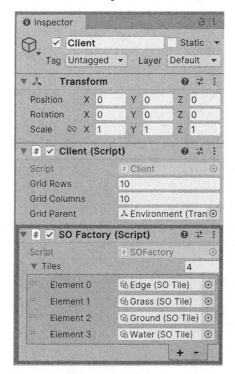

*Figure 18.11: Client object and SO Factory in the Inspector*

Since the publicly accessible parts of the SOFactory class are static and match up to what we're already using in the FlyweightFactory class, we can easily swap out the two factories by updating Client.cs to match the following code:

```
public class Client : MonoBehaviour
{
    //... No changes needed ...

    void Start()
    {
        //... No changes needed ...
    }

    private void GenerateTerrain()
    {
        for (int x = 0; x < gridRows; x++)
        {
            for (int z = 0; z < gridColumns; z++)
            {
                IFlyweight tile = null;
                _context.xCoord = x;
                _context.zCoord = z;

                // 1
                if(Random.Range(0, 5) == 0)
                {
                    tile = SOFactory.GetFlyweight(TerrainType.Grass);
                }
                else if(Random.Range(0, 10) == 5)
                {
                    tile = SOFactory.GetFlyweight(TerrainType.Water);
                }
                else
                {
                    tile = SOFactory.GetFlyweight(TerrainType.Ground);
                }
```

```
                        tile.Create(_context);
                }
            }
    }


    public void GenerateCorners()
    {
        List<Vector2Int> corners = Utilities.GetCorners(gridRows,
gridColumns);
        foreach(Vector2Int corner in corners)
        {
            _context.xCoord = corner.x;
            _context.zCoord = corner.y;


            // 2
            var cornerTile = SOFactory.GetCorner();
            cornerTile.Create(_context);
        }
    }
}
```

And yes, we also need to update our Corner.cs code to reference the new factory before we press **Play**, as shown in the following code snippet:

```
public class Corner : IFlyweight
{
    //… No changes needed …


    public Corner()
    {
        // 1
        _tile = SOFactory.GetFlyweight(TerrainType.Edge);
    }


    public void Create(ExtrinsicState context)
    {
        //… No changes needed …
    }
}
```

When we run the game again, everything works exactly the same, which is a testament to how flexible and interchangeable our IFlyweight interface is! But now we can actively edit the intrinsic state for each of our flyweight objects and create new ones on the fly.

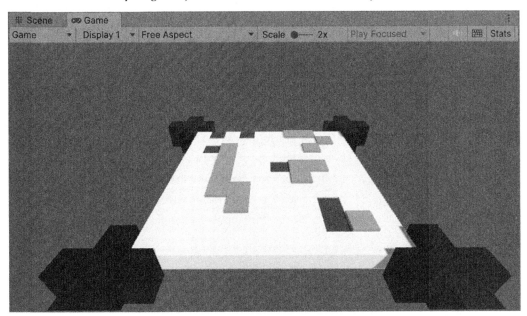

*Figure 18.12: Full randomly generated flyweight terrain*

That wraps up our code for the Flyweight pattern, but there's still one extremely important question to cover before we hit the end of the chapter – are you using a Flyweight or a Type Object?

# Flyweight or Type Object?

Both the Flyweight and Type Object patterns deal with performance and optimization in similar ways, and they're often taught all mashed together, which makes it difficult to understand the *intent* behind each one and the different solutions they offer.

With the Type Object pattern, the intent is to create new complex classes without using big inheritance hierarchies. This pattern is also about *data* rather than *behavior* (as Type Objects don't typically act on extrinsic state), but you'll see a fair bit of memory optimization as a side bonus. You also don't see factories come into play with the Type Object because they are structured to privately create and return new instances of themselves, so there's no additional need for this abstraction layer (which isn't to say you can't add it). Again, this is where the line gets murky between these two patterns, as they can be combined and still function, but the intent becomes blurred.

As we've seen with the Flyweight pattern, storage optimization is the *core intent* and the pattern structure can incorporate *data* and *behavior*. Acting on extrinsic state is a *core operation* of Flyweights, and adding factories greatly increases strong boundaries between the client and flyweight interface. The bottom line is there's no rule that says these two patterns can't work together, but it's especially important with these two structures that you're clear on what problem you need to solve and how you're solving it.

## Summary

Phew, that was an involved chapter (because why would performance optimization be easy, right?). But before you start looking for applicable spots to shoehorn the Flyweight pattern into your projects, let's review some key topics. First, you'll get the most out of the Flyweight pattern when you're creating lots and lots of objects with both context-independent and -dependent data, and when those two data categories can be easily partitioned. The pattern will also come in handy when the context-dependent data can be computed rather than stored.

The Flyweight pattern has five components: the Flyweight interface, concrete Flyweights, un-shared Flyweights, a Flyweight factory, and, of course, the client using it all. A clean flyweight interface is one that has operations that act on the object's extrinsic state, acting as an injection point for any context-dependent information. Concrete flyweight objects implement the flyweight interface and store all the intrinsic data that can be shared. Unshared flyweight objects don't give you any of the optimization benefits of shared state, but they can be useful when presenting a con-sistent interface for clients, especially if they're managing flyweight child objects in their classes. The flyweight factory acts as a clearing house for creating, storing, and returning flyweight objects on request, which is a nice boundary between what the client sees and the underlying flyweight structure. The client deals with the flyweight interface and the flyweight factory, making it easy to extend and maintain a large store of Flyweight types.

`ScriptableObject` assets are a phenomenal tool for creating flyweight objects, as they remove a lot of the boilerplate initialization code and can be used right from the **Inspector**. However, you may want to look at more efficient and Unity-approved ways of creating flexible `ScriptableObject` factories if you're going to be using multiple flyweight objects.

Keep in mind that the Flyweight and Type Object patterns both offer similar solutions with dif-ferent intents, and it's easy to get them mixed up and mashed together without even trying, but that shouldn't hinder your usage of either or both.

In the next chapter, we'll bring our journey full circle by considering a different approach to global access with the Service Locator pattern and explore how we can make ourselves a generic registry of services instead of using singleton classes!

# Further reading

- Interfaces are a great way to create groups of related functionalities (with or without default implementations) that can be adopted by any class or struct. These are especially handy when you want to have a class inherit from multiple groups of functionalities, which is called object composition. For more information, check out the documentation at `https://learn.microsoft.com/en-us/dotnet/csharp/fundamentals/types/interfaces`.

- ScriptableObjects are the perfect way to create data containers in your Unity projects (and we'll use them in almost every chapter going forward), but I'd also recommend checking out the documentation at `https://docs.unity3d.com/Manual/class-ScriptableObject.html`.

# Leave a review!

Enjoying this book? Help readers like you by leaving an Amazon review. Scan the QR code below to get a free eBook of your choice.

# 19

# Global Access with the Service Locator Pattern

In the last chapter, we used the Flyweight pattern to create a resource-efficient sharing system for objects created in large (sometimes massive) batches. In this chapter, we'll circle back to the very first topic of this book, global access, but instead of a Singleton solution, we'll explore what the Service Locator pattern has to offer.

Scenarios where the Service Locator pattern shines are eerily similar to areas where a Singleton would be a potential solution – allowing a very select few services or systems to be accessible anywhere in your project. While this kind of freewheeling access should be extremely limited (for coupling and safety reasons we'll discuss a little later), there are some use cases where a global service is a necessity (logging and data persistence come to mind). Think of the service locator as a wrapper for classes you would typically consider making into singletons – a registry of global services makes access safer and more defensible while also giving you the freedom to initialize those services (even if they have dependencies). Whenever you have more than one potential class that needs global access, we should consider the Service Locator pattern instead of multiple singletons running amok.

Correctly identifying service locator use cases is a point we'll hammer home throughout the chapter – singletons and Service Locators should ideally be context-free and unique, meaning they don't need to know when or where they're being used to work properly, and you should only need one. If you have a service that only works at certain times when your code is running (like a multiplayer session manager), it doesn't make sense to make it accessible to other parts of the project that will never use its features (like during local play).

We'll use this chapter to focus on the following topics:

- The pros and cons of the service locator design pattern

- Creating service contracts

- Building a Service Locator class

- Adding a generic solution

- Extra service locator features

Let's start off with the technical requirements for this chapter, then move to the pattern breakdown and get into code of our own!

# Technical requirements

To get started:

1. Download or clone the GitHub repository at `https://github.com/PacktPublishing/C-Design-Patterns-with-Unity-First-Edition`

2. Open the **Ch_19_Starter** project folder in Unity Hub

3. In **Assets | Scenes**, double-click on **SampleScene**

The starter project for this chapter is pulled right from *Chapter 2, Managing Access with the Singleton Pattern* (it's fitting that we start and end with similar scenarios and solutions). Our scene has a playable character that you can move and rotate using the *WASD* or arrow keys and three big red spheres that can be collected by running headlong into them!

As for the scripts:

- `Client.cs` is an almost empty script that has a placeholder `Awake` method for our service registrations. We won't be doing much work here other than testing our code.

- `Item.cs` is a simple collectible script that implements the `OnCollisionEnter` method and destroys the object it's attached to (**Item** Prefabs in the scene). We'll be getting and calling service methods from here.

- `Player.cs` controls the simple movement and rotation using the *WASD* and arrow keys – we won't be doing any work in this script (it just makes our example a little more fun).

We'll also be using some Unity and C# language features to take our code the extra mile. Don't worry if you're not familiar with them, I've included links for the basics, and I'll explain how they apply to our use cases as we go.

- Interfaces (`https://learn.microsoft.com/en-us/dotnet/csharp/fundamentals/types/interfaces`)

- Statics (https://learn.microsoft.com/en-us/dotnet/csharp/language-reference/keywords/static)

- Generics (https://learn.microsoft.com/en-us/dotnet/csharp/fundamentals/types/generics)

Our job is to create a set of services that can be registered and safely retrieved from a central access point while ensuring a minimum of coupling between the client and service code.

# Breaking down the Service Locator pattern

As part of the Structural family of design patterns, the Service Locator pattern is all about exposing services that need to be global while limiting information on the concrete service code doing the work and where the services are located. Think about *how* a service is implemented and *where* it's housed; these are your guiding stars for this pattern.

The Service Locator pattern is useful when:

- You have unique systems or services that need to be globally accessible regardless of context or scope.

- You want to provide a single access point to a service or services without coupling any client code to the concrete service class implementation.

Most of us use Service Locators every day, but let's examine a concrete example – getting paid electronically. In the past, you would have to give your payment details to anyone you wanted to request money from over the internet, which was a not-so-small logistical headache and wasn't super safe either. There was no barrier between your sensitive information and the people or businesses that needed to know about your data to send payments, as shown in *Figure 19.1*.

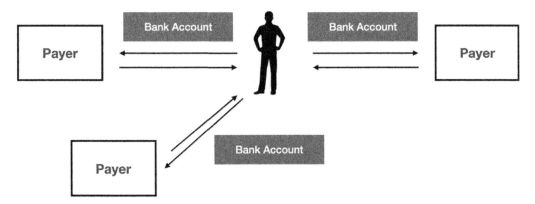

*Figure 19.1: Example of distributing banking details to clients*

When services like PayPal entered the game, they took care of locating you and hiding your sensitive information. All you have to do nowadays is register yourself with a service like PayPal, enter your respective banking details, and let anyone sending you money just look you up! Not only is this more secure (payees can't actually get to your banking data), but whenever you modify your concrete banking information, you don't have to tell anyone but PayPal about the change (and yes, this system also works for paying people yourself), as shown in *Figure 19.2*.

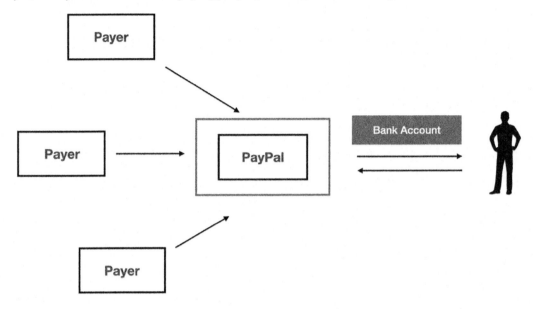

*Figure 19.2: Example of bank details behind a service layer*

In this example, PayPal is the service locator, and you are the service they are storing and locating. When you register yourself, you enter into a service contract with PayPal by providing information about where and how you want to receive your money, but when someone wants to pay you, they can simply search your name and hit the **Send Money** button. Your information is safe behind the service contract while the payment feature is exposed to your clients!

One thing we haven't covered yet is how and when each service gets registered, which can happen at compile time before your game starts or dynamically during actual gameplay. Both options are possible with the service locator – each depends on what your project requires but we'll cover both use cases in the chapter examples.

# Diagramming the pattern

The Service Locator pattern has four main components, as shown in *Figure 19.3*:

- The **Client** requests a service from the **Service Locator**, having no knowledge of where it's located or how it's found. To add a layer of security and abstraction, the client will only deal with **Service Contract** interfaces, not the concrete service implementations themselves.

- Each **Service Contract** is an interface with public methods for accessing the internal workings of its Concrete Service implementations.

- Each **Concrete Service** implements the Service Contract interface and adds concrete features.

- The **Service Locator** is responsible for registering and returning services, as well as dealing with missing or unregistered services. The locator will also work with **Service Contract** interfaces instead of **Concrete Service** types.

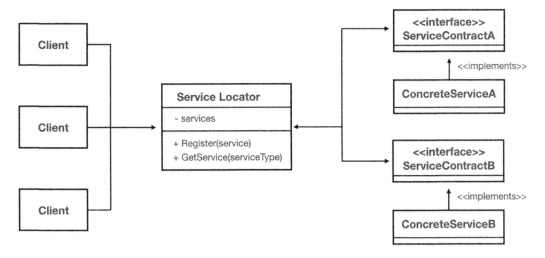

*Figure 19.3: UML diagram of Service Locator components*

The preceding structure allows us to store and return services *through* the **Service Locator** class using their respective **Service Contract** interfaces while keeping the **Client** decoupled from each **Concrete Service** class. For a globally accessible service, this is ideal for ensuring our concrete services can't be modified by the client code and provides a central registry of our services for easy querying.

# Pros and cons

Like all design patterns, there are pros and cons. Let's start with the potential benefits the Service Locator pattern can add to your project:

- **Simplifying global access by pooling** your services into a single point of access is the main benefit of the Service Locator pattern because it decouples client code from where services are located and what concrete services are being used. As with the singleton, providing global access this way is efficient and dangerous if safety precautions and proper usage are not applied (we'll get hands-on with both of those choices as we build out our locator structure).

- **Runtime and dynamic initialization** are a big plus because they give you more flexibility on when and where you register your services. However, this also means that services could potentially be missing (unregistered) or accidentally wired up with null objects. Both these scenarios can be planned for in advance, which we'll absolutely do in our example project.

However, be careful of the following pitfalls when using the pattern in your projects:

- Dependency and coupling aren't great and can lead to management headaches when your project becomes deeply intertwined with globally accessible objects. However, when service use cases are correctly identified (unique instances and context-free), the service locator benefits outweigh this downside.

- Unit testing can be a problem with global objects, but if we use service contract interfaces instead of just concrete service classes, we can easily swap in testable services or provide different service scopes for testing scenarios.

Looking at the pros and cons, a globally accessible service locator (singleton or not) is a better solution than having multiple singleton systems running around your project. Not only would there be fewer dependencies between your mechanics and these global systems, but the way we'll construct our locators offers an added abstraction layer between the calling code and the underlying concrete services (safety belts are always encouraged).

Now that we've covered the structure, benefits, and limitations of the Service Locator pattern, we can dive into service contracts and a locator service of our own!

# Creating services and contracts

Imagine you're building a 3D adventure game where your player explores a given area looking for loot. Since your game has several systems that need to be efficiently accessible from different parts of your project, you think singletons may be the right solution. However, you already know that too many singletons running around your code may be problematic, so you look for a way to keep track of the different systems under a common umbrella using a Service Locator!

If you've ever run into a service locator structure in the wild, you might have had trouble seeing through the elaborate setups, builders, lazy loading, bootstrapping, and general over-architected fluff that surrounds the core of what the pattern actually does. To avoid getting lost in the forest without seeing any beautiful trees, we're going to lay out a statically accessible service locator class to get the hang of what makes this pattern so simple and usable (and then move on to more scalable solutions).

## Logging and saving contracts

A Service Locator class wouldn't be much use without any services to manage, so the first part of our journey is to create interfaces for each kind of service – called service contracts. The service contracts hold all the methods that each type of service needs to implement and provide an abstract layer between the client and concrete services we'll be creating.

In our example, we'll have two services, one for logging and one for saving player data; these are both good candidates because they are largely context-independent (they should be accessible in pretty much every part of the game unless you have an extremely niche scenario) and could have several different concrete classes.

In the **Scripts** folder, create a new C# script named `ILogContract` and update its contents to match the following code block, which creates a logging service interface:

 The systems we'll be building and using are extremely simple because they are not the focus of the Service Locator pattern. However, the systems themselves don't matter as long as they have contract interfaces the locator class can work with, even in complex production environments.

```
using System.Collections;
using System.Collections.Generic;
using UnityEngine;

// 1
public interface ILogContract
{
    // 2
    void Log(string message);
    void Throw(string message);
}
```

Let's break down our first service:

1.  It declares a public interface for all logging services.

2.  It adds two methods that all logging services need to implement.

Now let's create another new C# script called SystemDebugger and update its contents to match
the following code, which creates a concrete implementation for simple debugging and exception
throwing:

```
using System.Collections;
using System.Collections.Generic;
using UnityEngine;

// 1
using System;

// 2
public class SystemDebugger : ILogContract
{
    public void Log(string message)
    {
        DateTime time = new DateTime();
        Debug.Log($"{time.Date}: {message}");
    }

    public void Throw(string message)
```

```
    {
        DateTime time = new DateTime();
        throw new Exception($"{time.Date}: {message}");
    }
}
```

Let's break down our simple concrete logging service:

1.  It adds the System using directive to access the DateTime class.

2.  It creates a concrete logging service class that implements the ILogContract interface methods and prints debug logs or throws an exception on demand.

Let's follow the same steps to set up our data persistence system by going back into the **Scripts** folder, creating a new C# script named ISaveContract, and updating its contents to match the following code block:

```
using System.Collections;
using System.Collections.Generic;
using UnityEngine;

// 1
public interface ISaveContract
{
    // 2
    void Save(string data);
    void Load();
}
```

Now we can set up a brand-new concrete saving service for cloud storage (even though we're not going to fully flesh it out here) by going to the **Scripts** folder, creating a new C# script named CloudStorage, and updating its contents to match the following code:

```
using System.Collections;
using System.Collections.Generic;
using UnityEngine;

// 1
public class CloudStorage : ISaveContract
{
    public void Save(string data)
```

```
    {
        Debug.Log($"{data} saved to database...");
    }

    public void Load()
    {
        Debug.Log($"Data loaded from database...");
    }
}
```

 In most cases, having service contract interfaces that don't share a common parent is perfectly fine. However, if you do need an additional abstraction layer that brings all your services under one roof, that's not a problem – just create an empty parent interface and have each service contract interface implement it, like so:

```
public interface IContract {}

public interface ISaveContract : IContract { … }
public interface ILogContract : IContract { … }
```

Because we're already in our services code (and we want to make our lives easier), let's put in a little front-loaded work by declaring concrete logging and saving services that don't do anything but that we'll use later in a later section, the Null Object pattern.

## Planning for missing services

One of the easiest and often overlooked parts of the Service Locator pattern is how to gracefully fail when handling nonexistent or missing services. We can't get into the actual code for that just yet, but we can build out two placeholder classes (one for each service) that will help us later.

Let's start with our logging service by creating a new C# script named NullLogger and updating its contents to match the following code snippet:

```
using System.Collections;
using System.Collections.Generic;
using UnityEngine;

// 1
public class NullLogger : ILogContract
```

```
{
    // 2
    public void Log(string message)
    {
        Debug.LogWarning($"{GetType().Name} service being used!");
    }

    public void Throw(string message)
    {
        Debug.LogWarning($"{GetType().Name} service being used!");
    }
}
```

Let's break down the new null logging service:

1.  It creates a new concrete class that implements the ILogContract interface.
2.  It adds the ILogContract interface methods and prints out warning messages.

This null concrete class makes errors and missing services easier to track down without breaking or stopping the application (or putting the error handling labor on our calling code) by debugging messages saying the null service is being used instead of the concrete instance we want.

Let's also create a new C# script called NullSaver to take the weight if our saving service isn't found and update its contents to match the following code snippet, which creates a placeholder saving service class:

```
using System.Collections;
using System.Collections.Generic;
using UnityEngine;

public class NullSaver : ISaveContract
{
    public void Save(string data)
    {
        Debug.LogWarning($"{GetType().Name} service being used!");
    }

    public void Load()
```

```
    {
        Debug.LogWarning($"{GetType().Name} service being used!");
    }
}
```

With service contracts and concrete services ready to go, we can lay the groundwork for a basic locator class, which we'll start in the next section.

# Building a Service Locator class

The core of any service locator class is the services in its care, so we'll start by storing private references for each service and exposing public static methods for registering and retrieving those references from anywhere in our project. In the **Scripts** folder, create a new C# script named BasicLocator and update its contents to match the following code block.

```
using System.Collections;
using System.Collections.Generic;
using UnityEngine;

// 1
public class BasicLocator
{
    // 2
    private static ILogContract _logging;
    private static ISaveContract _saving;

    // 3
    public static void RegisterLogger(ILogContract service)
    {
        _logging = service;
        Debug.Log("Logging service registered...");
    }

    public static void RegisterSaver(ISaveContract service)
    {
        _saving = service;
        Debug.Log("Saving service registered...");
    }
```

```
    // 4
    public static ILogContract GetLogService()
    {
        return _logging;
    }

    public static ISaveContract GetSaveService()
    {
        return _saving;
    }
}
```

Breaking down the new locator class:

1. It declares a new public locator class.

2. It adds two private static variables to hold each service reference.

3. It adds two methods for registering services.

4. It adds two methods for returning our services.

To test our services, let's update Client.cs to match the following code snippet, which performs the all-important registration step to ensure the services are ready to use in the Awake method.

```
public class Client : MonoBehaviour
{
    void Awake()
    {
        // 1
        BasicLocator.RegisterLogger(new SystemDebugger());
        BasicLocator.RegisterSaver(new CloudStorage());
    }
}
```

We also need to change our item collection logic to use the newly registered services, so update Item.cs to match the following snippet as well.

```
public class Item : MonoBehaviour
{
    // 1
    ILogContract _logging;
    ISaveContract _saving;
```

```
    void Start()
    {
        // 2
        _logging = BasicLocator.GetLogService();
        _saving = BasicLocator.GetSaveService();
    }


    void OnCollisionEnter(Collision collision)
    {
        if (collision.gameObject.tag == "Player")
        {
            Destroy(this.gameObject);


            // 3
            _logging.Log("Item collected!");
            _saving.Save($"1 point");
        }
    }
}
```

Let's break down our new collectable code:

1.  It adds two references to the services we want to use.

2.  It queries and sets each service reference.

3.  It calls methods from the ILogContract and ISaveContract interfaces when an item is collected.

Hit **Play** to test out our new service locator and you'll see our registration logs printed out to the console when the game starts, as shown in the following figure:

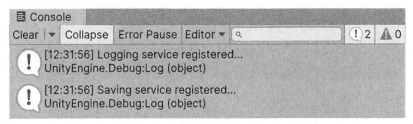

*Figure 19.4: Console logs for services being registered correctly*

When you start collecting items, the BasicLocator will be the central provider for all the operations we need, which you'll see in the additional console logs:

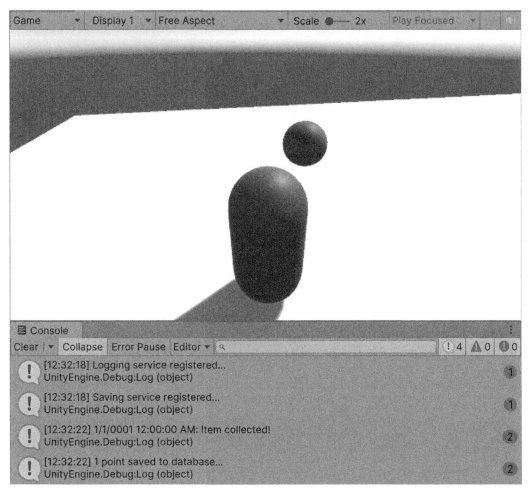

*Figure 19.5: Gameplay using registered services*

Before you throw the book down and speed off to your own projects, we should cover an extremely important scenario – what if a service wasn't properly registered and you get a null object when you try and request it?

# The Null Object pattern

A common solution to the unregistered service problem is to simply return a null object or throw an exception, but this presents a problem of its own – whose responsibility is it to handle the null object?

- If there isn't a one-size-fits-all policy for handling a missing service, throwing exceptions and letting the client decide what to do based on the context is fine.

- If the opposite is true and you don't need contextual exception handling every time your calling code tries to locate a service and comes up missing, you put yourself in a very dangerous position.

The one time you forget to check for a null object before using a service you've requested is when things break. And the worst part is, it's totally unnecessary in this case – if a null service should always be handled the same way, we should address it in the service locator and leave the calling code out of the loop.

For our example, we'll return an instance of one of our null service classes we created earlier to give our future selves less headaches. This solution doesn't require any assertions or checks outside of the service locator (and let's be honest, the extra class declaration is so little work it's one hundred percent worth it in most cases).

The solution we're using is called the Null Object pattern, which returns a placeholder object that has implemented the same interface as the object (service in our case) we're trying to retrieve. The Null Object pattern isn't complicated, which is why it doesn't get its own chapter, but you can and should add it to your architecture toolbox – it has widespread benefits in many of the patterns we've covered.

Update `BasicLocator.cs` to match the following code block, which initializes all our services to their null counterparts when the `Initialize` method is called and protects us from potentially registering a null service from the client side of things.

```
public class BasicLocator
{
    private static ILogContract _logging;
    private static ISaveContract _saving;
```

```
// 1
private static ILogContract _nullLogger = new NullLogger();
private static ISaveContract _nullSaver = new NullSaver();

// 2
public static void Initialize()
{
    _logging = _nullLogger;
    _saving = _nullSaver;
}

public static void RegisterLogger(ILogContract service)
{
    // 3
    if(service == null)
    {
        _logging = _nullLogger;
    }
    else
    {
        _logging = service;
        Debug.Log("Logging service registered...");
    }
}

public static void RegisterSaver(ISaveContract service)
{
    // 4
    if(service == null)
    {
        _saving = _nullSaver;
    }
    else
    {
        _saving = service;
        Debug.Log("Saving service registered...");
    }
```

```
        }

        public static ILogContract GetLogService()
        {
            return _logging;
        }

        public static ISaveContract GetSaveService()
        {
            return _saving;
        }
    }
```

Let's break down our new defensive programming additions:

1.  It stores new instances of each null service.
2.  It adds an initializing method and sets each service to a null service before registration.
3.  It checks for a null logging service during registration and sets a null service if found.
4.  It checks for a null saving service during registration and sets a null service if found.

> You may have noticed the null service objects are the only times when the service locator knows about how a service is constructed. Generally, you want to keep service construction far away from the locator, but in this case, since the null objects don't require any additional initialization, it's safe. If you wanted a more separated solution, you could have the service contract interfaces include a method for returning their respective null objects either by hardcoding that logic or using Reflection.

Update `Client.cs` to match the following code, which initializes our services with our null services and tests out our new defense against unregistered services:

```
public class Client : MonoBehaviour
{
    void Awake()
    {
        // 1
        BasicLocator.Initialize();
    }
}
```

When we hit **Play**, we can still pick up items as before but with the added bonus of not getting null reference errors because our services haven't been registered properly:

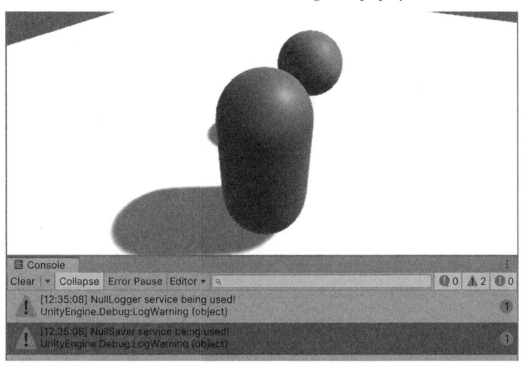

*Figure 19.6: Null services being used when services are registered*

We can also test to see if our code defends against registering a valid service and a null service with the following code:

```
public class Client : MonoBehaviour
{
    void Awake()
    {
        BasicLocator.Initialize();

        // 1
        BasicLocator.RegisterLogger(null);
    }
}
```

Now whether we forget to register a service or attempt to register a null service, both cases are handled with our null services correctly and nothing crashes when services are not initialized or initialized incorrectly, as shown in the following screenshot logs:

*Figure 19.7: Null services being used when null objects are registered*

Before we move on, let's revert our client script back to the way things are supposed to be with services being registered:

```
public class Client : MonoBehaviour
{
    void Awake()
    {
        BasicLocator.RegisterLogger(new SystemDebugger());
        BasicLocator.RegisterSaver(new CloudStorage());
    }
}
```

With everything working as expected, we can address the elephant in the room – so much duplicate code that does virtually the same thing! Well, now that we understand the structure of a good service locator, it's time to build a generic implementation that's a little more dynamic-friendly!

# Adding a generic solution

Our generic service locator is going to have the exact same features as the static locator we already built, but instead of knowing what services it's managing beforehand, we'll register services dynamically. Not only is this more flexible, but it also allows us to register and unregister services while our game is running!

In the **Scripts** folder, create a new C# script named GenericLocator and update its contents to match the following code block:

```
using System.Collections;
```

```
using System.Collections.Generic;
using UnityEngine;

// 1
using System;

// 2
public class GenericLocator
{
    // 3
    private static readonly Dictionary<Type, object> _services = new
Dictionary<Type, object>();

    // 4
    public static int Services
    {
        get { return _services.Count; }
    }
}
```

Let's break down the first portion of our generic locator solution:

1.  Declares the new Service Locator class
2.  Adds a private `Dictionary` of service objects stored by `Type` for easy lookup
3.  Adds a simple get property so we can check how many services are registered at any time.

For the registration method, we'll take in a generic type as long as it's a class and check for null objects:

You may notice we're using a helper method named `FindNullObject` that hasn't been implemented yet, but for now, just keep following along with the piecemeal structure and we'll get to it.

```
...

    // 1
    public static void Register<T>(T newService) where T : class
    {
```

```
    // 2
    Type key = typeof(T);

    // 3
    if(newService == null)
    {
        _services[key] = FindNullObject<T>();
        Debug.Log($"Null {key} registered...");
    }
    // 4
    else if (!_services.ContainsKey(key))
    {
        _services[key] = newService;
        Debug.Log($"{key} service  registered...");
    }
    // 5
    else
    {
        Debug.Log($"{key} service already registered...");
    }
}
```

Let's break down our generic registration method:

1.  It adds a new generic method that takes in a service parameter of type T where T  always needs to be a class.

2.  It converts the generic type T into a concrete Type.

3.  It checks if the service is null and registers a null service class if true.

4.  It checks if the service is already registered, and if it's not, we add the service to our _services dictionary.

5.  It prints out a debug log if the service has already been registered.

When we want to retrieve a service all we need to provide is the generic type and we'll either receive the service stored in our Dictionary or the respective null service of the generic type we're looking for.

```
...

// 1
public static T GetService<T>() where T : class
{
    // 2
    Type key = typeof(T);

    // 3
    try
    {
        return _services[key] as T;
    }
    catch
    {
        // 4
        return FindNullObject<T>();
    }
}
```

Let's break down the generic service request method:

1. It adds a new generic method that returns a service object of type T, where T is always a class.

2. It converts the generic type T into a concrete Type.

3. It uses a try statement to check if there is a registered service of type T in our _services dictionary and returns the service if found.

4. If there is no service found we use the catch statement block to return the appropriate null service using the FindNullObject method.

Now let's add the helper method we've already defined to output the appropriate null service objects for each case, which compares the name of the generic service type we're looking for with the service contract interfaces we've created.

```
...

// 1
static T FindNullObject<T>() where T : class
```

```
    {
        // 2
        Type key = typeof(T);

        // 3
        switch (key.Name)
        {
            case nameof(ILogContract):
                return new NullLogger() as T;
            case nameof(ISaveContract):
                return new NullSaver() as T;
            default:
                return new NullLogger() as T;
        }
    }
```

Let's break down our null service helper method:

1.  It adds a new `private` generic method that returns a service object of type T, where T is always a `class`.

2.  It converts the generic type T into a concrete `Type`.

3.  It uses a `switch` statement to match the generic type with each of our established null service classes by class name and returns the appropriate null service instance cast as type T.

> The `switch` statement approach may work for a few services, but it's not the most extendable approach. I'd recommend looking at how we structured our reflection factory in *Chapter 4, Creating Items with the Factory Method Pattern*, to see how this could be written for production code.

To test how we handle missing and null service registrations, update `Client.cs` to match the following snippet:

```
public class Client : MonoBehaviour
{
    void Awake()
    {
        // 1
        GenericLocator.Register<ISaveContract>(null);
```

```
            Debug.Log($"Services registered: {GenericLocator.Services}");
    }
}
```

And then update Item.cs to match the following code, which uses the new GenericLocator class instead of BasicLocator:

```
...

void Start()
{
    // 1
    _logging = GenericLocator.GetService<ILogContract>();
    _saving = GenericLocator.GetService<ISaveContract>();
}
```

If we run the game again, we'll see that our NullSaver object was saved when we registered a null service, which is why our console log only shows a single registered service:

*Figure 19.8: Console logs for generic service locator using missing and null services*

When we go to pick up any of the items in the scene, we'll receive a NullLogger object because we didn't register any logging class at all!

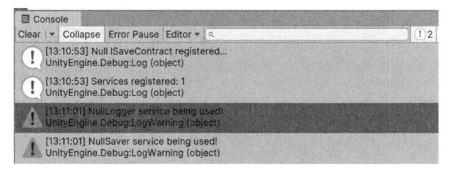

*Figure 19.9: Console logs showing null services being used*

OK, now that we know our safety net is correctly installed, let's also test the positive use cases where we've correctly registered our systems (because it's always nice to see your system running the way it should):

```csharp
public class Client : MonoBehaviour
{
    void Awake()
    {
        // 1
        GenericLocator.Register<ILogContract>(new SystemDebugger());
        GenericLocator.Register<ISaveContract>(new CloudStorage());

        Debug.Log($"Services registered: {GenericLocator.Services}");
    }
}
```

When the game starts, both services are correctly registered and when we collect our prizes the valid concrete service classes take control and do their work, as shown in the following screenshot:

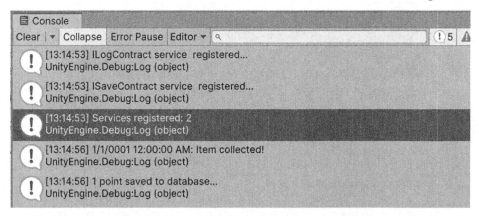

*Figure 19.10: Console logs showing valid services being registered and used*

That wraps up the core of the Service Locator pattern, but the foundation we've built not only safeguards us from registering null services or no services at all, it keeps the concrete service implementations completely separate from the calling code by using service contract interfaces (the *how*) and hides how we find the service (the *where*). But we're not done yet! There are still a few variations and powerups we can add to our code to make things even more flexible and useful, which we'll do in the last section.

# Extending locator functionality

Even though the foundation of the Service Locator pattern isn't as complicated as some of the other systems we've tackled throughout our journey, it's important to think about extended features that add to its usability, which we'll do in this last section.

## Initializing services

As far as automatically registering or initializing your services before a client needs them, Unity has a wonderful set of callbacks that can be invoked at different points in the runtime startup. All we need is a static method, the RuntimeInitializeLoadMethod attribute, and a selected RuntimeInitializeLoadType.

In the **Scripts** folder, create a new C# script named ServiceBootstrapper and update its contents to match the following code block:

```
using System.Collections;
using System.Collections.Generic;
using UnityEngine;

// 1
public static class ServiceBootstrapper
{
    // 2
    [RuntimeInitializeOnLoadMethod(RuntimeInitializeLoadType.
BeforeSplashScreen)]
    public static void Init()
    {
        Debug.Log("Registering services...");

        // 3
        GenericLocator.Register<ILogContract>(new SystemDebugger());
        GenericLocator.Register<ISaveContract>(new CloudStorage());

        Debug.Log("Services registered");
    }
}
```

Let's break down our bootstrapping class:

1.  It declares a new static class.

2.  It uses the RuntimeInitializeOnLoadMethod attribute to run the method block before the splash screen loads and any objects in the scene are loaded.

3.  It registers our services and prints out debug logs to show our service registration progress.

 You can find all the different RuntimeInitializeLoadType options and detailed explanations at https://docs.unity3d.com/ScriptReference/RuntimeIniti alizeOnLoadMethodAttribute.html.

To test this functionality, go into Client.cs one last time and comment out the registration calls to the GenericLocator, but leave the debug log that shows how many services have been registered when the scene loads. Hit **Play** and you'll see our new debug logs printed out as shown in the following screenshot:

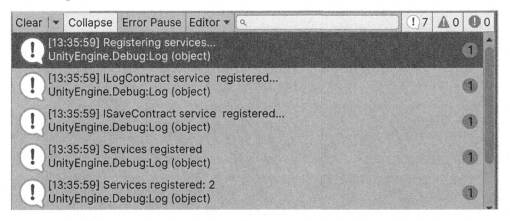

*Figure 19.11: Console logs showing services being registered before splash screen loads*

Now our services are registered *before* anything in our scene can get to them first, which is a great way to make sure none of our services are queried before they've had a chance to settle into the locator.

## Explicitly registering services

There may be situations where one of your services has more than one type (which would still work with our generic solution) but you want to explicitly choose what type it's registered as in the service locator registry.

In those cases, you could add a new method to your generic Service Locator classes as shown in the following code snippet (this isn't mandatory for the chapter example, so feel free to use this as a reference):

```
...

    public static void RegisterExplicit(Type type, object newService)
    {
        if(!type.IsInstanceOfType(newService))
        {
            throw new Exception($"Service type [{type.FullName}] doesn't
match service interface [{nameof(newService)}]!");
        }

        if (!_services.ContainsKey(type))
        {
            _services[type] = newService;
            Debug.Log($"{type.FullName} service  registered...");
        }
        else
        {
            Debug.Log($"{type.FullName} service already registered...");
        }
    }
```

Note that we're checking if type and the newService have matching types so we don't accidentally register nonconforming services. You may also have to rewrite or overload the FindNullObject helper method since we're not using generic types here, but I'll leave that stretch goal up to you!

## Unregistering services

You might also need to remove services from your generic service locator for testing or if they're no longer needed, which you could do with the generic method in the following code block:

```
...

    public void Unregister<T>()
    {
        Type key = typeof(T);
```

```
        if (!_services.ContainsKey(key))
        {
            Debug.Log($"{key.FullName} service has not been registered...");
        }
        else
        {
            _services.Remove(key);
        }
    }
```

Nothing too crazy here, just checking if we have the service already registered or not, and if we do, we'll remove it from our registry.

# A word on scope

The last topic we'll cover in our service locator deep dive is scope, which comes down to how you manage *what* services are being registered, *where* the registration is happening, and *how* the locator is accessed – all depending on context.

## Singleton Service Locators

For starters, everything we did with our BasicLocator and GenericLocator classes can be made into a singleton. This approach would give you more control over how the locator object is created and configured, which is especially helpful in Unity if you want to create GameObject locators from scratch. Since we've already gone through the myriad ways of accomplishing such a feat in *Chapter 2, Managing Access with the Singleton Pattern*, I'd encourage you to head back to the beginning of our adventure and see what new perspective hits you.

## Grouping services

If you go the Singleton route, we'll run into issues when testing because we'll always get the same registered services no matter what (it's a singleton after all). However, we can get around this by reverting our service locator class back to a non-static object and providing an abstract scope class that wraps a service locator instance and configures services, but can be extended with multiple concrete class implementations. This would allow us to specify which sets of services a singleton would be using, making it testable and extendable at the same time!

There is a wonderful article about this process and I'd highly recommend checking it out at `https://medium.com/@taha.m.gokdemir/design-patterns-for-unity-developers-service-locator-124cd4628c43`.

## A service for every level

Lastly, you may want to have different service registries for different levels of your project (another way to think of scope). For instance, you could have a global singleton locator that has a service registry for the entire game, but you could also have per-scene and even per-component service registries. This approach requires a lot more configuration that falls outside of the Service Locator pattern, but it can be extremely beneficial when taking your code to the next level.

There is a great video tutorial on this process that I highly recommend watching, as it takes you through the specific Unity theory and implementation of such a system. You can find the resource at `https://www.youtube.com/watch?v=D4r5EyYQvwY&list=PLnJJ5frTPwRMCCDVE_wFIt3WIj163Q81V&index=10&ab_channel=git-amend`.

## Summary

Congratulations on making it to the end of the last hands-on chapter! We've been through a lot, from creating service contract interfaces and a simple static service locator class, all the way to a flexible and extendable generic implementation with null service and null object protection (because it's always good to have insurance).

Remember, the Service Locator pattern is best used in situations where you have systems or services that are unique (they only need one instance in the project) and context-free (they don't depend on a situation or section of the game to run). You can build them manually if you know what services you want ahead of time, or you can spin up a generic solution to dynamically register and query your services while your program is running. When it comes to service scope, you have a few paths open to you, but your choice will depend on what you're trying to accomplish with your project.

Keep in mind that service locator classes work best when they defend against unregistered services or null service objects being mistakenly registered. We've taken precautions against those wrong turns in our example, which means your program won't break because of an assumed service being located, but it's important to build in those defenses – especially in globally accessible systems where your client code is completely decoupled *but* expecting a nice juicy service when it calls.

In the next and final chapter, we'll end our adventure into design patterns and set you off on your own journey with a hand-packed lunch full of helpful tips, resources, and the road ahead!

## Further reading

- Interfaces are a great way to create groups of related functionalities (with or without default implementations) that can be adopted by any class or struct. These are especially handy when you want to have a class inherit from multiple groups of functionalities, which is called object composition. For more, check out the documentation at `https://learn.microsoft.com/en-us/dotnet/csharp/fundamentals/types/interfaces`.

- Generics open up a whole new world of programming possibilities, (which is why I included a generic solution in this chapter), but I'd recommend reading up further on the topic at `https://learn.microsoft.com/en-us/dotnet/csharp/fundamentals/types/generics`.

## Join our community on Discord

Join our community's Discord space for discussions with the author and other readers:

`https://packt.link/gamedevelopment_packt`

# 20

# The Road Ahead

First, a big thank you for pushing through and making it this far in our adventure – writing this book took more than two years of research, testing, and writing, which is hopefully two years you don't have to spend finding your way through the maze of design patterns and their real-world applications! If you're a budding software developer at the beginning of your career (and happened to find yourself here), you've gained a lot of ground. If you're an established engineer or game programmer and already knew this stuff, I congratulate you still and hope you found a few new and compelling tools for your toolbox!

When I talk to uninitiated developers about design patterns for the first time, more often than not I see an immediate gleam of hope in their eyes, as if I've shown them a magic trick that would be a big hit at their company parties. When we talk a little more, I see the gleam dim and die out when they realize design patterns aren't magic after all and don't solve *all* problems *all* of the time.

The trick isn't to memorize design patterns (because that won't help anyone), but to exercise your ability to truly see code, from components all the way to high-level systems and everything in between – see how everything communicates, interacts, and depends on each other. Apply what you've learned, experiment, and remake your future projects into effective and beautiful systems – intentionally!

And because no book or teaching resource is ever really complete, we're going to spend this last chapter looking to the future of your software design journey with the following topics:

- SOLID principles
- The design patterns not covered

- Further resources
- Getting involved in the community

# SOLID principles and you

If design patterns are the engineering classes aimed at solving problems repeatedly found in the wilds of programming, then the SOLID principles are philosophy seminars. If SOLID is a new acronym for you, don't worry – here's a quick breakdown of what's in store:

| | |
|---|---|
| **S**ingle-responsibility principle | There should never be more than one reason for a class to change, every class should only have one responsibility! |
| **O**pen-closed principle | In a perfect world, entities (classes, functions, modules) should be open to extension but closed to modification, meaning new behaviors are allowed if the source code isn't tampered with. We've seen this first-hand with abstract classes and interfaces that allow concrete implementations to be switched out anytime without breaking the client! |
| **L**iskov substitution principle | Base classes must be able to use objects of derived classes without knowing it, meaning if a `Weapon` class is a subtype of an `Item` class, then an `Item` can be replaced with a `Weapon` without breaking the game. |
| Interface segregation principle | Clients should never be forced to depend on interfaces they never use, which means interfaces work best when they contain small subsets of functionality that classes can choose from a la carte. Let's say we have an `Item` interface that has features for equipping and consuming. If a `Weapon` class only needs to be equipped but not consumed, it shouldn't have to implement the entire `Item` interface when there's no chance the weapon will ever be eaten – `Item` should be split into two interfaces and `Weapon` or other objects can choose what they need! |

| Dependency inversion principle | We should always depend on abstractions over concrete implementations because those abstractions should never depend on concrete details. The reverse is true for better working software – details should depend on abstractions. |
| --- | --- |
| | Our game code is much more flexible when client code doesn't care about concrete `Item` or `Weapon` objects but instead relies on `Equippable` or `Consumable` interfaces. |

These design principles are focused on making object-oriented software more maintainable, flexible, and understandable – sound familiar? And before I see you throw your hands up in frustration, I'll address why these weren't included in this book. While I could say that these principles are extensively documented elsewhere (which they are), the honest and maybe controversial answer is that I've found teaching SOLID principles *before* design patterns is often more confusing for new inductees than the other way around (blasphemy, I know).

And because these principles are somewhat overarching and widely applicable, it's more efficient and useful to fold them into your design perspective once you have enough data (problem scenarios) and solutions (design patterns) to apply them to. You can know all the theory in the universe, but without a dataset to practice with, there's not much work getting done.

If you want to dive further into SOLID principles, I'd highly recommend going straight to the source with *Clean Code* (`https://www.amazon.com/Clean-Code-Handbook-Software-Craftsmanship/dp/0132350882`) and *Clean Architecture* (`https://www.amazon.com/Clean-Architecture-Craftsmans-Software-Structure-ebook/dp/B075LRM681`) by Robert C. Martin. While the examples are mostly theoretical (and the technical ones are not written in C#), these books are the best stepping stones I've found in the wild.

For Unity-specific content, I'd recommend watching this playlist by Jason Weimann at `https://www.youtube.com/playlist?list=PLB5_EOMkLx_WjcjrsGUXq9wpTib3NCuqg`.

So, add these principles to your toolbox, and the next time you're working with solutions from this book, I'm confident new connections will start firing!

# The patterns left out (but not forgotten)

Picking which patterns to include in this book wasn't easy – they all have a place in software design because they all solve a specific problem. However, some patterns either solve similar problems, have similar solutions with different details, or are built into C# already (remember, the original book on design patterns was written in 1994). I picked the most common and most useful patterns of the bunch for a strong foundation, but being a bit of a completist, here is a list of additional patterns for you to investigate (mixed together from game programming and software design scenarios).

Structural patterns:

| Composite | Allows objects to have a tree-like structure so clients can handle individual objects and compositions of objects the same way. |
|-----------|--------------------------------------------------------------------------------------------------------------------------------|
| Bride | Decouples abstractions from implementations so they can each change without any dependencies. |
| Proxy | Uses a placeholder as a stand-in for an object, which gives you finer-grained access control to the underlying target. |

Behavioral patterns:

| Mediator | Defines an object as a wrapper for how a set or group of objects interact with each other and prevents those objects from explicitly referring to each other. |
|----------|-------------------------------------------------------------------------------------------------------------------------------------------------------------|
| Template | Defines the overall structure of an algorithm in an operation while letting subclasses redefine portions of the algorithm without changing the base structure. |
| Subclass Sandbox | Defines behaviors in subclasses from a set of operation blueprints in a base class. |
| Chain of Responsibility | Decouples request senders from request receivers by giving multiple sequential objects the chance to handle the request. |
| Interpreter | Defines a representation of a language's grammar and provides an interpreter to translate sentences using the grammar representation. |
| Iterator | Allows sequential access to elements of aggregate objects without showing the underlying representation. |
| Bytecode | Encodes behavior as data instructions for a virtual machine to execute. |
| Event Queue | Decouples when a message or request is sent from when it is processed. |

| Component | Allows a single entity to exist in multiple domains without the domains being coupled to each other (Unity is built on this pattern). |
|---|---|

Optimization patterns:

| Spatial Partition | Stores objects in data structures organized by position (in 2D or 3D space) to make querying faster and more efficient. |
|---|---|
| Data Locality | Uses CPU caching to maximize data access speed and efficiency. |
| Dirty Flag | Defers unnecessary work until the results are needed. |

 If you're an observant learner, you may have noticed our list of design patterns we didn't cover is rather long. While I would have loved to include all 32 in this first edition, the book would have broken both bookshelves and Amazon delivery trucks alike. However, if the content resonates with enough software craftspeople out in the wild, the second edition will include a few more patterns and we'll go from there (maybe by the third edition we'll have it all down on paper without too much trouble).

After working through this book, the missing patterns won't hold much mystery for you, and I encourage you to find them and experiment away!

# Resourceful resources

When I'm developing games or applications in C#, I always have the Microsoft documentation open in a window I can get to easily. If I can't find an answer to a specific question or problem, I'll head to the resource sites I use most often:

- C# Corner: https://www.c-sharpcorner.com
- Dot Net Perls: http://www.dotnetperls.com
- Stack Overflow: https://stackoverflow.com

Since our topic coverage throughout this book relates to Unity so much, I tend to have the following resource tabs open as well:

- Unity Forum: https://forum.unity.com
- Unity Learn: https://learn.unity.com
- Unity Answers: https://answers.unity.com
- Unity Discord: https://discord.com/invite/unity

There is also a huge video tutorial community on YouTube related to game architecture and design patterns, so here are my top three:

- Game Programming Patterns: `https://www.youtube.com/playlist?list=PLB5_EOMkLx_VOmnIytx37lFMiajPHppmj`

- Advanced Game Programming Patterns: `https://www.youtube.com/playlist?list=PLnJJ5frTPwRMCCDVE_wFIt3WIj163Q81V`

- Unity Game Architecture: `https://www.youtube.com/playlist?list=PLnJJ5frTPwROdR23GWZskQPM8w9iFh0oc`

If books are more your speed (like me), here are a few great places to continue your journey:

- *Design Patterns: Elements of Reusable Object-Oriented Software* by Gamma, Helm, Johnson, and Vlissides: `https://www.amazon.com/Design-Patterns-Object-Oriented-Addison-Wesley-Professional-ebook/dp/B000SEIBB8`

- *Game Programming Patterns* by Robert Nystrom: `https://www.amazon.com/Game-Programming-Patterns-Robert-Nystrom-ebook/dp/B00P5URD96`

- *Clean Architecture* by Robert C. Martin: `https://www.amazon.com/Clean-Architecture-Craftsmans-Software-Structure-ebook/dp/B075LRM681`

- *The Pragmatic Programmer* by David Thomas and Andrew Hunt (`https://www.amazon.com/Pragmatic-Programmer-journey-mastery-Anniversary-ebook/dp/B07VRS84D1`)

The Packt library also has a wide variety of books and videos on Unity, game development, and C#, which you can find at `https://www.packtpub.com/all-products`.

## Getting involved

As your last task (and one that tends to last the lifetime of your career), put your new software architecture tools to work – and most importantly, share the results! There are tons of wonderful developers and communities out in the wild who eat, breathe, and generally sweat the topics you've just dipped your pinky toe into; join them:

- Use GitHub (`https://github.com`)
- Get active on Stack Overflow, Unity Answers, and Unity Forums
- Build your own custom C# and Unity architecture tools

Whatever you're building, remember that you don't have to walk the path alone.

## Summary

It's always a challenge to end something you've put a great deal of time and intention into, so I'll close with an observation: all the things we've learned about software architecture, design patterns, and flexible, reusable, and maintainable code during our time together are about perspective. While there are definite concrete tools and implementations of these concepts (and I'd like to think we learned a fair few here), the real work (and revelations) inherent in software craftsmanship takes place when looking through these special lenses.

I want to thank you again for joining me on this journey, because every word I've written, every line of code I've compiled, every time I've thought about stopping, has all been with you, the reader (and my younger self), in mind. I hope you enjoyed the ride as much as I did.

As always, happy coding!

## Leave a review!

Enjoyed this book? Help readers like you by leaving an Amazon review. Scan the QR code below to get a free eBook of your choice.

packt.com

Subscribe to our online digital library for full access to over 7,000 books and videos, as well as industry leading tools to help you plan your personal development and advance your career. For more information, please visit our website.

## Why subscribe?

- Spend less time learning and more time coding with practical eBooks and Videos from over 4,000 industry professionals
- Improve your learning with Skill Plans built especially for you
- Get a free eBook or video every month
- Fully searchable for easy access to vital information
- Copy and paste, print, and bookmark content

At www.packt.com, you can also read a collection of free technical articles, sign up for a range of free newsletters, and receive exclusive discounts and offers on Packt books and eBooks.

# Other Books You May Enjoy

If you enjoyed this book, you may be interested in these other books by Packt:

**Hands-On Unity Game Development – Fourth Edition**

Nicolas Alejandro Borromeo

Juan Gabriel Gomila Salas

ISBN: 978-1-83508-571-4

- Build a game that includes gameplay, player and non-player characters, assets, animations, and more
- Learn C# and Visual Scripting to customize player movements, the UI, and game physics
- Implement Game AI to build a fully functional enemy capable of detecting and attacking
- Use **Universal Render Pipeline (URP)** to create high-quality visuals with Unity

- Create win-lose conditions using design patterns such as Singleton and Event Listeners
- Implement realistic and dynamic physics simulations with the new Physics System

**Learning C# by Developing Games with Unity – Seventh Edition**

Harrison Ferrone

ISBN: 978-1-83763-687-7

- Understanding programming fundamentals by breaking them down into their basic parts
- Comprehensive explanations with sample codes of object-oriented programming and how it applies to C#
- Follow simple steps and examples to create and implement C# scripts in Unity
- Divide your code into pluggable building blocks using interfaces, abstract classes, and class extensions
- Grasp the basics of a game design document and then move on to blocking out your level geometry, adding lighting and a simple object animation
- Create basic game mechanics such as player controllers and shooting projectiles using C#
- Become familiar with stacks, queues, exceptions, error handling, and other core C# concepts
- Learn how to handle text, XML, and JSON data to save and load your game data

**Unity Cookbook – Fifth Edition**

Matt Smith

Shaun Ferns

Sinéad Murphy

ISBN: 978-1-80512-302-6

- Craft stylish user interfaces, from power bars to radars, and implement button-driven scene changes effortlessly
- Enhance your games with AI controlled characters, harnessing Unity's navigation meshes, surfaces, and agents
- Discover the power of Cinemachine in Unity for intelligent camera movements
- Elevate games with immersive audio, including background music and dynamic sound effects
- Bring your games to life with captivating visual effects, from smoke and explosions to customizable particle systems
- Build your own shaders using Unity's Shader Graph tool

**Practical Game Design – Second Edition**

Ennio De Nucci

Adam Kramarzewski

ISBN: 978-1-80324-515-7

- Define the scope and structure of a game project
- Conceptualize a game idea and present it to others
- Design gameplay systems and communicate them clearly and thoroughly
- Build and validate engaging game mechanics
- Design successful games as a service and prepare them for live operations
- Improve the quality of a game through playtesting and meticulous polishing

# Packt is searching for authors like you

If you're interested in becoming an author for Packt, please visit authors.packtpub.com and apply today. We have worked with thousands of developers and tech professionals, just like you, to help them share their insight with the global tech community. You can make a general application, apply for a specific hot topic that we are recruiting an author for, or submit your own idea.

# Share your thoughts

Now you've finished *Learning Design Patterns with Unity*, we'd love to hear your thoughts! Scan the QR code below to go straight to the Amazon review page for this book and share your feedback or leave a review on the site that you purchased it from.

https://packt.link/r/180512028X

Your review is important to us and the tech community and will help us make sure we're delivering excellent quality content.

# Index

# Download a free PDF copy of this book

Thanks for purchasing this book!

Do you like to read on the go but are unable to carry your print books everywhere?

Is your eBook purchase not compatible with the device of your choice?

Don't worry, now with every Packt book you get a DRM-free PDF version of that book at no cost.

Read anywhere, any place, on any device. Search, copy, and paste code from your favorite technical books directly into your application.

The perks don't stop there, you can get exclusive access to discounts, newsletters, and great free content in your inbox daily.

Follow these simple steps to get the benefits:

1.  Scan the QR code or visit the link below:

https://packt.link/free-ebook/9781805120285

2.  Submit your proof of purchase.
3.  That's it! We'll send your free PDF and other benefits to your email directly.

Printed in Great Britain
by Amazon

43818701R10375